Pro Power BI Architecture

Sharing, Security, and Deployment Options for Microsoft Power BI Solutions

Reza Rad

Apress®

Pro Power BI Architecture

Reza Rad
Meadowbank, Auckland, New Zealand

ISBN-13 (pbk): 978-1-4842-4014-4 ISBN-13 (electronic): 978-1-4842-4015-1
https://doi.org/10.1007/978-1-4842-4015-1

Library of Congress Control Number: 2018963592

Managing Director, Apress Media LLC: Welmoed Spahr
Acquisitions Editor: Jonathan Gennick
Development Editor: Laura Berendson
Coordinating Editor: Jill Balzano

Cover image designed by Freepik (www.freepik.com)

Distributed to the book trade worldwide by Springer Science+Business Media New York, 233 Spring Street, 6th Floor, New York, NY 10013. Phone 1-800-SPRINGER, fax (201) 348-4505, e-mail orders-ny@springer-sbm.com, or visit www.springeronline.com. Apress Media, LLC is a California LLC and the sole member (owner) is Springer Science + Business Media Finance Inc (SSBM Finance Inc). SSBM Finance Inc is a **Delaware** corporation.

For information on translations, please e-mail rights@apress.com, or visit http://www.apress.com/rights-permissions.

Apress titles may be purchased in bulk for academic, corporate, or promotional use. eBook versions and licenses are also available for most titles. For more information, reference our Print and eBook Bulk Sales web page at http://www.apress.com/bulk-sales.

Any source code or other supplementary material referenced by the author in this book is available to readers on GitHub via the book's product page, located at www.apress.com/9781484240144. For more detailed information, please visit http://www.apress.com/source-code.

Printed on acid-free paper

To Leila

For always being with me, encouragement, and motivation

To my Mother

For teaching me how to live

To my Father

For teaching me to work hard, and be courageous

To You: my book reader

For teaching me not to give up

Table of Contents

About the Author

 **Reza Rad** is based in New Zealand. He is a Microsoft Regional Director and a Microsoft Most Valuable Professional for Data Platform since 2011. He runs his own consulting business named RADACAD. He writes books and blogs and speaks at many conferences. He has been a developer for Microsoft technologies and worked as a consultant for many companies throughout the world. In 2014 he founded RADACAD as a training and consulting business focusing on Microsoft data analytics technologies. He publishes videos on his RADACAD YouTube channel.

Reza has written many books on Power BI and SQL Server. He is a trainer on Microsoft BI technologies, focusing on Power BI. He has authored a Power BI course, From Rookie to Rockstar, and trained many people around the world. Reza has been a featured speaker at many conferences all over the world on data analytics topics. He has presented at Microsoft Ignite, PASS Summit, TechEd, TechDays, and Microsoft Business Application Summit, and he has run workshops in many countries. Reza is a Power BI All-Star winner of PUG (Community for Power BI User Groups).

Reza can be reached via his blog (`http://radacad.com`) or YouTube or LinkedIn (`https://www.linkedin.com/in/rezarad`) or Twitter (`https://twitter.com/Rad_Reza`). His mission is to help others to make changes in the world.

About the Technical Reviewers

Patrick LeBlanc is a currently a Data Platform Solutions Architect at Microsoft and a contributing partner to Guy in a Cube. Along with his 20+ years' experience in IT, he holds a Master of Science degree from Louisiana State University. He is the author and co-author of five SQL Server books. Prior to joining Microsoft, he was awarded a Microsoft MVP award for his contributions to the community. Patrick is a regular speaker at many Domestic and International SQL Server Conferences and Community events.

Currently working as a Power BI & Data Analytics Consultant, **Gilbert Quevauvilliers** has over 10+ years' experience working with data of any size and any source. By leveraging his skills, he is able to provide insights into customers' data quickly and efficiently. And this has enabled his customers to gain a better understanding of their business, which relates to better sales or significant cost savings.

Gilbert was recently awarded a Microsoft MVP award for Power BI. Power BI, in his opinion, is the logical choice in terms of creating insights, being cost effective, and providing dashboards and reports on Web, Mobile, or in Apps out of the box.

Belinda Allen is a Microsoft Most Valuable Professional for Power BI (MVP). Belinda is currently the Business Intelligence and Training Programs Manager for the Azure Cloud-based SaaS ERP offering, PowerGP Online, and the author of two books on Business Intelligence and Microsoft Dynamics GP.

Belinda is also the B in the MBS Podcast, where three Microsoft MVP's talk about Microsoft, Business, and Stuff.

Prior to joining Njevity, Belinda was a principal at Smith & Allen Consulting, Inc. (SACI) in New York City. SACI was a Dynamics GP partner for over 25 years. She has always had a passion for reporting and business intelligence. Her skills include Microsoft SQL Server, Microsoft Power BI, Microsoft PowerApps and Flow, Microsoft Excel, and of course Dynamics GP. For many years, Belinda held a Microsoft Certified Trainer credential for all aspects of Dynamics GP.

Belinda is also well known for her blog, `www.BelindaTheGPcsi.com`, and she is starting her new blog, `www.BIBelindacom.com`. On her blog, she shares really useful information about the product both quickly and succinctly. With followers from all over the globe, she can share knowledge and achieve her mission: "To improve the lives and business success of my followers."

Nikhil Gaekwad is a Product Manager on the Power BI team at Microsoft. Born in India and raised in Toronto, Canada, Nikhil attended the University of Waterloo to earn his bachelor's degree in Systems Design Engineering. His journey at Microsoft started off in 2015 as a Technical Program Manager on the Windows Wireless team. While there, he was responsible for envisioning, building, and delivering features in the Wi-Fi and IoT space to millions of customers around the world. He has always had a strong passion for working with data and leveraging them to generate actionable business insights. With an aspiration to be a leader and a major influence in the upcoming business intelligence platform at Microsoft, Nikhil joined the Power BI product team in 2017. Since then, Nikhil has a core role in evolving and transforming the Power BI service. He has authored many product blogs and featured as a speaker in major industry conferences around the world.

Adam Saxton is just a guy in a cube doing the work! He is on the Power BI product team at Microsoft working with customers to help adopt Power BI. Adam is based in Texas and started with Microsoft supporting SQL Server connectivity and Reporting Services in 2005. He has also worked with Power BI since the beginning, on the support side, and with documentation. In addition, he produces weekly videos for his Guy in a Cube YouTube channel.

Acknowledgments

Writing this book was a big mission: finding time to do it along with my busy consulting, training, and mentoring schedule on one side; and getting help from all the kind people around me from the other side. I would like to thank everyone who helped me through this process. This book was not possible without their help.

Writing any books on the cloud technologies is always a risk, because of the always fast-changing nature of those technologies. Power BI between all those technologies is probably one of the fastest paced changing ever. Every month we get updates and features. It took me a long time to incorporate features of the technology in the book, and at every phase and review, new features announced. You as the reader of the book may see some features by the time of reading, which is not explained in this book. The reason is that at some point we had to pull the trigger to publish the book. We could not simply stand still for Power BI features to all come through, because there will always be another coming soon! However, as the author of this book, I always keep up-to-date materials in my blog (`http://radacad.com`), and I also will work on having further editions of this book with updated materials in the near future.

Thanks to Leila, my lovely wife, for being always beside me in all situations, in the hard times and good times, to encourage me to continue when there is no light.

Thanks to my mother and father, who thought me how to live, and how to work hard, and be open to challenges in my life.

Thanks to the Apress team for their support through this process, especially Jonathan and Jill for the big help through the book. Finding reviewers for this book was not easy. This book covers a wide range of Power BI features, and finding experts on some of them was not easy.

Thanks to all reviewers of my book: Adam, Patrick, Gilbert, Belinda, Nikhil, and others who helped me in fine-tuning this book with their invaluable reviews and comments. They were all super busy with their tasks and jobs, and I appreciate every single moment of their time for this book.

Finally, thanks to you, my blog readers, book readers, LinkedIn and Twitter followers. All of you, one by one, encouraged me always. Writing this book was months of work, which I couldn't have done it if it was not because of you. Thanks, always, for your kind words and motivation.

Introduction

I've been teaching and consulting on Power BI for many years. My students and clients always ask me, "What is a good reference for Power BI architecture?," and I always refer them to my blog posts. Then I got a proposal from Apress to write a book on Power BI architecture, which has always been on my to-do list.

This is not a book for beginning Power BI, nor is it for data analysts or developers. It is a book for someone who wants to design the strategy and architecture of Power BI so it can be used in an organization or as a solution. This is a book that talks about components and their collaboration with each other. This is a book that gives you blueprints of different architectures and the pros and cons of each.

If you are a developer or an analyst, you still will benefit from this book, but you will notice that this book does not explain how to create reports with Power BI. For that, you can read my online book, "Power BI from Rookie to Rockstar." This is a book focusing on architecture topics such as sharing, security, integration, administration, etc.

After finishing this book, you will have full knowledge of all Power BI components and will be able to design the architecture to use Power BI in your organization (or for your client's organization) while considering all existing requirements.

How the Book Is Organized

Part I gets you started. The book starts with an introduction to Power BI components. Even if you are new to Power BI, you can understand this book. Chapter 1 explains the key components and how they work together in a Power BI solution.

Chapter 2 covers what you need to install or set up to follow the instructions, demos, and examples through this book.

Part II begins with Chapter 3 and teaches you about the Power BI website and the three main Power BI object types: Dashboard, Report, and Dataset. You will learn the difference between the dashboard and report. And you will understand why the dataset is separated from the report.

Chapter 4 explains the role of Gateway in a Power BI solution. You will understand what types of data sources need gateway setup. You will also learn the process of setup and configuration of the gateway. You will see how a report can be scheduled to refresh through the gateway. This chapter will give you a full understanding of the gateway.

Chapter 5 covers the three modes of connection in a Power BI report. In this chapter, you will learn about the Import Data or schedule refresh mode. You will learn the advantages of this mode and the limitations. This is the default mode in many scenarios when you use Power BI. However, it may not always be the best option. You will learn about the scenarios when Import Data is the preferred mode of connection.

In Chapter 6 you will learn about the second mode of the connection named DirectQuery. You will learn when to use DirectQuery vs. Import Data and the benefits of each. You will also learn the side effects of using DirectQuery. DirectQuery is not a possible option for all data sources; you will learn that some data sources, such as SQL Server, support this type of connection.

Chapter 7 covers the third mode of connection called Live Connection. This type of connection is limited only when you are connecting to Analysis Services. You will learn all the details about this type of connection, and the situation in which you may use this mode of connection. Through an example, you will see the features available compared to the other two modes of connection.

Chapter 8 gives you a full comparison of the three modes of connection in Power BI: Import Data, DirectQuery, and Live Connection. You will learn their differences and the best practices to use them.

Part III covers sharing methods in Power BI. As a reporting solution, you do need to know all the different methods of sharing. Chapter 9, starts the sharing topic by going through the simple dashboard or report sharing. You will learn how this scenario can be used for test scenarios, and why it is not ideal for sharing with end users or developers.

Chapter 10 explains the second method of sharing named workspaces. You will learn that workspaces can create an environment for developers, and it can be useful as a collaborative space for the Dev team. You will learn the advantages of this option.

In Chapter 11, you will learn the disadvantages of workspaces when it comes to sharing with end users, and you will learn another method of sharing called Power BI Apps. In this chapter, through an example, you will see how this method is one of the best methods of sharing Power BI content with end users and creates the isolation of the dev team and user environment.

Chapter 12 explains a free method of sharing in Power BI called Publish to Web. However, this free method of sharing should not be used in all scenarios. Because of the security considerations, you would need to use this method only in limited scenarios.

Chapter 13 explains one of the methods of embedding Power BI content into another application, which is SharePoint online. You will learn, through an example, that Power BI can be embedded easily and is accessible to SharePoint users.

Chapter 14 takes it one step further and explains how you can embed Power BI content in any web application. You will learn about the requirements and setup for Power BI Embedded. You will also learn that you will need a web developer to take care of this work for you.

In Chapter 15, you will read a full review of all methods of sharing and their pros and cons. You will learn the best scenario to use as a sharing method, and the scenarios when you have to avoid a particular method of sharing.

Part IV of this book covers another important part of the book, which is about the security of the data in Power BI. You will learn how one report can be shared with multiple audiences, but they see only the part of data in the report that they have been authorized to by admin.

Chapter 16 starts the row-level security discussion with a very simple example called static row-level security. You will learn how a simple scenario of security can be implemented, and how it works regardless of the data source you are using in Power BI.

In Chapter 17, you will learn the overhead of static row-level security, and you will learn how to overcome it by developing a dynamic row-level security pattern. In this chapter, you will learn how to identify the logged in users in the system, and authorize them to use the only part of the model that they have access to from the data model and relationships.

Chapter 18 takes it one step further and explains three of the most common scenarios of implementing dynamic row-level security. You will learn about these patterns through examples: manager-level access, users and profiles, and the organizational hierarchy.

In Chapter 19, you will learn how the row-level security works when you have a Live Connection to a data source such as Analysis Services Tabular. You will learn the requirements and configuration for setting up the security in such an environment through an example.

In Part V you will learn everything about the administration in Power BI. The administration section starts with Chapter 20. In this chapter, you will learn the configuration options that you have as a Power BI administrator and the important options to be careful of when you are setting up your Power BI tenant.

Chapter 21 explains the metric usage report in Power BI service and how it can be used and even customized. You will learn the factors you can read on the usage metrics and their relationship to the Power BI tenant admin settings.

Chapter 22 covers licensing. Power BI licensing can sometimes be challenging. In this chapter, you will learn the licensing options for Power BI, which are per user and per capacity licensing. You will learn everything that you need to know to make the right decision about the licensing of your Power BI implementation.

Chapter 23 dives into one of the licensing models, which is designed for enterprises, called Power BI Premium. Through this chapter, you will learn the differences of that model vs. other licensing models, the benefits for licensing, and when you should switch to a particular licensing model.

Part VI is all about the integration of Power BI with other tools and services. This integration starts with Integrating Power BI with PowerPoint in Chapter 24. You will learn about sample usage of this option, and all the limitations available when using this feature.

Integration of Power BI with Excel is more than just integration. You will learn about the collaboration of these two tools and services in Chapter 25. You will learn that Excel and Power BI can integrate with each other in four ways. And you will learn all the details about these methods of integration.

Chapter 26 explains how Power BI can be used in a fully on-premises solution. The on-premises solution of Power BI is called Power BI Report Server. You will learn how to set up the report server and configure it. You will also learn about the limitation of the report server compared with the Power BI service through an end-to-end example.

Power BI and Report Service services of SQL Server can interact with each other. This is the topic of Chapter 27. In this chapter, you will learn how SSRS report elements can be pinned to Power BI dashboards and the considerations.

In Chapter 28, you will learn a real-time streaming solution with Power BI dashboard showing live data from an input of Azure Stream Analytics. This is a method that can be used in many IOT solutions. You will see an end-to-end example of a real-time streaming solution with Power BI.

Chapter 29 explains the Developer features in Power BI service. You will learn about Power BI REST API. REST API is an API that you can use in .NET code to write scripts and interact with Power BI objects in the service. You will see some examples of how the REST API can be used to extend Power BI functionality for administration.

The book then finishes with some guidelines and blueprints in Chapter 30 about architecture. You will learn some architecture best practices for sharing, self-service, and enterprise usage of Power BI.

PART I

Getting Started

CHAPTER 1

Power BI Components

Power BI is a combination of some components. You will need to learn about these
components and their role in the solution before any further steps. It is not possible to
talk about architecture when you don't yet know about Power Query or Power BI Service.
Each component is playing an important part in the Power BI solution; it is essential
to know them as the very first step. In this chapter you will learn what Power BI is and
components of it such as Power BI Desktop, Power Query, DAX, Power BI Service, and
Power BI Mobile App. You will also learn about Power BI Report Server, Gateway role in
the solution, the API for developers, and how all these components work together.

What Is Power BI?

Power BI is a cloud-based technology from Microsoft for reporting and data analysis.
This reporting technology is built in a way that is not only useful for developers to create
reports, but also for power users and business analysts. Power BI created a simple, easy
to use, and user-friendly environment for creating reports. And on the other hand, it is
based on several powerful components that help in creating reports and data analysis for
complex scenarios.

Every component of Power BI is responsible for a specific part of the technology.
There are components for building reports, connecting to data sources, doing analytics
calculations, sharing reports, etc. The following sections explain what each component
is. Some of these components are explained in detail in this book. However, other
components need their own book to explain, and it is outside of the scope of this book to
go through them all.

© Reza Rad 2018
R. Rad, *Pro Power BI Architecture*, https://doi.org/10.1007/978-1-4842-4015-1_1

Power BI Desktop

The most common tool when talking about Power BI is Power BI Desktop. This tool is the report development or report authoring editor for Power BI reports. This tool is free to download, install, and use. This tool is lightweight, about ~150MB, and can be easily downloaded and installed. There is no configuration when installing this tool. Power BI Desktop support installation is only on Windows machines at the time of writing this book. There are some ways of installing it on non-Windows machines such as Mac using some utility tools, but that topic is outside of the scope of this book.

As the target for this book is not building or authoring reports, we will not go through details of Power BI Desktop. You should read other books to learn how to develop reports. However, in this chapter, the main purpose is to give you an idea of what every component of Power BI is and how it works. Hence, let's have a quick look at Power BI Desktop.

To download Power BI Desktop, you can use this link: `https://powerbi.microsoft.com/en-us/desktop/` You might be asked to log in to Power BI Desktop after installing it. However, Logging into the tool is not mandatory, so you can skip that part. Log in is mainly required when interacting with the Power BI website. For the majority of the examples of this book, you won't need Power BI Desktop. However, some examples need this tool. So please download the tool from the above URL, and install it. The installation process is very simple and straightforward.

Figure 1-1 is a screenshot of Power BI Desktop at the time of writing this book (Note that with the fast pace of updates in Power BI components, pictures used in this book may get outdated very fast).

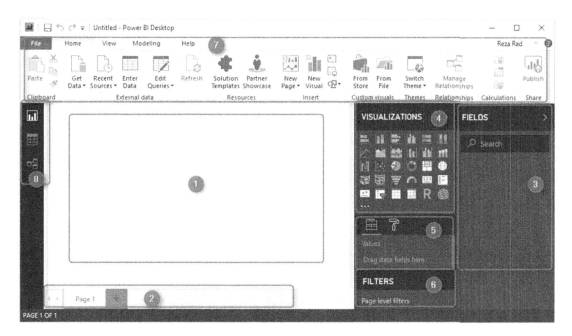

Figure 1-1. *Power BI Desktop sections*

Power BI Desktop is not a complex tool to use to build your first report. Everything is close together in an easy reach and designed to be very user friendly. Let's look at different parts of the tool:

1. Report design area; here you add visuals to your report and design the layout.

2. Page navigation; one Power BI report can have multiple pages. Here is where you add or remove pages, or navigate between pages.

3. Field's pane; every report comes from a set of fields coming from a dataset. Here is where you see all fields under tables, and you can select from them to add to your visuals.

4. Visuals pane; to select a visual and add it to your report, you can select it from this list. You can also add more visuals to this list.

5. Visual's configuration pane; for every visual, there is a need for configuration. The configuration includes adding fields to the visual and setting the format of it. This area is where you apply these configurations.

6. Filter's pane; if the data in the page, report, or the visual needs some filtering, the filter's pane is where to apply these filtering criteria.

7. Home Menu; there are several common actions needed when working with Power BI Desktop, such as connecting to data sources, getting data from them, adding a static image or text to your report, adding more visuals to the report as custom visual, and many other actions. These are usually available in the menu options at the top.

8. The report, Data, Relationship navigation; you can navigate to see the report layout, data in the dataset, or relationship between tables using this pane.

Power BI Desktop is the first tool you would need. Let's now take a look at other components.

Power Query for Data Transformation

As one of the key components of every reporting tool is connecting to data sources and preparing data (or in other words. data transformation), there is a specific component for that in Power BI: named Power Query. Power Query is also called Get Data and Transform. Power Query is the component that connects to different types of data sources, gets data from those, gives you the ability to apply transformations, and finally loads the data into your Power BI dataset.

Power Query comes in different shapes and sizes. It is not just within Power BI Desktop. You can even find it in Excel. However, for this book, we only consider the Power Query inside Power BI Desktop. This component is part of Power BI Desktop. It means that when you install Power BI Desktop, Power Query automatically installed with it. You can start working with that by choosing Get Data from Power BI, as shown in Figure 1-2.

Figure 1-2. *Get Data*

There are many data sources that you can get data from with Power Query. You can even create connectors yourself (which is outside of this book's scope). Power Query has its window for development, called the Query Editor. Query Editor is the place that you apply all data transformations, and it prepares data to load into Power BI. This process usually happens before data loads into Power BI. Figure 1-3 shows a screenshot of Query Editor.

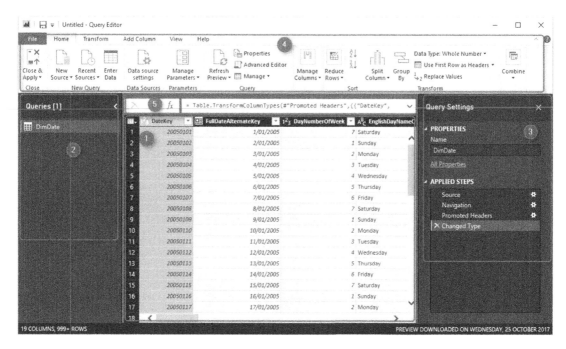

Figure 1-3. *Power Query Editor Window*

Following are some key points to notice in the Query Editor's user interface:

1. Data preview's pane; in Query Editor, there is always a few numbers of rows loaded as a preview, which helps you to see how transformations apply to the data.

2. Queries pane; list of all queries from different tables and datasets will be listed here.

3. Query settings pane; every query has several steps applied. These are data transformation steps, which you can go back and forth between. Also, some other configurations at the query level are placed here.

4. Data transformation's menu options; there are many data transformation options you can apply in Query Editor. In the menu at the top, you will see a list of the majority of them.

5. Formula's pane; you can view or modify the formula behind every transformation step here. This formula is in a language named M.

Power Query is the component that we will refer to in some of the examples of this book. However, you don't need to install it separately, because it is already part of Power BI Desktop installation from the previous section.

DAX and Modeling

This component is the analytical core and engine of Power BI. It installs as part of Power BI Desktop itself, and there is no specific editor window for that. All modeling, calculations, and configurations of that will be in the Power BI Desktop window itself. DAX and Modeling are built in within Power BI Desktop in a way that the majority of people consider as the non-detachable part of Power BI Desktop. However, there are some situations that this component detaches from Power BI, and we will have some examples of that later in this book.

DAX and modeling are not just parts of Power BI, they are also part of Excel Power Pivot and SQL Server Analysis Services Tabular Model. For the Power BI version of it, you don't need to install any special component; it is all built in and ready to use.

Your main interaction with this component is when you design a relationship diagram for the dataset in Power BI Desktop, or when creating some calculations. Figure 1-4 shows a relationship diagram.

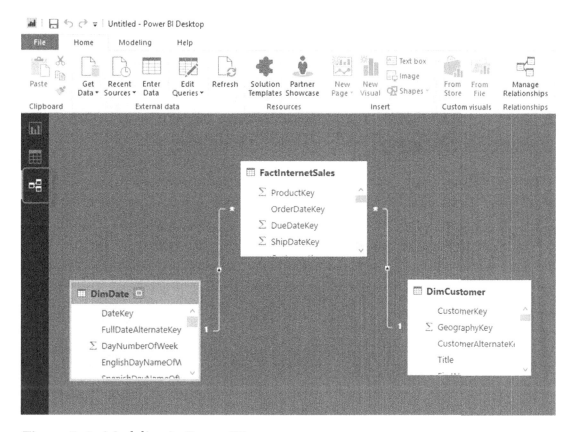

Figure 1-4. *Modeling in Power BI*

And in Figure 1-5 is a screenshot showing the writing of a calculation in DAX. Don't worry if you don't understand what this DAX expression does.

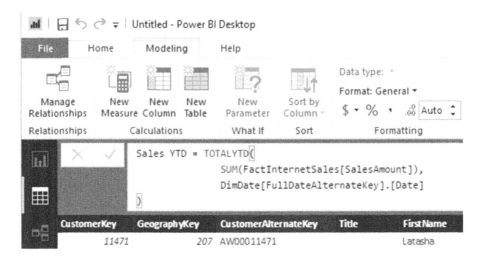

Figure 1-5. *Calculations in Power BI*

DAX stands for Data Analysis Expression language. It is a language to write calculations in Power BI. This language is very powerful and gives you a lot of analytical power through your model.

Power BI Service

Power BI Desktop, Power Query, and DAX are all components for creating and developing reports. After developing reports, it's the time to publish them and share them with others. Power BI Service is an online service hosted in the Power BI website for hosting reports, and of course sharing it afterward. For working with Power BI Service, you need to have a Power BI account. There are a few options when choosing an account, and we will talk about that in full details later in the licensing chapter of this book. For getting started with this book, you can start with a Power BI free account and apply for a 60-day trial.

Your reports after publishing to the website will be accessible via Power BI service (or website) through `http://powerbi.microsoft.com`. Figure 1-6 shows such a report.

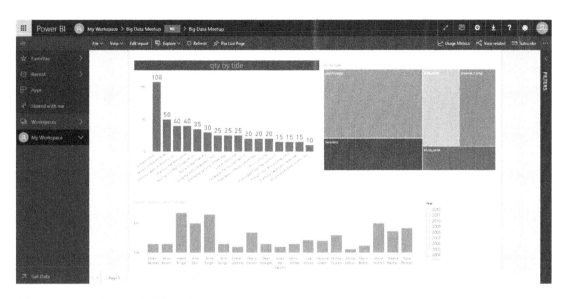

Figure 1-6. *Power BI Service*

Power BI Service is one of the components that we will go through it in full details through this book. In this getting started section, it is just enough to know that Power BI service is a place for hosting reports, sharing them with others, and configuring the usage and security.

In Power BI service, you can even edit or author reports. However, report development features in the service are limited only to visualizations. You will not have the Power Query component or DAX and the modeling component of Power BI Desktop available on the website. Power BI service for report development only gives you visualization and the report pane.

Power BI service can be accessed via all different types of browsers if you use their recent versions. Power BI service works based on the HTML5 standard, which supported in all new browsers: IE, Edge, Safari, Chrome, Firefox, etc.

Power BI Mobile App

Besides using browsers to connect to Power BI service and browse reports, there is another way to access reports interactively. There is a Power BI Mobile App available in the Windows Store or Microsoft, App Store of Apple, or Google Play store. The app is free; you can easily download and install it. After logging into the app, you will be able to browse Power BI reports from your mobile devices. Mobile reports can be designed to be different from normal reports. Figure 1-7 shows a screenshot of a Power BI report opened in a mobile app.

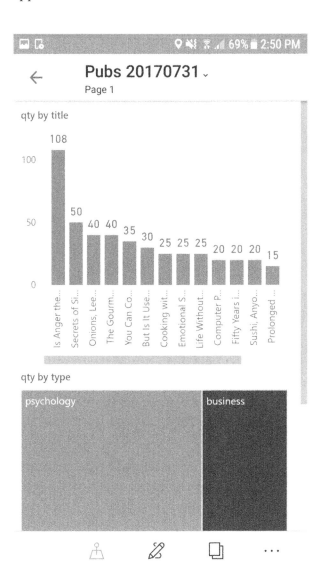

Figure 1-7. *Power BI Mobile*

Having the report in the mobile app will give you some specific features such as annotations and the ability to share those annotations with others. See Figure 1-8 for an example.

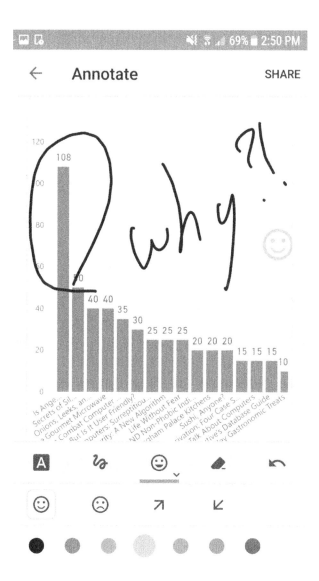

Figure 1-8. *Annotation in Power BI Mobile App*

Power BI Report Server

Many businesses still prefer to keep their solutions and data on-premises. Power BI is a cloud-based technology. However, it has a version that works on-premises. This edition of Power BI keeps the report, data and everything on-premises if required. Power BI on-premises leverages a component named Power BI Report Server. Power BI Report Server is a specific version of SQL Server Reporting Services developed for hosting Power BI reports. Reports shared with other users through this environment. There are a lot of features in Power BI service, which not yet implemented on the report server. However, this solution gets users to the on-premises experience of Power BI reports. Through this book, we will go through Power BI report server in detail, and you will learn installation, configuration, and using the report server.

Gateway

Gateway is another component of Power BI specifically for creating a connection between Power BI service (which is a cloud-based technology), and the data source on-premises. This component is an application that installs on a server on the on-premises domain and manages the connection for Power BI reports. Gateway is not required if the data source is cloud based (such as Azure SQL Database).

Gateway installation has some options and configurations that need careful consideration. This book will go through details of installing gateway, configuring it, adding data sources to it, and finally scheduling datasets to be refreshed through a gateway connection. Gateway is an important part of a Power BI architecture, and that is why we have dedicated chapters about it in this book.

Developer API

Power BI is not just a tool for report developers; it is also for application developers or programmers. There are few APIs in Power BI that developers can interact with it. REST API is an API for .NET (C#, or VB) and developers can use it through ASP.NET or Mobile applications. You can interact with the report in Power BI service through this API. You can embed a report into an application, refresh the dataset in Power BI service, or change gateway configuration, etc. We will have a section about REST API of Power BI in this book.

There are also other SDKs that developers can work with: an SDK for creating custom connectors in Visual Studio, or another SDK for creating custom visuals. This book doesn't cover the topics of custom connectors or custom visuals.

How the Components Work Together

Now that you know about all components, you might wonder how they all work together. The diagram in Figure 1-9 shows the placement of every component and explains how they work together.

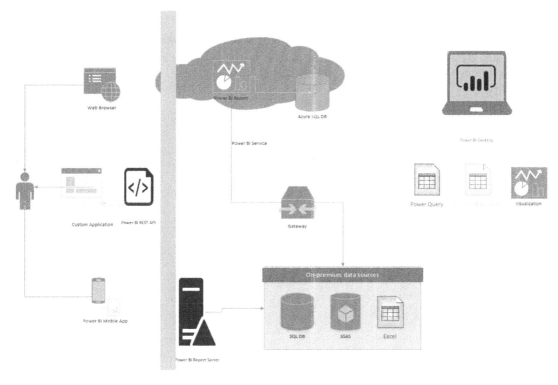

Figure 1-9. *All Components of Power BI*

We will get back to Figure 1-9's diagram many times through this book, and will go through different sections of it in every chapter and explain how components work with each other.

CHAPTER 2

Tools and Preparation

This book is full of examples. To be able to run these examples, you need to set up your working machine. The tools that are needed will have to be downloaded and installed, accounts that are needed will be acquired, and data files needed are all explained. You will get the Power BI Desktop installation guide through this chapter, the Power BI accounts setup; and you will learn how to install Power BI mobile app and download the code files for this book.

Getting Power BI Desktop

There are two ways of getting the Power BI Desktop onto your local PC. One is the traditional method of downloading an installer from a website, and running that installer on your PC to install Power BI. The other and more modern approach is to visit the Windows Store and select the Power BI Desktop app. You'll need Windows 10 or higher for the latter option to work.

Installing from Website

Power BI Desktop is a free report development tool that you can download it for free from this URL: `http://powerbi.microsoft.com`. There are usually two installation formats: 32-bit and 64-bit. The installation process is very simple and straightforward. After installing the application, you can open it from the start, Programs.

Power BI Desktop App

There is another way of installing Power BI Desktop. This method works in Windows 10 and everywhere that Windows Store Apps are available. This method installs the Power BI Desktop as an App, and Figure 2-1 shows how it looks to do that. For installing it in this way, you must go to Microsoft Store in your Windows operating system machine.

© Reza Rad 2018
R. Rad, *Pro Power BI Architecture*, https://doi.org/10.1007/978-1-4842-4015-1_2

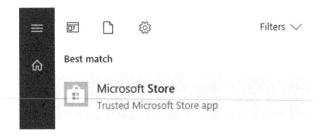

Figure 2-1. *Installing from Microsoft Store*

In the Microsoft Store window, search for Power BI Desktop. Figure 2-2 highlights what you are looking for and should select.

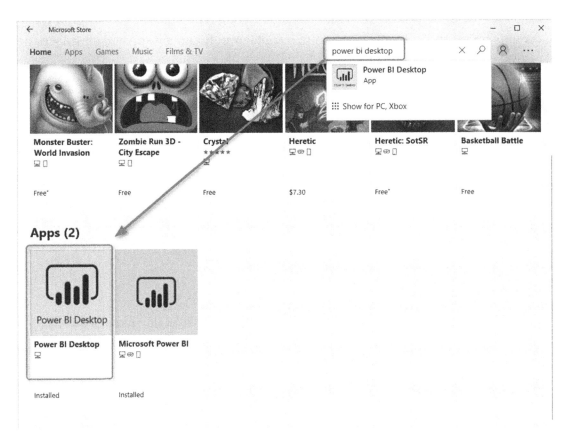

Figure 2-2. *Finding the Power BI Desktop App in Store*

You will find two apps: Power BI Desktop and Power BI. Select Power BI Desktop. Note that the Power BI app is an app just for browsing, not for report development. Power BI Desktop is an app for report development.

An Important Note is that if you install Power BI Desktop as an app, it will update automatically each time a new update is available. The Power BI team at Microsoft is doing a great job on updating Power BI Desktop every month. With the Power BI Desktop App, you always get the latest update automatically.

Setting Up Power BI Accounts

For going through examples of this book, you also need to have Power BI accounts. You don't need only one; you need more than one account to test some of the functions such as sharing and security. Power BI accounts can be Free or Pro. Free accounts do not support sharing (it should be part of a paid subscription, which is Pro or Premium only).

For examples of this book, you can create a Free account and apply for a 60-day Pro Trial. The Pro Trial lasts for 60 days and doesn't cost you anything. The process of creating a Power BI account is as below (Only go through this process if you don't have a Power BI account already).

Go to Power BI website: `http://powerbi.microsoft.com` and click on Sign up as shown in Figure 2-3.

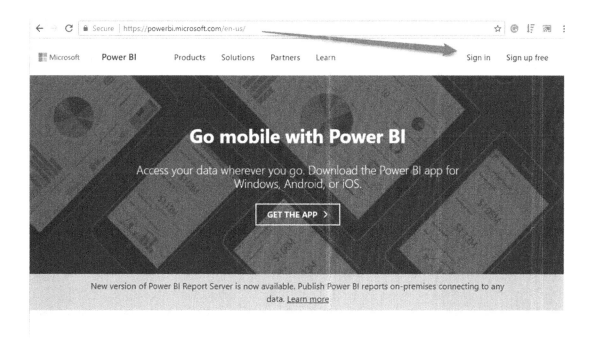

Figure 2-3. *Setting Up Power BI accounts in the Power BI website*

In the next window, shown in Figure 2-4, you have options to download Power BI Desktop (which we already did in the previous step), to download Report Server (which we will do it later in this book), and to sign up for an account.

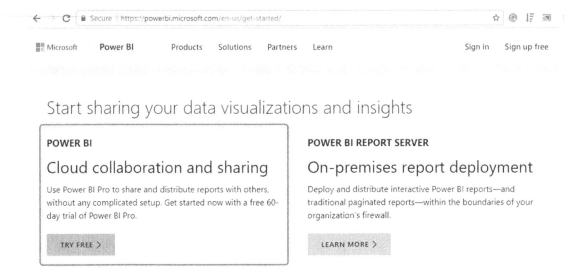

Figure 2-4. *Creating Power BI Accounts*

Click on Try Free as indicated in Figure 2-4. You'll be taken to the window in Figure 2-5, and there you should enter your email address.

Figure 2-5. *Use your organizational email account to create a Power BI account*

The email used in this step should NOT be a public domain email address. You can NOT use emails such as Gmail, Yahoo, Live, or domains like that. You can use your organizational, company, or university account for this easily. After entering the email, click on Sign up.

After clicking on Sign up, you will receive an email from support@email. microsoftonline.com; make sure that your company firewall doesn't block this email as a sender. This email will contain a verification code, which you need to enter in the next step of sign-up. Figure 2-6 shows the dialog into which you will type the verification code when you receive it. The textbox for the verification code is underneath those for your name and password selections.

Create your account

| Reza | Rad |

••••••••

••••••••|

We sent a verification code to **student3@radacad.com**. Enter the code to complete signup.

| | resend signup code |

☐ Microsoft may send me promotions and offers about Microsoft products and services for businesses.

By choosing **Start**, you agree to our terms and conditions and understand that your name and email address will be visible to other people in your institution. Microsoft Privacy Policy

Start ⊙

Figure 2-6. *Entering information to sign up in Power BI website*

After this step, you will get a message that your account set up correctly. You can then go to Power BI service at `http://powerbi.microsoft.com` and log in with your account. One way to understand that your account set up correctly is to see the welcome page as shown in Figure 2-7.

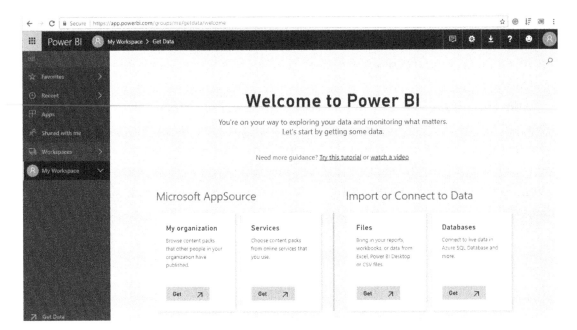

Figure 2-7. *When you logged in to the Power BI website, your account is ready to use*

Creating Power BI Accounts from Office 365

Another way of assigning Power BI licensing is through the Office 365 portal. If you have administrator access to an Office 365 tenant, you can log in to http://portal.office.com, find the user in the list of users, and assign Power BI Free for the user (or Power BI Pro if you want). Power BI Pro is also included with the Office 365 E5 subscription. Figure 2-8 shows licenses being assigned to a student.

Figure 2-8. *Assigning Power BI Pro Licenses to Office 365 users*

Checking Whether Your Account Is Pro or Free

One way to check if your account is a Pro account or Free account is through the Power
BI service. Do so by clicking on the setting icon, and then clicking on the Manage
Personal Storage as shown in Figure 2-9.

Figure 2-9. *Manage Personal Storage to check your Power BI account*

Figure 2-10 shows the result that you'll get, and the Student 3 user in the figure is currently assigned a free account. You can see that by the words "Free user" following the username. From this window, you can select try the Pro level for free for a period of time, or you can simply go ahead and upgrade your account to that level.

Figure 2-10. *Checking the Power BI license*

Installing the Power BI Mobile App

Another component that we need through this book is the Power BI Mobile app. With Windows, Apple, or Android devices, you can simply search for the app, and install it. Figure 2-11 shows the app as it appears in one of the popular app stores.

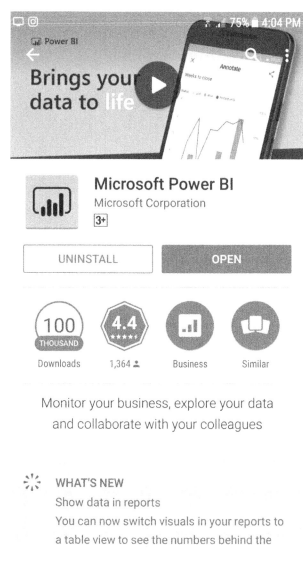

Figure 2-11. *Installing Power BI mobile app*

After installing the app, you can log in using the same account you have created in the previous step.

Downloading Dataset Files

All sample files, including datasets, and sample Power BI (*.pbix) files are available from the Apress website. Visit this book's catalog page at https://www.apress.com/us/book/9781484240144. From there, you should find a link to the source code for the book.

PART II

Power BI Service

CHAPTER 3

Power BI Service Content

Power BI content, when published to Power BI, splits into three different content types: Dashboard, Report, and Dataset. Each content type has some properties of its own. Further, in the next chapters, you will be referred to the content of this chapter. In this chapter, you learn about these three components and their specific properties: Power BI report, dashboard, the dataset, and the difference between these items.

Publishing Reports from Power BI Desktop

This book is not about developing a report on Power BI. Don't expect to see an explanation about how to create a report in Power BI. For that, I do recommend reading my blog series and the online book *Power BI from Rookie to Rock Star* here: `http://radacad.com/online-book-power-bi-from-rookie-to-rockstar`.

This book is about the Power BI service and architecture. You will learn about the architecture of a report and how it works on the website. For learning this, open a Power BI sample report available in the source code folder of Chapter 3. The report is a file with a *.pbix extension named as Pubs.pbix. When you open the file, it will automatically open with Power BI Desktop and you should a window similar to that in Figure 3-1.

© Reza Rad 2018
R. Rad, *Pro Power BI Architecture*, https://doi.org/10.1007/978-1-4842-4015-1_3

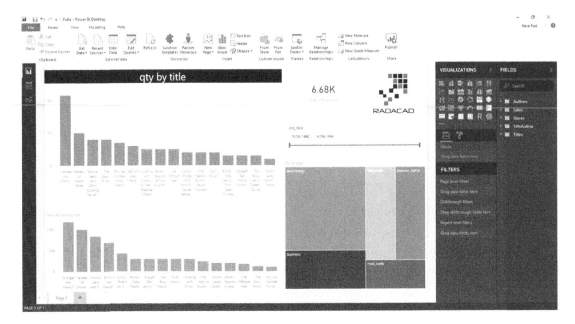

Figure 3-1. *Sample Power BI Report*

Every Power BI report, when stored, stores the data and the layout of the report in a *.pbix file. The data is encoded and compressed in the file; you cannot read it from there. Let's see what happens when you open the file.

When you open a *.pbix file, or as long as you have the Power BI Desktop open with a data model and report in it, there will be an instance of Microsoft SQL Server Analysis Service running on your machine. If you go to the services list in the Task Manager, shown in Figure 3-2, you will find this service running. To go to the task manager, use the Ctrl+Shift+Esc key combination.

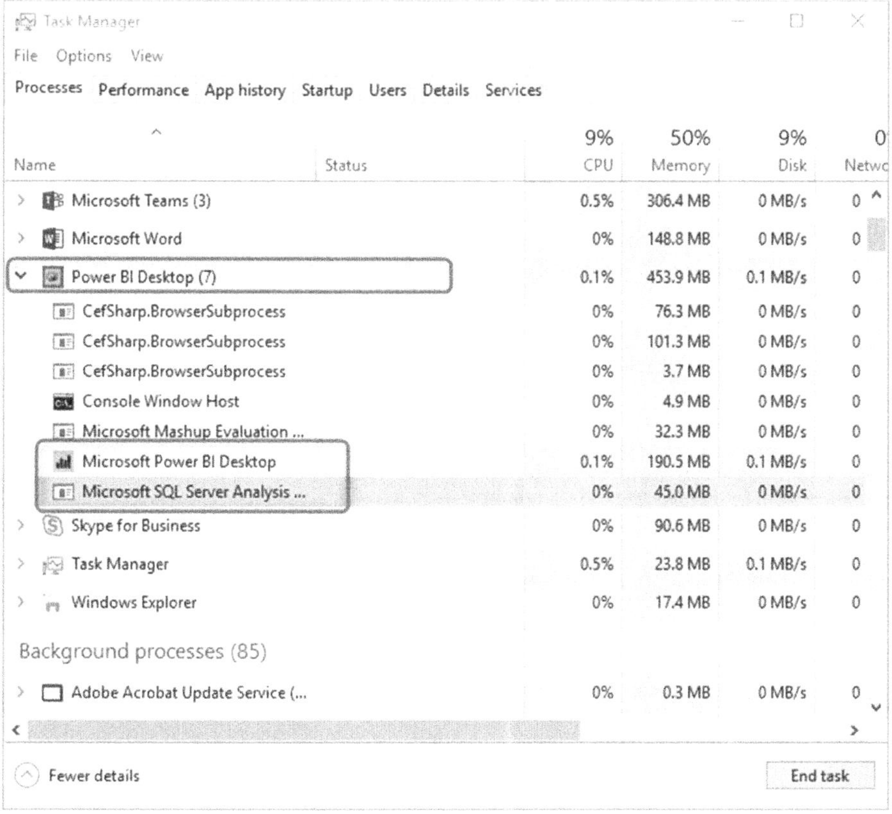

Figure 3-2. *SQL Server Analysis Services is running behind the scene*

You can see in the list of processes above, there is a process for Microsoft Power BI Desktop, which is obvious. However, there is another service there, named Microsoft SQL Server Analysis Services. This service is the modeling engine of Power BI. Whenever you load data into the Power BI model, this service keeps the data in memory.

Power BI is an in-memory technology, and it means every data you load into the report will be loaded into the memory. There are other ways of working with Power BI that doesn't load data into the memory. We will talk about those methods in the next few chapters. However, the default way of working with Power BI (also called Import Data, cached data, or Scheduled Refresh) always loads data into the memory.

Understanding the SQL Server Analysis Services service behind the scene makes you think that there are two layers when talking about Power BI, Report, and the Dataset. When you look at the *.pbix file, you will see only one file. However, when you open it in Power BI Desktop, you have the Power BI Desktop application, and the SQL Server Analysis Services service (let's call it as its abbreviation from this point forward SSAS). Power BI Desktop application keeps the report, and SSAS keeps the model or dataset.

31

If you have the Power BI Desktop file open, the report and dataset are separate. When you save it and close the application, the data in the model and the layout of the report all will be persisted and saved in a *.pbix file.

When you publish a *.pbix file to thr Power BI website, you publish both the report and the data at the same time. The publishing process in Power BI is simple; you just need to click on Publish option (highlighted in Figure 3-3) in the home tab menu in Power BI Desktop as the below screenshot illustrates.

Figure 3-3. *Publish a Power BI report*

When you click on Publish, you need to be logged in to Power BI desktop. To ensure that you are logged in, you can check the top right-hand side part of your Power BI Desktop application and see if you can find your username there. If you see your username, it means you are logged into Power BI desktop. Otherwise, just click on the sign-in option there and log in with your account.

If you are not logged into Power BI desktop, when you click on the Publish button, it will bring up the sign in the window for you. In any scenario, you need to sign in to the Power BI Desktop for publishing.

In case you see a message about selecting a destination for publishing, just select "My Workspace" as shown in Figure 3-4. Later in this book, you will learn about other options here and what is the meaning of those. If this is your first time publishing a report into Power BI, it is very likely that you don't see this message at all.

Figure 3-4. *Selecting a personal workspace for publishing the report*

After this step, you will see a message shortly that mentions the report published and indicates that publication was successful. See Figure 3-5 for an example. You can click on the link for the report to open it in Power BI website. Congratulations! You have published your first report on the Power BI website (or service).

Figure 3-5. *Publish successful*

Click on the Open Pubs.pbix in Power BI link. The Power BI website will open in a new browser window. After logging in with the same Power BI account, you will be able to see the report in the browser, and it should resemble that shown in Figure 3-6.

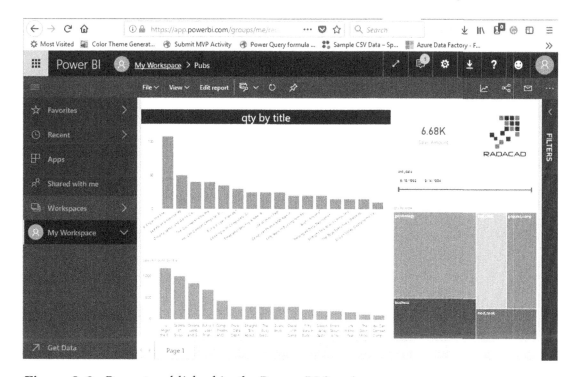

Figure 3-6. *Report published in the Power BI Service*

Reports that you publish are only accessible to you at this point. No one except you has access to see the report and data of this report.

Power BI Report

After publishing Pubs.pbix file into the Power BI service, you've seen that the report can be opened through a web browser. A Power BI report is a visualization content (sometimes split into multiple pages in one report) that gets the data from a dataset.

You can even edit a report on the website by clicking the Edit report button shown in Figure 3-7. And remember that the report is a visualization element. If you click on the Edit icon on top of the report on the website, you can go to edit mode, where you can make any changes in the visualization layer.

Figure 3-7. *Editing the report is possible through Power BI Service*

After going to edit mode, you can see an interface very much like the Power BI desktop interface for editing the visualization. Figure 3-8 shows this interface, and it is just for editing the visualization. You cannot modify the data model or dataset from here.

Figure 3-8. *Edit report is giving you Visualization pane of the editor in the Power BI service*

If you compare this view in Figure 3-8 with the Power BI Desktop view, you can see that the Power BI Desktop, has two other sections, which are not available in the service: the Data tab and the Relationship tab. You can only do modeling changes in Power BI Desktop. The website only allows you to do data visualization changes. Figure 3-9 shows the icons to click in order to make changes to your model.

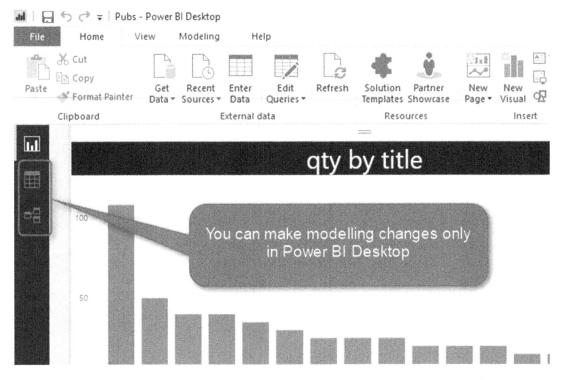

Figure 3-9. *Modeling changes are only available through Power BI Desktop*

Dataset

Dataset is where the model, structure, and the data resists in Power BI. Dataset and report are two separate elements. One dataset can be used to create multiple reports or can be created only in one report. There are different types of the dataset as well (we will explore that more in detail later in this book). A report cannot exist without a dataset (with the import data option). Dataset is the place that the connection to the data source is set up.

To find a dataset related to a report, you can simply click on theView-Related option in the report to navigate to the dataset. Figure 3-10 shows the View-related option.

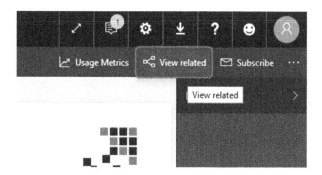

Figure 3-10. *View related in the Power BI service gives you all related objects to the current object*

After clicking on View related, you can see the dataset for the report. (One report can only connect to one dataset.) See Figure 3-11 for an example.

Figure 3-11. *Dataset related to the current report and the latest refresh time for it*

Another way to find datasets is to go to object explorer in "My Workspace." Clicking on "My workspace" itself will bring up a list of dashboards, reports, workbooks, and datasets. Figure 3-12 illustrates.

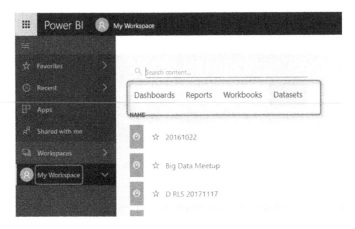

Figure 3-12. *Accessing all datasets under your workspace*

Every dataset can have several configuration options, as illustrated in Figure 3-13. These configurations can be security setting, dataset schedule refresh setting, refreshing dataset right now, creating a blank new report from the dataset, and a few other options.

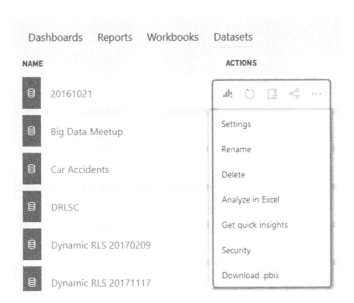

Figure 3-13. *Actions on the "More options" menu for each dataset*

Later in this book, we will go through every single element in the configuration of the dataset. You will learn how to set up a dataset to refresh automatically on a scheduled basis, or how to use a security configuration to implement row-level security and restrict data access. One of the most important settings for the dataset is to set it to refresh. Depending on the type of data source, you might need extra elements for that such as Gateway, which we will go through details of in the next few chapters.

One dataset can be the source for multiple reports. When clicking to create a new report as in Figure 3-14, you can create another report from the same dataset.

Figure 3-14. *Creating a report from an existing dataset in the Power BI service*

Figure 3-15 provides a mental image illustrating the structure of dataset, report, and data source that is fundamental to Power BI. Every dataset can connect to one or more data sources, and every dataset can be used as the source for one or more reports.

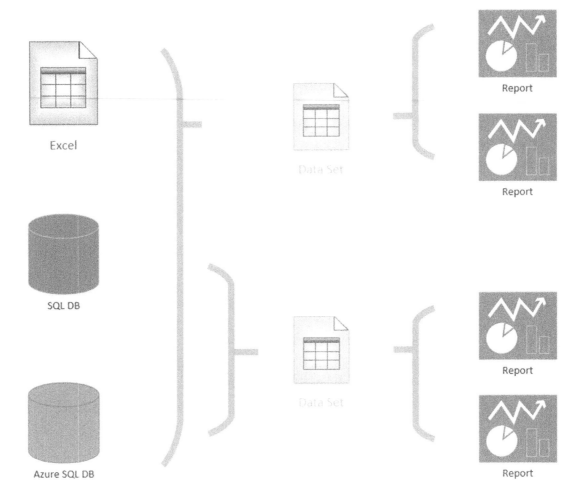

Figure 3-15. *Structure of Dashboard, Report, and Dataset in Power BI service*

Dashboard

Another element of Power BI Service is Dashboard. The dashboard is a visualization element. However, there are some differences between dashboard and report, which you will learn about later in this chapter. The dashboard is usually the navigation point and high-level view of the content in Power BI. A dashboard can be created on top of one or more reports.

To create a dashboard in Power BI, you can start from a report. Click on the Pubs. pbix report in the service, then with your mouse hover on top of one of the visualizations (except slicer); then you will see few icons, one of which is Pin. Figure 3-16 shows the Pin icon, which is toward the very right-hand side of the image.

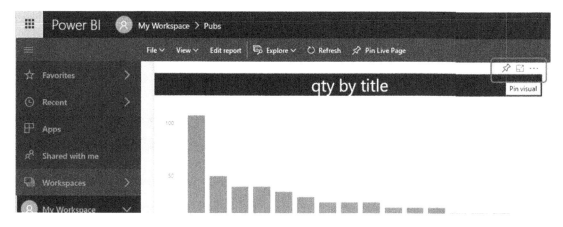

Figure 3-16. *Pinning visuals from report to a dashboard*

You may now Pin the element to a new or existing dashboard. Figure 3-17 shows the dialog in which to choose between existing and now.

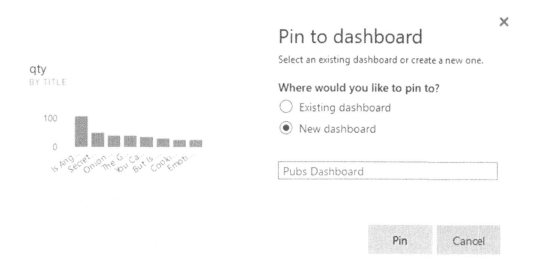

Figure 3-17. *Pinning to a new dashboard or an existing one*

After pinning an item to the dashboard, you can navigate to the dashboard by going to My Workspace, under Dashboards, and clicking on the Pubs Dashboard. The view of the dashboard looks like a normal report, and Figure 3-18 provides an example. However, the behavior is different.

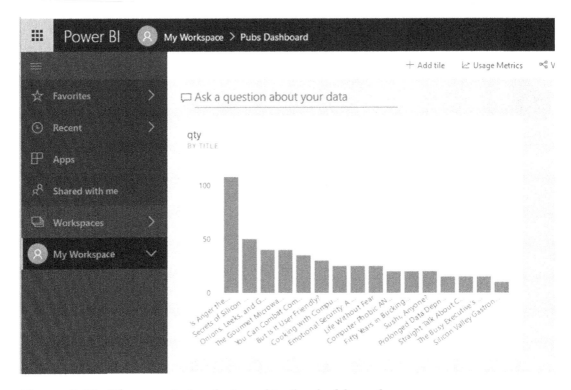

Figure 3-18. *The report visual pinned to the dashboard*

When you click on a chart in the dashboard, instead of highlighting or slicing and dicing, you will be redirected to the report page. This behavior is different from that of a report. There are more differences between the report and dashboard, which will be explored in the very next section.

Every Dashboard can have an element from one or more reports. As a result, every dashboard can get data from multiple datasets. Figure 3-19 is the diagram view of how the dashboard, report, and dataset work with each other.

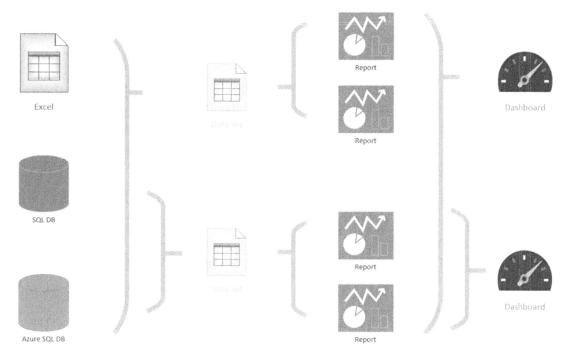

Figure 3-19. *Each dashboard can contain visuals from multiple reports*

Dashboard vs. Report

This question is one of the main questions that people ask when they are in the preliminary stages of building a Power BI solution. There is a misconception that Report is a detailed tabular report, and the dashboard is interactive visualizations with charts. However, this definition isn't for the Power BI reports and dashboard. There are differences in these two main components of a Power BI solution; understanding differences will help you to leverage their power in the best way. In this section, you will learn what are the differences are between these two and Where, When, Why, and which is the best to use?

Definitions

Following are two definitions to help you distinguish between reports and dashboards:

- A Power BI Report is a combination of multiple visual elements (charts, texts, values…) on a page that can be interrelated with each other. Data visualized in the report can be sliced and diced with slicers. Power BI report is fully interactive for user interaction. And It can be filtered based on some criteria.

- A Power BI Dashboard is a high-level view of key performance indicators from one or more reports. The purpose of the dashboard is not slicing and dicing, but merely to present a fast view of existing reports in order to aid in executive decision making.

Beyond the Definitions

The following sections describe reports and dashboards in somewhat greater detail. The added detail goes beyond the mere definitions to flesh out the picture of how reports and dashboards differ from one another.

Power BI Reports

Reports in Power BI can have multiple pages. In each page, there might be multiple visualization elements such as you see in Figure 3-20. Slicing and dicing, hovering and highlighting are possible in the Report. You can drill down through a hierarchical data structure, or you can select a column in a column chart and see the related data to it in other visualization elements.

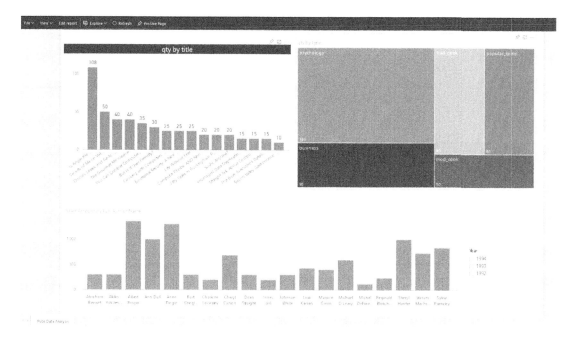

Figure 3-20. *Sample Power BI Report*

Reports are for end users to manipulate with different slicers and visuals and filters to hone on in the data they are interested in seeing. For example, a user might want to understand why the Sales Amount in month August is lower than in another month? Or a user might wonder which product is selling best, and how it is distributed through branches.

Power BI Dashboards

A Dashboard in Power BI is a navigation point to reports and provides a high-level day-to-day view of key performance indicators. With dashboard visualization, elements from multiple reports and pages can be *pinned* to one main place where they can be viewed together at a glance. See Figure 3-21 for an example. This place then will work as a navigation point. By clicking on each of the visuals, the user will be redirected to the report and page that has this element.

Figure 3-21. *Sample Power BI Dashboard*

Unique Features of a Power BI Report

The following subsections describe features and aspects of Power BI that are unique to reports. These features and aspects differentiate reports from dashboards.

Slicers

You can slice and dice the data in the report with slicers, as shown in Figure 3-22. Slicing and dicing is unique to reports, and the functionality is not generally available from dashboards.

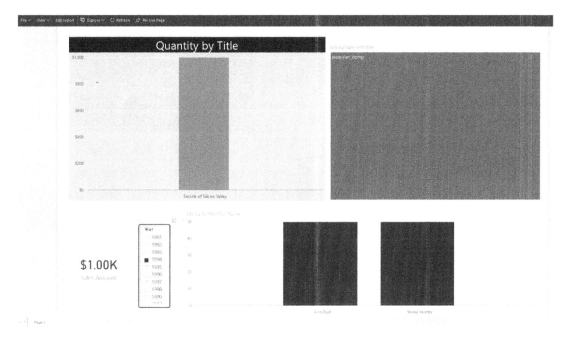

Figure 3-22. *Slicers give you the ability to slice and dice data in the report*

Multiple Pages

You can have multiple pages in a report. Navigation between pages is simply possible through the navigation pane (see Figure 3-23) at the bottom of the report. In a dashboard, you can have as many as tiles you want, but there is no concept of pages.

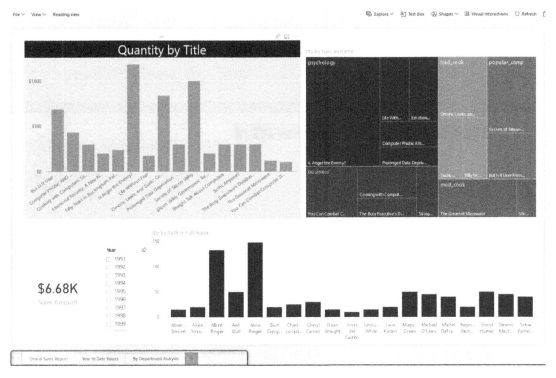

Figure 3-23. *Having multiple pages is possible in a Power BI reports*

Interactivity

Users can interact with report elements and get more insight from them. For example, you can select an element in a chart and it will highlight other elements that are related. Figure 3-24 shows a report having multiple elements in it.

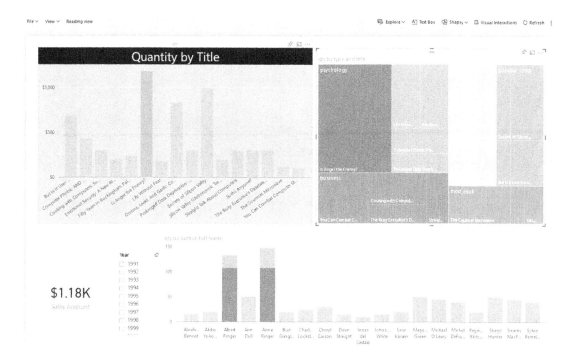

Figure 3-24. *Power BI reports are interactive for slicing and dicing and highlighting*

Drill Down/Up

In Power BI, you can have hierarchies; such as Product Group, or Calendar. And you can drill down or up in different levels of hierarchy through some of the visualization elements. However, in Dashboard drill down/up is not possible. Figure 3-25 shows a sales amount report that is currently showing sales by year.

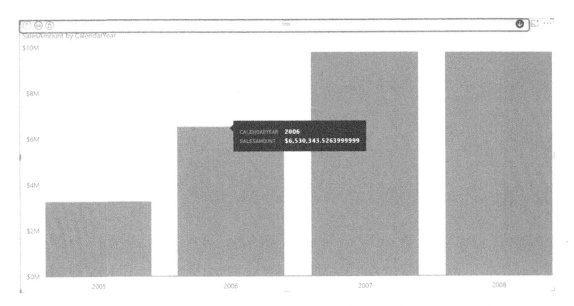

Figure 3-25. *You can drill down or up in some of the visuals in Power BI report*

Publish to Web

Publish to Web is a specific feature of Power BI reports. With Publish to Web, a report can be published as a public web page or can be embedded (see Figure 3-26) in a publicly available web page. Dashboards, at the time of writing this post, cannot be published publicly on the web. To read more about Publish to Web, go to the Sharing chapter of this book.

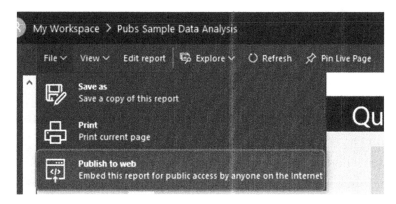

Figure 3-26. *A Power BI report can be shared through the publish to web*

Exploring Data

Users can explore the data behind a visual element in a report with options in Explore Data or See Records. These options help users to drill even down to the record level and see the roots of a given value in a report or a chart. Figure 3-27 shows the sort of detail that you can see in a report, which might lie behind a visual.

⟨ Back to Report   **QUANTITY BY TITLE**

title	Sales Amount ▼	stor_id	ord_num	payterms	title_id
Is Anger the Enemy?	$821.25	7066	QA744...	ON invoice	PS20...
Is Anger the Enemy?	$219.00	7131	N914008	Net 30	PS20...
Is Anger the Enemy?	$109.50	7067	D4482	Net 60	PS20...
Is Anger the Enemy?	$32.85	6380	722a	Net 60	PS20...

Figure 3-27. *Exploring data is possible through Power BI report*

Unique Features of a Power BI Dashboard

Just as there are features and aspects unique to reports, there are also some that are unique to dashboards. The following subsections describe features and aspects unique to dashboards, helping you to choose appropriately when to use a dashboard versus a report.

Automatic Refresh

Automatic refresh is one of the main benefits of dashboards vs. reports. A dashboard can be designed in this way that it be open for many hours and it will refresh automatically (depends on elements explained later). On the other hand, if you open a report, and if dataset of that report gets refreshed, you need to refresh your report manually; otherwise your report won't be refreshed automatically.

Many students in my courses ask why reports are not refreshed automatically like dashboards are. I believe the main reason for the behavior is in scenarios like this: consider that an analyst has opened an inventory report, and the analyst is checking an inventory value against a static report that sits in Excel or even on paper. The Excel or paper report is static, and the analyst is doing a sanity check to see whether the numbers match. If a report is dynamic, then nothing can be checked. There might be other reasons as well, but the foregoing scenario is I believe the main reason that reports are not refreshed automatically.

Power BI Dashboards refresh whenever the underlying dataset refreshes (when we import the data into Power BI). If the dataset is scheduled to refresh, or if we refresh it manually, the dashboard will refresh automatically. Power BI Dashboards for DirectQuery datasets refresh automatically every 15 minutes or more.

Customization by Users Is Easy

It is easy to change the size of dashboard tiles and to change the order of them, also to add new tiles (see Figure 3-28) on the dashboard. That said, it is also possible to make changes to a report as well. But that requires clicking on the Edit report, going to edit mode, applying changes, and saving. The dashboard is like a user's view of the world, so it simply can be adjusted to what he/she wants to see.

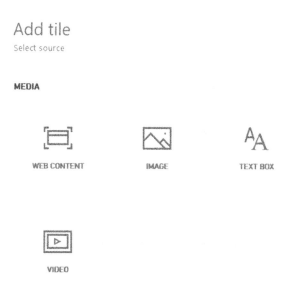

Figure 3-28. *Adding static tiles in Power BI dashboard*

Featured Dashboards

A dashboard can be set as a landing page by setting that dashboard as the Featured Dashboard. There can be only one featured Dashboard. Figure 3-29 shows the setting.

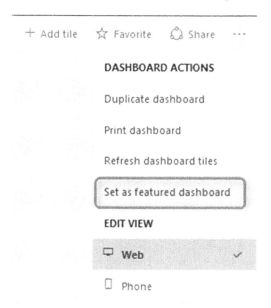

Figure 3-29. *Featured dashboard will be the landing page when you log in to the Power BI service*

Q&A Support

Q&A is an engine of the top of Power BI model that will respond to your natural English language questions. The Q&A box is only available on top of certain types of dashboards. See Figure 3-30.

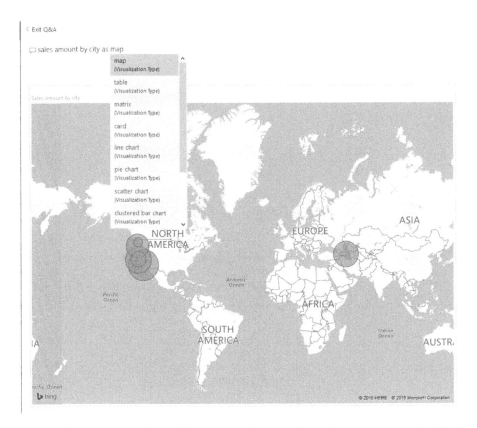

Figure 3-30. *Q&A option for asking questions and getting responses in the Power BI dashboard*

Real-Time Monitoring

Power BI Dashboards can monitor real-time data. Figure 3-31 shows an example of such a dashboard. Datasets for real-time monitoring now can be sourced from PubNub, Azure Stream Analytics, or REST API. Real-time monitoring means using a PUSH approach to refresh a dashboard as you view it. Anytime new data in the source is available, the dashboard immediately shows the data.

Figure 3-31. *Real-time dashboard*

Alerts

You can define alerts for each data-driven tile in a dashboard. Alerts can be as simple as if the number goes above or below something, send an email to me. Figure 3-32 shows a new alert being added.

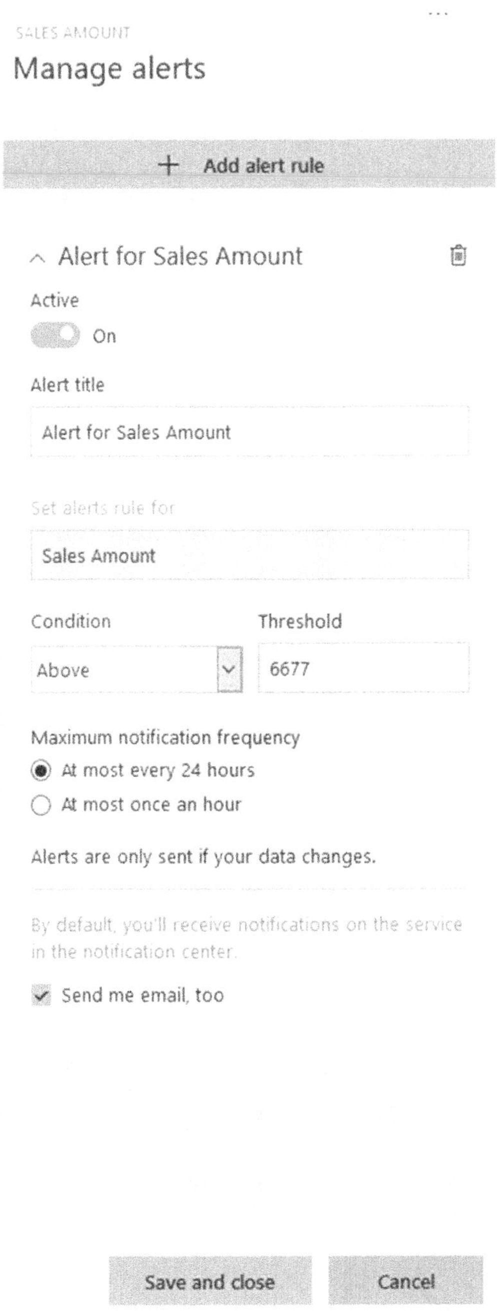

SALES AMOUNT

Manage alerts

+   Add alert rule

∧ Alert for Sales Amount   🗑

Active

⬤▢ On

Alert title

Alert for Sales Amount

Set alerts rule for

Sales Amount

Condition   Threshold

Above   ∨   6677

Maximum notification frequency

◉ At most every 24 hours

◯ At most once an hour

Alerts are only sent if your data changes.

By default, you'll receive notifications on the service
in the notification center.

☑ Send me email, too

Save and close   Cancel

Figure 3-32. *Defining alerts in the Power BI dashboard*

Get Related Insights

In dashboards, you can get more insight by selecting the Related Insights feature of a given tile. This option causes Power BI to search through patterns in the dataset and visualize them automatically. Figure 3-33 shows what the results might look like, and the insights are in the rightmost area in the figure.

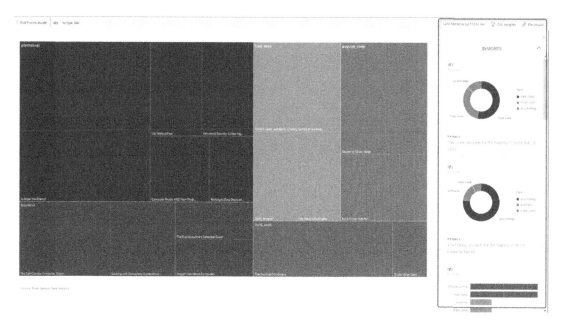

Figure 3-33. *Getting extra insight in the Power BI dashboard*

Differences at a Glance

Dashboards and reports are not the same. There are many major differences to consider. Dashboards provide a day-to-day, single page view of main KPIs, which can be refreshed automatically and can visualize real-time events. Dashboards can be used to navigate to reports. Reports are interactive data visualization elements that can be used to slice and dice, and to highlight and interact with data in order to investigate numbers and develop insight.

Summary

In this chapter, you learned about the components of Power BI Service: Dashboard, Report, and Dataset. You've learned the way that these components work with each other, and the difference between a dashboard and a report. The very next chapter is about focusing more on dataset configuration and gateways.

CHAPTER 4

Gateway

The On-premises Data Gateway is the required component that creates the relationship between Power BI cloud service and on-premises data sources. In this chapter, the difference between two types of gateways will be explained. You will go through the process of installing and setting up the gateway. The gateway then will be used in the next chapters for setting up data set refresh. You will learn what the gateway is and the difference between the personal and on-premises mode of the gateway. You will learn about installation and configuration of the gateway, and also an example of setting a schedule refresh.

Power BI is a data analysis tool that connects to many data sources. If the data source for Power BI is located in an on-premises location, then the connection from the cloud-based Power BI service and on-premises located data source should be created with an application called the On-Premises Data Gateway. In this post, you will learn what the Gateway is, what the types of the gateway are, their differences, installing the gateway, and scheduling a dataset with that gateway.

What Is Gateway?

The On-premises Data Gateway creates the connection between Power BI cloud-based data analysis technology and the data source located on-premises. The gateway is an application that can be installed on any servers in the local domain. The gateway is responsible for creating the connection and passing data through. Figure 4-1 shows the role of a gateway in connections.

© Reza Rad 2018
R. Rad, *Pro Power BI Architecture*, https://doi.org/10.1007/978-1-4842-4015-1_4

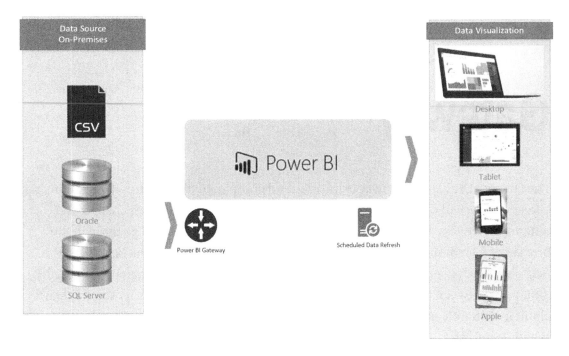

Figure 4-1. *What is Gateway*

You don't need a gateway in all scenarios. You need it only if a data source is located on-premises. For online or cloud-based data sources, no gateway is required. For example: if you are getting data from CRM Online, you don't need a gateway. However, if you are getting data from an SQL Server database located on your local domain server, then you need a gateway. For Azure SQL Database you don't need a gateway. However, a SQL Server database located on Azure Virtual Machine is considered as on-premises and needs a gateway.

Types of Gateways

Gateways come in two different modes: Personal Mode and Enterprise (labeled as On-premises Data Gateway). The difference between these two is not the paid or licensing plan. Both gateways are free to use. The difference is the way that you want to use the gateway. The personal mode is mainly used for one-person use, not for a team. Enterprise mode, on the other hand, is a choice when you want to work in a collaborative environment. Table 4-1 highlights some of the differences.

Table 4-1. *Types of Gateways*

	Personal Mode	Enterprise Mode (Recommended)
Target Persona	Business Analyst who wants to set up and use gateway to run his/her reports.	BI Admins to set up the gateway for their companies. Multiple BI developers to use the gateway for their reports.
Usage	Analyst	BI Admin Developer
Connection Type	Import Data or Scheduled Refresh	Import Data or Schedule Refresh Live Connection DirectQuery
Management	Per-user data source management	Central data source management
Monitoring/ Control	No monitoring/Control	Central Monitoring and Control
Services Supported	Power BI only	Power BI PowerApps Microsoft Flow Azure Logic Apps Azure Analysis Services

Personal Mode

When you install an On-premises Data Gateway in personal mode, you can use it yourself only. You can connect it to local data sources such as SQL Server, Excel, and other data sources. However, the gateway installed as personal mode only supports one type of connection: import data or schedule refresh (We will talk about these types of connections in the next few chapters). This gateway is only used for Power BI; you cannot use it for other applications.

Because the personal mode gateway is personal, you cannot use it in a team development scenario. Multiple developers cannot leverage this gateway. You can create reports and connect it to this gateway and share it with multiple users. However, only one developer can use the gateway. That is why it is named personal mode.

Installing personal mode and configuring it is easier than the enterprise mode. When you install a gateway in personal mode, you don't have the configuration option to set data sources for it. There is no place to configure it after installation. This mode of gateway is meant to be used for business analysts with the least amount of hassle to get their report published and get refreshed.

This type of gateway is usually for one business analysis that you want to publish Power BI reports and schedule it to refresh and share it for users to use easily. Not many configurations options, easy to set up and single developer features of it make it a good option for such scenarios.

Enterprise Mode (Recommended)

The On-premises Data Gateway's enterprise mode is what I recommend that you install. This mode of installation supports a multi-developer environment. Multiple developers can use the gateway installed. This type of gateway is built for team development; you can have a gateway administrator. For adding data sources and controlling it, there is a central configuration section for gateways.

Enterprise mode supports not only Power BI but also PowerApps, Azure Logic Apps, and Microsoft Flow, which are other Microsoft cloud-based technologies. This mode also supports all types of connections from Power BI. Not only is the import data or scheduled refresh supported, but also DirectQuery and Live Connection are supported with this gateway.

This type of gateway is for enterprise usage of Power BI, or where Power BI needs to be used alongside with other applications such as PowerApps. Multiple developers can work with the same gateway if the gateway administrator authorizes them to use it. More centralized control and monitoring exist for this type of gateway.

Gateway Architecture

The understanding of architecture can be helpful in using the gateway. Figure 4-2 illustrates some of the architectual details.

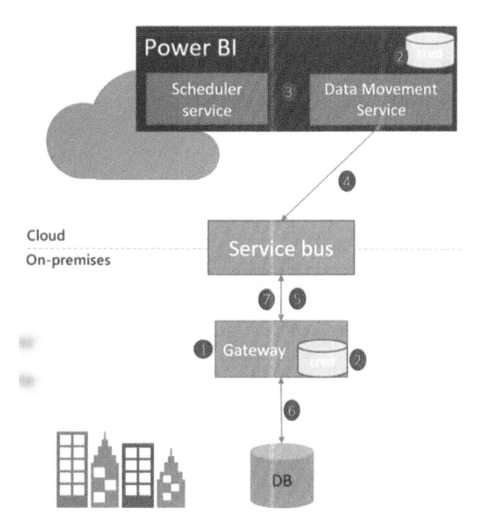

Figure 4-2. *Gateway Architecture*

Following are some aspects of gateway architecture to be particularly aware of. The numbers indicate steps in an overall process.

1. Gateway installed on a machine in the on-premises domain. During this installation, credentials are stored in the local and Power BI service.

2. Credentials entered for the data source in Power BI are encrypted and then stored in the cloud. Only the gateway can decrypt the credentials.

3. Power BI service kicks off a dataset refresh; this happens through a service named Scheduler service in Power BI.

4. Data Movement Service analyzes the query and pushes it to the appropriate service bus instance.

5. There is a queue of requests in the service bus. Gateway polls bus for pending requests.

6. Gateway gets the query and executes it on the data source.

7. After getting the result, the gateway pushes that back to Power BI.

Item 5 is very important. Gateway is polling the bus to check if there are any pending requests. The bus cannot trigger a gateway. The reason for this architecture is security. If the bus can trigger the gateway, the inbound security ports need to be open, which is not a good practice for security. So, we can say that gateway connection is very secure because it is only using outbound ports.

Considerations Before Installing the Gateway

The gateway can be installed on any machines in the on-premises domain. However, it is not recommended for it to be installed on the Domain Controller itself. Here are requirements for gateway installation:

Minimum Requirements:
.NET 4.5 Framework
64-bit version of Windows 7 / Windows Server 2008 R2 (or later)

Recommended:
8 Core CPU
8 GB Memory
64-bit version of Windows 2012 R2 (or later)

How Many Gateways Are Required?

One gateway should be enough for many situations. However, there are sometimes that you would get more benefit with having more gateways. As an example, if you have a gateway that is used for scheduled data refresh, and the same gateway is used for a Live Connection, then you get slow performance for the live connection if there is a scheduled data refresh in process at that time. So, in this scenario, you might consider having one gateway for your Live Connection and another one for a scheduled refresh.

If you install a gateway in personal mode, and then you decide to install in Enterprise mode on that machine, you need to clean the registry. This process is not an easy process to go through. My recommendation is to choose the version of the gateway that you need on that machine carefully. If this is a server, then I highly recommend installing Enterprise mode on it rather than personal.

The gateway can be installed only on s 64-bit Windows operating system. The Gateway machine should be always up and running to cater for data refresh queries. Do not install the gateway on a machine that is connected through a wireless network. A gateway will perform more slowly on a wireless network. Ports that need to be open for a gateway are all outbound ports: TCP 443 (default), 5671, 5672, 9350 thru 9354. The gateway does not require inbound ports.

Installing Gateway

You can download Gateway from this link:

```
https://powerbi.microsoft.com/en-us/gateway/
```

Or you can find the link when you log in to Power BI service by clicking the Download arrow, and then selecting Data Gateway, as shown in Figure 4-3.

Figure 4-3. *Where to get Gateway from*

There is only one gateway installer to download. At the time of installation, you choose the type of gateway that you wish to install. Figure 4-4 shows the dialog confirming that you wish to download the installer.

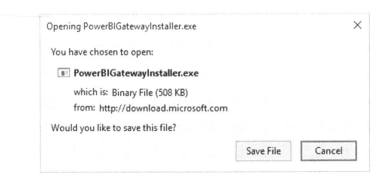

Figure 4-4. *Downloading Gateway's installation file*

After running the installation file, you will see the option to choose the gateway type. Figure 4-5 shows this option.

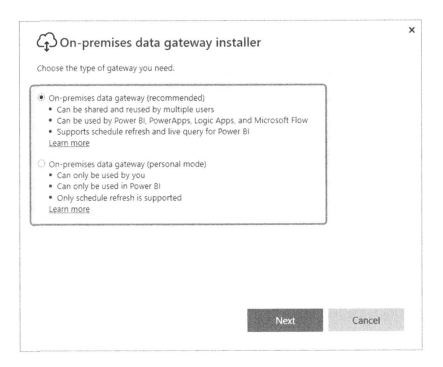

Figure 4-5. *Choosing the type of gateway*

We are going to install Enterprise mode (labeled as On-premises Data Gateway), because it supports Live connections and DirectQuery connections, which we will talk about it in future chapters. Personal mode will not be listed if you downloaded the On-premises Data Gateway from a service other than Power BI.

After choosing the gateway type, the installer downloads the remaining files required for install, and then you can continue the installation. You need to choose the folder to install the gateway. For this example, we'll keep the folder as is with no change. The installation process is simple. After installation, you need to register your gateway.

To register your gateway, you need to use your Organizational email account, and then sign in. See Figure 4-6 for an example.

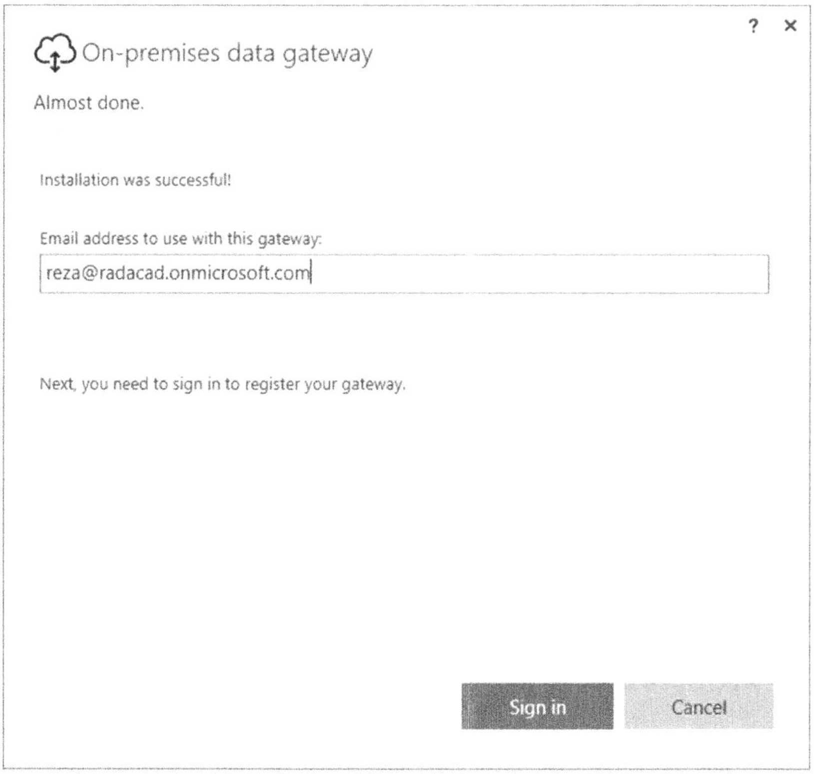

Figure 4-6. *Registering Gateway*

You can then Register a new gateway or migrate or restore an existing gateway. If you are installing for the first time, Select Register a new gateway and continue. You will need to enter two important pieces of information:

- **Gateway name**: a name that can remind you where this gateway is installed. For example, Reza-Vaio-Gateway or something like that.

- **Recovery Key**: this is a very important key and is required for recovering the gateway later. If you want to uninstall it and install again, or if you want to move the gateway from one machine to another without the hassle of changing all connections, then keep the gateway name and recovery key in a safe place.

You can also add the gateway to an existing gateway cluster. This option is added recently for having high availability through gateways. You can see the option in Figure 4-7. For this book, leave that option unchecked.

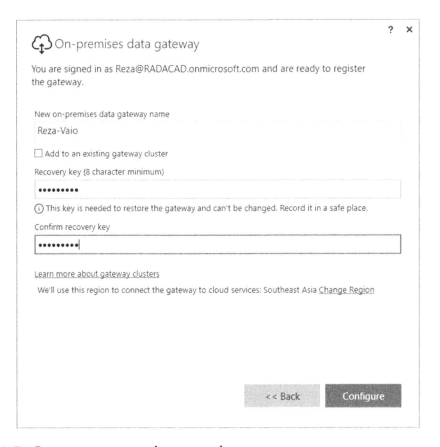

Figure 4-7. *Gateway name and recovery key*

After successful registration of your gateway, you should see a message that says the gateway is online and ready to go. Figure 4-8 shows an example of this message.

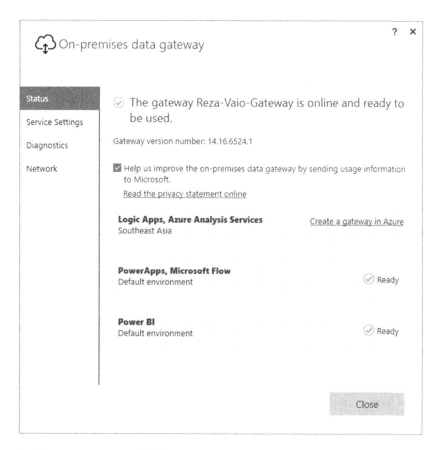

Figure 4-8. *Gateway successfully set up*

Now you can see the gateway in the Power BI service under your account as well. Look under Power BI Service, click on Setting Icon, and then click on Manage Gateways as shown in Figure 4-9.

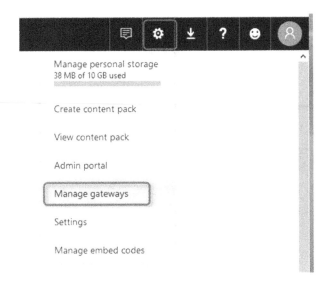

Figure 4-9. *Manage Gateways*

You should see all gateways set up under your account. From Figure 4-10, you can see that I have four gateways under my account, and only one of them (Reza-Vaio-Gateway) is up and running and ready to be used.

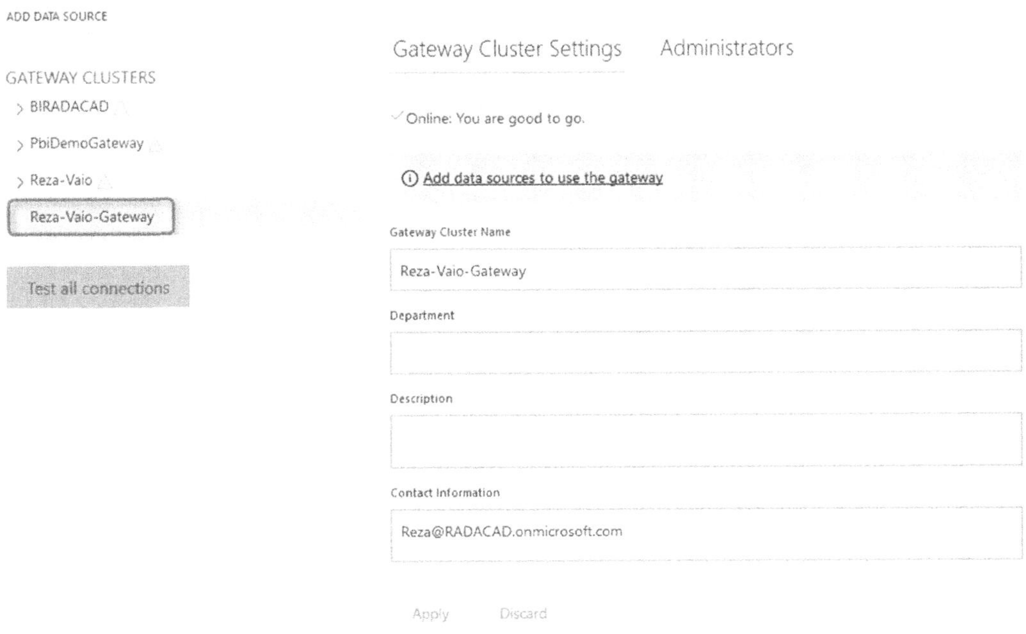

ADD DATA SOURCE

GATEWAY CLUSTERS
> BIRADACAD
> PbiDemoGateway
> Reza-Vaio
Reza-Vaio-Gateway

Test all connections

Gateway Cluster Settings   Administrators

✓Online: You are good to go.

ⓘ Add data sources to use the gateway

Gateway Cluster Name

Reza-Vaio-Gateway

Department

Description

Contact Information

Reza@RADACAD.onmicrosoft.com

Apply   Discard

Figure 4-10. *Gateway up and running*

If you install a gateway in personal mode, you don't need to register the gateway with a name and recovery key. And you cannot see your gateway in the Manage Gateway section in the Power BI service. However, I recommend always using enterprise mode.

Adding Data Sources

The gateway itself is just for creating the connection from the cloud to the local domain. For your datasets to refresh through this gateway, you need to add Data Sources. Data sources are connections to every on-premises database, file, folder, etc., that have been used in Power BI as a connection.

To add data sources to the gateway, first, you need to check the Power BI file and see what data sources have been used. One easy way of finding that out is to open the *.pbix file in the Power BI Desktop.

After opening the file, click on Edit Queries ➤ Data Source Settings, as shown in Figure 4-11.

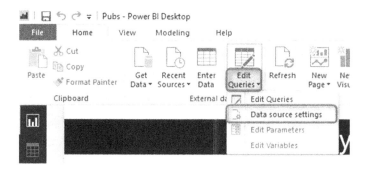

Figure 4-11. *Data Source Settings in Power BI Desktop*

In the Data Source Settings, you will see all data sources used in the current file. Click on every data source, click on Change Source, and copy the path for the file. Figure 4-12 shows the path.

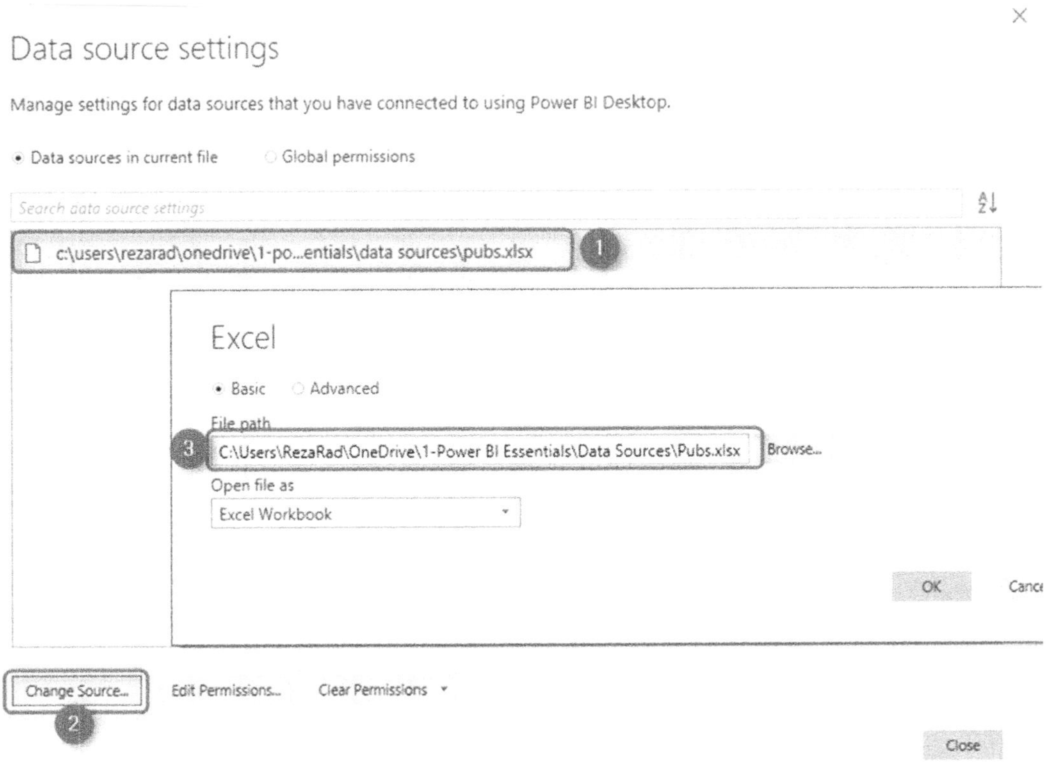

Figure 4-12. *Finding every data source*

Now you can go to the Power BI service, Manage Gateway section. There, select the gateway installed previously. Then click on Add Data Source as shown in Figure 4-13.

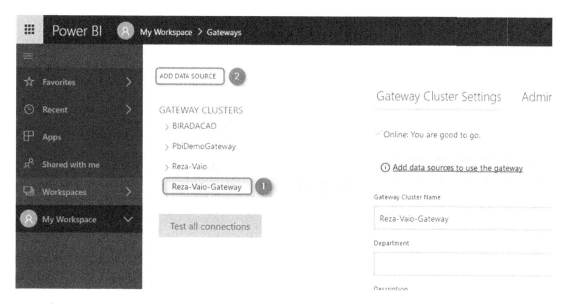

Figure 4-13. *Adding Data Source*

In the Add Data Source tab, you need to set some options. These are shown next in Figure 4-14.

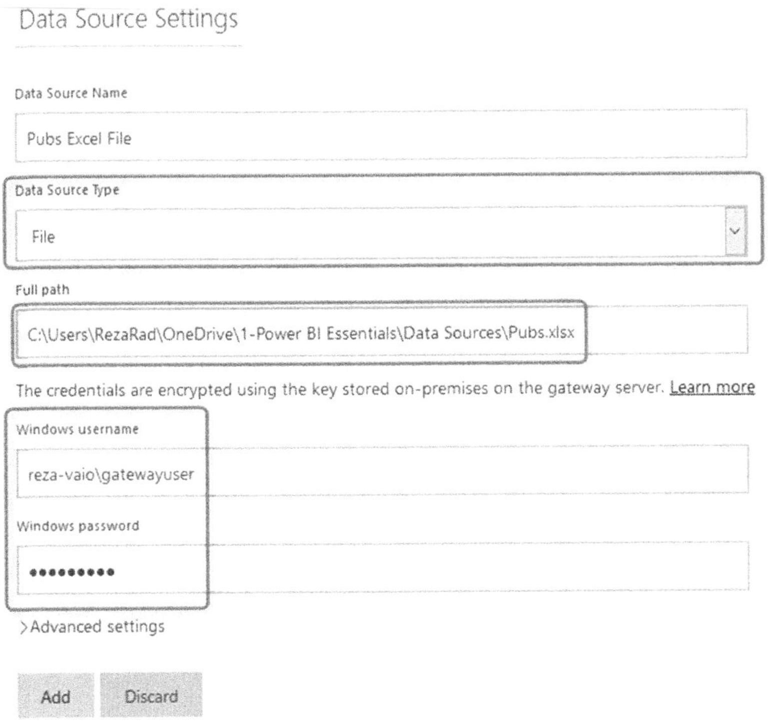

Figure 4-14. Data Source Configuration

The Data Source Name is only important for jogging your memory later. The first important option is the Data Source Type. In this example, because my source is an Excel file, I choose File. However, this can be an SQL Server database or any other data sources.

After choosing the data source type, you need to enter other configurations for that source. We have used the file, so we need to specify the full path of the file. This path should be the path of the file from the machine that the gateway is installed on. If the file is in a shared folder path, then that path should be accessible from the machine that the gateway is installed on it. And this should also be the same path that has been used in the data source configuration of Power BI Desktop.

You need to enter the username and password to access the data source as well. In this case, because we have used a file, then the username and password should be the local username and password that have access to that data source from the machine that the gateway is installed on it. Username should always have a domain name leading it (domain\username) like the screenshot below.

If everything is set up correctly, you should see a message that mentions the Connection Successful. See the right side of Figure 4-15 for an example of this message.

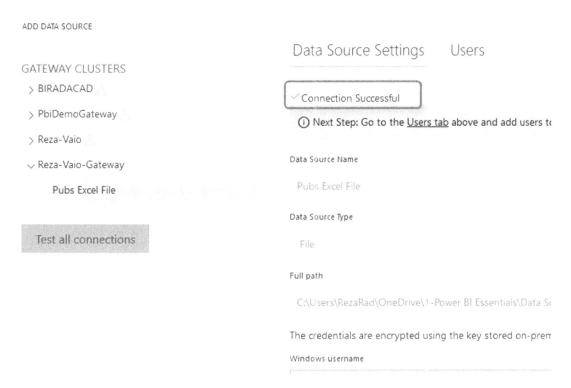

Figure 4-15. *Data Source set up successfully*

Important note   If you have multiple sources, then you must do this process for every single one of them.

Connecting Through the Gateway

After adding the required data sources, then you can create the connection through the gateway. You should select the data source that you want to configure the Power BI service. First, go to Settings in Power BI service as shown in Figure 4-16.

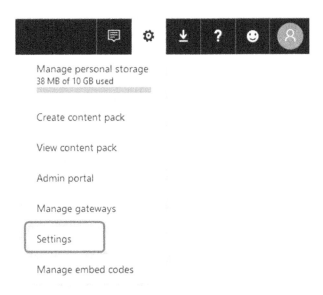

Figure 4-16. *Settings of datasets*

Click on Datasets, find your dataset, then click on Gateway Connection as shown in Figure 4-17. If your gateway has all the data sources needed for this dataset, then you will see it under Use a data gateway, and you can select it, then click on Apply.

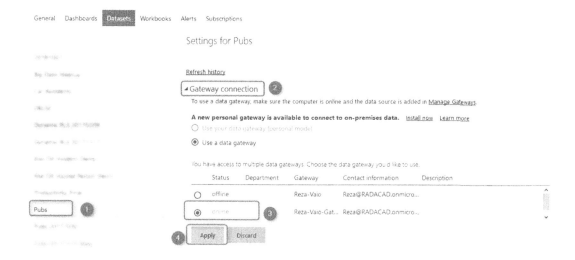

Figure 4-17. *Binding gateway to a dataset*

You have now configured your dataset to refresh through the gateway. You can now test by manually refreshing your dataset. To manually refresh your dataset, first find it in your workspace as illustrated in Figure 4-18.

Figure 4-18. *Refreshing Dataset manually*

After finding your dataset, you then can click on refresh. The refresh icon is the circular, arrow icon in Figure 4-18. If everything set up correctly, the last refresh time should update with no error occurred. Congratulations! You have set up the gateway for your dataset.

Troubleshooting

There are a few scenarios in which you may face an issue when setting up the gateway. One is that you may not be able to see the gateway listed when you go to your dataset setting. The reason is most probably because you did not add all data sources needed for that dataset. Go to Power BI Desktop and check that you have added all data sources.

Gateway has a logging system that can be helpful when an issue comes up. You can enable logging, and access the gateway logs from the on-premises data gateway. Figure 4-19 shows the settings to enable logging.

Figure 4-19. Logging for gateway

There are a few known issues with the on-premises gateway, which you can read more about here: `https://docs.microsoft.com/power-bi/service-gateway-onprem-tshoot`. There are a few known issues with the personal gateway, which you can read more about here: `https://docs.microsoft.com/power-bi/personal-gateway`.

Summary

In this chapter, you've learned about the On-premises Data Gateway. The gateway is a connection between the Power BI cloud-based dataset and the data source on-premises. You learned that the gateway is only required for on-premises connections. There are two modes to install gateway: personal and enterprise (recommended) You learned that the enterprise mode of the gateway can serve more than one developer at a time; be used for Power BI, PowerApps, and a few other applications; and it also supports multiple connection types.

We went through installation and configuration of the gateway and the connecting one Power BI dataset to it. The key to using gateway is to add all required data sources under it, and then map it to the dataset. In next few chapters, we are going to talk about the different types of connections in Power BI and how a gateway works with them.

CHAPTER 5

Import Data or Scheduled Refresh

Power BI is one of the BI tools in the market that supports more than one type of connection. Each connection type has pros and cons. In this section, we are going to cover everything about the Import Data or Scheduled Refresh type of connection. You will learn about how Power BI stores data into the in-memory engine, and what are the scenarios to use this connection method.

Connection Type Is Not Data Source Type

Connection type doesn't mean the data source type. Apparently, Power BI supports hundreds of data source types. Connection Type is the way that the connection is created to the data source. One data source can support many types of connections. For example, you can connect to SQL Server database with Import Data or DirectQuery. It is the same data source, however, just different types of connections.

Every Connection type has some advantages and disadvantages. One connection type is suitable for smaller datasets, one for big, one connection type is useful for better flexibility, the other for not needing the scheduled refresh, etc. You cannot change the type of connection in the middle of your Power BI development cycle. Choosing the connection type is one of the decisions that should be made at the beginning. Otherwise, you might end up with a lot of reworking.

© Reza Rad 2018
R. Rad, *Pro Power BI Architecture*, https://doi.org/10.1007/978-1-4842-4015-1_5

Importing Data

Import Data is the first type of connection, which I explain here in this chapter. This type of connection imports the whole dataset into the memory. This memory will be the memory of the machine that hosts the Power BI report. If you have Power BI report opened in Power BI Desktop, then it will be the memory of the machine that Power BI Desktop is running on it. When you publish your report into Power BI website, it will be the memory of that machine in the cloud.

Loading data into the memory also means something more: data needs to be refreshed. The process of updating the data needs to be scheduled if you are using this method of connection. Otherwise, data will be obsolete. That is why this technique is called Import Data, or Scheduled Refresh.

To have a closer look at importing data, create a suitable report. Open Power BI Desktop, click on Get Data, and finally choose Excel from the drop-down. Figure 5-1 illustrates.

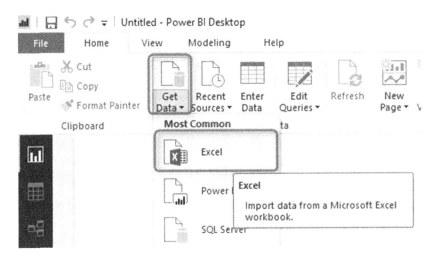

Figure 5-1. *Get Data from Excel*

Select the Excel file Pubs Descriptions.xlsx. You should see the screen in Figure 5-2. Place check marks to select all the tables in the list. Then click on Load.

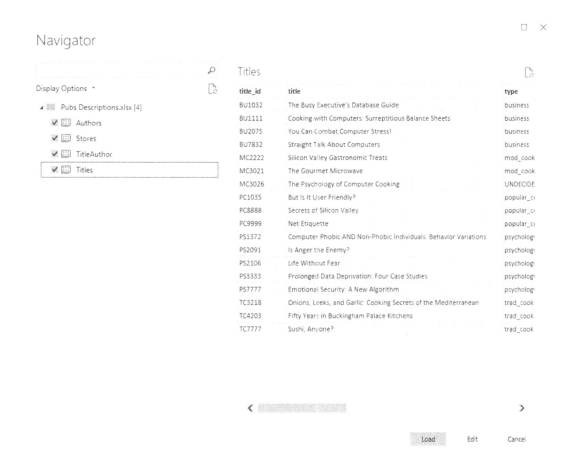

Figure 5-2. *Select all tables*

You will see that Power BI loads this data into the model. You should see a status screen like that in Figure 5-3 during the load process.

Figure 5-3. *Data Loads into memory*

As you probably guessed already, the example in this chapter shows the Import Data Connection Type. The Excel data source only supports an Import Data Connection type. If a data source supports multiple connection types, then you can choose which connection type you prefer when you are connecting to that source. For example, if you are connecting to SQL Server database, you will see an option to choose Import or DirectQuery, as shown in Figure 5-4.

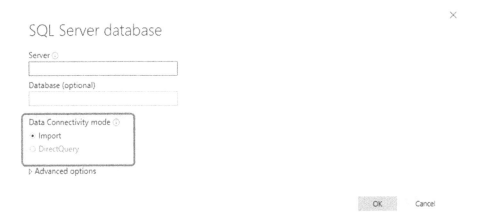

Figure 5-4. *SQL Server database supports multiple connection types*

How Power BI Stores Data into Memory

The very first question that comes to your mind is then this: How big does the memory need to be? What if I have hundreds of millions of records? Or many gigabytes of data? How does Power BI store data into the memory? To answer that question, you need to learn first a little bit about an in-memory engine named xVelocity.

Power BI, SQL Server Analysis Services Tabular, and Power Pivot are three technologies that are using the same engine for storing data: an in-memory engine named xVelocity. xVelocity is storing data in the memory. However, it applies a few compression steps to the data before storing it. The data stored in the memory would not be the same size as your data source in the majority of the cases. Data will be compressed significantly. However, the compression is not always at the same rate. Depending on many factors, it might behave differently.

How xVelocity Compresses the Data

To learn the whole concept of data compression in xVelocity, you need to read a book. However, in this section, very briefly I'm going to explain to you what happens when xVelocity engine works on compressing the data.

Traditional database technologies stored data on disk because disk was the only suitable option at the time. Consider a table such as in Figure 5-5.

4 bytes	4 bytes	4 bytes	8 bytes	3 bytes	16 bytes	16 bytes		Total each row: 100 bytes
Order ID	Quarter	Quantity	Sales Amount	Oder Date	uniqueidentifier	text	other columns	
1	1	5	43254	7/01/2017				
2	1	2	123423	8/01/2017				
3	1	67	234	9/01/2017				Number of rows: 100 Million
4	1	1	523	10/01/2017				
5	1	7	132	11/01/2017				Total space needed: 100M * 100bytes= 10GB
6	1	34	675	12/01/2017				
7	1	3	79678	13/01/2017				
8	2	8	90780	10/05/2017				
9	2	45	89	11/05/2017				
10	2	9	868	12/05/2017				

Figure 5-5. *Traditional way of storing data*

As you can see in Figure 5-5, every column consumes space depending on the data type of the column. An entire row could end up consuming, say, 100 bytes. Then for 100 million rows in the table, you will need 10 gigabytes of space on the disk. That large volume of data is why traditional database technologies stored their data on disk.

xVelocity uses Column-store technology combined with other performance-tuned compression algorithms. In simple words, xVelocity stores data column by column, and it will first sort every column by its values. Then it will create a mapping table for it with indexes at the beginning and end of each section. Figure 5-6 illustrates this column-centric approach.

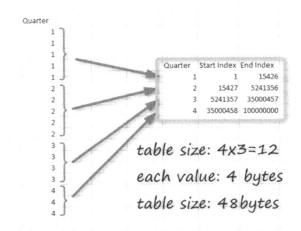

Figure 5-6. *xVelocity compression and mapping table*

The whole point of this compression is that when you have a huge column, a lot of values are repetitive in that column. For the Quarter column in the example above, you can have only four unique values. So instead of storing that for 100 million times, which takes about 400MB space (4 bytes every value, multiplied by 100 million rows will be equal to 400MB), you can store unique values and their start and end indexes.

The mapping table showed in the above image, is a table of three columns, and four rows mean 12 values. Even considering 4 bytes for each; this table would end up being 48 bytes only. The method explained in the above paragraphs is roughly how the compression engine works in xVelocity.

Compression has other levels as well, but the mapping table illustrated in Figure 5-6 is the core of compression. Learning this means you know that the data before Power BI loads it into memory will be compressed. The size of data in Power BI is probably not the same size of the data in your source database or file. You might have an Excel file with 800MB size, and that data might consume only 8 MB after you load it into Power BI. Such compression obviously depends on many things, including the cardinality of the data and the number of unique values in each column.

Important   If you have a column with a lot of unique values, then the compression engine of Power BI suffers, and Power BI memory consumption will be quite large. Examples are the ID of the fact tables (Not ID of dimensions that used in the fact table as a foreign key), and also certain created or update timestamp columns that even sometimes contain dates and times to the millisecond.

Where Data Is Stored in Memory

Your next question maybe is where the data is stored in the memory. Power BI models are always loaded into an Analysis Services engine. Even if you don't have Analysis Services installed, it will be in your system when you use Power BI with an Import Data connection type.

To check and see that Analysis Services is really installed, go to Task Manager on the machine on which you have open Power BI Desktop with an Import Data connection mode. You'll find on that machine, that the Microsoft SQL Server Analysis Services engine is running. (See Figure 5-7). Here is where your data is stored in memory. Analysis Services keeps the in-memory. When you save and close your Power BI file, then that data will be persisted in a *.pbix file. The next time you open the file, data will be loaded again into Analysis Services to an in-memory engine.

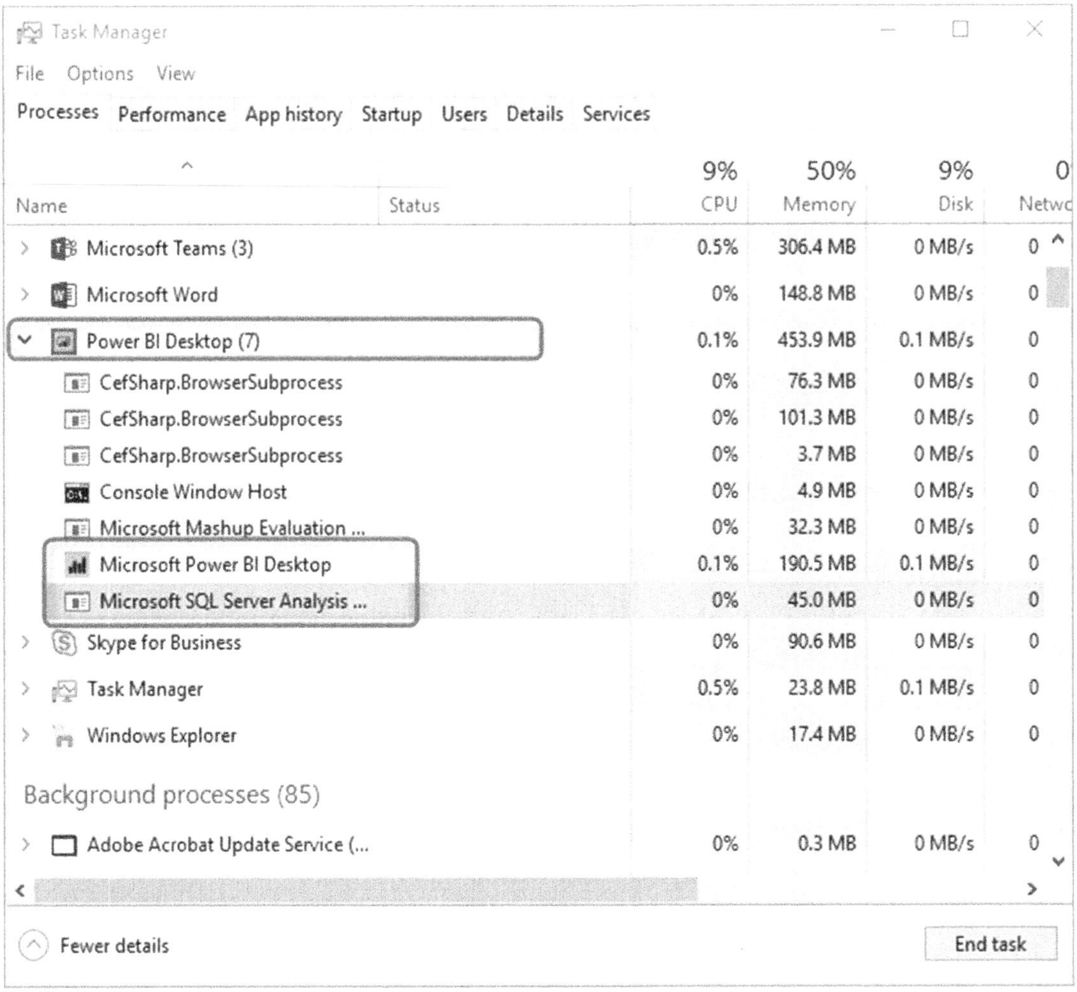

Figure 5-7. *SQL Server Analysis Services stores the data into the memory*

In your Power BI Service, you can also see how much every dataset consumes from the available memory. Just click on the Setting Icon and then on Manage Personal Storage. Figure 5-8 illustrates.

Figure 5-8. *Manage Personal Storage*

Having selected Manage personal storage, you will be taken to the screen in Figure 5-9. There you can look at all datasets and their sizes.

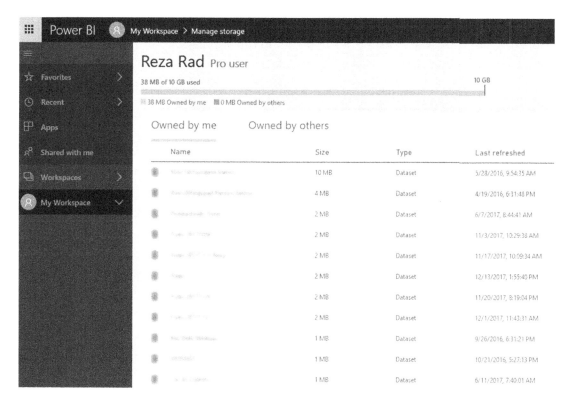

Figure 5-9. *Check dataset sizes in Power BI service*

Is There a Limitation on the Size?

If you are developing Power BI files and then publishing them to the service, there is a limitation on the sizes of the files. Because Power BI service is a cloud-shared hosting service for Power BI datasets, then it needs to limit the access so that everyone can use the service with a reasonable response time.

At the time of writing this chapter, the limit for Power BI file size is 1GB per model (or dataset in other words). You will have 10GB space in your account, but every file cannot be more than 1GB. If you load your data into Power BI, and the file size ends up being more than 1GB, then you need to think about another connection type.

Power BI Premium is a subscription that offers dedicated capacity in Power BI service. With Power BI Premium, you can have much more extensive datasets. At the time of writing this chapter, the dataset size for Power BI premium models can be 10GB for a P3 SKU. It is also on the road map of the Power BI team to increase this size and bring larger datasets to the service.

Combining Data Sources

So far you know how the Import Data connection type works. Now let's see scenarios that this type of connection is suitable for. One of the advantages of this type of connection is the ability to combine any types of data sources. Part of data can come from Excel, and another part from SQL Server database, or from a web page. With an Import Data connection type, Power Query is fully functional.

In the same Power BI file that you have been using so far (which has data from Pubs Descriptions.xlsx Excel file in it), click on Get Data and choose from Text/CSV. Figure 5-10 illustrates.

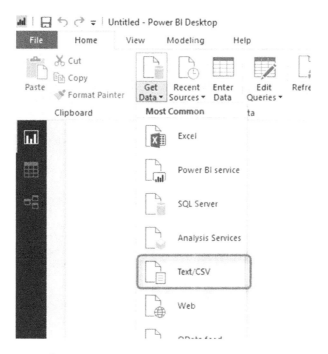

Figure 5-10.   *Get Data from Text/CSV*

Now select the Pubs Transactions.csv file, and then click on Load. Then click on the relationship tab. The relationship tab is on the left-hand side panel, the bottom option. You will see a view like that in Figure 5-11 showing that tables from both data sources are connected to each other.

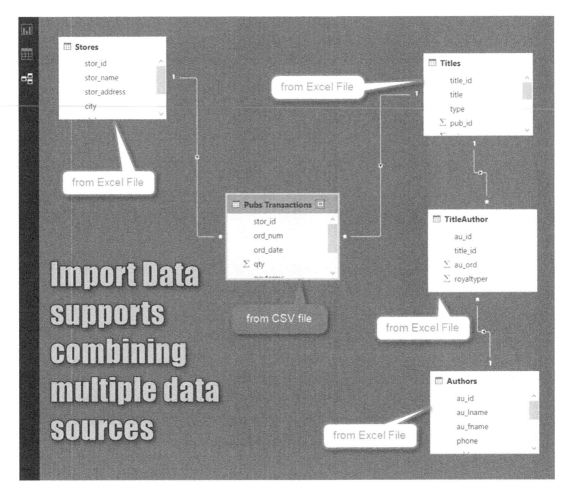

Figure 5-11. *Relationship Diagram; Import Data supports combining multiple data sources*

One of the main benefits of the Import Data is that you can bring data from any data sources, and combine them with each other. You can also leverage full functional Power Query with this connection type. You can do many data transformations and calculations with Power Query. To see the Power Query transformations, click on Edit Queries as shown in Figure 5-12.

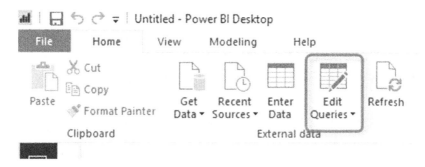

Figure 5-12. *Edit Queries*

You can then see the Query Editor with many transformations built in to use. To learn Power Query, you should read one of the many books focused on that specific topic. One option is my free book, "Power BI from Rookie to Rockstar," available from my website at radacad.com. Figure 5-13 shows the Query Editor window.

Figure 5-13. *Query Editor window*

Analytical Expression Language

Another powerful functionality of Power BI that you have access to when using Import Data is DAX. DAX is the language that you can leverage to do analytical calculations. Calculations such as Year to Date, rolling average 12 months, and many other calculations become super efficient to be done in DAX. DAX is a language that is supported in all xVelocity technologies of Microsoft (Power BI, Power Pivot, and SQL Server Analysis Services Tabular). You can write any DAX calculations in Import Data mode, such as Quantity Year to date as shown in Figure 5-14.

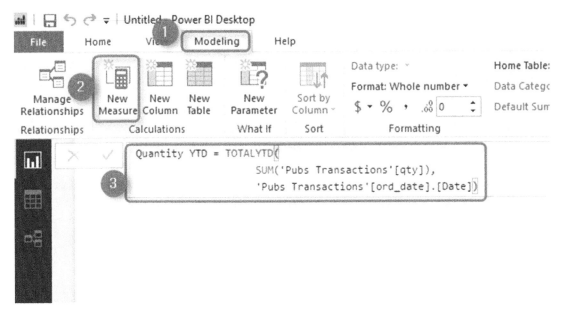

Figure 5-14. *DAX calculation for Year to Date*

The calculation in Figure 5-14 is a measure. You define such measures in DAX, and the following code is used in the figure:

```
Quantity YTD = TOTALYTD(
                SUM('Pubs Transactions'[qty]),
                'Pubs Transactions'[ord_date].[Date])
```

The result from the operations in this code is the year-to-date value of the quantity. Figure 5-15 shows the result in the Query Editor.

Year	Quarter	Month	Day	qty	Quantity YTD
1994	Qtr 3	September	13	78	78
1994	Qtr 3	September	14	85	163
1994	Qtr 3	September	15		163
1994	Qtr 3	September	16		163
1994	Qtr 3	September	17		163
1994	Qtr 3	September	18		163
1994	Qtr 3	September	19		163
1994	Qtr 3	September	20		163
1994	Qtr 3	September	21		163
1994	Qtr 3	September	22		163
1994	Qtr 3	September	23		163
1994	Qtr 3	September	24		163
1994	Qtr 3	September	25		163
1994	Qtr 3	September	26		163
1994	Qtr 3	September	27		163
1994	Qtr 3	September	28		163
1994	Qtr 3	September	29		163
Total				493	163

Figure 5-15. *Year-to-date calculation visualized in a table*

DAX is another powerful component of Power BI. This component is fully functional in Import Data. There are many calculations you can write using DAX, and I cover the language in my online book, "Power BI book from Rookie to Rock Star."

Publishing a report is all the same for Import Data or other types of connections. You can click on Publish in the home tab, and publish it to your workspace.

Gateway Configuration

For Import Data connection types that uses on-premises data sources, you need to have a gateway. If your data sources are all cloud based (such as Azure SQL database, etc.), you don't need a gateway for that.

Because in an Import Data connection type, you can easily combine multiple data sources to each other, it is very likely that your Power BI file has more than one data source in it. You need first to check all data sources in your Power BI Desktop and define them all under the gateway.

To find data sources in Power BI Desktop, click the Home tab, go under Edit Queries, then choose Data Source Settings. Figure 5-16 illustrates.

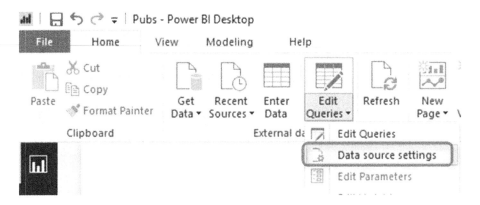

Figure 5-16. *Data Source settings*

Under Data source settings is where you will find all data sources listed. Figure 5-17 shows the results on my PC as I write this book, and you can see that I have two data sources available.

Data source settings

Manage settings for data sources that you have connected to using Power BI Desktop.

⦿ Data sources in current file   ○ Global permissions

Search data source settings

c:\users\rezarad\dropbox (rada...05\code\pubs descriptions.xlsx
c:\users\rezarad\dropbox (rada... 05\code\pubs transactions.csv

Figure 5-17. *All data sources in the current file*

In the previous chapter, I explained how to add data sources in the gateway. You need to make sure that all data sources in the *.pbix file are defined under the same gateway as shown in Figure 5-18. Otherwise, you won't be able to use the gateway for the dataset.

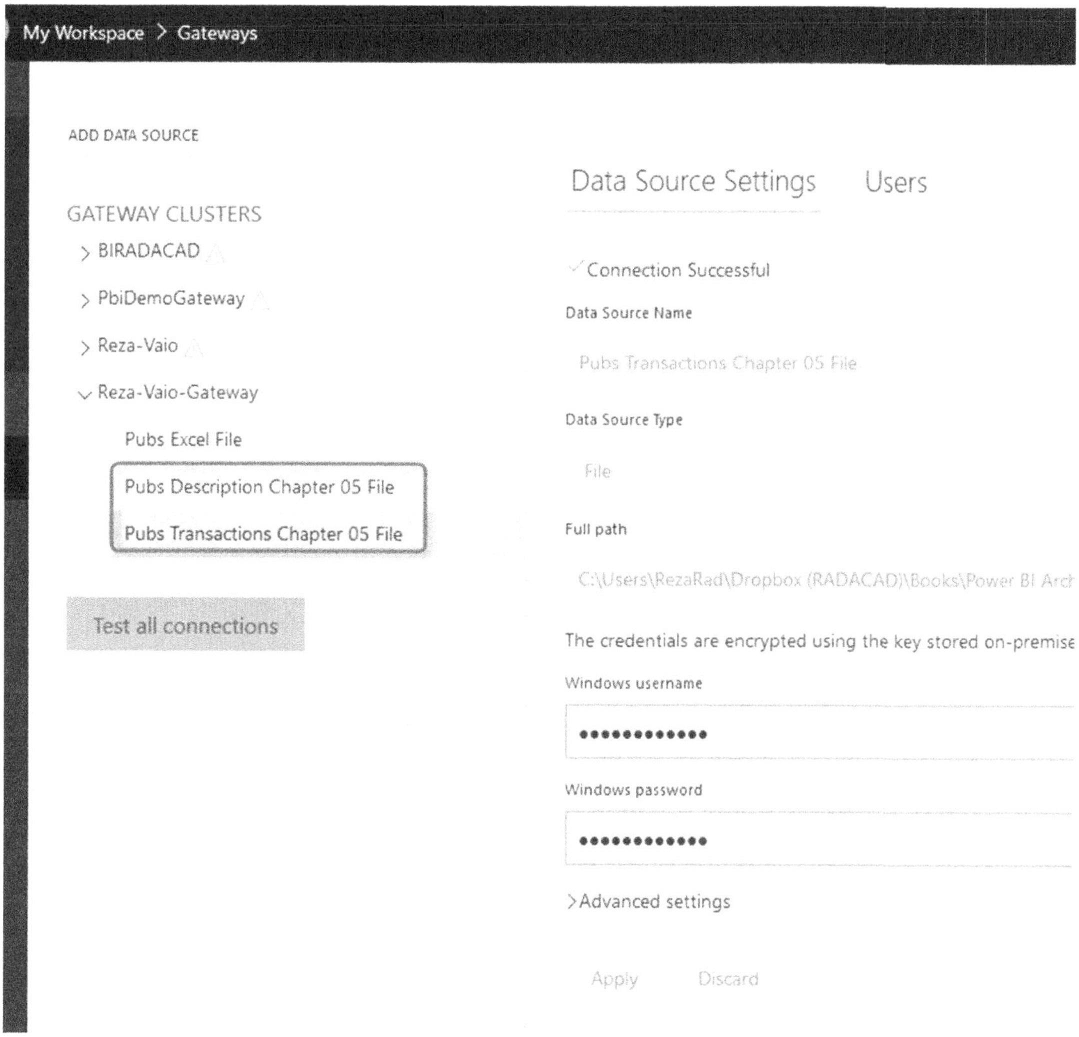

My Workspace > Gateways

ADD DATA SOURCE

GATEWAY CLUSTERS

> BIRADACAD

> PbiDemoGateway

> Reza-Vaio

∨ Reza-Vaio-Gateway

   Pubs Excel File

   Pubs Description Chapter 05 File

   Pubs Transactions Chapter 05 File

Test all connections

Data Source Settings   Users

✓ Connection Successful

Data Source Name

   Pubs Transactions Chapter 05 File

Data Source Type

   File

Full path

   C:\Users\RezaRad\Dropbox (RADACAD)\Books\Power BI Arch

The credentials are encrypted using the key stored on-premise

Windows username

   ••••••••••••

Windows password

   ••••••••••••

>Advanced settings

Apply   Discard

Figure 5-18. *Add all data sources under the gateway*

Schedule Refresh

After adding all sources, then you can connect the gateway to the dataset. You can also schedule the refresh of the dataset on a recurring basis. To schedule a refresh, click the highlighted icon at the right side of Figure 5-19.

Power BI
My Workspace
Favorites
Recent
Apps
Shared with me
Workspaces
My Workspace
import
Dashboards
Reports
Workbooks
Datasets
NAME
ACTIONS
Pubs Import Data

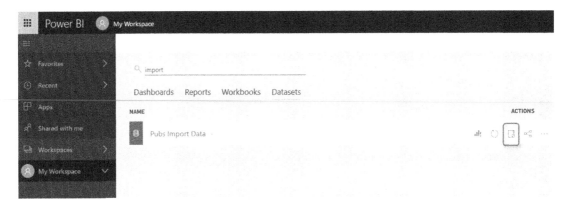

***Figure 5-19.** Schedule Refresh*

Refreshes can be scheduled weekly, or daily, as shown in Figure 5-20. You can schedule a maximum of eight refreshes per day, However, with Power BI Premium, you are not limited and may schedule any number of refreshes per day.

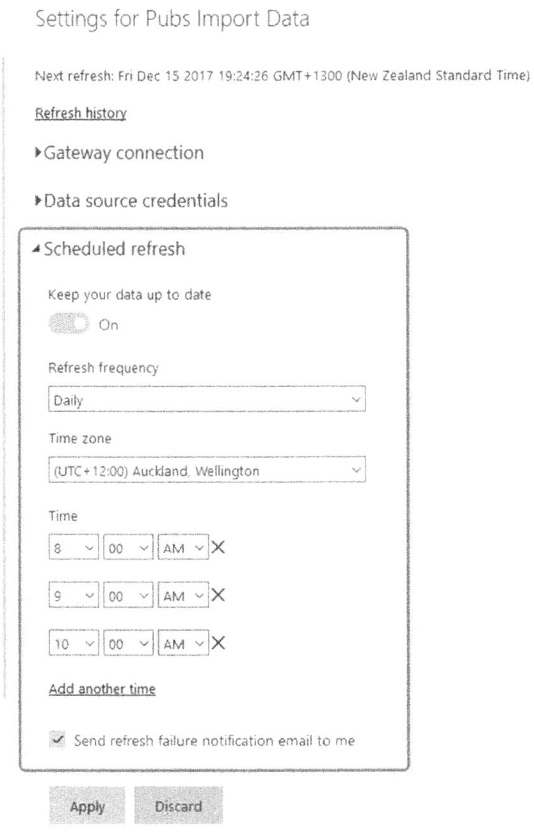

Settings for Pubs Import Data
Next refresh: Fri Dec 15 2017 19:24:26 GMT+1300 (New Zealand Standard Time)
Refresh history
Gateway connection
Data source credentials
Scheduled refresh
Keep your data up to date
On
Refresh frequency
Daily
Time zone
(UTC+12:00) Auckland, Wellington
Time
8 00 AM
9 00 AM
10 00 AM
Add another time
Send refresh failure notification email to me
Apply
Discard

***Figure 5-20.** Schedule Refresh configuration*

After setting up the scheduled refresh, you can see the next refresh and the last refresh time in the dataset properties. See Figure 5-21 for an example.

Figure 5-21. *Checking times for next and last refresh*

Advantages and Disadvantages of Import Data

Let's wrap up things up by recapping the advantages and disadvantages of Import Data. Following are the advantages:

- Speed from the In-Memory Database Engine: the Import Data connection type comes with w super-fast response time. Remember that it is an in-memory technology, and querying data from memory is much faster than querying from disk. The Import Data method of connection is the fastest method of connection in Power BI.

- Flexibility from DAX and Power Query: you have DAX and Power Query fully functional. These are two dominant components of Power BI. In fact, Power BI without these two elements is just a visualization tool. The existence of Power Query and DAX make Power BI an extraordinary tool that can cover all analytics requirements. If you use Power BI with other types of connections, you don't have these two components fully functional. Import Data gives you the flexibility to do data manipulation with Power Query and analytical calculations with DAX.

Nothing is without trade-offs. Disadvantages of Import Data connection types include the following:

- Requirement to Schedule Refresh: in many BI scenarios, data will be refreshed overnight or on a scheduled basis. However, sometimes the demand is to have data without delay. Import Data is not capable of doing that. With Import Data, there is a need for the dataset to be refreshed. And it can be scheduled to refresh up to 8 times a day (or 48 times a day with Power BI Premium).

- Large Scale Data: if your dataset is massive, let's say petabytes of data, and the compression engine of Power BI cannot fit your data into the allowed size of 1GB per model, then you must change the type of connection. Alternatively, you can choose to be part of a Power BI Premium capacity and leverage a larger dataset allowance with that option.

Summary

In this chapter, you learned about Import Data or Scheduled Refresh. With this type of connection, the data will be imported into the memory. However, data will be compressed, and the copy of the data in memory would be usually smaller than the actual data source size. Because this method copies the data into the memory, you do need to set a scheduled refresh for this model.

Import Data or Scheduled Refresh is the fastest method, the agilest way of working with Power BI, and the most thoroughly functional connection type in Power BI. It allows you to combine multiple data sources with Power Query, write analytical calculations with DAX, and finally visualize the data. This method is super- ast because reading data from memory is always faster than reading from disk.

However, The Import Data mode has a couple of limitations: the need to refresh data is one of them, and the other one is the size limitation of Power BI files. Size limitation can be lifted using Power BI premium capacity, or by changing to other types of connections, which I explain in the few next chapters.

CHAPTER 6

DirectQuery

In the last chapter, you learned about Import Data as a connection type. In this chapter, you'll learn about the second type of connection named DirectQuery. This type of connection is only supported by a limited number of data sources, and mainly targets systems with a huge amount of data. DirectQuery is different from another type of connection, which I'll talk about in the next chapter, named Live Connection.

When a dataset is very large, loading data into Power BI might not be an option. Some data sources support a DirectQuery connection. In this chapter, you learn about this type of connection. DirectQuery will be explained through an example and demo of connection SQL Server on-premises' connection to Power BI. This chapter also explains the pros and cons of this type of connection at the end.

What Is DirectQuery?

DirectQuery is a type of connection in Power BI that does not load data into the Power BI model. If you remember from the previous chapter, Power BI loads data into memory (when Import Data or Scheduled Refresh is used as a connection type). DirectQuery doesn't consume memory because there will be no second copy of the data stored. DirectQuery means Power BI is directly connected to the data source. Anytime you see a visualization in a report, the data comes straight from a query sent to the data source.

© Reza Rad 2018
R. Rad, *Pro Power BI Architecture*, https://doi.org/10.1007/978-1-4842-4015-1_6

Which Data Sources Support DirectQuery?

Unlike Import Data, which is supported in all types of data sources, DirectQuery is only supported by a limited number of data sources. You cannot create a connection as a DirectQuery to an Excel File. Usually, data sources that are relational database models, or have a modeling engine, support DirectQuery mode. Here are all data sources supported through DirectQuery (as of today):

- Amazon Redshift
- Azure HDInsight Spark (Beta)
- Azure SQL Database
- Azure SQL Data Warehouse
- Google BigQuery (Beta)
- IBM Netezza (Beta)
- Impala (version 2.x)
- Oracle Database (version 12 and above)
- SAP Business Warehouse (Beta)
- SAP HANA
- Snowflake
- Spark (Beta) (version 0.9 and above)
- SQL Server
- Teradata Database
- Vertica (Beta)

This list may change with every new update in Power BI connectors, and some new data sources may be added to the DirectQuery-supported lists of Power BI. To view the up-to-date list always use this link:

`https://docs.microsoft.com/en-us/power-bi/desktop-directquery-data-sources`

From the list above, those connections that are Beta or Preview are not yet supported in the Power BI service.

How to Use DirectQuery

For running this example, you need to have an SQL Server instance installed. You can download SQL Server Developer edition from here:

https://www.microsoft.com/en-us/sql-server/sql-server-downloads

Then set up AdventureWorksDW database on it. You can get that database from here:

https://github.com/Microsoft/sql-server-samples/releases/download/
adventureworks/AdventureWorksDW2016.bak

This book is not about installing and configuring SQL Server or setting up a database on it. So, I'm not going to explain how to do those things. We'll only talk about the Power BI part of the picture in this chapter.

Get started by opening Power BI Desktop and choosing to Get Data from SQL Server. Figure 6-1 shows how to choose that option.

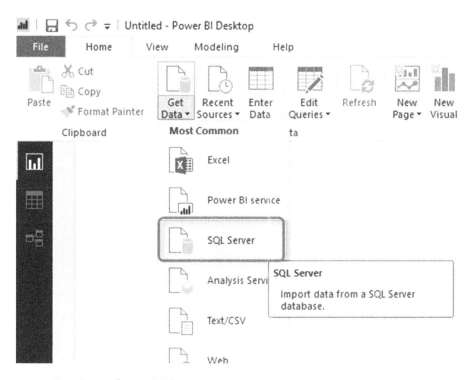

Figure 6-1. *Get Data from SQL Server*

The very first query you will get when connecting to SQL Server includes an option for choosing the Data Connectivity mode. Select DirectQuery for this chapter's example, as shown in Figure 6-2. Also, you need to put your server name. If your SQL Server instance is the default instance on your machine, you can type a dot (.) for the server name.

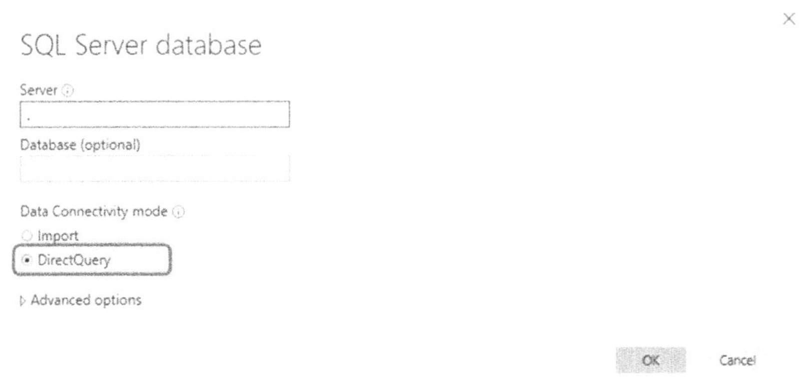

Figure 6-2. *Selecting DirectQuery Mode*

Any data source that supports DirectQuery also supports Import Data.

In the Navigator window, you can select some tables from AdventureWorksDW database. Choose the DimDate and FactInternetSale tables as shown in Figure 6-3.

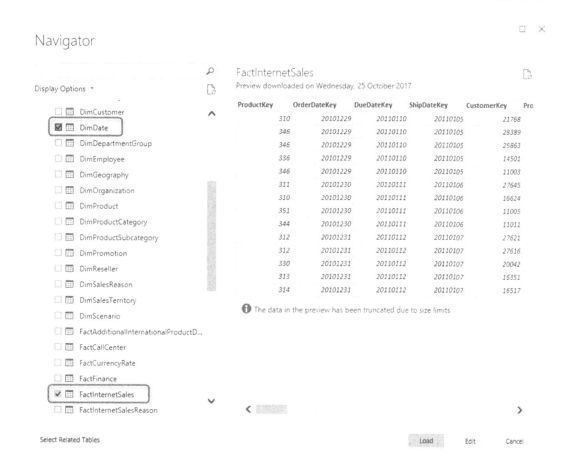

Figure 6-3. *Select Tables in DirectQuery mode*

After selecting tables, click on Load. The data load dialog in this connection mode will be much faster because there is no process of loading data into the memory. This time, only metadata will be loaded into Power BI. The data remains in the SQL Server.

No Data Tab in DirectQuery Mode

One of the very first things you will notice in the DirectQuery Mode is that there is no Data Tab (the middle tab on the left-hand side navigations of Power BI). Notice in Figure 6-4 that the Data Tab is absent from the left side.

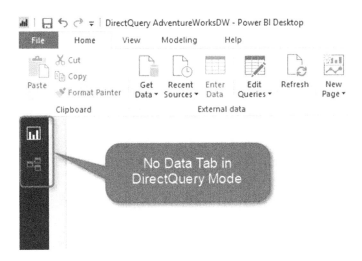

Figure 6-4. *No Data Tab in the DirectQuery Mode*

The Data tab shows you the data in the Power BI model. However, with DirectQuery, there is no data stored in the model. Also, at the bottom right side of the Power BI Desktop, and as shown in Figure 6-5, you will notice that there is a note about the connection being a DirectQuery connection.

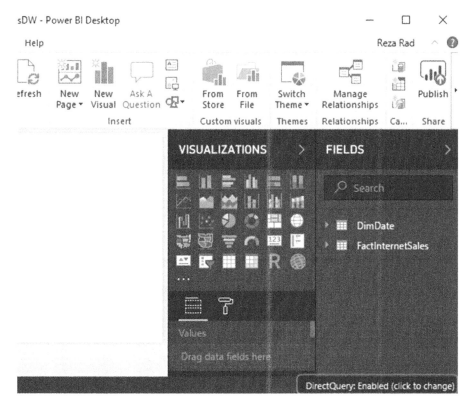

Figure 6-5. *DirectQuery is enabled*

How DirectQuery Works

With DirectQuery enabled; every time you see a visualization, Power BI sends a query to the data source, and the result of that comes back. You can check this process in SQL Profiler. SQL Profiler is a tool that you can use to capture queries sent to a SQL Server database.

Figure 6-6 shows an example Power BI report visual on a DirectQuery model.

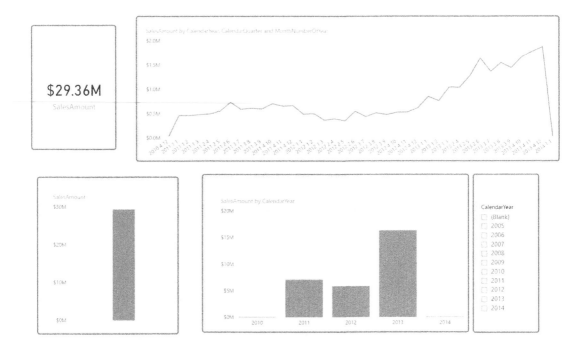

Figure 6-6. *Sample Power BI Report*

Running SQL Profiler will show you that every time you refresh that report page or change something that forces the page to refresh, there will be one query for every single visualization! See Figure 6-7 for an example.

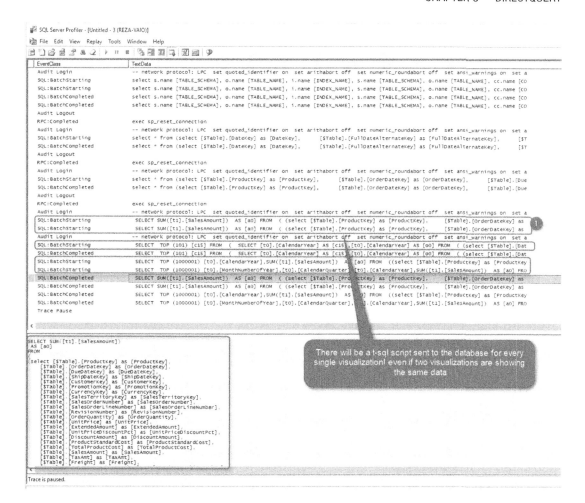

Figure 6-7. *Capturing queries sent to the database with SQL Profiler*

You can see that in the SQL Profiler, five queries have been sent to the database. That works out to one query for each of the five visualizations shown in Figure 6-6. Even if two visualizations are showing visuals from the very same data, as shown in Figure 6-8, they still send separate queries to the database.

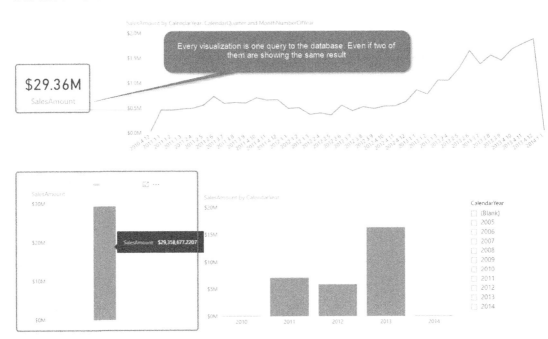

Figure 6-8. *Every Visualization will send a query to the database*

Performance

DirectQuery performs much slower than the Import Data option. Import Data loads data into memory. It is always faster to query data from memory (Import Data), rather than querying it from disk (DirectQuery). Whenever you decide to use DirectQuery, you must immediately think about performance tuning for your database.

Using DirectQuery without performance tuning the source database is a mistake that you should avoid.

To understand the need for performance tuning, let's go through an example. Assume that we have a large table in an SQL Server database, a table with 48 million rows in it. Further assume that we are querying the Sum of Sales column from that table. Figure 6-9 shows the performance I get when I have a normal index on my table with 48 million records. Notice the elapsed time of 4 minutes and 4 seconds.

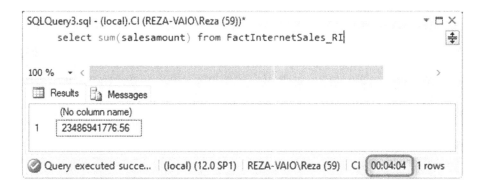

Figure 6-9. *Table with Regular Index*

A simple summation of sales amounts from my table of 48 million records takes 4 minutes and 4 seconds to run. However, Figure 6-10 shows the same query responding in less than a second when I have a clustered column-store index on the table.

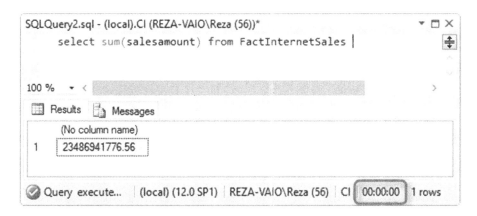

Figure 6-10. *Table with Clustered Column-Store Index*

Whenever connecting to DirectQuery sources, it's worth taking some time to think about how to optimize query execution on those sources. After all, why spend 4 minutes and 4 seconds when you can return the same results in less than a second?

Query Reduction

One of the newest features added in Power BI is to help to reduce the number of queries sent to the database in DirectQuery mode. The default behavior of a slicer or filter in Power BI is that by selecting an item in a slicer or filter, other visuals will be filtered immediately. In the DirectQuery mode, it means it will send multiple queries to the database with every selection in filter or slicer. Sending multiple queries will reduce the performance of your report.

You may want to select multiple items, but with only selecting the first item, five queries will be sent to the database. Then with selecting the second item, another five queries will be sent to the database. The speed, as a result, will be two times slower. To fix this issue, you can set a property in Options of your Power BI file.

Click on File menu in Power BI Desktop, then select Options and Settings, and from there select Options. This is all as shown in Figure 6-11.

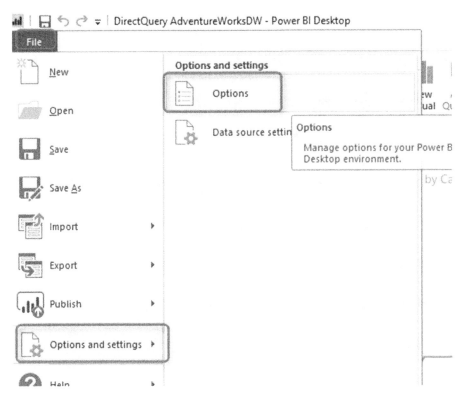

Figure 6-11. *Options in Power BI*

Then click on Query Reduction on the left-hand side under the Current File section. You will see the Options window shown in Figure 6-12.

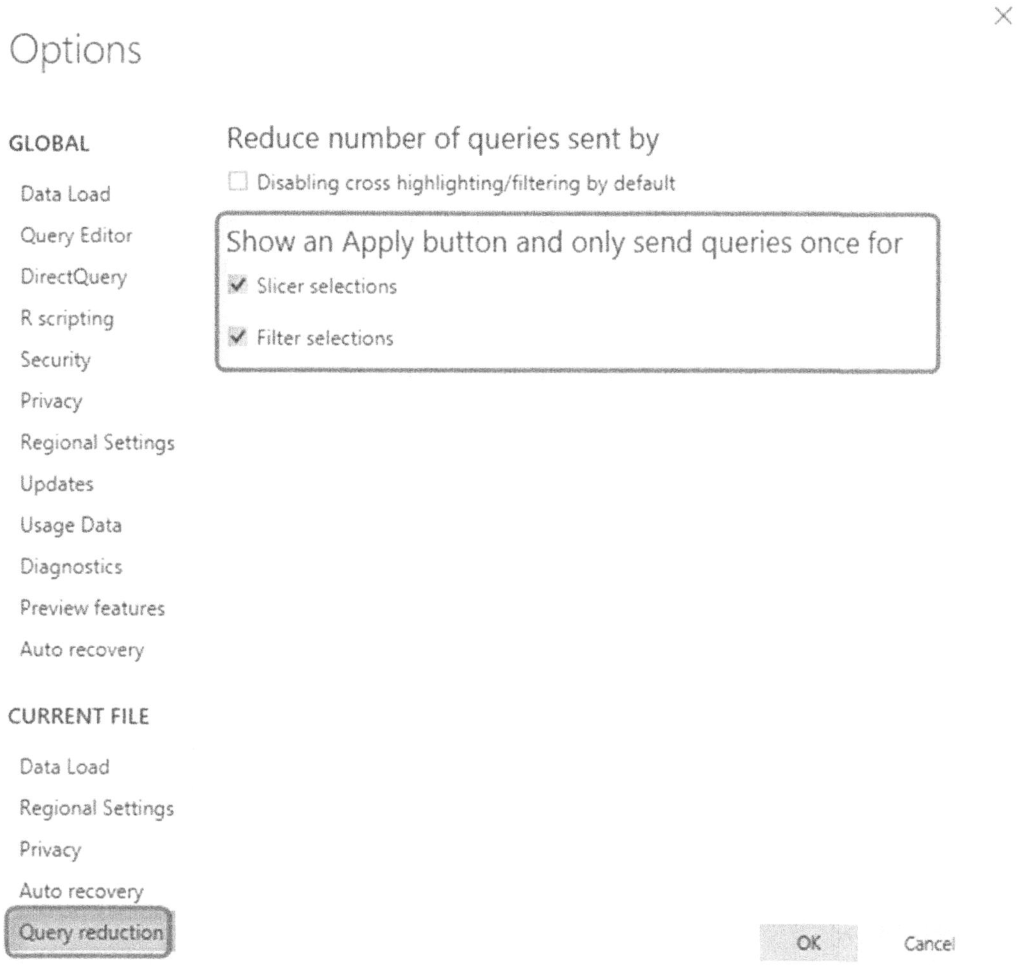

Options   ×

GLOBAL   Reduce number of queries sent by

Data Load   ☐ Disabling cross highlighting/filtering by default

Query Editor   Show an Apply button and only send queries once for

DirectQuery   ☑ Slicer selections

R scripting   ☑ Filter selections

Security

Privacy

Regional Settings

Updates

Usage Data

Diagnostics

Preview features

Auto recovery

CURRENT FILE

Data Load

Regional Settings

Privacy

Auto recovery
                                              OK   Cancel
Query reduction

Figure 6-12. *Query Reduction*

There are two sections in the query reduction. The first item is what I do not recommend in most of the cases. The first item will disable cross-highlighting/filtering by default. Selecting the first option causes the main functionality of Power BI, which is cross-highlighting/filtering, to not work by default. Cross-highlighting/filtering means that when you click on a visual, other visuals will be either filtered or highlighted. This feature is what makes the Power BI an interactive visualization tool. The option for removing it for most of the cases is not useful. However, if you have some visuals that don't need to interact with each other, enabling this option will reduce the number of queries sent to the database.

The second option, however, is beneficial, especially if you have multi-select slicers. When you choose this option, then your filters or slicers will have an Apply button on them. Changes will not apply until you click on the apply button, and then all queries will be sent to the database. This option is highly recommended when you have a multi-selection slicer or filter. See Figure 6-13 for an example of the Apply button, which appears toward the lower right in the figure.

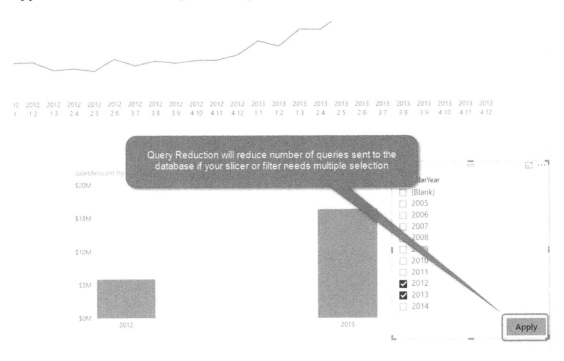

Figure 6-13. *Query Reduction sends queries only once the Apply has been clicked*

Single Data Source

One of the fundamental limitations of DirectQuery mode is single data source support. With this mode, because data is not loaded into a secondary storage, you can only connect to one single data source. If you are connected to an SQL Server database, then you cannot bring another query from another SQL Server database or any other data sources. If you try to do that, you'll get a message such as in Figure 6-14 that says this feature is only supported in Import Data and you have to switch to that.

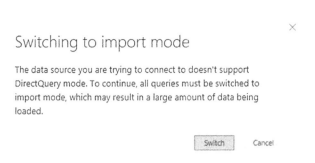

Figure 6-14. *Single Data Source Limitation in DirectQuery*

The concept of using DirectQuery works with having an enterprise data warehouse. You need to bring all data that you need to analyze in your Power BI report, into an enterprise database, and then use that as the source in Power BI with a DirectQuery connection. Using DirectQuery, as a result, means that you have to use other ETL tools to take care of many data transformations.

Limited Power Query

With DirectQuery, you can apply some data transformations in the Query Editor window. However, not all transformations are supported. To find out which transformations are supported and which are not, you have to check the data source first. Some of the data sources are not supporting any transformation at all, such as SAP Business Warehouse. Some of the transformations, such as SQL Server database, support more transformations.

If you use a transformation that is not supported, you'll get an error message such as in Figure 6-15 that says, "This step results in a query that is not supported in DirectQuery mode."

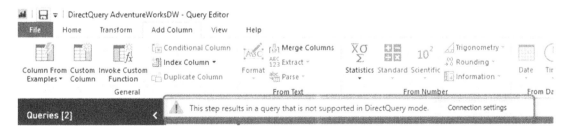

Figure 6-15. *Not all data transformations in Power Query are supported with DirectQuery Mode*

Transformations in Power Query are limited in DirectQuery mode. Depending on the data source, some transformations or sometimes no transformations at all are supported.

As I mentioned earlier; when you use a DirectQuery connection, then you usually should think of another data transformation tool, such as SQL Server Integration Services, etc., to bring data transformed into a data warehouse before connecting Power BI to it.

Limited Modeling

DAX and Modeling are also limited in DirectQuery mode. You cannot create calculated tables because these are in-memory generated tables, and DirectQuery doesn't store anything in memory. You cannot use the built-in Date hierarchy in Power BI. The date hierarchy in Power BI is based on an in-memory date table created when you use Import Data. With DirectQuery such table cannot be built, and as a result, the built-in hierarchy doesn't work in DirectQuery. Figure 6-16 shows some of the grayed-out options that are not available for DirectQuery connections.

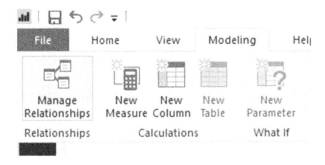

Figure 6-16. *Limited Data Modeling in the DirectQuery mode*

DAX Limitations

You can write DAX calculations as a New Column or New Measure. However, you cannot use all DAX functions. A limited number of functions are available to use. For example; you cannot use PATH functions to create hierarchies on an organizational chart or chart of accounts type of solution. You cannot use many of the Time Intelligence functions such as TotalYTD that calculates an insight out of a DateTime field.

Every DAX expression will be converted to T-SQL script and will run on the database. Here is, for example, a DAX expression to calculate sales for productkey=528:

```
Measure = SUMX(
    FILTER(
        FactInternetSales,
        FactInternetSales[ProductKey]=528
    ),
    FactInternetSales[SalesAmount]
)
```

And here is the T-SQL script cached in SQL Profiler for that expression:

```
SELECT SUM([t1].[SalesAmount])
 AS [a0]
FROM
(
(select [$Table].[ProductKey] as [ProductKey],
    [$Table].[OrderDateKey] as [OrderDateKey],
    [$Table].[DueDateKey] as [DueDateKey],
    [$Table].[ShipDateKey] as [ShipDateKey],
    [$Table].[CustomerKey] as [CustomerKey],
    [$Table].[PromotionKey] as [PromotionKey],
    [$Table].[CurrencyKey] as [CurrencyKey],
    [$Table].[SalesTerritoryKey] as [SalesTerritoryKey],
    [$Table].[SalesOrderNumber] as [SalesOrderNumber],
    [$Table].[SalesOrderLineNumber] as [SalesOrderLineNumber],
    [$Table].[RevisionNumber] as [RevisionNumber],
    [$Table].[OrderQuantity] as [OrderQuantity],
    [$Table].[UnitPrice] as [UnitPrice],
```

```
    [$Table].[ExtendedAmount] as [ExtendedAmount],
    [$Table].[UnitPriceDiscountPct] as [UnitPriceDiscountPct],
    [$Table].[DiscountAmount] as [DiscountAmount],
    [$Table].[ProductStandardCost] as [ProductStandardCost],
    [$Table].[TotalProductCost] as [TotalProductCost],
    [$Table].[SalesAmount] as [SalesAmount],
    [$Table].[TaxAmt] as [TaxAmt],
    [$Table].[Freight] as [Freight],
    [$Table].[CarrierTrackingNumber] as [CarrierTrackingNumber],
    [$Table].[CustomerPONumber] as [CustomerPONumber],
    [$Table].[OrderDate] as [OrderDate],
    [$Table].[DueDate] as [DueDate],
    [$Table].[ShipDate] as [ShipDate]
from [dbo].[FactInternetSales] as [$Table])
)
 AS [t1]
WHERE
(
[t1].[ProductKey] = 528
)
```

The conversion of DAX to T-SQL is not always that simple. With some DAX expressions, the conversion is not good at all. That is why some of the DAX functions are not available to use. There is an option in the Option window – see Figure 6-17 – to choose to use unlimited DAX functions. However, I do not recommend this option.

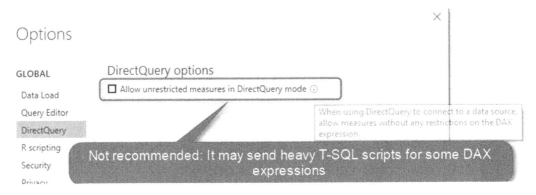

Figure 6-17. *Allow unrestricted measures in DirectQuery Mode*

This option will allow you to use unrestricted measures and DAX expressions. However, I do not recommend it as it will send heavy T-SQL scripts for some of the expressions.

No Refresh Needed

One of the advantages of DirectQuery is that there is no need for data refresh to be scheduled. Because every time a user looks at the report, there is a query sent to the database, and the recent data will be visualized, son there is no need for a data refresh schedule.

For Dashboards when the automatic refresh happens, the DirectQuery connection will be refreshed every 15 minutes or more. For reports, data will be updated anytime a new query is sent to the database, refreshing the report or filtering or slicing and dicing.

Large Scale Dataset

The main benefit of DirectQuery is to use it over a massive amount of data. This feature is in fact, the main reason that you may need to consider DirectQuery. Because the data is not loaded into the memory, there is no limitation on the size of the data source. The only limitation is the limitation that you have in the data source itself. You can have petabytes of data with a DirectQuery connection. However, you need to consider performance tuning in the data source as mentioned before in this chapter.

No size limitation is the main benefit and, in many cases, the only reason why some scenarios use DirectQuery. What you've learned in this chapter is that DirectQuery is slower, less flexible, with fewer features in Power Query, and DAX. Overall, DirectQuery is the only option if the other two types of connections (Import Data, or Live Connection) cannot be used.

Summary

Power BI supports three types of connection. In this chapter, you've learned about DirectQuery which is one of the connection types. DirectQuery is not storing a second copy of the data into memory. It will keep the data in the data source. With DirectQuery, anything you see in the report will be sent to the database through T-SQL scripts. If you have 10 visualizations in your report, it means posting 10 queries to the database and getting the result of that back.

DirectQuery supports a huge amount of data. Because the data is not stored in the memory, the only limitation on the data size is the limitation of the data source itself. You can easily have petabytes of data in a database and connect to it from Power BI. The limitation that we have in Import Data does not apply here, and you can have s large scale dataset for connecting to it. Another advantage of DirectQuery is no need for a scheduled refresh. Because with this mode the data will be updated anytime the report is refreshed with queries sent to the database, there is no need for scheduling refresh.

DirectQuery has many limitations and downsides. With DirectQuery, the speed of Power BI reports is much slower. DirectQuery is limited in using modeling features of Power BI such as DAX, calculated tables, built-in date table, and Power Query functionalities. DirectQuery is, as a result, less flexible with fewer features. Using DirectQuery means you get slower reports, with less functionality on the Power BI side.

DirectQuery, because of the limitations mentioned above is only recommended if the other two types of connections (Import Data or Live Connection) cannot be applied. In the next chapter, I'll explain about Live Connection. If you decided to use DirectQuery, it is then better to use another integration tool and do all the data transformation before loading data into the source database. Also, it is better to take care of all the calculations in the data source itself.

DirectQuery is only recommended if the other two types of connection (Import Data or Live Connection) cannot be applied.

Here is a list of pros and cons of the DirectQuery:

Advantages

– Large Scale Dataset; Size limitation only for the data source itself

– No need for data refresh

Disadvantages

– Single Data Source only

– Power Query transformations are limited

– Modeling is limited

– DAX is limited

– Lower speed of the report

CHAPTER 7

Live Connection

Live Connection is another type of connection in Power BI. This type of connection is somehow similar to DirectQuery because it won't store data in memory. However, it is different from DirectQuery, because it will give you the analytical engine of SQL Server Analysis Services Tabular. With this method, you get benefits of both worlds: large-scale model size and the analytical power of Analysis Services. In this chapter, you'll learn the details of this type of connection, things that you need to consider, and how to set it up working with a gateway.

This chapter focuses on Live Connection. You will learn about this type of connection in detail through an example. You will learn what types of data sources are supported, and what are the considerations for this type of connection. Through the example of this chapter, you learn all details for this type of connection.

What Is Live Connection?

Live Connection is a type of connection only to three types of data sources. This type of connection does not store a second copy of the data into the memory. Data will be kept in the data source, and visualizations will query the data source every time from Power BI. The only three types of data sources supported by this type of connection are:

- SQL Server Analysis Services Tabular

- SQL Server Analysis Services Multi-Dimensional

- Power BI Service Dataset

These three types are SQL Server Analysis Services (SSAS) technology. You cannot have a Live connection to an SQL Server database engine itself. However, the SSAS technology can be cloud based (Azure Analysis Services), or on-premises (SSAS on-premises).

© Reza Rad 2018
R. Rad, *Pro Power BI Architecture*, https://doi.org/10.1007/978-1-4842-4015-1_7

Creating a Report with Live Connection

To create a Live Connection example, you need to have the SQL Server Analysis Services Tabular model installed. You can download the SQL Server trial 180 days edition from this link:

```
https://www.microsoft.com/sql-server/sql-server-downloads
```

After installing SSAS Tabular instance, then you can restore the AdventureWorks Tabular model on it. The database can be accessed and downloaded from here:

```
https://msftdbprodsamples.codeplex.com/downloads/get/353143
```

In this chapter, we are not going into details of how to set up or install SQL Server, or the SSAS tabular model.

To begin, open a Power BI Desktop, select Get Data, then select Analysis Services as shown in Figure 7-1.

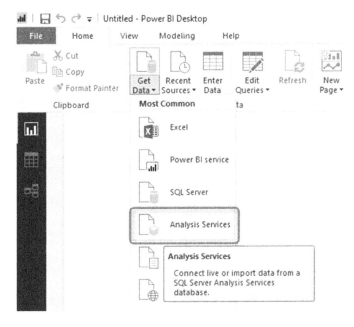

Figure 7-1. *Get Data from Analysis Services*

When connecting to the SQL Server Analysis Services database, you can choose "Connect live." Figure 7-2 shows an example of making this choice.

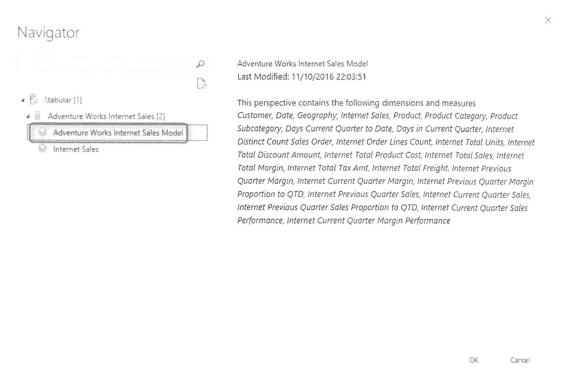

Figure 7-2. *Connect Live to Analysis Services*

The SSAS installed on my machine is in the tabular instance name. That is why I put the server name as ".\tabular". For your machine, the setup might be different. In the Navigator window, you can select the Adventure Works Internet Sales model as shown in Figure 7-3.

Figure 7-3. *Select the Model from Analysis Services*

You just choose a model, not tables. And the model includes multiple tables that, with their relationships, hierarchies, and calculations, will be connected to Power BI. You can see on the right bottom side of Power BI Desktop in Figure 7-4 that the connection in question is mentioned as Live Connection.

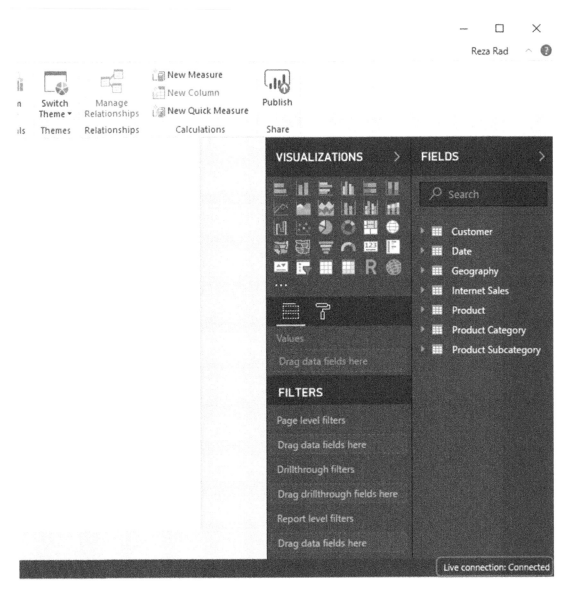

Figure 7-4. *Live Connection enabled*

How Live Connection Works

Consider that we have a Power BI report like in Figure 7-5.

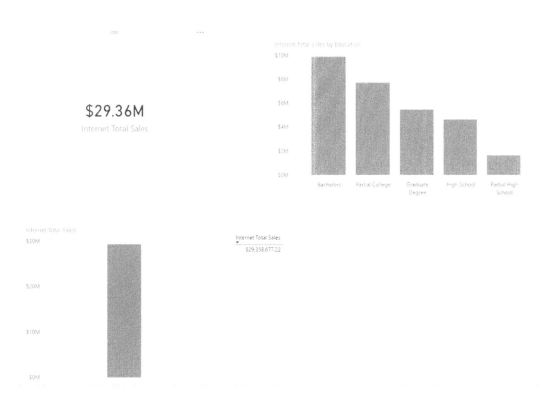

Figure 7-5. *Sample Power BI report*

You can run the SQL Profiler on Analysis Services to capture all DAX queries sent to the database. Figure 7-6 shows the queries posted to the database of the report in Figure 7-5.

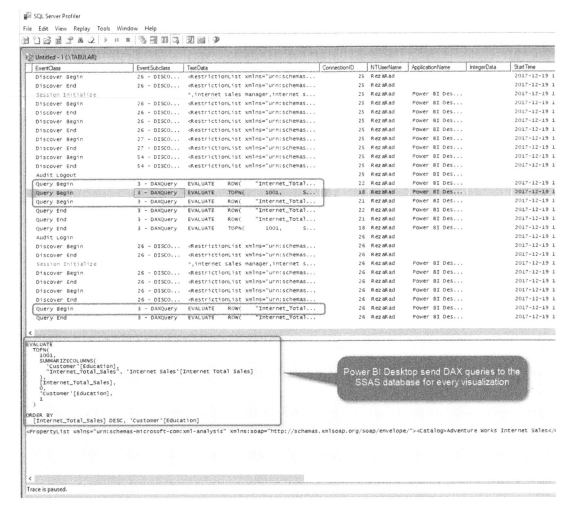

Figure 7-6. *DAX Codes sent to the Analysis Services database*

Like the DirectQuery mode, Power BI Desktop will send a query to the database for every single visualization. However, because these queries run on an analytical engine, you can expect faster results. I should say that you can *usually* expect faster results, because circumstances may vary.

Performance

Live Connection can work faster than DirectQuery in many scenarios. However, in every implementation, many factors affect the performance, and there are always exceptions. In general, because Live connection connects to an analytical engine, then calculations and analytical results come faster than a query from the database.

Using a Live connection to SSAS tabular is usually faster because the data is stored in the memory of the machine that runs SSAS Tabular. However, it depends on the network bandwidth, how calculations and model are implemented, and how it might change.

Live Connection, however, is not as fast as Import Data. Import Data is the fastest possible option regarding performance in Power BI. A Live connection is the second in the list, and DirectQuery is the last one and the slowest one.

Although the performance of the Live Connection is usually better than the DirectQuery, however, I highly recommend performance tuning of the SSAS Model. SSAS Model can perform fast if the server specification is at the right scale, the data model is designed well, and calculations are written a proper way. If any of the items mentioned above don't apply, then the performance of SSAS server and the Live connection will decrease.

Performance Tuning in Live Connection is a Must to do.

Like the DirectQuery mode, Live Connection is only supporting one source for a connection. If you want to have more than one source for a connection, then you need to bring them all into the SSAS model.

No Power Query

With Live Connection, Power Query transformations are not available at all. In fact, the Edit Queries and all related options of that are disabled in the Live Connection mode, and you can see as much in Figure 7-7.

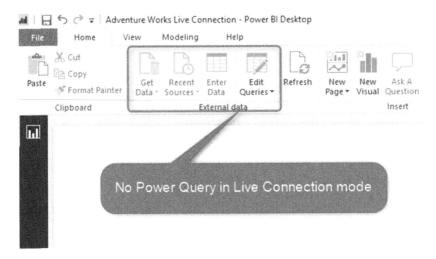

Figure 7-7. *No Power Query in the Live Connection mode*

All data transformation needs must be handled before loading data into SSAS model. Because SSAS is not a data transformation tool, you can leverage SSIS to do the data transformation before loading data into the data warehouse, and then process data from the data warehouse into an SSAS data model. Figure 7-8 illustrates a sample scenario.

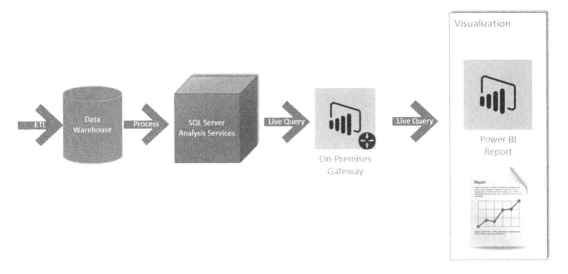

Figure 7-8. *Enterprise usage of Live Connection with a Data Warehouse and ETL*

With the Live Connection, you don't have the relationship tab as well. Power BI becomes a mere visualization tool in this mode. You can see in Figure 7-9 the paucity of options in the left-side menu for a Live Connection data source.

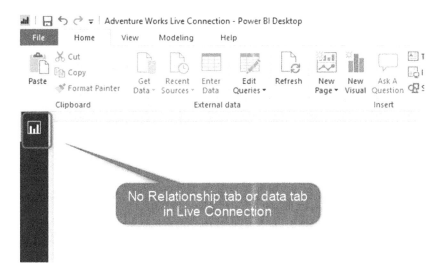

Figure 7-9. *No Relationship tab in the Live Connection*

Modeling and Report Level Measures

With the Live connection, your modeling in Power BI is very limited. You can only create measures. The type of measure that you create a Live Connection is called Report Level Measures. Report Level Measures, as the name of it explains, are only for this Power BI report. If you create another Power BI report connected live to the same data source, you cannot use the report level measures built in a previous Power BI report.

To create a report level measure, click on Add New Measure in the Modeling tab, as shown in Figure 7-10.

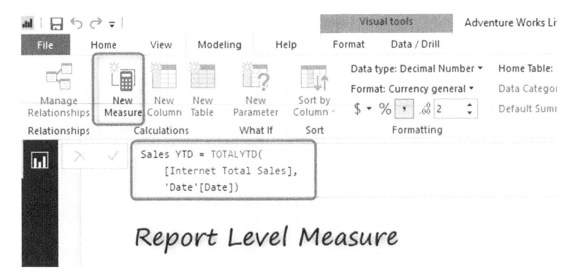

Figure 7-10. *Report Level Measure*

As you can see in Figure 7-10, I have created a report level measure for calculating sales year to date. The code is as follows:

```
Sales YTD = TOTALYTD(
    [Internet Total Sales],
    'Date'[Date])
```

The code that then ends up being sent to SSAS can be fetched using SQL Profiler. That code appears as follows:

```
DEFINE MEASURE 'Customer'[Sales YTD] =
  (/* USER DAX BEGIN */
TOTALYTD(
    [Internet Total Sales],
    'Date'[Date])
/* USER DAX END */)

EVALUATE
  TOPN(
    502,
    SUMMARIZECOLUMNS(
      ROLLUPADDISSUBTOTAL('Date'[Date], "IsGrandTotalRowTotal"),
```

```
    "Internet_Total_Sales", 'Internet Sales'[Internet Total Sales],
    "Sales YTD", 'Customer'[Sales YTD]
  ),
  [IsGrandTotalRowTotal],
  0,
  'Date'[Date],
  1
)

ORDER BY
  [IsGrandTotalRowTotal] DESC, 'Date'[Date]
```

Report Level Measures are not bound to the SSAS model. Report level measures are only for the current Power BI file. In other files they must be created again.

Report Level measures are useful for flexibility and giving the user self-service functionality. However, they will reduce the governance and centralized modeling feature of Live connection.

Publishing and Gateway Configuration

Let's now have a look at how to publish and configure Figure 7-10's report in the Power BI service. Publishing the report is like publishing any other report. You also know from previous chapters how to set up the gateway. Therefore, let's go straight to the point of adding data sources.

Create Data Source

You might think that one gateway is enough for connecting to all data sources in a domain. That is right. However, you still need to add a data source to that gateway per each source. Each source can be an SQL Server database, Analysis Services database, etc. For this chapter's example, we are building a data source for SQL Server Analysis Tabular on premises. Before going through this example, I have installed AW Internet Sales Tabular Model 2014 on my SSAS Tabular and want to connect to it.

For creating a data source, click on Add Data Source in manage gateways window (you have to select the right gateway first). Figure 7-11 illustrates.

Figure 7-11. *Create a Data Source*

Then enter details for the data source. I named my data source as AW Internet Sales Tabular Model 2014, and you can see that name about halfway down in Figure 7-12. I also entered my server name and database name. Then I used Windows authentication by specifying my domain user username and its password.

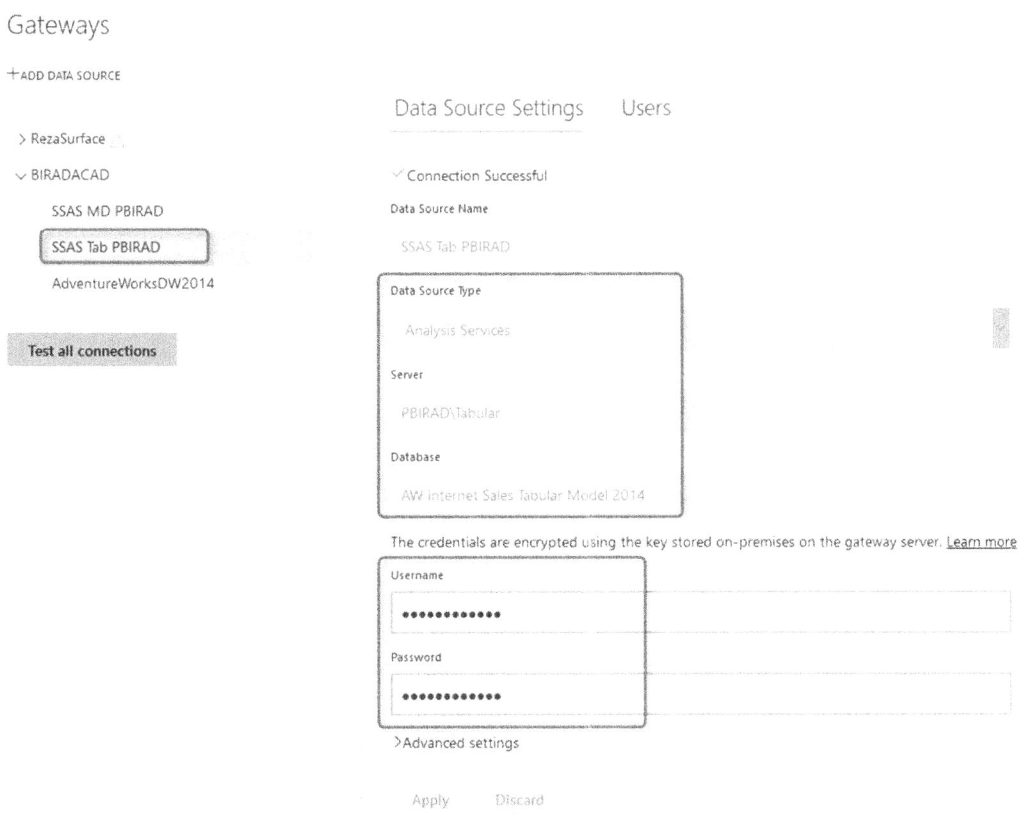

Figure 7-12. *Data Source Configuration*

You should see a successful message after clicking on Apply. The domain name that I use is BIRADACAD (my SSAS Tabular domain), and the user is PBIgateway, which is a user of BIRADACAD domain (username: BIRADACAD\PBIgateway) and an administrator for SSAS Tabular (explained in the next few paragraphs).

Note that the user account that you are using here should meet these conditions:

- It should be a Domain User.

- The domain user should be an administrator in SSAS Tabular.

You can set administrator for SSAS Tabular by right-clicking on the SSAS Tabular instance in SSMS and Properties window, as shown in Figure 7-13.

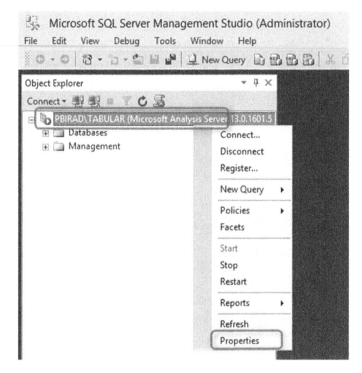

Figure 7-13. *Properties of SSAS Server*

In the Security settings tab, add the user to the administrators list. See Figure 7-14, and notice the BIRADACAD\PBIgateway user that's highlighted in the Server administrators' text box.

Figure 7-14. *Security settings in SSAS server*

Effective User Names

A Gateway account is used for accessing Power BI cloud services from on-premises SSAS Tabular. However, this account by itself isn't enough for the data retrieval. The gateway then passes the EffectiveUserName from Power BI to on-premises SSAS Tabular, and the result of any query will be returned based on the access of EffectiveUserName account to SSAS Tabular database and model. Figure 7-15 illustrates this process.

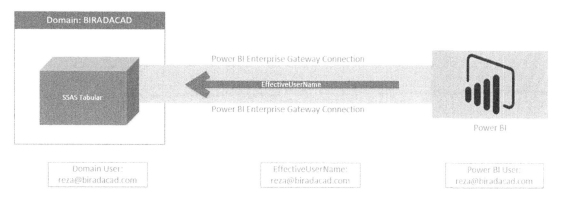

Figure 7-15. *EffectiveUserName*

By default, EffectiveUserName is the username of the logged-in user to Power BI, or in other words EffectiveUserName is the Power BI account. The Power BI account should have enough access to the SSAS Tabular database to fetch required data. If Power BI account is the account from the same domain as SSAS Tabular, then there is no problem, and the security configuration can be set in SSAS Tabular. However, if domains are different, then you have to do UPN mapping.

UPN Mapping

SSAS Tabular is part of a domain (it should be actually because that's how Live connection works), and that domain might be the domain that your Power BI user account lives in. If you are using the same domain user for your Power BI account, then you can skip what's described in this section. If your Power BI user account is in a separate domain from SSIS Tabular, then you have to set the UPN Mapping as illustrated in Figure 7-16.

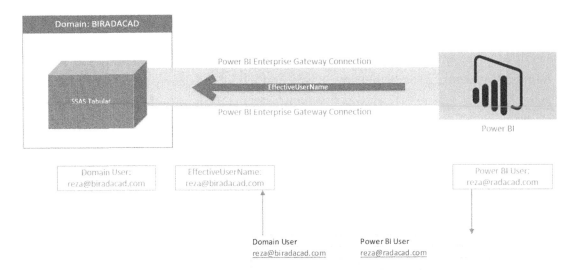

Figure 7-16. *UPN Mapping Table*

UPN Mapping, by simple definition, will map Power BI accounts to your local on-premises SSAS Tabular domain accounts. Because in my example I don't use the same domain account for my Power BI account, I am able to set up UPN as shown in Figure 7-17.

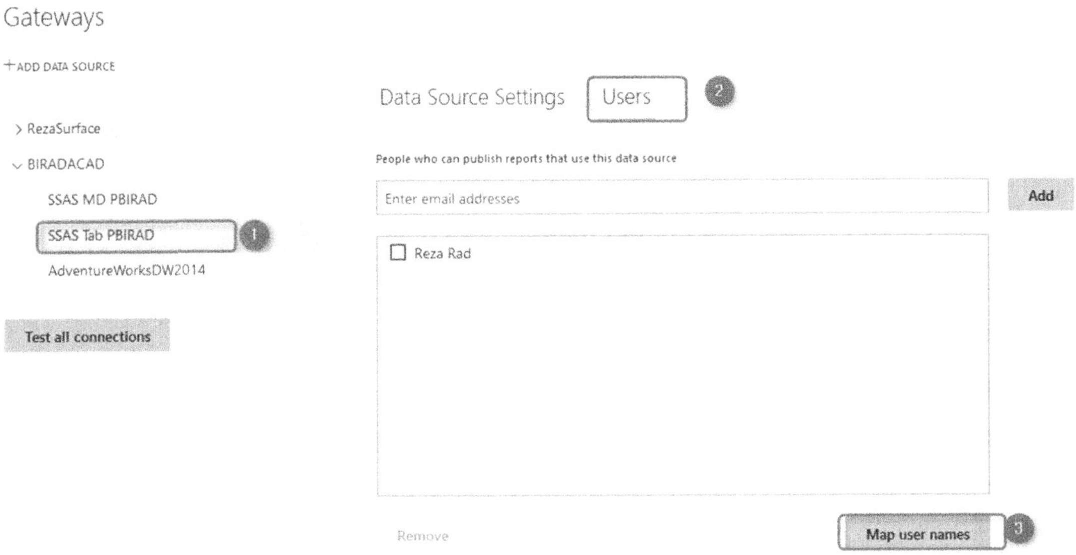

Gateways

+ADD DATA SOURCE

> RezaSurface

∨ BIRADACAD

   SSAS MD PBIRAD

   SSAS Tab PBIRAD   **1**

   AdventureWorksDW2014

Test all connections

Data Source Settings   **Users**   **2**

People who can publish reports that use this data source

Enter email addresses   **Add**

☐ Reza Rad

Remove   **Map user names** **3**

Figure 7-17. *Map User Name in the data source*

Then in then Mapping pane, I create a new mapping that maps my Power BI user account to reza@biradacad.com, which is my local domain for SSAS Tabular server. See Figure 7-18 for an example of how I do this.

Figure 7-18. UPN mapping setting in Power BI service

Now with this username mapping, reza@biradacad.com will be passed as EffectiveUserName to the SSAS Tabular.

Live Connection to Power BI Service

Another type of Live connection is to connect to a dataset published in Power BI service, as shown in Figure 7-19. This dataset will be treated as an SSAS instance. The dataset in Power BI service is hosted in a shared SSAS cloud environment. When you connect to it from Power BI Desktop, it is like connecting to an instance of SSAS with a Live connection.

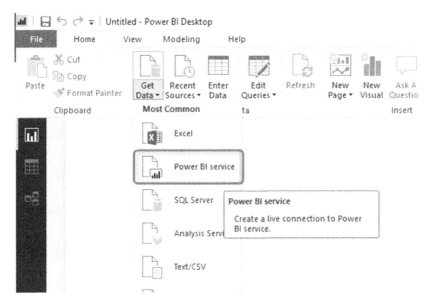

Figure 7-19. *Get data from Power BI service*

For this option, you need to be logged in to the Power BI Desktop. You will see list of all datasets that you have Edit access on. Then you can choose one of them as illustrated in Figure 7-20.

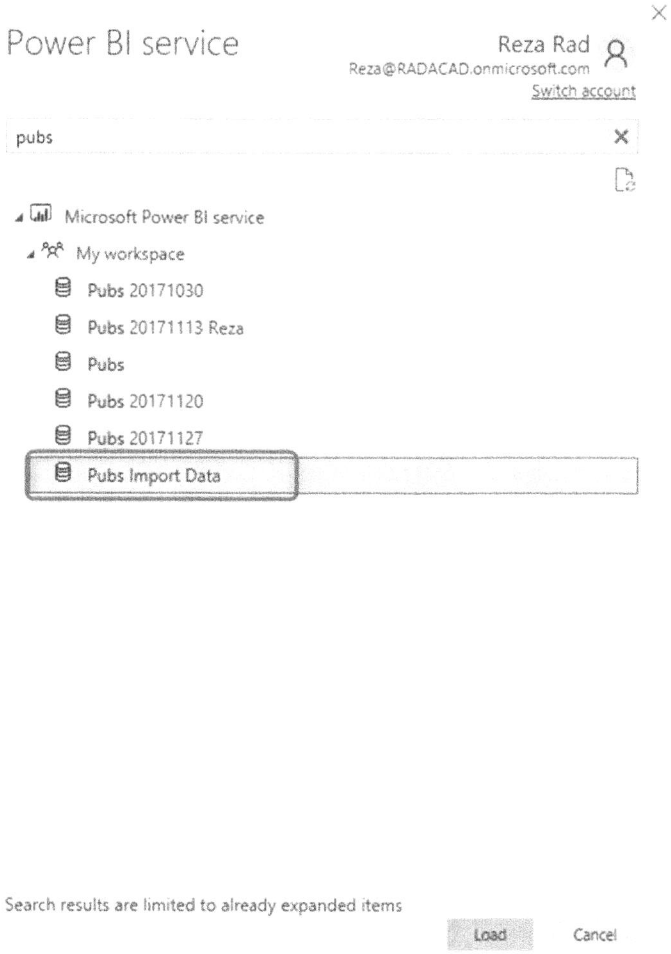

Figure 7-20. *Access to the list of datasets available in the service*

After connecting to the dataset, you will see the Live Connection message at the bottom right-hand side of the Power BI Desktop. (Look toward the bottom right in Figure 7-21). This method will work precisely similar to connecting to SSAS with the Live connection.

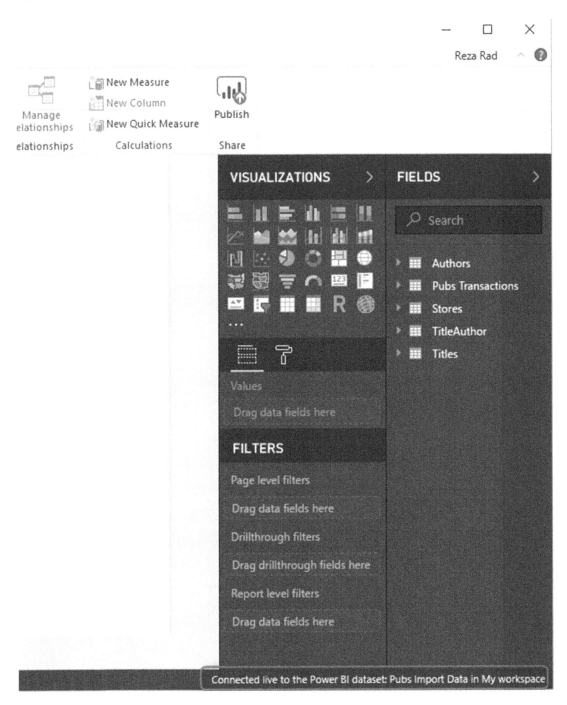

Figure 7-21. *Get data from Power BI service is a Live Connection type*

Connecting to another dataset in Power BI service with Live Connection is a right approach for multi-tenancy development. One user can build the model, and another user can work on another Power BI file for the visualization part of it. I'll explain more about this in future chapters.

Live Connection versus DirectQuery

One of the mistakes that a lot of Power BI developers make is to consider DirectQuery and Live Connection the same. These two types of connections are different in many aspects. Here is a list of differences between these two types:

- DirectQuery is a connection mainly to a non-Microsoft database or analytical engines, or to relational databases (such as SQL Server, Teradata, Oracle, SAP Business Warehouse, etc.).

- Live Connections is a connection to three sources: SSAS tabular, SSAS multi-dimensional, and Power BI dataset.

- DirectQuery for some of the data sources (such as SQL Server database) still has a limited Power Query functionality available.

- Live Connection has no Power Query features in it.

- You can create simply calculated columns in DirectQuery; these will be converted to T-SQL scripts behind the scene.

- You cannot create calculated columns in Live Connection.

- You can use Report Level measures with the ability to leverage all DAX functions in Live connection.

- In the DirectQuery mode, you can have limited measure abilities. For more complex measures, you must use the option to allow unrestricted measures in DirectQuery mode, which is not recommended, because it will slow down the performance for some expressions significantly.

- DirectQuery mode usually is slower than Live connection.

- A Live connection is usually less flexible than the DirectQuery.

As you see. the list above explains that these two types of connection are entirely different.

Summary

In this chapter, you've learned about Live Connection. This type of connection is only available for three data sources: SSAS tabular, multi-dimensional, and Power BI dataset. This type of connection is much more limited than the DirectQuery because you have no access to the Power Query or relationship tab.

However, the Live Connection is providing a better solution than the DirectQuery, because the ability to write DAX code is fully possible if the SSAS tabular is used as a data source. With Live Connection, you get the benefit of both worlds; because data is not stored in the Power BI, the size limitation of Import Data does not apply here, and the data size can be big. Also, because SSAS tabular can leverage DAX, and the analytical power of Power BI is based on DAX, then the analytical engine of this solution is also very efficient.

A Live Connection is faster than DirectQuery in most of the cases. However, it is still slower than Import Data in the performance. The recommendation is to start with Import Data, and if not, then the second option would be Live Connection. If none of them can be applied (for example, if you are working with huge amount of data, and the SSAS licensing is not available because the Microsoft toolset is not used for analytics in your company), then you can choose the last option. which is DirectQuery.

CHAPTER 8

Choosing the Right Connection Type

Power BI supports different methods for connecting data. That is why the decision to choose the right way is always a tough decision. You have heard of DirectQuery, Live Connection, and Import Data. What do these three mean? And what is the situation that you should choose one over the other? What are the pros and cons of each? What are the best practices to choose each? Which one is faster? Which one is more flexible? Is DirectQuery and Live Connection one thing? Or two separate methods? And many other questions. I always get a lot of questions like this in my courses, conference talks, and blog posts. In this chapter, you are going to get the answer to all questions above. This chapter helps you to choose the right data connection methodology and architecture for your Power BI solution.

The Decision Is Difficult

If Power BI only had one way to connect to data sources, then everything would be easy. You would never need to choose between methods and find the right method for yourself. However, Power BI supports three different methods for connecting to data: DirectQuery, Live Connection, and Import Data (or some call it Scheduled Refresh). Many of you might still think that DirectQuery and Live Connection are the same. However, they are different. You will learn later in this chapter about their differences. Each method has some benefits and also some disadvantages. Depending on the scenario that you are implementing Power BI for, you might choose one way over the others. Changing from one method to another method can be a time-consuming task after a while in the implementation process. So, it would be best to choose the right method from the beginning.

© Reza Rad 2018
R. Rad, *Pro Power BI Architecture*, https://doi.org/10.1007/978-1-4842-4015-1_8

Choosing the right method is an essential step for your Power BI Solution Architecture, which you need to decide about usually in the early phases before starting implementation. In this chapter, you are going to learn in detail what every method is and the answer to all the questions below:

- What is Import Data/Schedule Refresh?

- What is DirectQuery?

- What is Live Connection?

- What is the Difference between Live Connection and DirectQuery?

- Pros and Cons of Each Method

- Which method is the performing best and fastest?

- Which method is more flexible?

- Which method is more scalable?

- What are Architecture Scenarios to use for Each Method?

- What is the Gateway Role?

What Is Import Data?

This method has two names; some call it Import Data, some call it Scheduled Refresh. Both names explain the behavior of the method. With this method, data from the source will be loaded into Power BI. Loading in Power BI means consuming memory and disk space. As long as you are developing Power BI on your machine with Power BI Desktop, then it would be memory and disk space on your machine. When you publish the report on the website, then it will be memory and disk space of yjr Power BI cloud machine.

If you have 1 million rows in a source table, and you load it into Power BI with no filtering, you end up with having the same amount of data rows in Power BI. If you have a database with 1,000 tables, however, you only load 10 of those tables in Power BI, then you get memory consumption for just those 10 tables. The bottom line is that you spent memory and disc space as much as you load data into Power BI.

Compression Engine of xVelocity

The very first assumption that you might make after reading the above explanation about Import Data is that if you have a database with 100GB, then if you import it into Power BI, you will get a 100GB file size in Power BI. The statement above is not true. Power BI leverages the compression engine of xVelocity and works on a Column store in-memory technology. Column store in-memory technology compresses data and stores it in a compressed format. Sometimes you might have a 1GB Excel file, and when you import it into Power BI, your Power BI file ends up with only 10MB. The reason is mainly that of compression engine Power BI. However, the compression rate is not always that. The compression rate depends on many things: the number of unique values in the column, sometimes data types, and many other situations. To learn more about the xVelocity compression, read the chapter about Import Data earlier in this part of the book.

The short read for this part is this: Power BI will store compressed data. The size of data in Power BI would be much smaller than its size in the data source.

Pros and Cons of Import Data

Following are some of important trade-offs to be aware of when choosing Import Data or when considering whether you might choose it.

- Pro. Power BI Full Functionality: You get Power BI's full functionality. You can use Power Query to combine data from multiple sources, or DAX to write advanced time-intelligence expressions of the visualization. There will be no limitation on the functionality of Power BI with this method. You can use all components.

- Con. Size Limitation: You have a limitation on the size of the model. Your Power BI model (or let's say the file) cannot be more than 1GB. You usually have up to 10GB size in your account. However, every file should be up to 1GB of the size. There is an exception for this: Power BI Premium allows you to have up to 10GB size of model loaded in the Power BI website with a P3 SKU. Without a Premium maximum file size, you can have 1GB. However, remember that 1GB in the Power BI file is not equal to 1GB data in the source (as mentioned in the compression engine section).

- Pro. Import Data is the fastest Method: The Import Data connection method is the fastest option possible. Data is loaded into the memory of the server. Reports and queries are evaluated from the data loaded into the memory.

What Is DirectQuery?

DirectQuery is a direct connection to a data source. Data will NOT be stored in the Power BI model. Power BI will be a visualization layer and then query the data from the data source every time. Power BI will only store metadata of tables (table names, column names, relationships...) but not the data. The Power BI file size will be much smaller, and most probably you never hit the limitation of the size because there is no data stored in the model.

DirectQuery is only possible through a few data sources. At the time of writing this chapter, these are supported data sources for DirectQuery:

- Amazon Redshift
- Azure HDInsight Spark (Beta)
- Azure SQL Database
- Azure SQL Data Warehouse
- IBM Netezza (Beta)
- Impala (version 2.x)
- Oracle Database (version 12 and above)
- SAP Business Warehouse (Beta)
- SAP HANA
- Snowflake
- Spark (Beta) (version 0.9 and above)
- SQL Server
- Teradata Database

To get the most up-to-date list, look at this post.

Important Pros and Cons of DirectQuery

DirectQuery brings a somewhat different set of trade-offs and conditions. The following sections describe some of the more notable ones.

Scalability: The Main Advantage

The DirectQuery method has no limitation on the size of the dataset. This lack of limitation is because no data is stored in the Power BI file, so you never encounter any issues due to the amount of data under analysis. You can have data sources with Petabytes of data in SQL Server, Oracle Database, or in any other supported data sources, and you can connect to that data from Power BI.

Limited Functionality: Mainly Visualization

The DirectQuery method will not have full functionality of Power BI. With this method, you have only two tabs in Power BI Desktop: Report and Relationship. You can change only the relationship in this mode, as illustrated in Figure 8-1.

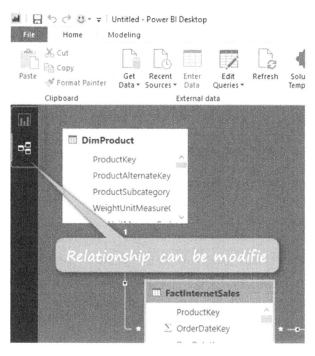

Figure 8-1. *Relationship can be modified in the DirectQuery*

In Power Query, you are limited in the operations you can perform. Operations that cannot be folded cannot be used. To learn more about query folding, read this post at `http://radacad.com/not-folding-the-black-hole-of-power-query-performance`. If you want to combine data sources, then you cannot do that in this mode. You get a message like that in Figure 8-2 if you try and combine data sources.

Figure 8-2. *Single Data Source support in DirectQuery*

You are also limited in your DAX expressions; you cannot write all types of expressions. Many functions are not supported. As an example, and as shown in Figure 8-3, time-intelligence functions are not supported.

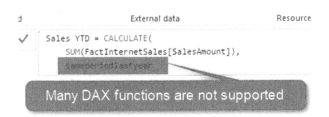

Figure 8-3. *Limited DAX and Modeling in DirectQuery*

Slow Connections

A big disadvantage of the DirectQuery method is that the connection is slower than other types of connections. Every visual sends a query to the data source from which data comes back. You must think through and work out performance issues at the data source when using the Direct Query method.

Just for a very small example of performance tuning, Figure 8-4 shows the performance I get when I have s normal index on my table with 48 million records.

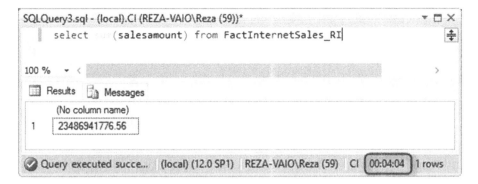

Figure 8-4. *Large table with regular index*

A regular select sum from my table with 48 million records takes 4 minutes and 4 seconds to run. And the same query responds in less than a second when I have clustered s column store index. You can see the shorter execution time in Figure 8-5. This difference is entirely due to configuration changes made in the data source.

Figure 8-5. *Large table with clustered column store index*

What Is Live Connection?

Live Connection is very similar to DirectQuery in the way that it works with the data source. It will not store data in Power BI, and it will query data source every time. However, it is different from DirectQuery. Live Connection is only supported for these datasets:

- SQL Server Analysis Services (SSAS) Tabular

- SQL Server Analysis Services (SSAS) Multi-Dimensional

- Power BI Service

Because these data sources are modeling engines themselves, Power BI only connects to these and fetch all model metadata (measure names, attribute names, relationships...). With this method, you need to handle all your modeling requirements in the data source, and Power BI just surfaces that data through Visualization.

Important Pros and Cons of Live Connections

Live Connection is the last of the three connection types under discussion. The following subsections describe some trade-offs associated with this method.

Big Size Model with OLAP or Tabular Engine

The big benefit of the Live Connection model is that you can have a big-sized data model (not limited to 1GB), and also you can leverage the modeling layer of SSAS. SSAS Tabular will give you DAX, and Multi-Dimensional will provide you MDX. With any of these two languages, you can cover all your calculations and modeling needs. This method has a better modeling feature than DirectQuery because in DirectQuery, there is no DAX or MDX as the analytical language to help. All calculations need to be done on the database side. Sometimes doing calculations on the database side is much more complicated than doing it in the analytical expression language.

No Power Query Support

The big disadvantage of the Live Connection is that you will not have even Power Query simple transformations available. With this method, you will only have the Report tab, as shown in Figure 8-6.

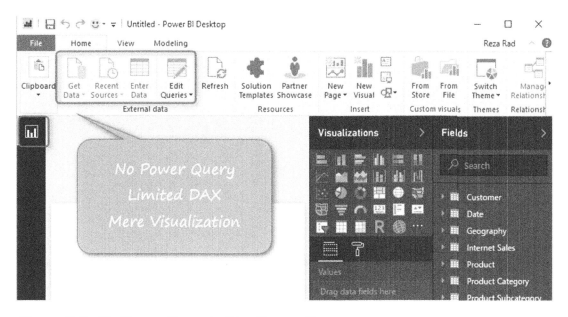

Figure 8-6. *No Power Query in Live Connection*

Report Level Measures

With the SSAS Tabular Live Connection only, you get report level measures such as the ones shown in Figure 8-7. Report Level Measures give you the ability to write DAX expressions. However, you might want to keep such measures in the data source to keep your model consistent. This feature is not yet available in connection to SSAS Multi-Dimensional at the time of writing this chapter.

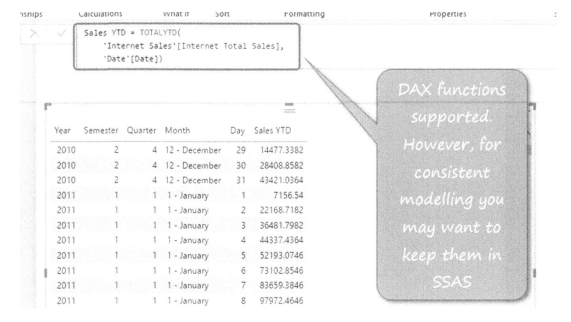

Figure 8-7. *Report Level Measures*

Report Level Measures are a great feature because users can create measures without the need to call a BI developer to do that. However, these measures will not be added to the dataset. These are just for the report. So, for the consistency of your model, you might want to keep measures creation as part of your SSAS data source model.

Pros and Cons of Each Method

Import Data is the method supporting all Power BI features. It provides the following advantages:

- Fastest Possible Connection

- Power BI Fully Functional

- Combining Data from different sources

- Full DAX expressions

- Full Power Query transformations

The one disadvantage is the Power BI file size limitation of 1GB (higher if you pay for a premium account).

DirectQuery is a direct connection to a database such an SQL Server or Oracle Database, and it brings the following advantages:

- Large Scale data sources supported. No size limitation.

- Pre-Built models in some data sources can be used instantly.

The price for DirectQuery's benefits consists of the following disadvantages:

- Very Limited Power Query functionality

- DAX very limited

- Cannot combine data from multiple sources

- Slower Connection type: Performance Tuning in the data source is MUST DO

Live Connection is a direct connection to an SSAS model, and it has these advantages:

- Large Scale data sources supported. No size limitation as far as SSAS Supports.

- Many organizations already have SSAS models built, and these can be used from Live Connection without the need to replicate them into Power BI.

- Report Level Measures are available.

- MDX or DAX analytical engines in the data source of SSAS can be a great asset for modeling compared to DirectQuery.

Disadvantages of Live Connection include:

- No support for Power Query

- Cannot combine data from multiple sources

- Slower Connection type: Performance Tuning in the data source is MUST DO

Which Method Performs Fastest?

Import Data is the fastest possible option. Data is loaded into the memory of the server, and all queries will be resolved immediately.

Live Connection is the next option on this list, primarily if SSAS Tabular or Power BI Service is used. This is because these two are in-memory technologies and perform faster than multi-dimensional models.

DirectQuery is the slowest type of connection. You have to consider performance tuning of your data source when using DirectQuery.

The performance winner is the Import Data method.

Which Method Is More Flexible?

With Import Data you get the full functionality of Power BI. This includes full Power Query transformations and DAX measures, as well as visualizations.

Direct Query and Live Connection both are next on this list because each of them gives you something. DirectQuery gives you a few Power Query options. Live Connection will give you Report Level Measures.

The winner in flexibility is the Import Data method.

Which Method Is More Scalable?

The Import Data method has a size limitation of 1GB per model unless you pay for a Power BI Premium account. Without using Power BI Premium, the Import Data method does not scale to large amounts of data.

With DirectQuery and Live Connection, you get better scalability. Data sources support a large amount of data. There is effectively no size limit.

The scalability winners are Live Connection and DirectQuery.

Architecture Scenarios

The following sections describe some architecture scenarios that, when recognized, should help you to make the right choice of connection method.

Import Data for Agility and Performance

Import Data has the fully functional Power BI with a great performance. So If your data set is not a huge dataset, then you can easily use the Import Data method and produce reports in a very fast time frame.

Live Connection for Enterprise Solution

Many enterprises already have pre-built models in SSAS tabular or multi-dimensional. These models can be easily used in a Power BI Live Connection.

Even if your company hasn't yet started an SSAS solution, and you are dealing with a huge dataset, this option is better than DirectQuery. This is because in SSAS you have analytical expression languages of MDX or DAX to cope with lots of calculations and modeling challenges. Figure 8-8 shows a sample architecture that can be used with the Live Connection method.

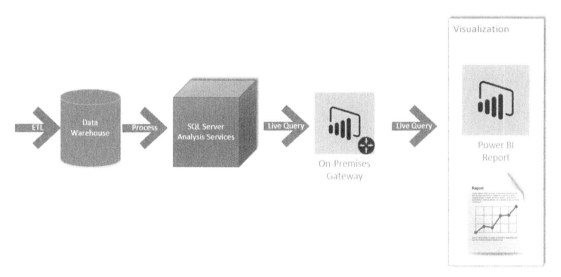

Figure 8-8. *Enterprise usage of Power BI with Live Connection*

Another approach is to use Power BI service as the central hub of development. In this approach, data is sourced from various Power BI reports. This approach is shown in Figure 8-9.

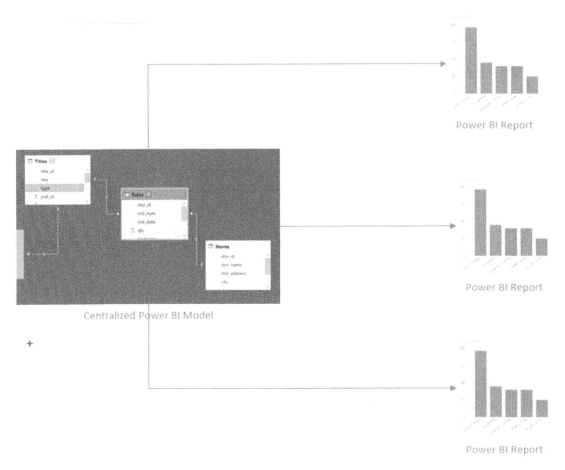

Figure 8-9. *Centralized Power BI Model with Get Data from Power BI*

Direct Query for Non-Microsoft Sources

The DirectQuery connection is not used that much in Microsoft solution architecture. The main reason is that if you have a Microsoft-based solution architecture, you probably will use SSAS as mentioned above to leverage the analytical engine of it. The DirectQuery mode is mainly used in Non-Microsoft architecture such as when the data is sourced from Oracle Database, IBM DB2, SAP Hana, or some similar system.

What Is the Gateway Role?

Regardless of the type of connection you use (Import Data, DirectQuery, or Live Connection), if the data source is located on-premises, you will need a gateway to it. Otherwise not. To learn more about setting up for a gateway, read the Gateway chapter earlier in the book.

Summary

In summary, you've learned what three different types of connections are: Live Connection, Import Data, and Direct Query. In previous chapters, we went through details of each connection type. This chapter wrapped everything up together in one comparison summary. You've learned their differences, pros and cons, and scenarios of when each should be used. There are still a lot of details for each method, which you have already read about in previous chapters. In this chapter, you gained a holistic view of everything.

Now, you have a good understanding of which scenarios are good for which type of the connection. Your first decision point of Power BI should be made by now, so let's go to the next architectural decision point of Power BI: sharing and security of Power BI, which will be discussed in the following few chapters.

PART III

Sharing

CHAPTER 9

Dashboard and Report Sharing

Power BI provides multiple ways of sharing the content with users. Each sharing method has pros and cons and can be used for specific scenarios. Some of the sharing methods can be used together to build a framework for sharing. In this chapter, I will talk about the most basic way of sharing Power BI content. This method is called Dashboard Sharing. Dashboard sharing is the easiest way of sharing; however, it is always the best way of sharing. In this chapter, you'll learn how this method works, the pros and cons of this method, and scenarios of using it.

The first method of sharing Power BI content is dashboard and report sharing. This is also the easiest method for sharing. This chapter walks you through the process of using this method. Limitations of this method and advantages of using it will be explained.

Power BI Content Owner

Before going through dashboard sharing, you need to understand the content security in Power BI. When you publish a *.pbix report into Power BI website, especially when you publish it under "My workspace," no one else will see or have access to your report. It would be only you who has access to it. Then you can decide whom you want to share this report with.

Every Power BI content (report, dashboard, or dataset) has an owner; the content owner is the person who created and published that content into Power BI. The owner has full access to the content of Power BI. One of the accesses that the owner has is to share the content with others.

© Reza Rad 2018
R. Rad, *Pro Power BI Architecture*, https://doi.org/10.1007/978-1-4842-4015-1_9

How Does Dashboard Sharing Work?

Dashboard sharing, as the name of it explains, is based on a dashboard. You can only share a dashboard with this method, not a report. Consider that you have a dashboard like the below screenshot, and you want to share it. There is a share link at the top-right corner of the dashboard, as shown in Figure 9-1.

Figure 9-1. *Sample Dashboard, Starting with Share*

Dashboard sharing has very few options to set and is very simple to configure. You just need to add the email addresses of people whom you want to share this report. See Figure 9-2 for an example. You can also write a message for them to know that this report is shared with them. There are two options to set:

- Allow recipients to share your dashboard.

- Send email notification to recipients.

You can decide if people that you shared this dashboard with are also allowed to share it with others or not? And you can also choose if you want them to receive an email notification when you shared the dashboard with them or not.

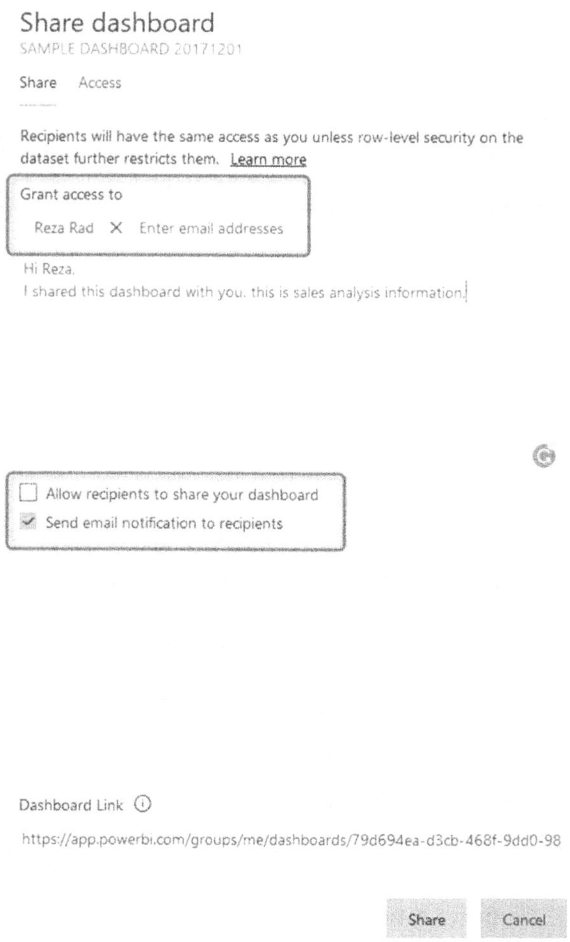

Share dashboard
SAMPLE DASHBOARD 20171201

Share   Access

Recipients will have the same access as you unless row-level security on the dataset further restricts them. Learn more

Grant access to

Reza Rad   ✕   Enter email addresses

Hi Reza,
I shared this dashboard with you. this is sales analysis information.

☐ Allow recipients to share your dashboard
☑ Send email notification to recipients

Dashboard Link ⓘ

https://app.powerbi.com/groups/me/dashboards/79d694ea-d3cb-468f-9dd0-98

Share   Cancel

Figure 9-2. *Dashboard Sharing configurations*

After configuration, then you can click on the Share button. The recipient will immediately have access to the report. If you selected "Send email notification to recipients," they will receive an email. Otherwise, they get a notification in Power BI itself. When they log in to the service (`http://powerbi.microsoft.com`), they can find the shared dashboard under "Shared with me" section, shown in Figure 9-3. The recipient can then click on a dashboard to view it.

Figure 9-3. *Users can access the dashboard through "Shared with me" section*

Two Levels of Access

With dashboard sharing, users will have two levels of access: Read, or Read and reshare. These are shown in Figure 9-4. If you give access without selecting the option "Allow recipients to share your dashboard," then the access is Read. If you choose the Read and reshare, then the access allows the recipient to both read and to further share the access with others.

You can also remove this access anytime you want, by going to the Share option in the same dashboard, and clicking on the Access tab. You will see a list of all users who have access to this dashboard, and their access level (Owner, Read, Read and reshare), and then you can click on more options (…) and change it.

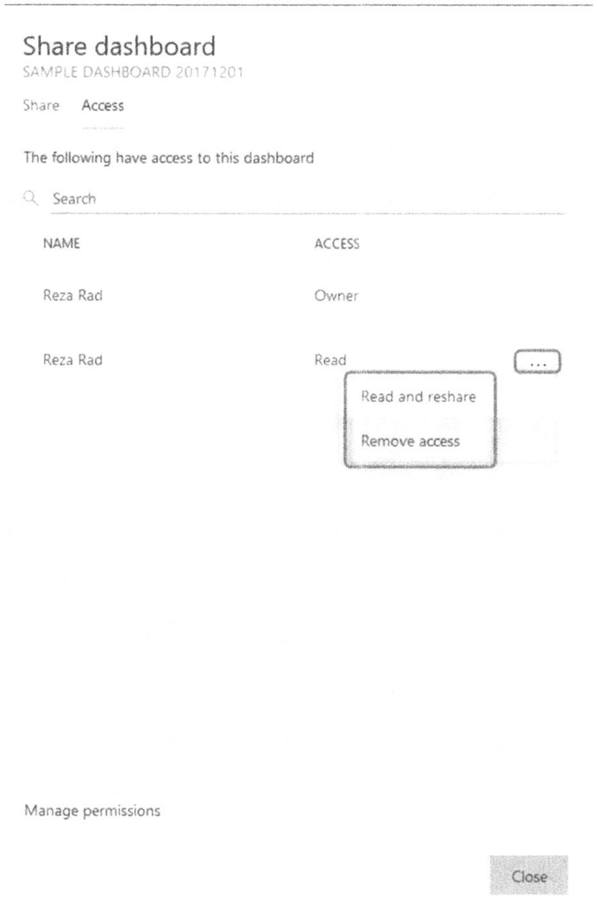

Share dashboard
SAMPLE DASHBOARD 20171201

Share   Access

The following have access to this dashboard

Search

NAME	ACCESS
Reza Rad	Owner
Reza Rad	Read

Read and reshare

Remove access

Manage permissions

Close

Figure 9-4. *Removing access*

Manage Permissions

Another way of setting access is through manage permission in the dashboard, report, or dataset. If you share a dashboard, by default the report and the dataset will also be shared as read-only for users. Figure 9-5, for example, shows that the Edit report option is dimmed in the toolbar. Users can click on dashboard and go to the report; they can interact with the report quickly. However, they cannot Edit the report. Access to edit a report cannot be provided via sharing of a dashboard.

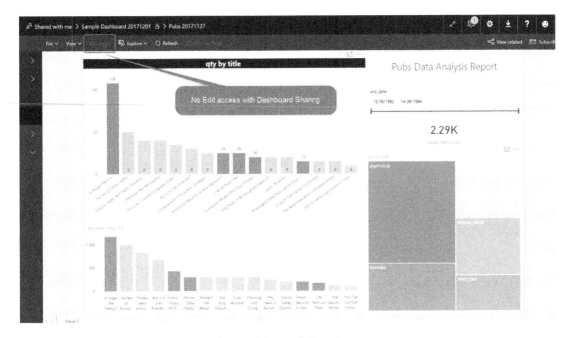

Figure 9-5. *No Edit access with Dashboard sharing*

To manage permission on every item (dashboard, report, or dataset) individually, you can go to Manage Permission in the Access tab of Share window for the dashboard. See Figure 9-6 for an example of the Share dashboard options.

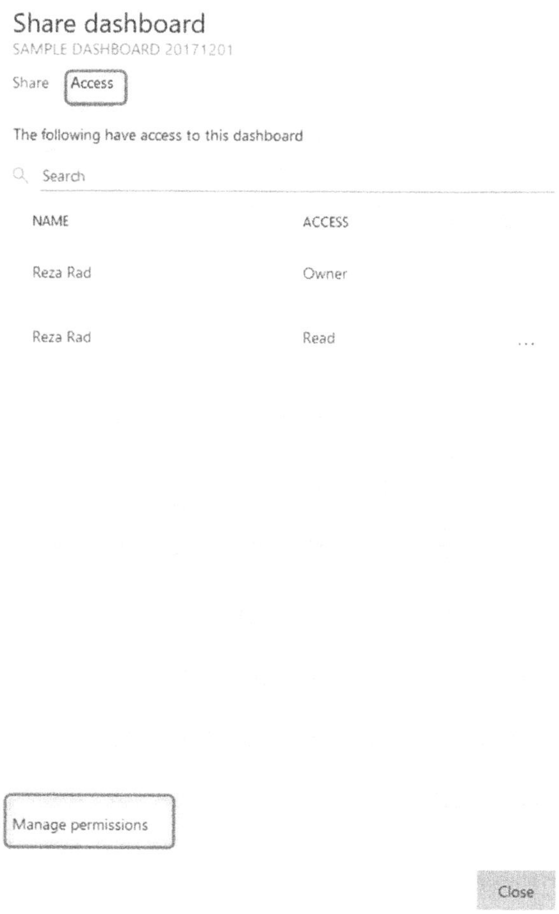

Figure 9-6. *Manage Permissions*

Manage permissions will show you a detailed list of access to the dashboard, reports, and datasets. In the left-hand side of the Manage Permissions section, shown in Figure 9-7, you will see related reports and datasets. You can click on that report.

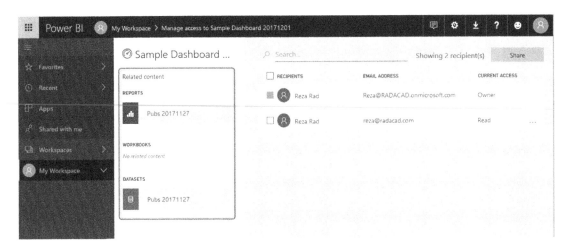

Figure 9-7. *Manage permissions at every object level*

By clicking on a report or dataset, you will see the permission specified for that object. And you can change it. For example, user reza@radacad.com has access as Read to the report in the below screenshot (because we shared this dashboard with him, so the report sharing happened automatically after that). You can remove that access by clicking on more options, which is the triple-dot menu shown toward the lower right in Figure 9-8.

Figure 9-8. *Removing access to a report for a user through Manage permissions*

You will see the Remove access window (Figure 9-9), which asks do you also want to remove the access to some of the related content as well or not. Let's just remove access to this report now, so click the Remove access button.

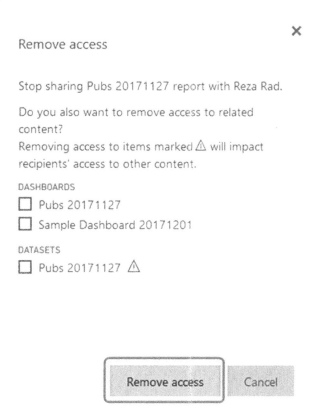

Figure 9-9. *Checking related content when removing access*

If you are removing access to some of the other items, you should be careful, because an item might be used in multiple other objects. For example, if you remove the access to a dataset, that dataset might be used in multiple reports.

If you shared a dashboard with a user but removed the access to the report or dataset, the user when logged in and accessing the dashboard will see the error message for tiles that are coming from that report. Users cannot drill into the report because they don't have access to it. Figure 9-10, near the very top, shows the error message that users will see.

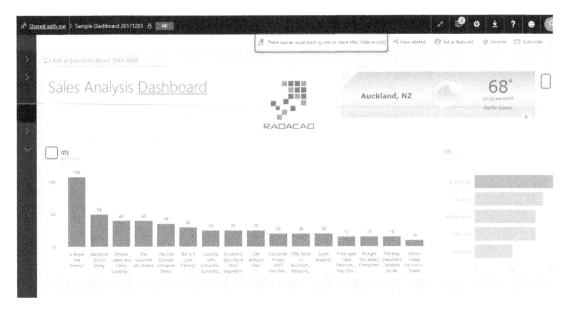

Figure 9-10. *Access to a dashboard, when users don't have access to the underlying report*

Licensing Part Sharing

Dashboard sharing, like many other methods of sharing in Power BI, is a paid feature. The account that is sharing the content should be a Power BI pro account, and people who are using the shared content should be part of a paid account (Power BI Pro accounts, of Power BI free accounts under a Power BI premium capacity). I'll talk about licensing more in the licensing chapter of this book. Free users with no connection to Power BI premium cannot leverage content shared with this method of sharing.

Advantages of Dashboard Sharing

Dashboard sharing is the most basic way of sharing content in Power BI. This method is quick and easy to set up. You don't need to have a lot of steps to set up sharing of the dashboard. The ability to share it very quickly makes this method the most common method of sharing for testing.

If you have created a Power BI content and want to share it with others easily just for Testing, this is one of your first options in Dashboard sharing.

Disadvantages of Dashboard Sharing

Dashboard sharing is simple; however, it has many drawbacks, which makes it hard to be used in production. I do not recommend using this method to share Power BI content with users in a production environment because of the reasons mentioned below.

No Edit Access

With Dashboard sharing, you cannot specify edit access. For end users, you never want to give edit access; however, if you are working with a team of developers, and you want to provide them with access to edit the content, you cannot do that with dashboard sharing. You have to use other methods of sharing, which will come in the next few chapters.

Share Objects One at a Time

You can only share one dashboard at a time. What if you wanted to share hundreds of dashboards? You must go to each dashboard, and share items individually. Sharing every single dashboard would add a lot of maintenance overhead to your work. It would be best to have all content under a group and share it with others at once.

Summary

Dashboard sharing is straightforward; it has two levels of access, Read, or Read and reshare. You can use this method efficiently for test scenarios. When you want to share a dashboard with a user for testing, Dashboard sharing can be one of the best options to choose.

Dashboard sharing, however, has some disadvantages. There is no Edit access to this way of sharing; and on the other hand, if you want to share multiple items, you have to go to each dashboard and share individually from there. Because of these two significant limitations, dashboard sharing is never used in the development or production environment of Power BI implementation. Other methods, which I'll write about in the next few chapters, can cover these limitations.

CHAPTER 10

Workspaces as a Collaborative Environment

Workspaces are another way of sharing Power BI content with other people. The benefit of this approach of sharing is that you can share content with a group of people and create a development environment that everyone has edit access to it. Workspaces are also aligned with Office 365 groups, which can be very helpful. Content will be shared with Power BI groups, and managing members are easily possible through the Power BI service or Office 365 admin panel. In this chapter, I get you through sharing with workspaces, what the limitations and advantages are, and how it is different from dashboard sharing. At the end of this chapter, you will have a full understanding of which scenarios are suitable to be used with this method of sharing.

There is a second, much better method for sharing when content should be shared with a group of people working together as a team. In this chapter, you will learn about Workspaces in Power BI. This chapter will clarify the benefit of workspaces through an example and explain how workspaces can be useful in some scenarios of sharing.

What Is a Workspace?

Workspace is a shared environment for a group of people. You can have multiple Power BI content in a workspace. One workspace can have hundreds of dashboards, reports, and datasets in it. You can add people (or Power BI account, in other words) to the workspace and give them access to edit or read the content.

One account may be part of multiple workspaces such as in Figure 10-1 or various accounts to have access to one workspace. You can even consider workspaces as shared folders. Everyone has a workspace named "My Workspace," and this is similar to your "My Documents" folder on your machine. "My workspace" never should be used for sharing content with others except for testing, basically, because it is your personal workspace.

© Reza Rad 2018
R. Rad, *Pro Power BI Architecture*, https://doi.org/10.1007/978-1-4842-4015-1_10

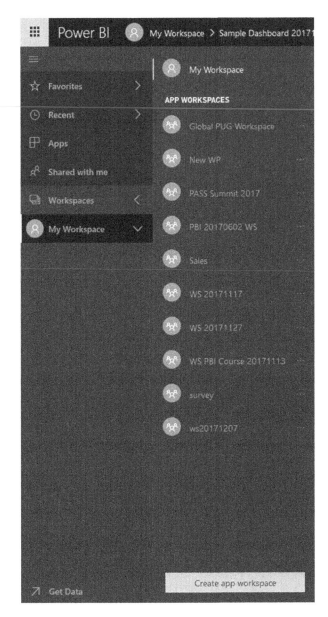

Figure 10-1. *Workspaces in Power BI*

If you want to share content with others, your starting point can be creating another folder, which in Power BI terminology, we call it workspace. Workspaces are called "App workspace" because you can create an app based on it (you will learn about the app in future posts).

Workspaces are best to be used as a collaborative environment to share content between people of a team. Let's now look at how we can use workspaces.

How to Create Workspaces

Creating workspaces are easy. You need to do that from the Power BI service. Log in to the service (http://powerbi.microsoft.com), and click on workspaces as shown in Figure 10-2.

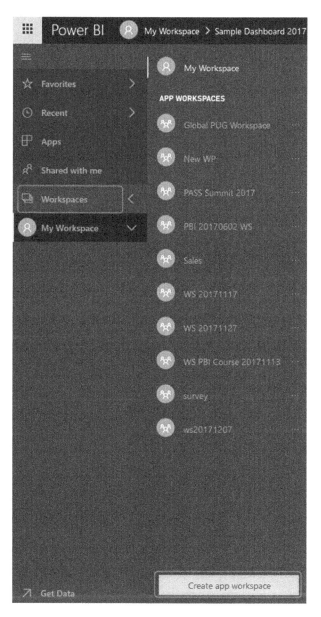

Figure 10-2. *Create app workspace*

If you are already part of one or more workspaces, you'll see them in the list of workspaces. Click on Create app workspace, and you'll be taken to the dialog in Figure 10-3. When you create a new workspace, you need to assign a name to it. The name of workspace would be the name that others will see when joined to this workspace.

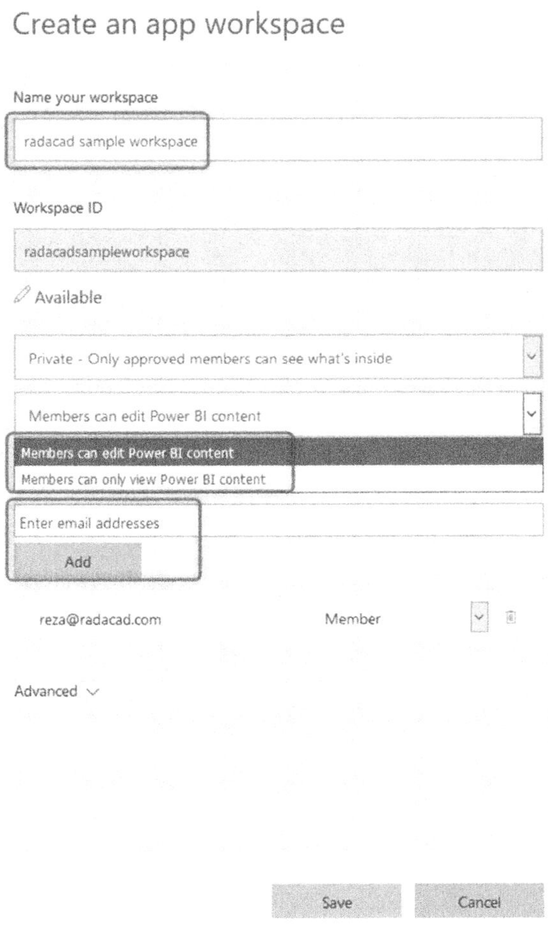

Figure 10-3. Configuring Workspace

You can define the group to be private or public. The public will be available for anyone in your organization to join. Private would be for the group of people whom you add in this section or Office 365 as members of this workspace. You can also choose to give users Edit or Read-only access. If a member is an Admin, then he/she will have edit access automatically.

After defining the group, you will be automatically taken to a view of your new workspace similar to what you see in Figure 10-4. However, your new workspace doesn't have any content (dashboard, dataset, or report) in it yet.

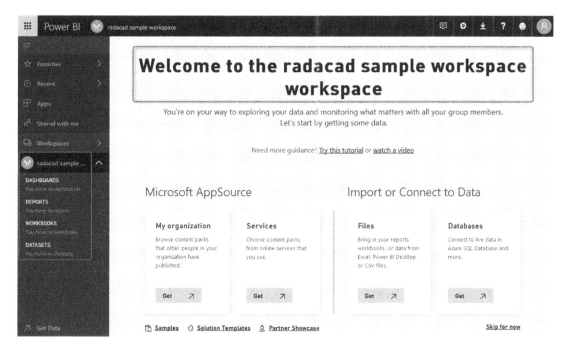

Figure 10-4. *New workspace is like an environment*

How to Add Content to a Workspace

At the time of writing this chapter, the only way to have content in a workspace is to publish it from the Power BI Desktop. The Microsoft team is working on a feature to move/copy content from one workspace to another in their road map, but there is no timing available here that I can share now.

When you have a Power BI report opened in Power BI Desktop, you can simply click on Publish (see Figure 10-5), and if you are part of a workspace, then you will see a pop-up window asking which workspace you want to publish the report to it. You can select "radacad sample workspace" that we've created above.

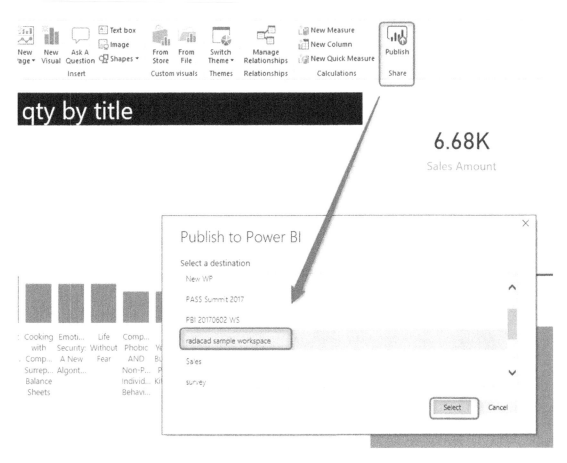

Figure 10-5. *Publishing to a workspace*

After publishing the content to the workspace, you and anyone else who is part of that workspace will see that content. Figure 10-6 shows a user's view of the workspace published in Figure 10-5. Members can edit the content because I specified edit access for members when creating the workspace.

Figure 10-6. *Edit access in the workspace*

Two Levels of Access

With workspaces, you can provide two levels of access (except administrator of the workspace, of course): Edit and Read-only. The access levels here are one level beyond what Dashboard sharing provides. With Dashboard sharing, you could only share read-only, but with workspaces. you can have read-only or Edit access levels.

Advantages of Workspaces

There are advantages to using workspaces, and most of them have to do with scaling the use of Power BI beyond just one person. The following subsections describe some of these advantages.

Sharing Multiple Contents with Team

You may have shared a dashboard with a couple of your colleagues in your organization, and after a few weeks a need for a new dashboard comes up, so you share that dashboard with them. A couple of months later, another member of your team asks for access to a dataset in Power BI to be able to create a report and share with some others. Power BI workspaces enable you to share content (dashboard, report, and dataset) with all members of a group. You don't need to share each dashboard with each user; groups made it easy for you.

Multiple Workspaces

It is a hectic environment when you are part of multiple teams, and each team has their own set of dashboards, reports, and datasets. Your "shared with me" section in Power BI will be hundreds of items and finding something there would be a problem. Power BI workspaces create a separate environment for all members of the group. You can easily switch between workspaces in Power BI.

Isolated User/Group Administration

When you share content with an individual in the organization, if that person leaves the company or is replaced by someone else from another team, then you have to remove sharing from a previous user account and assign it to the new user account. A best practice is to share content with groups. And members of groups then easily can be managed by an administrator. Power BI workspaces are fully synchronized with Office 365 groups. Once you use a group in Power BI, then it is only an admin's task to add/remove members from it.

Best Developer Environment

For a team of developers, you need an environment to share multiple Power BI content. Everyone needs to have edit access to the content provided by the team. Power BI workspace is the perfect solution for the development environment. You can create a workspace as a development environment and then share it with other members of the developer team with Edit access. Then you all have access to the same content in your development workspace.

Power BI workspaces are the perfect solution for development environments

Disadvantages of Workspaces

Workspaces are not good places to share content with end users. You may wonder why is that? You can give users of the workspace read-only access to the content. However, this is half of the requirement. In an end-user sharing environment, one of the primary requirements is to have development and user environments separated from each other.

Assume that you have created a workspace and shared it with end users. If you suddenly make changes in the workspace while they are using it, then their view of the world breaks and changes.

With one workspace, your development and user environment are the same.

You cannot use one workspace to be shared between developers and users. Creating multiple workspaces also brings another challenge, and that is overhead.

If you have multiple workspaces, then moving or copying content between workspaces is not possible. This limitation means you must re-create your dashboards in every workspace. The overhead maintenance costs of such a scenario are high. (Future editions of Power BI may eliminate this issue, however.)

Office 365 Synchronization

Power BI groups are fully synchronized with Office 365 groups. If you go to the O365 admin panel, you will see groups that you have created in Power BI. You can manage groups and their members in this admin panel, as shown in Figure 10-7.

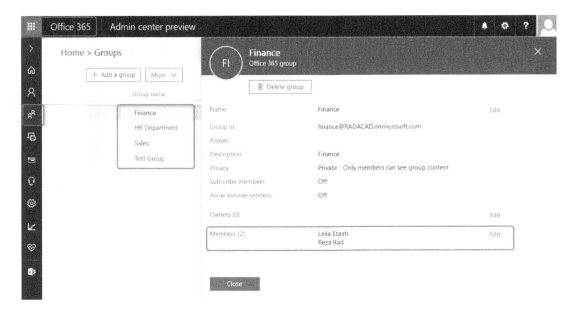

Figure 10-7. *Workspaces in Office 365*

This functionality is beneficial in enterprise solutions, where you share content with a group of Power BI, and then members of the group will be managed by an Office 365 admin. Groups also can be created from an Office 365 admin panel. For example, you can create a group as shown in Figure 10-8.

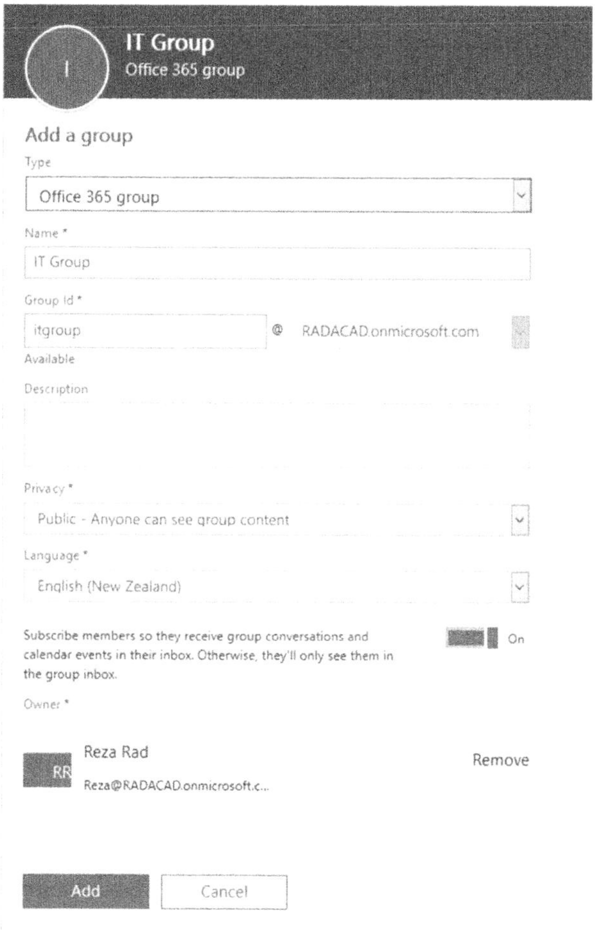

Figure 10-8. *Managing Workspaces as an Office 365 group*

Groups will be visible in Power BI service of all members (who have Power BI subscription added to their Office 365 subscription options). That means if you already have Office 365 groups created for your organization, then you don't need to create Power BI groups for them again; they will be visible for users who have a Power BI subscription.

Power BI Pro

Power BI workspaces are a Pro option and are not part of the Power BI free user account. Figure 10-9 shows the option to upgrade from the free to a Pro-level account.

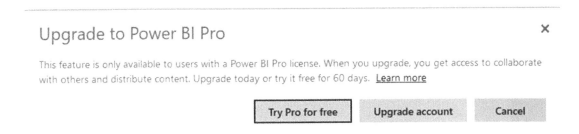

Figure 10-9. *Pro account required for creating workspaces*

Summary

Power BI workspaces are a great way of sharing multiple Power BI content with users. If you have hundreds of dashboards, reports, and datasets, you can easily share it through a workspace with others. Workspaces are also isolating the administration part of the work. An Office 365 admin can take care of adding members to the group or removing from it because Power BI workspaces are bound to Office 365 groups behind the scene.

Workspaces provide Edit access and Read-only access. Because of that, Workspaces are a great way to create a collaborative development environment. Multiple developers can have access to the same content in a workspace with edit access.

Workspaces are better used for a development environment but not for the end-user environment. The main reason is that having one workspace for a dev or user environment makes it hard to develop if a developer makes a change; the end user will be affected immediately. Managing multiple workspaces is not also an easy job. The discussion about workspaces brings us to the next way of sharing, which I'll talk about it in the next chapter.

CHAPTER 11

Power BI Apps

You've learned previously about some of the methods of sharing content in Power BI, such as Workspaces and Dashboard Sharing. In this chapter, I'll explain everything about new Power BI Apps: a mechanism to share the content in Power BI in a way that has security and governance together. Power BI App is an enhancement version of two methods: Workspaces, and Content Packs (which is an obsolete method and replaced by Power BI App) together! This chapter provides a full detailed guide on this method and explains best practices for using it.

Power BI Apps

Power BI Apps are a way of sharing content with end users. You already know about the limitations of Dashboard Sharing and Workspace Sharing. The Power BI App method is providing an extensive approach to sharing content for end users. With Power BI Apps, you can share content with end users, without the worry to change something in the development environment. Managing multiple environments is much easier with this approach. An app can be shared with a group of people or the entire organization.

187

© Reza Rad 2018
R. Rad, *Pro Power BI Architecture*, https://doi.org/10.1007/978-1-4842-4015-1_11

App Workspace

To start creating an app, you'll need a workspace. The reason that workspaces in Power BI are called App workspace is that you can create an app on top of a workspace. The content that you will have in this workspace can be selected for the App to be shared with users. In the previous chapter, you've learned how to create and manage workspaces. Figure 11-1 shows how to start the process for creating a new one.

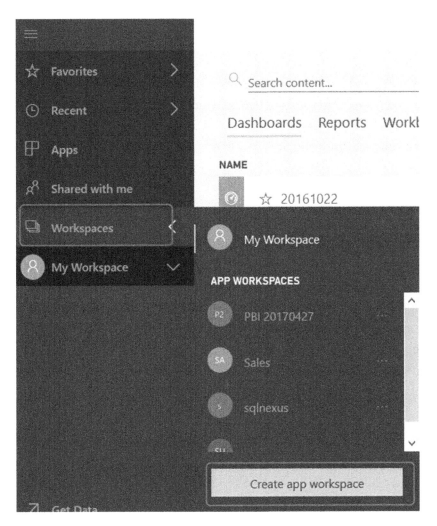

Figure 11-1. *Create App Workspace*

App workspace is like a folder that is shared with a group of people. Set a name for the app workspace. You can specify if users have access to this workspace via edit or read-only. Please note that this way of access is only for people that you add to the group directly, not for users of this App. Figure 11-2 shows a group being created, through which you may provide users access to the new workspace.

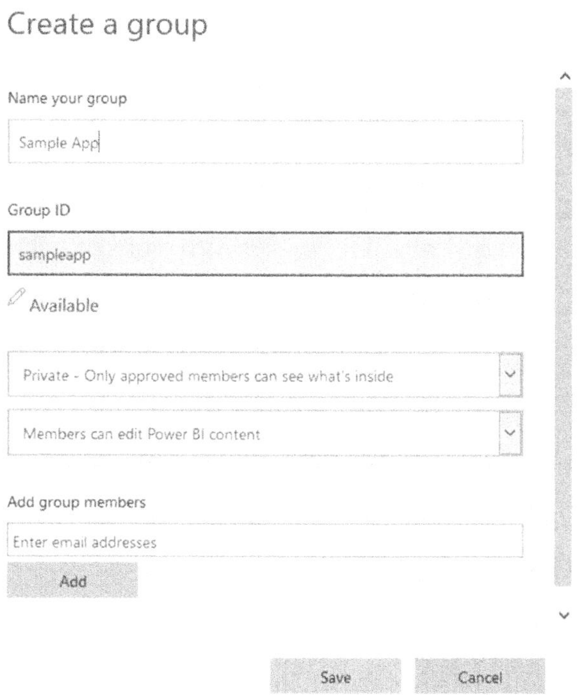

Figure 11-2. Workspace Configuration

After creating the app workspace, you should see a new workspace that is blank at first. That blank workspace will resemble that in Figure 11-3.

Figure 11-3. *Workspace Created*

Publish Content to App

For publishing content to the app, just simply publish it to the app workspace. Open Power BI Desktop, go to Publish as shown in Figure 11-4, and select the app workspace created. After publishing content into the new app workspace, you should be able to publish an App as described in the next section.

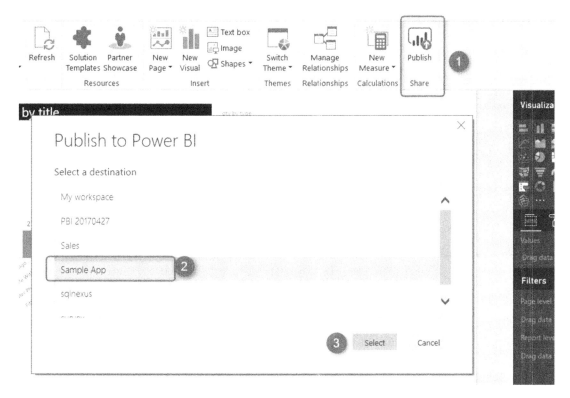

Figure 11-4. Publish Power BI report to the workspace

Publish App

You can easily publish an app from the app workspace. Just click on the workspace, and then from the list of dashboards and reports (see Figure 11-5), select any item you want to be included in the app in the "included in app" column.

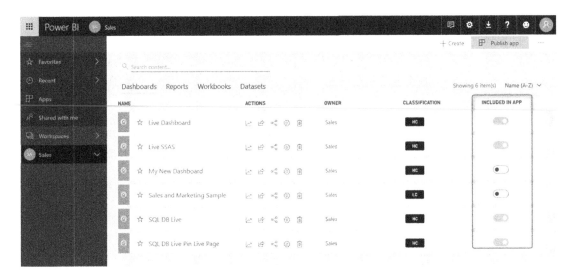

Figure 11-5. *Select content to include in the app*

Then at the top right-hand side, select Publish App. Do that by clicking the highlighted button that is shown in Figure 11-6.

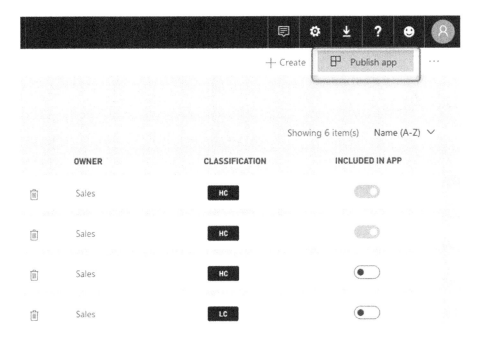

Figure 11-6. *Publish App*

Set a description and color for the app, as shown in Figure 11-7. You can also see how many reports, dashboards, workbooks, and datasets are part of this app.

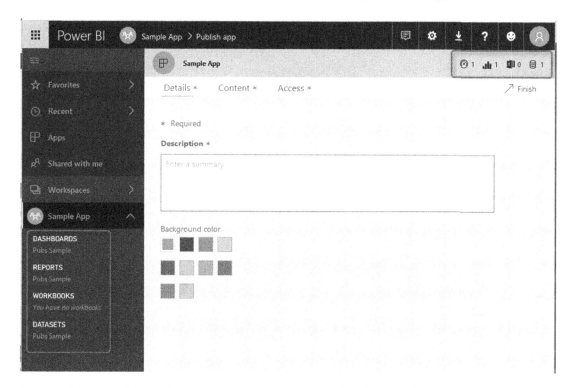

Figure 11-7. *Adding description and background color for the App*

In the next tab, you will see the content. And you are also able to select the landing page for the Power BI App. Figure 11-8 shows that being done.

Figure 11-8. *Setting the Landing page for app*

You can also set a group of people that you want the app to be shared with. That group may be your entire organization, or it may be a specific subset of people. Figure 11-9 shows how to grant permissions. When you're done, click on Finish in the upper right.

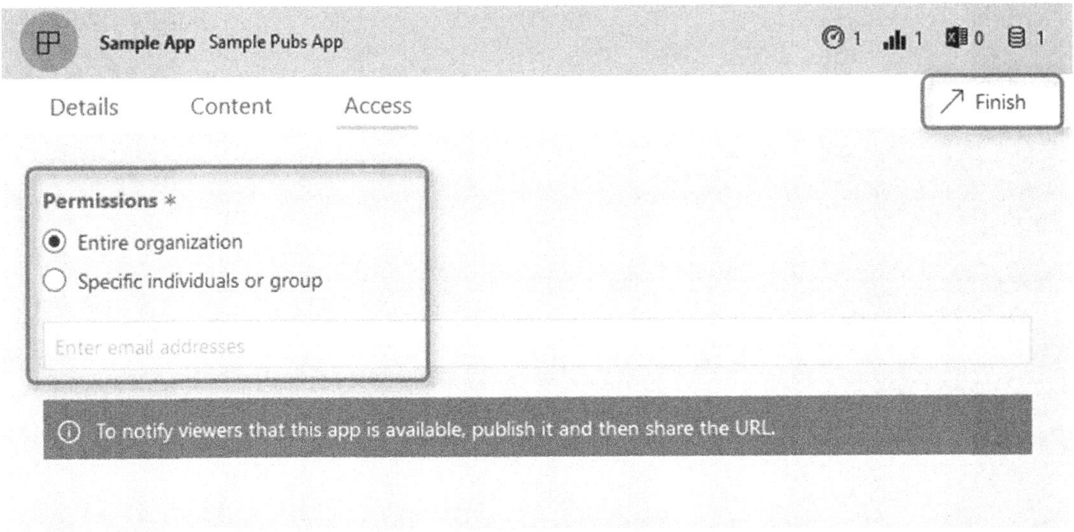

Figure 11-9. *Access Control for the App*

After publishing the app, users will be able to access it immediately. However, you can share a link with them to make the app easier for them to access. Figure 11-10 shows the link being shared.

SUCCESSFULLY PUBLISHED

Sample App

You can now share this link with everyone you have given access to. Users that were given access can also install the app by visiting Get Apps.

https://app.powerbi.com/Redirect?action=OpenApp&appId=225f   Copy

Go to app

Figure 11-10. *App published*

Getting an App

Users can go to their Power BI account page and click on Apps, and then Get Apps. They will be able to see all apps shared with them, as illustrated in Figure 11-11.

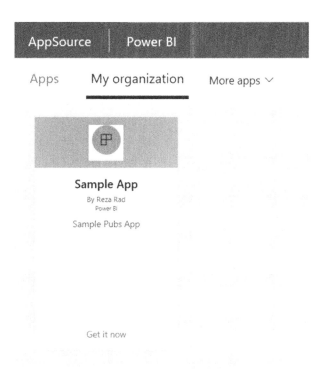

Figure 11-11. *Seeing list of apps*

Users can simply Get an app of interest as shown in Figure 11-12. Then once the app is installed, users are able to execute the app right away.

Figure 11-12. *App Installed*

By clicking on the app, users will be redirected to the landing page (see Figure 11-13). From there, users can explore the content in the app.

Figure 11-13. *Landing page for the app*

Changes in the App

You can apply any changes you want to the content in the app workspace. The changes on workspace will NOT affect users until you "update app". With the new update, they will get the updated content. You can also "Unpublish" the app, and Figure 11-14 shows the menu option for that purpose.

Figure 11-14. *Unpublish App*

Isolated Environments for Developers and Users

One of the most useful advantages of using Power BI Apps is the ability to have two separate environments: for Developers and for Users. The concept works merely based on the fact that a Power BI App is always associated with a workspace. Workspace acts like a developer environment, and Power BI App serves as an end-user environment.

Workspaces are developer environments, and Power BI Apps are end-user environments.

If you are a member of the developer team, you would have Edit access to the workspace. Providing edit access can be done easily in the workspace configuration by adding members to the edit access list as shown in Figure 11-15.

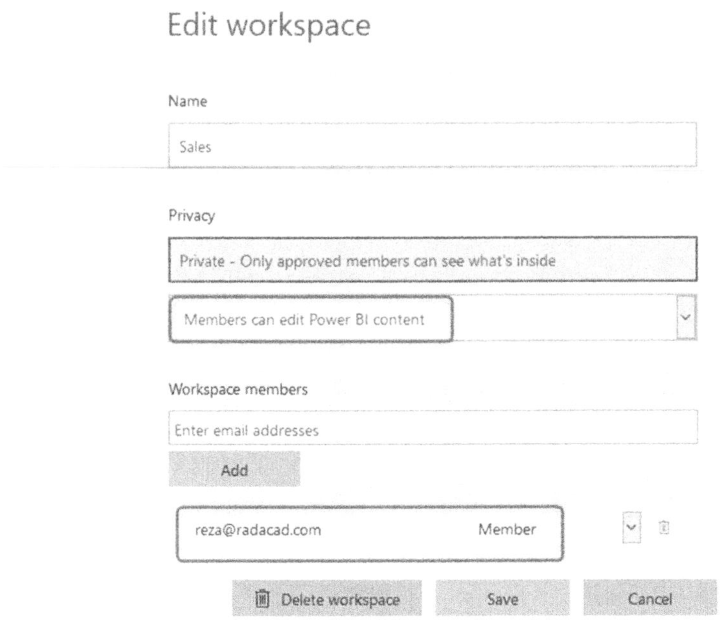

Edit workspace

Name

Sales

Privacy

Private - Only approved members can see what's inside

Members can edit Power BI content

Workspace members

Enter email addresses

Add

reza@radacad.com   Member

Delete workspace   Save   Cancel

Figure 11-15. *Edit access for workspace members in the developer environment*

All users who have edit access can change the content in the workspace. Their changes do not apply to the end-user environment until they Update the app.

Changes in a workspace do not affect the end-users' environment until the app is Updated.

As a developer, you might make some changes in the workspace. For example, you might remove a chart from a report, and then save it. This process is illustrated in Figure 11-16.

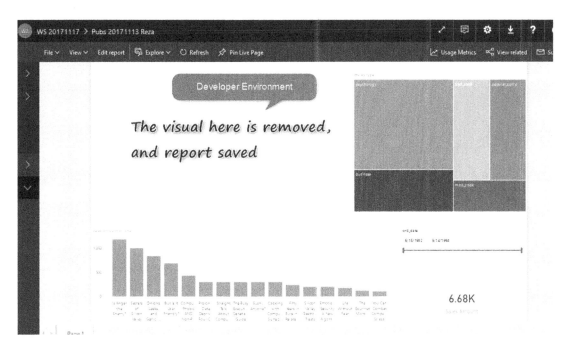

Figure 11-16. *Developers can make any changes in the report in the development environment*

The end user will not be affected by such a change. End users will still see the full report. For example, end users will still see the report as in Figure 11-17, even though the first bar chart has been removed in Figure 11-16.

Figure 11-17. *End-user environment (Power BI App) will not be affected by changes in the workspace until the app is updated*

To sync the Developer and End-User environments, you need to update the app to get the changes applied to the end-user side. Figure 11-18 shows such an update being initiated.

Figure 11-18. *Update App will apply latest changes*

What About Data Refresh?

Data refresh and access to up-to-date data is always a big question that comes through my presentations: Would I need to update the app, so end users get the updated data? How would they access the data refreshed or up to date? The answer is that data will be updated, if it is scheduled to refresh with a scheduling process determined at the dataset level, or if it is LiveQuery or DirectQuery. Regardless of users or developers, the dataset refresh is a different process.

If you have set up your dataset to be refreshed, then users will always have access to up-to-date data. You don't need to update the app for data changes. You just need to update the app for structural changes (adding, modifying or removing tables, fields, relationships, calculations), or visualization changes (adding, modifying or removing visuals on the report).

Pros and Cons of Power BI Apps

Following are some advantages of using Power BI Apps:

- Separate Environments for Developer and End User: The largest benefit of this method is to have two separate environments: an environment for developers to edit the Power BI content in a collaborative workspace and another environment for end users to consume the report. End users will be able only to view the reports, and developers will be able to make changes.

Power BI App is the best solution to have an Isolated developer and end-user environment.

- Controlling multiple Power BI content: Similar to the workspace, with the Power BI App, you can share multiple dashboards, reports, and datasets at the same time. Controlling multiple contents means less maintenance overhead compared to dashboard sharing, which is one dashboard at a time.

- External Sharing: Another great benefit of Power BI App is the ability to integrate that with Azure B2B services and provide external sharing. If you want to share Power BI content with people outside of your company, you can do that with a combination of the Azure B2B and Power BI App. Here is the blog post from Microsoft Product team about it: `https://powerbi.microsoft.com/en-us/blog/power-bi-expands-access-to-intelligence-for-external-guest-users/`

Power BI App is one of the newest ways of sharing in Power BI, and because of that there are still some flaws to be resolved:

- Power BI Apps is not a full replacement of Content Pack: Users cannot Make a Copy as they could in content pack. You might say: What is the benefit of copying? The answer is: Power BI is all about self-service. There are always some users who want to be able to create their version of the report. With Content Pack, that was simply possible. They could make a copy and change their copy without touching the original report. (read this blog post to learn how). With the new app; they cannot change anything. They cannot make a copy. Or if they are part of the group with edit access to the workspace, then they CAN CHANGE the original! It is either too much power for them or nothing.

- Immediate need for the app workspace administrator: Users who are not the admin of the group, but only have Edit access, can publish an app! Updating or publishing an app is too much access. Consider a situation that users are using a published app, and suddenly someone by mistake updates the app! It is critical that the admin of app workspace be the only person who can publish the app or at least can give this permission to a specific group of people.

- Changes in the Dataset Applies immediately: Power BI App is separating developer and end-user environments, and the changes in a report in a workspace don't affect the end user until you update the app. However, this functionality doesn't work with the dataset in that way. Power BI App and the workspace are sharing the same datasets, so any changes on the schedule refresh or structural changes will apply on both.

Summary

Power BI Apps comes to replace the content pack and workspaces with one better solution, and it is very promising. With this new combination, you will have the power of both. You can use workspaces to group the content and give edit access to your power users. And you can also use the content pack to share the content with the end users.

Power BI App is a very new feature, and many updates will come for this shortly, including the following:

- Disassociating from Office 365 groups.

- Push app to uses without the need for them to install (get) it.

- Copying content between workspaces.

The above list is based on what Power BI team's blog post mentioned as the roadmap for Power BI apps.

CHAPTER 12

Publish to Web

You've learned about three different ways of sharing content in Power BI so far. All of the methods that we talked about before (Dashboard Sharing, Workspaces, and Power BI Apps) need paid Power BI subscriptions for consuming reports. Users need to be either a Power BI Pro or free account under Power BI premium capacity. Publish to Web is another way of sharing Power BI content, which is free. Yes, you read that right; with this method, you can share Power BI content with users who even don't have a Power BI account.

Publish to the Web is an easy way of sharing for public data. However, it has some disadvantages as well. In this chapter, you will learn about this feature more in detail, and you will learn what this feature is and how it is different from Power BI Embedded. It will be a very long chapter if you want to learn about both Power BI Embedded and Publish to the Web and compare them here. So, in this chapter, I'll explain Publish to Web, and in the next chapters, you'll learn about Power BI embedded and their differences. In this chapter, you will learn how easy is to share your report with the public through a web page that can be your blog post, an HTML page, or any other web pages. Some questions about this feature are also answered through the content of this chapter.

What Is Publish to Web?

Once you have published your Power BI report into Power BI Service (or website), then you can share it with others through creating a dashboard, or workspaces in Power BI. What if you want to share it with the public through the Web? Let's say you want everyone to see the report and play with it (with all the interactive features that you have in Power BI). The answer is: use Publish to Web. Publish to Web allows you to create an embedded code for a Power BI report, and use that code in a web page. This simple

© Reza Rad 2018
R. Rad, *Pro Power BI Architecture*, https://doi.org/10.1007/978-1-4842-4015-1_12

feature will enable everyone to access the report. They won't be able to edit the report, but they will see the report, and the report will be fully interactive for them so they can highlight items, select slicers, and drill down.

How to Do It?

Using the Publish to Web feature is very simple. All you need to do is first deploy or publish the report into the Power BI website or service. And there click on the report (not dashboard). Once you have opened the report, click on the File menu option and choose to Publish to Web, as shown in Figure 12-1.

Figure 12-1. *Publish to Web on the report*

Then you will be informed about this feature in a message box that mentions this step will create a link and embed code for you to share with the world through a website or even email. Click on Create embed code as shown in Figure 12-2.

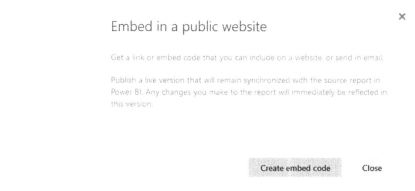

Figure 12-2. *Creating embed code*

Because publishing to the web is all about sharing a report and apparently the data in the report, you will be informed again to check the confidentiality of the data and report and make sure you are sharing the content that is not harmful for an organization or someone when it is viewable to the public. Figure 12-3 shows the confirmation screen warning you to think twice about releasing confidential or proprietary information.

Figure 12-3. *Warning; embed in a public website*

After clicking on Publish, you will see the embed code plus a link to share through email if you want. See Figure 12-4. You can also choose the size of the screen for the embed code.

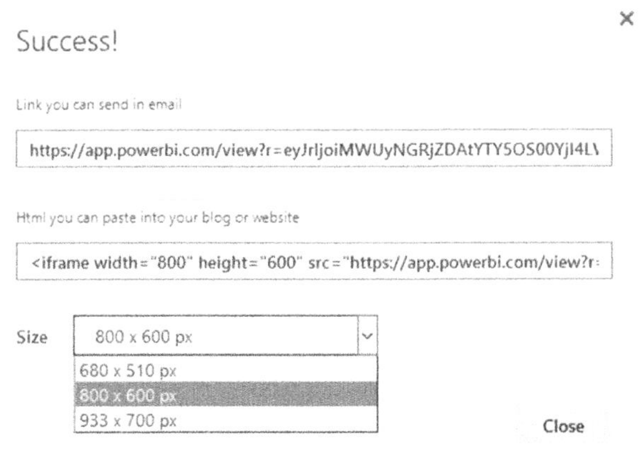

Success!
Link you can send in email
https://app.powerbi.com/view?r=eyJrljoiMWUyNGRjZDAtYTY5OS00YjI4L\
Html you can paste into your blog or website
<iframe width="800" height="600" src="https://app.powerbi.com/view?r=
Size
800 x 600 px
680 x 510 px
800 x 600 px
933 x 700 px
Close

Figure 12-4. *Embed code is created*

You can browse the link immediately to see the report in your browser. Figure 12-5 shows the report that I've just published.

qty by title
108
50
40
40
35
30
25
25
25
20
20
20
15
15
15
10
psychology
business
mod_cook
popular_comp
ord_date
6/15/1992
9/14/1994
6.68K
Sales Amount
17/11/2017 2:09:58 PM +13:00
Microsoft Power BI

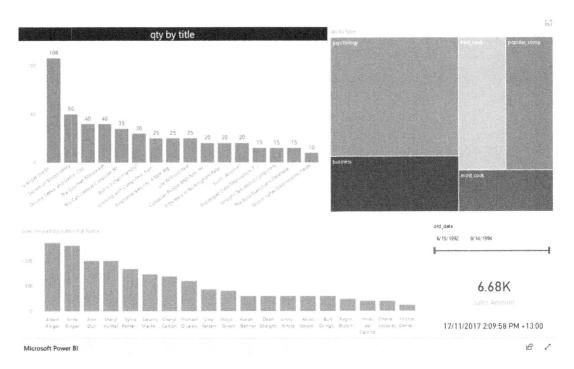

Figure 12-5. *Access the report with the link produced*

For browsing the report, you don't need to log in to Power BI service. In fact, people viewing this report won't need anything. As you see in the screenshot, the report is fully interactive, and users can highlight, select, or deselect items.

You can also use the embed code and add it to your HTML page, or blog post or wherever you want them to see in the report. Figure 12-6 shows an iframe tag, which is the embedded code that places the report into an existing HTML page. After adding the embed code, the full interactive report will be visible on the web page in question.

Figure 12-6.   *Embedding into a blog post's web page*

Security Thoughts?

Think carefully about security and what you share, because what you share is out there for anyone to access. The following sections highlight some issues to think about before publishing to the Web.

What You Share Is for Everyone!

The first thing you might think of is usually security. How can you manage security on this? The short answer is there is no security here. The report is shared through the Web, or email, with EVERYONE. So everyone who has the link or embeds code can access the report. They cannot edit it. But they can view it with no restriction.

Users Can Share It with Others!

A report that is published to the Web has a share section at the right bottom-hand side, which is highlighted in Figure 12-7. Everyone can share this report with anyone else through all social media channels: Facebook, Twitter, LinkedIn, sharing the link directly! This method of sharing is not secure. I do only recommend using this method of sharing the data that you want to publish as a public report on your company's or organization's website.

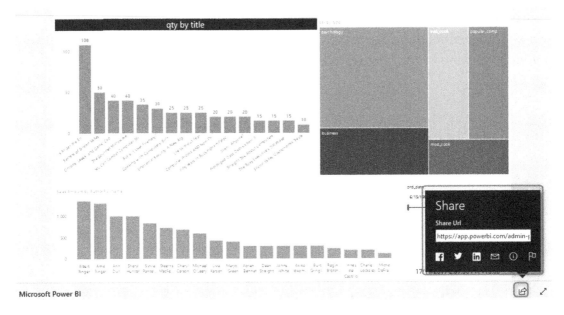

Figure 12-7. *All Sharing options from a Published to Web report*

All Report Pages Are Visible

If you have a report with 10+ pages, all of them would be visible to browsers. You cannot limit which pages you want to show and which you don't. As an example, the report you see above has more than one page, and you can view all of them. I recommend creating different reports if you want to restrict some pages and share them separately.

Publish to Web is only recommended for public data sharing in your organization's website with the public. There is no security option for Publish to Web; this method should not be used for reports of the confidential data of businesses.

Link or Embed Code Is Synchronized with the Report

If you make any changes to the report, all changes will be synchronized, because of the link or embed code is just a reference to this report. So, people will always see the latest version of your report. If you also want to keep the report up to date, you can schedule it for data refresh.

Removing the Access Is Easy!

If, for some reasons, you want to revoke the access for everyone to the report, you can do it easily. Just go to Power BI website or service, and under Setting, click on Manage Embed Codes. Figure 12-8 illustrates.

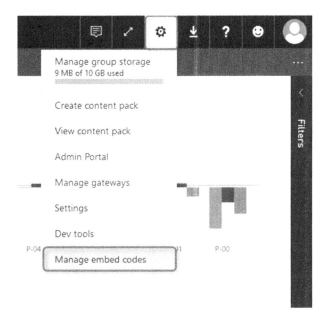

Figure 12-8. *Manage Embed Codes under your account*

Then you will see the embed code created, and you can delete it by clicking the Delete button highlighted in Figure 12-9.

Figure 12-9. *Delete the embed code*

Please note that once you delete the embed code, no one would be able to access this report from the public web. You will see a notification message like that in Figure 12-10 to that effect.

Figure 12-10. *Confirmation for Deleting the code*

If you go ahead and delete the embed code, the link and the embed code will show a message to public web users that the content is not available. Figure 12-11 shows this message.

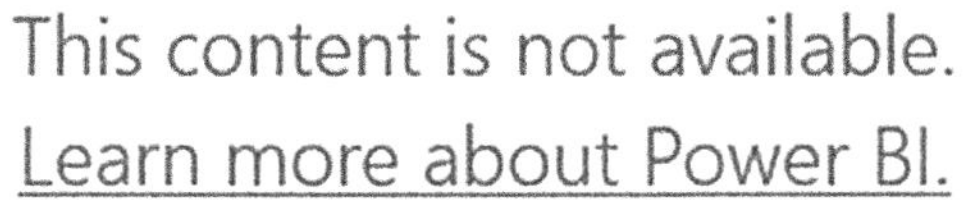

This content is not available.
Learn more about Power BI.

Figure 12-11. *Publish to Web is removed, and page is not accessible anymore*

Central Monitoring for all Embed Codes

Publish to Web seems a frustrating option with all the explanation so far. There is a need for an administration page to manage all embed codes there across the Power BI tenant. The Power BI team recently added this feature to the admin portal of Power BI. Here is the place that you can find all reports that are published to the Web, and you can remove those from being published to the Web.

To go to the admin portal, click on the setting icon in Power BI service. Then go to Admin Portal as shown in Figure 12-12.

Figure 12-12. *Admin Portal*

Click on Embed Codes on the left-hand side, and you will see all embed codes published by anyone from your organization (to access to the admin portal, you need to be the Power BI administrator; you will learn about that in another chapter). Figure 12-13 shows what the embed code listing looks like.

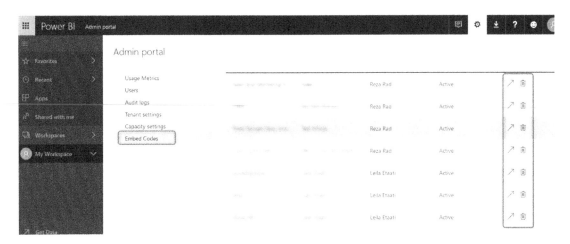

Figure 12-13. *Manage all embed codes in the Power BI tenant*

For each report that is published to the web, there are two options: to view the published report, or to delete it. Once you delete it, no one will be able to use the published to web's link.

Differences from Other Sharing Methods

If you played with Power BI before, you know that you can share your dashboards with people in your organization. This feature is different from embed code. Here are some differences between sharing dashboard and embed code:

- You Share a Dashboard, not a Report.

- Only those who have access to the dashboard will see the content.

- Dashboard link that is shared with the public won't show anything if they are not authorized to see it.

- Power BI Workspace or App is For Authorized Group of Users inside or outside of Your Organization, not for everyone!

- Power BI Embedded is different from Publish to Web.

You Share a Dashboard, Not a Report

If you click on the ellipses button beside a dashboard, you can share it with others in your organizations with their Power BI accounts. Figure 12-14 illustrates.

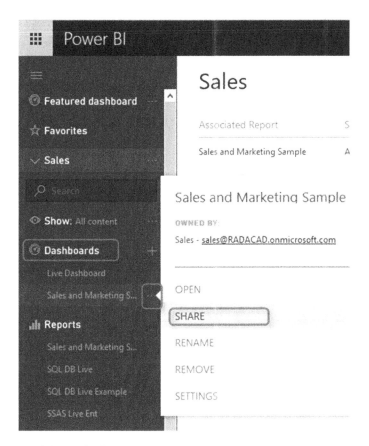

Figure 12-14. *Dashboard Sharing*

Only Those Who Have Access to the Dashboard Will See the Content

Once you share a report, you can choose who has access to see it based on their Power BI accounts. You can give them Edit access if you want as well. Figure 12-15 shows the dialog from which you provide authorization for others to access a dashboard

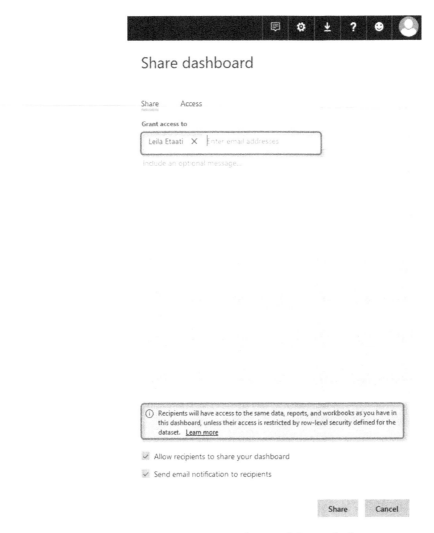

Figure 12-15. *Authorizing users in the Dashboard Sharing*

Dashboard Link Works Only for Authorized Users

Despite of having the dashboard link available in the Access tab of the sharing pane, only authorized users can see the content when browsing the link. Otherwise, they will see a message such as in Figure 12-16 that says they don't have permission to view this dashboard.

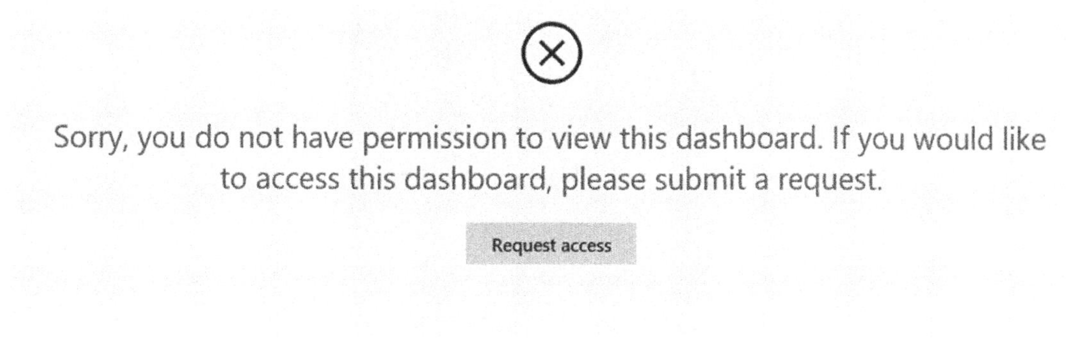

Sorry, you do not have permission to view this dashboard. If you would like
to access this dashboard, please submit a request.

Request access

Figure 12-16. *Unauthorized users don't have access to the content in other
sharing methods*

Power BI Workspace or App Is for Authorized Group of Users Inside or Outside of Your Organization, Not for Everyone!

You can share dashboards, reports, and datasets with a workspace that is an Office 365
group in your organization. Figure 12-17 shows a number of such workspaces. Users
of the group associated with a workspace will have access to all content shared by the
group. Also, you can use Power BI apps to share content within your organization or
even outside of your organization with Azure B2B services. However, with Publish to
Web, any users who have access to the page will see the report, regardless of having a
Power BI account or not.

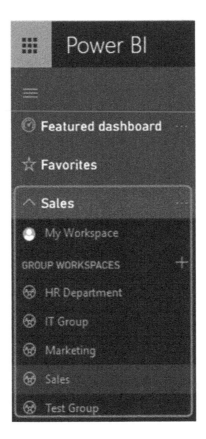

Figure 12-17. *Workspaces*

Public Access or Organizational Sharing

Last but not least, the difference between Publish to Web and Sharing is all about the difference between giving public access or sharing content through the organization.

With Sharing dashboards or using Power BI workspaces and apps, you can share content with other users. These users SHOULD BE Power BI users; they cannot access content anonymously. They need to log in to Power BI service to access the content.

With Publish to Web, EVERYONE accesses the report even if they don't have a Power BI account. They don't need to log in. They can browse the page that contains the Power BI embed code with no restriction on viewing the report.

Power BI Embedded Is Different from Publish to Web

Now that you know about Publish to Web, I can explain how Power BI embedded works in a nutshell. Power BI Embedded brings Power BI into applications. Yes, you can share your Power BI report through an application with API Keys. And you share the report with application users, even if they don't have Power BI accounts. However, you are much more flexible here. You can choose which reports you want to share with which users in the application. Power BI Embedded is the way to bring Power BI experience into an application with a security configuration enabled for users. I will explain in a separate chapter how to use Power BI Embedded. Stay tuned.

Publish to Web is not a secure, but is a free way of sharing and is for the public. Power BI embedded is a secure, paid service, and for specific people that you authorize.

Summary

In summary, Publish to the Web is the only free way of sharing Power BI content. This method of sharing doesn't have any security bound to it. As soon as you publish a report to the Web, anyone with that link will be able to access the report and the data. This method of sharing is easy; however, is not recommended for confidential data. This method is an only good option if you want to share some public reports on your company's public website.

Publish to the Web is entirely different from Power BI Embedded, so these two methods should not be considered the same. In the next few chapters, I'll explain what Power BI embedded is and how it works.

CHAPTER 13

Embed in SharePoint Online

So far, you've learned about four ways of sharing Power BI content. In this chapter, you'll learn about another method of sharing, which is named Embed in SharePoint online. Embedding in SharePoint online is an excellent method to share Power BI content through a SharePoint portal. Because Power BI and Office 365 accounts are bound to each other, this method of sharing is prevalent for SharePoint users. You can use SharePoint as a portal for users to refer to it. Power BI content then can be easily shared through that portal with Office 365 users.

How to Embed in SharePoint Online

To use this method, you need to have a Power BI report published in the service. This method only works for Power BI reports (Not Dashboard). To share a report with this method, log into the service and open a Power BI report. Click on the File menu and choose: Embed in SharePoint online as shown in Figure 13-1.

© Reza Rad 2018
R. Rad, *Pro Power BI Architecture*, https://doi.org/10.1007/978-1-4842-4015-1_13

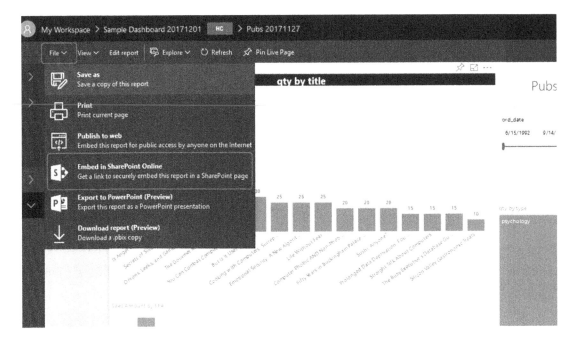

Figure 13-1. *Embed in SharePoint Online menu item in the Power BI Report*

The next step will generate a link that can be used in SharePoint. Just copy the link from this step, as shown in Figure 13-2.

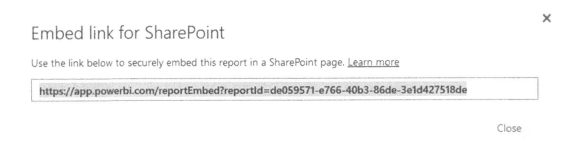

Figure 13-2. *Get the Embed URL*

The URL from Figure 13-2 is needed in the SharePoint online for embedding the Power BI Report. Log in now to your SharePoint Online tenant. You can go to the Pages section as shown in Figure 13-3.

Figure 13-3. *Navigate to the Pages section of a SharePoint site*

Create a New Site Page, or you can edit an existing page. Figure 13-4 shows creating a new page.

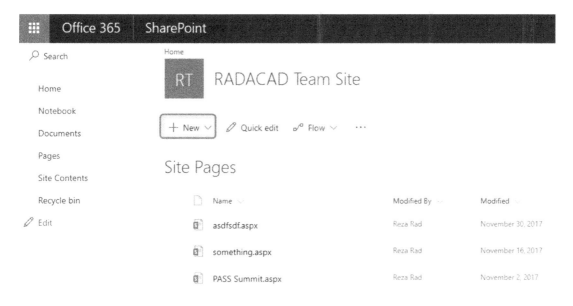

Figure 13-4. *Create a new SharePoint Site Page*

Name the new page. For this chapter's example, I'll name the page as "Power BI Embedded into SharePoint Online." Then click the Add icon to add a new object, and select Power BI from the items list as indicated in Figure 13-5.

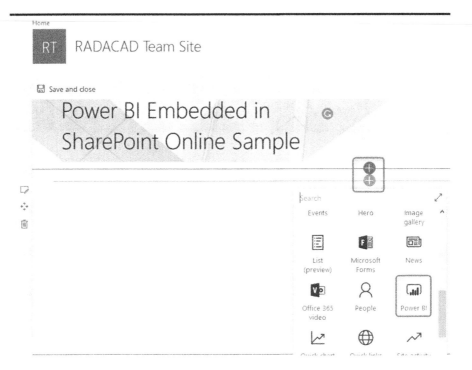

Figure 13-5. *Add a Power BI Object in the SharePoint page*

The Power BI component is now inserted to your page. Click on Add Report (At the time of writing this chapter, you can only embed report, not dashboard, into SharePoint online) as shown in Figure 13-6.

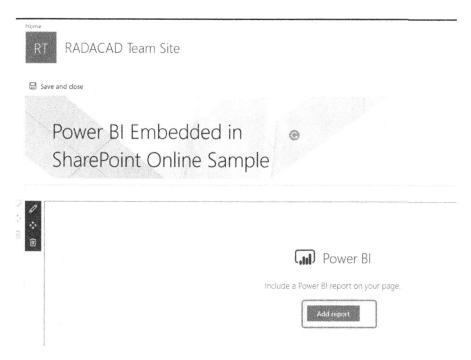

Figure 13-6. *Add the Report in Power BI Object*

You can now paste the embedded URL from the previous step into this section. Do so, and select the page (if Power BI report has multiple pages). See Figure 13-7 for an example.

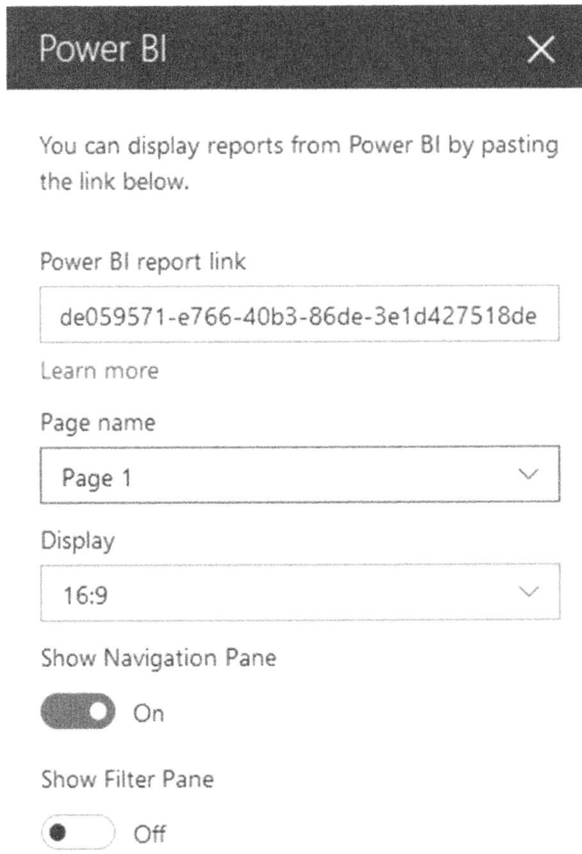

Figure 13-7. *Embed using the link*

As soon as you make these changes, you'll see the preview of the report on the page. Figure 13-8 shows what that preview looks like.

Figure 13-8. *Report embedded in the SharePoint page*

You can now publish the page. Once the page is published, the Power BI embedded part will be part of the published page, as shown in Figure 13-9. The Power BI report embedded in the SharePoint online page will be interactive like a standard Power BI report.

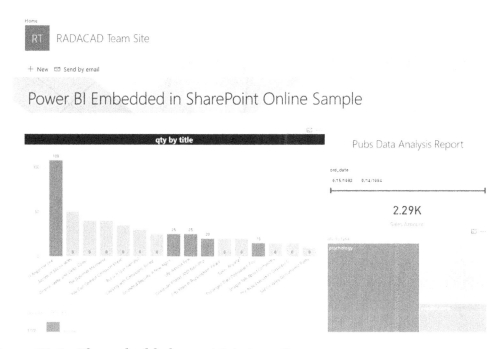

Figure 13-9. *The embedded report is interactive*

Sharing a SharePoint Page with an Embedded Power BI Report

After embedding the Power BI report into the page, let's see how you can share it with others. A SharePoint page can be shared with other SharePoint online users (which usually are also Office 365 users). However, one important note is that if a Power BI report is embedded in this page, then users need to have Power BI accounts to see it, and also their account should have access to that Power BI report as well. It means you need to manage permission in two locations: the SharePoint online page and Power BI report.

Access to SharePoint

You can share the page with other users. Simply click the Share icon at the top right-hand side of the page, as shown in Figure 13-10.

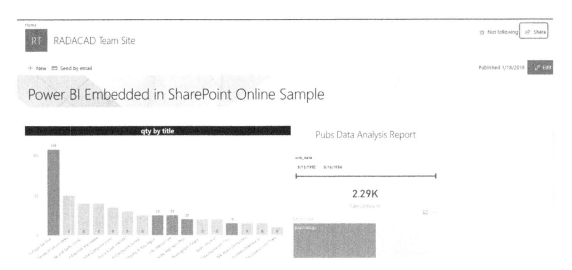

Figure 13-10. *Sharing the SharePoint page*

You can then add people from Office 365 accounts into the list. Figure 13-11 shows three people being added, and you can specify a personal message to go along with the invitation.

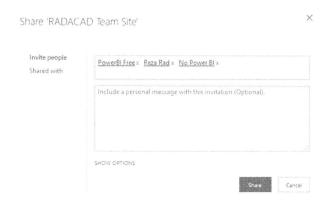

Figure 13-11. *Sharing Options in the SharePoint*

Figure 13-11 shows that the page I'm sharing is with the following three accounts:

- Power BI pro account; this is the account named "Reza Rad" in screenshot.

- Power BI free account.

- An Office 365 account with no Power BI license in it.

Power BI Permission

Users also need to be permitted to access the Power BI report. To handle their permission, you can use the Manage Permission part of dashboard sharing. Figure 13-12 highlights the button.

To manage permission on every item (dashboard, report, or dataset) individually, you can go to the Dashboard in Power BI service, click on share, and go to the Access tab. Then click on Manage permissions.

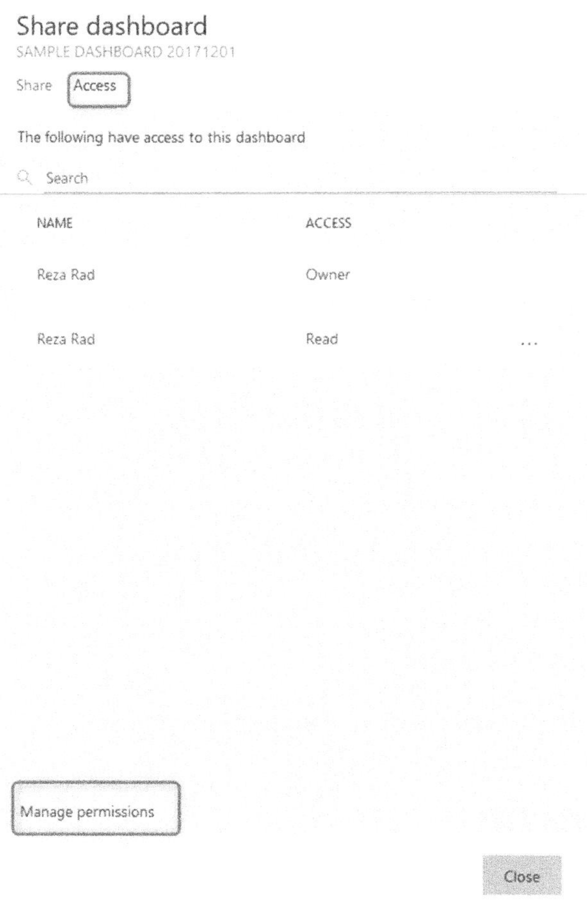

Share dashboard
SAMPLE DASHBOARD 20171201

Share [Access]

The following have access to this dashboard

🔍 Search

NAME	ACCESS	
Reza Rad	Owner	
Reza Rad	Read	...

[Manage permissions]

[Close]

Figure 13-12. *Manage Permissions in Power BI Service*

Manage permissions will show you a detailed list of access to the dashboard, reports, and datasets. On the left-hand side of the Manage Permissions section, highlighted in Figure 13-13, you will see related reports and datasets. You can click on the report.

Figure 13-13. *Managing access to each individual content object (Dashboard, report, dataset)*

By clicking on a report or dataset, you will see the permissions specified for that object. And you can change the permissions. For example, Figure 13-14 shows that user reza@radacad.com has Read and reshared access to the report being examined.

Figure 13-14. *Add user to the permission list of the report*

Now, let's see what each user will see when they log in to their page. A user who is a Pro user, and the content is shared with him/her in Power BI service, and the page is shared with him/her in SharePoint Online, will see the page fully visible as in Figure 13-15.

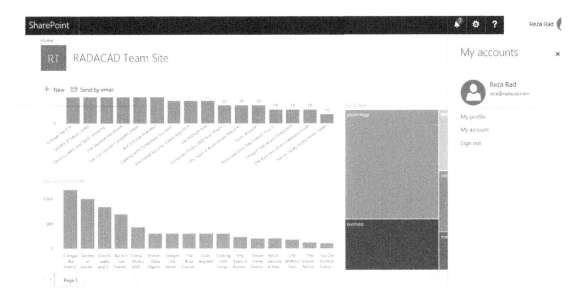

Figure 13-15. *Power BI user with right licensing and right permission will see the report and page fully visible*

Other users, however, can't see the page entirely. If users don't have a Pro subscription, or if they are not part of a Power BI premium subscription, they can't see the content and will see an error as shown in Figure 13-16.

Figure 13-16. *Non-Power BI user, or users with no paid licensing won't be able to access the report*

The important takeaway from this chapter's example is that users need to have a Power BI account. The Power BI report should be shared with them in the service, and the SharePoint page should be shared with them. Power BI accounts only can use a page if they are part of a premium capacity or a Power BI pro account.

Advantages and Disadvantages

Like all other methods, this method also has pros and cons. Advantages of Embed in SharePoint Online include the following:

- One portal for all content: With SharePoint online, you can share other documents as well, so why not use it for all other documents, and also the Power BI report? You can have one portal that is the central sharing portal for your Office 265 tenant. Users usually love the integrity.

- Embedding is simple: Unlike Power BI Embedded, embedding in SharePoint online is easy. You just get the URL and embed it into a Power BI object in the SharePoint online. You don't need to write a single line of code for that purpose, but with Power BI Embedded you do need a developer.

Disadvantages of Embed in SharePoint Online are that:

- Power BI Service Golden Plate is missed: One of the great aspects of Power BI components is the service. If you use embedding in the SharePoint, then users will use that as the portal for reports. Power BI Service has many exciting features, which may not be well used in this scenario, such as Alerts, feature dashboards, the dashboard itself, Q&A, and many other items. Users can still log in to Power BI service and see the report, but the experience that you create for them with SharePoint online would not be there.

- You have two places for managing permissions: At the time of writing this chapter, you need to manage permission in Power BI Service, and also in SharePoint online. This would take some time for maintenance, and also some reconciliation to check on those people who have access to the page are always permitted to read the report or not. Hopefully, this issue resolves quickly in the next few version upgrades of Power BI Service.

Summary

In summary, embedding in SharePoint Online is an easy way of adding an interactive Power BI report into a SharePoint online page. This method gives you the ability to have a central SharePoint portal for all your content as well as Power BI reports. Users do need to be part of a paid Power BI subscription to use this feature. However, they will lose the functionalities available for them in the Power BI service, because those are not available in SharePoint. In the next chapter, you'll learn about Power BI Embedded.

CHAPTER 14

Power BI Embedded

Power BI leverages a very powerful method of sharing named Power BI Embedded. This method of sharing is important because of mainly two specific features of it. With this method of sharing, you can share Power BI content in your custom application, and you can share it with your custom application users, regardless of if they have or don't have Power BI accounts. In this chapter, you will learn everything about Power BI Embedded, including but not limited to scenarios of using it and how to implement it.

What Is Power BI Embedded?

Power BI Embedded is embedding an entire or part of a report, dashboard, or dataset with Q&A in a custom application. This way of embedding is fully secure because it will leverage authentication keys and tokens. This way of embedding is not like Publish to the Web. Publish to the Web is not a secure method. However, Power BI Embedded is a fully secure method and customizable.

When to Think of Power BI Embedded?

You usually need to think of this method when you have main scenarios like these:

- You want to share a Power BI report with users who do not have Power BI accounts.

- You want to embed Power BI report inside your custom application.

Examples of these scenarios involve an ISV company, which has customers from all other companies; their Office 365 tenant might be entirely different for every single company. If the ISV company wants to share a Power BI report to all clients, then it means it has first to create Power BI accounts for each client in their tenant, and then publish the Power BI report separately to each tenant. This process involves lots of extra work.

© Reza Rad 2018
R. Rad, *Pro Power BI Architecture*, https://doi.org/10.1007/978-1-4842-4015-1_14

Power BI Embedded is a big help for our ISV company mentioned above. An ISV company simply can embed Power BI reports in a custom ASP.NET application, and then create users and passwords as part of the application. The username and password of the application are not Power BI users, of course. Everyone who has access to that page would be able to review the report.

What to Know?

There are a few things you need to know before choosing Power BI Embedded as your method of sharing:

- Licensing of Power BI Embedded is Different, it is calculated based on buckets of Page Renders.

- Power BI Embedded doesn't have all the features of Power BI services (such as subscription, alerts, etc.).

- You do need a web developer to take care of embedding and any further changes.

Power BI Licensing in normal form is per user; Pro user must pay a monthly fee to use Power BI. Power BI Embedded is different. Page renders are counted and depend on which bucket of the page render you fall into as there is a different licensing plan for it. You will read more about licensing a bit later.

When you use Power BI Embedded, you won't be using Power BI service. As a result, you will not have features such as Usage Metrics report, Alerts, subscriptions, and features like those which are specific to the service. You can obviously implement anything you want, but for those, you need to have a good web developer on your team.

Power BI Embedded is embedding a report into an application, and it needs a web developer to take care of this process. It is not just about the embedding itself, which may be a one-off process. When you embed the report into your application, then all other requests come after that. You would need to manage user and membership for your web application. You may want to have usage analysis of the report; you may want to have different levels of access to each report. Every single extra feature comes as a request for a web developer to implement. It is obviously possible to implement, but these are all coming at the cost of hiring a web developer.

Myths

Power BI Embedded enhanced significantly recently. There are many myths about this method that need clarification:

- Power BI Embedded only works with Live Connection, not with Import Data nor scheduled refresh. This statement is a myth.

- Power BI Embedded does not support all data sources. This statement is a myth.

- You can only embed Power BI report, not a dashboard nor Q&A. This statement is a myth.

- Row-Level Security is not possible with Power BI Embedded. This statement is a myth.

Many of the above statements were correct at the very beginning phase of the Power BI Embedded. However, with heaps of updates recently and enhancements in this technology recently, you can achieve all items mentioned above with Power BI Embedded. For your peace of mind; there is a team in Power BI only focused on Embedded features, and they are working hard to bring more features to this technology regularly.

Licensing of Power BI Embedded

Power BI Embedded is based on page renders. Every time you open a page with a Power BI object on it, that action of opening triggers what is considered as a page render. If you click on a slicer, then the page renders again. If you click on a column chart, and that click causes another part of the report to slice and dice, then that too counts as another page render.

You can view the current pricing at from `https://azure.microsoft.com/en-us/pricing/details/power-bi-embedded/`. It's important to think through your usage patterns so that you can make the right choices around pricing.

Implementing Power BI Embedded

If you are a developer and want to learn how to use Power BI Embedded, then start by downloading the example code used in this chapter. That example code is available from the following URL:

`https://github.com/Microsoft/PowerBI-Developer-Samples/tree/master/App%20Owns%20Data`

This example is one that Microsoft makes freely available.

Power BI REST API

We will be using Power BI REST API, which is at the moment version 2. If you download the sample code above, then you don't need to download API separately. However, if you are starting a new project, you can go to Nugget Manager in Visual Studio and search for Power BI REST API.

The new version of Power BI REST API has MANY features. In fact, there are so many features that they cannot fit into a single chapter. In this chapter, we'll focus on a few functionalities that are useful for integrating a report into your application.

Step 1: Register Your Application

The first step is to register your application. What does that mean? Any application that wants to interact with Azure should be registered and authorized through a process. There are two ways to register your application: one is simpler to start, the other one is simpler to maintain. :)

Register Through App Registration Website

Go to `https://dev.powerbi.com/apps` and register your application from there. It is a very easy process, so let's have a look. Log in to your Power BI account first, as shown in Figure 14-1.

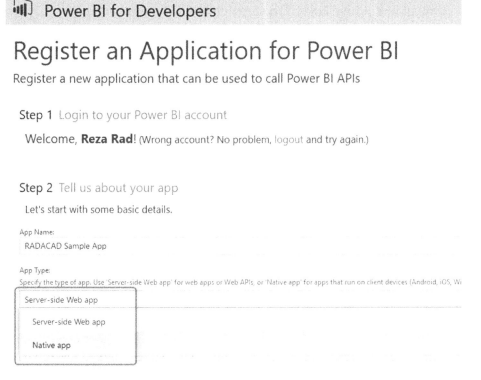

Power BI for Developers

Register an Application for Power BI

Register a new application that can be used to call Power BI APIs

Step 1 Login to your Power BI account

Create a new application with just a few simple steps. Once created, you can make any subsequent changes to your app details via the Azure Management Portal.

Sign in with your existing account | Don't have an account? Get one for free.

Figure 14-1. *Register an Application for Power BI*

After signing in, you can specify a name for your application (just to be able to find it easier in a list of applications). Also, select the application type. Figure 14-2 shows both name and type.

Power BI for Developers

Register an Application for Power BI

Register a new application that can be used to call Power BI APIs

Step 1 Login to your Power BI account

Welcome, **Reza Rad**! (Wrong account? No problem, logout and try again.)

Step 2 Tell us about your app

Let's start with some basic details.

App Name:
RADACAD Sample App

App Type:
Specify the type of app. Use 'Server-side Web app' for web apps or Web APIs, or 'Native app' for apps that run on client devices (Android, iOS, Wi

Server-side Web app

Server-side Web app

Native app

Figure 14-2. *Server-side Web App Selection*

There are two types of applications: Server-side web app, and Native app. What is the difference?

- Server-side Web App: An application that runs on a server, and is browsed through by clients, such as web applications and mobile applications in most of cases.

- Native App: an application that builds to run in a specific environment, such as a Console application.

Types of Integrating Power BI Content into Your Application

Before selecting the right application type, you need to understand that there are two types of integrating Power BI content into an application:

- Integrating without a Token: You are integrating content into your application, and you will be using Power BI users for access to the content. The above statement means that everyone who wants to look at the content should have a Power BI account.

- Integrating with a Token: You are integrating content into your application, and you are NOT using Power BI users. You will be managing user authentication through your application. Users may not even have Power BI accounts.

In this example, we are talking about integration WITH a Token.

Very Important: If you are using the method of integration "With a Token," then no matter what type of application you are writing, you have to choose Native App from the type of application above, even if you have a web/mobile application.

After selecting a Native app, then set a redirect URL. For this example, you can simply set it to be: http://localhost:13526

This redirect URL is not that important; it is about where to redirect. You can even set it to be other URLs.

The next step is to decide what permissions you want for this application. As you can see in the below image, there are different levels of permissions you can apply. It is not usually a good idea to give full permission to an application; however, for test purposes, you can select all permissions in the list, as shown in Figure 14-3. For this example, you might only need Read All Reports.

Redirect URL:
A valid URL

http://localhost:13526

Step 3 Choose APIs to access

Select the APIs and the level of access your app needs.

Dataset APIs	Report and Dashboard APIs	Other APIs
✓ Read All Datasets	✓ Read All Dashboards	✓ Read All Groups
✓ Read and Write All Datasets	✓ Read All Reports	✓ Create Content
	✓ Read and Write All Reports	

Figure 14-3. *Choosing API access*

Register Your Application

The last step is to click on Register your application; you will get a Client ID. Figure 14-4
shows how that Client ID will be presented, and I have elided my own ID from the image
in order to keep my ID secure.

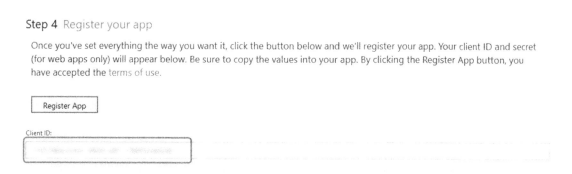

Step 4 Register your app

Once you've set everything the way you want it, click the button below and we'll register your app. Your client ID and secret
(for web apps only) will appear below. Be sure to copy the values into your app. By clicking the Register App button, you
have accepted the terms of use.

Register App

Client ID:

Figure 14-4. *Client ID*

If you register a server-side app, you will also receive a Client Secret along with Client
ID. Client ID (and Client Secret) are important factors for your application to be able to
interact with Azure and Power BI service.

Register Application Through Azure Portal

Another method of registering application is through Azure Portal. Go to `http://portal.azure.com` for this way of registration. The previous method of registration is easier and more user friendly. This method is much better for maintaining an application. With the previous method, there is no way of maintaining an application. You can only initiate registration from there. If you want to change permissions or anything related to the application, later on, the only way is through this method: Azure Portal.

In the Azure Portal, go to Azure Active Directory. Figure 14-5 shows the directory dashboard.

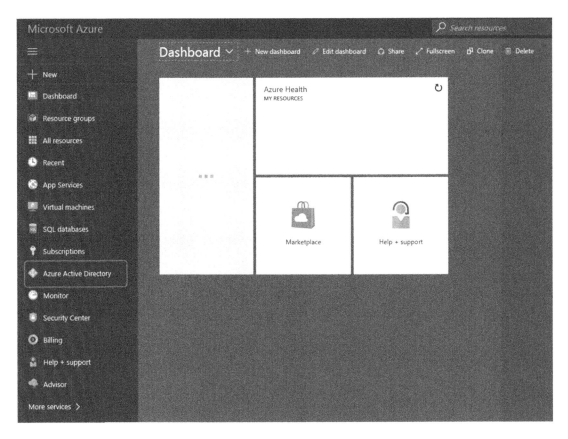

Figure 14-5. *Azure Active Directory*

Then go to App Registrations, as in Figure 14-6.

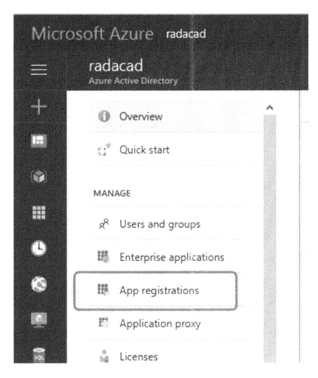

Figure 14-6. *App Registrations in Azure Portal*

Here you can register your application. Or you can even find your existing application. The screenshot in Figure 14-7 shows the RADACAD Sample Application that I registered earlier.

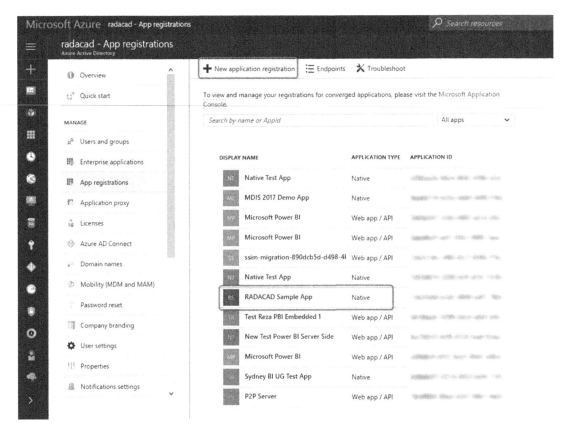

Figure 14-7. *App Registration Configuration*

After selecting the application, you can go to Required Permissions as shown in Figure 14-8. There, you can set up permissions for the app.

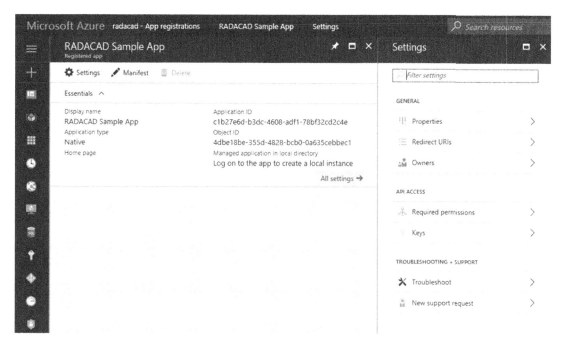

Figure 14-8. *Permission settings for App*

For Power BI apps you will find two sets of Permissions: for Power BI and for Azure Active Directory. After selecting the set, then you can select permissions as required, and as shown in Figure 14-9. Then save your settings. Don't forget to click on Grant Permissions after saving. Otherwise, permissions won't be granted!

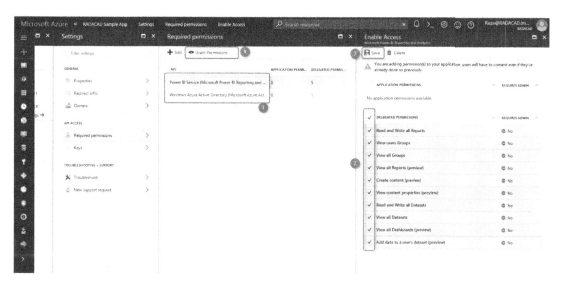

Figure 14-9. *Granting permission for App*

You can check permissions assigned in the list later if you want. Just bring up the page again, as shown in Figure 14-10.

Figure 14-10. *Permissions granted*

The process of registering your application is done, so now the next step is to start scripting and coding of your application with Power BI REST API.

Step 2: Authenticate

Every application that wants to interact with the Azure environment should go through an authentication process. This authentication process is passing Client ID (and sometimes Client Secret) to Azure and getting an authentication code. From this authentication code, an access Token can be fetched. This access token is a property that should be involved in every request sent from your application to Power BI and Azure afterward. Without this access token, your requests will fail.

Get Access Token

You need to get an access token to interact with Power BI REST API. This access token can be fetched through a process of authentication with Azure. The process itself requires at least a full chapter to explain. Figure 14-11 shows a flow diagram of the process.

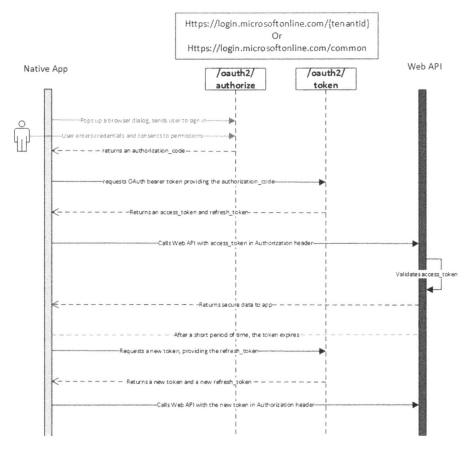

Figure 14-11. *Process to get Access Token*

I'm not going to explain details of this flow in this book. If you are interested in the details, read the following document:

https://docs.microsoft.com/en-us/azure/active-directory/develop/
v1-protocols-oauth-code

You don't really need to know all the details that are behind the scenes. It takes only a few lines of code to do the needed work.

Get Access Token from C# Code

After opening the sample code, go to the Web.Config file. Look for the lines of code that are highlighted in Figure 14-12.

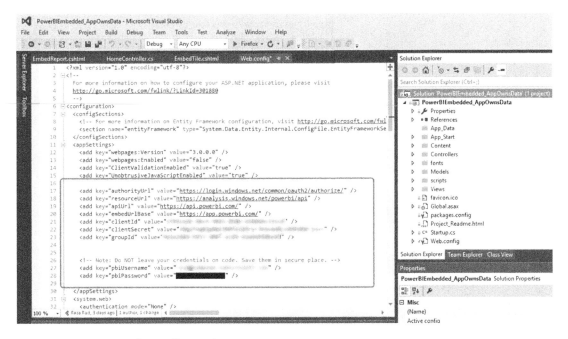

Figure 14-12. *Web.config settings*

In the web.config file, you will see some settings such as API URL and EmbedURL and some other configurations. Leave these as is. Then put your CLIENT ID there (the one you got from the previous step of registering your application). For this example, you don't need Client Secret. Also, you need to specify your Power BI username and password. Make sure that these are saved in a secure place, and are fetched from there when needed.

Sample Application Structure

The sample application used here is an MVC application that has three layers: Model, View, and Controller. I'm not going to explain details of that; you need to read a book to understand how MVC works. As a very basic definition; View is a presentation layer, Controller is a business layer and code logic, and Model is the content passed from Controller to View. The Authentication process and getting Access Token in this scenario happen in the controller.

Authentication Process

If you open HomeController.cs under Controllers folder, then you will find the first method EmbedReport(), which is doing the authentication process in the very first few lines that are highlighted in Figure 14-13.

Figure 14-13. *Getting the access token through C# Code*

The authentication process, in general, includes passing credentials to AuthorityURL and getting the result back if the application has the access, and authentication goes through correctly, and then you will get a result that you can fetch Token from it. The token then will be used in creating a new instance of Power BI Client. Power BI Client is the main object that should be created from REST API to interact with Power BI service.

Power BI Client Object

Power BI Client object is the main object that needs to be created to interact with Power BI Service. As you've learned above, you need to have the access token for this step. You just need parameters to create a Power BI Client object: ApiURL (which is static) and token (which is gained through the authentication process above). For example:

```
var client = new PowerBIClient(new Uri(ApiUrl), token credentials);
```

After creating the PowerBIClient object as shown in this code snippet and in Figure 14-14, you have access to a massive amount of information from Power BI Service, and you can implement many actions through it.

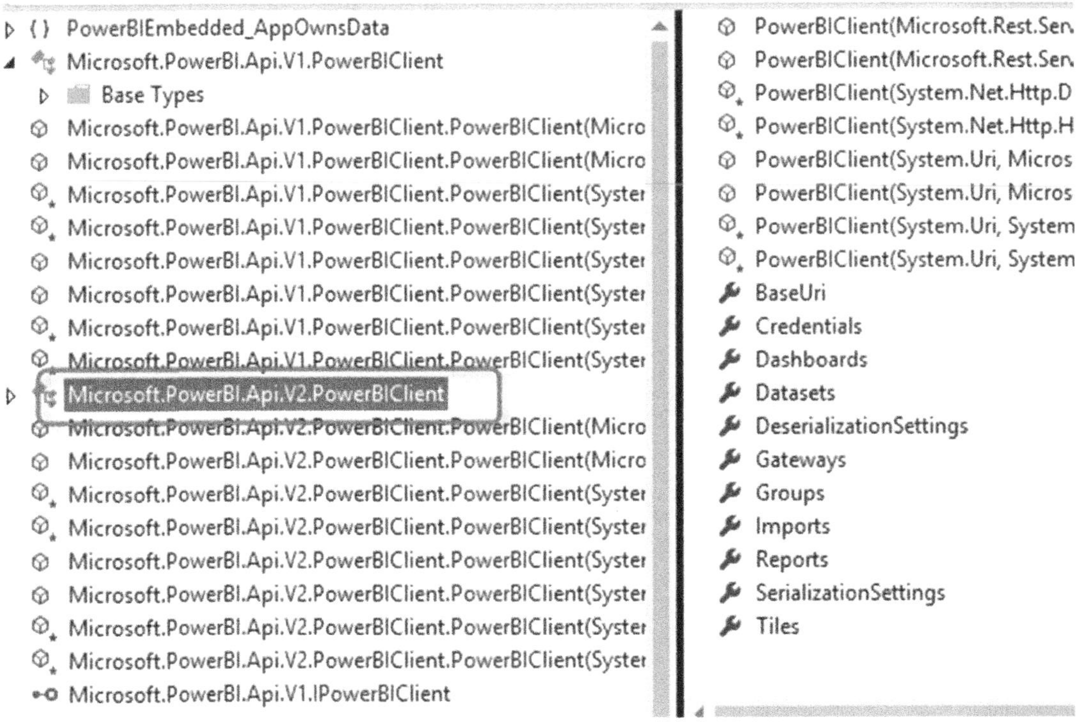

Figure 14-14. *PowerBIClient Object*

Step 3: Embed Content

In this step, you will learn about codes and the method to embed the content into your application after registration and authentication of the application.

Get List of Reports

For this example; I'm going to Embed a report into a web page, so I will get a list of reports first (you can even directly mention the report Id). I'll use the following code for that purpose:

```
// Get a list of reports.
            var reports = await client.Reports.GetReportsInGroupAsync
            (GroupId);

            // Get the first report in the group.
            var report = reports.Value.FirstOrDefault();
```

```
if (report == null)
{
    return View(new EmbedConfig()
    {
        ErrorMessage = "Group has no reports."
    });
}
```

As you can see, the function used is GetReportsInGroupAsync. This function simply returns all reports under a group. Group Id is specified in the web.config file. Notice that Id is not the name of the group. The names that you see for group, dashboard, report, and dataset are just display labels. Each object in Power BI has an ID that is a unique identifier (GUID). You can easily find it when you browse the group in Power BI Service through URL, as shown in Figure 14-15.

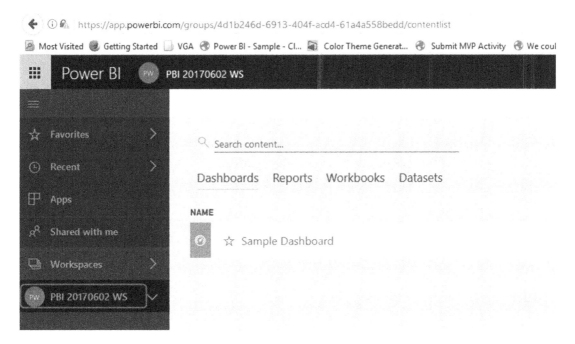

Figure 14-15. *Getting the workspace ID*

These Ids can then be used for Power BI REST API functions.

The function above will return the first report on that list because I've used FirstOrDefault() function. You can easily mention any other reports if you want to.

Creating Embed Content

In the MVC application, the next step is to create the embed content and push it to the view. The following lines of code generate the embed content:

```
// Generate Embed Token.
            var generateTokenRequestParameters = new GenerateToken
            Request(accessLevel: "view");
            var tokenResponse = await client.Reports.
            GenerateTokenInGroupAsync(GroupId, report.Id,
            generateTokenRequestParameters);

            if (tokenResponse == null)
            {
                return View(new EmbedConfig()
                {
                    ErrorMessage = "Failed to generate embed token."
                });
            }

            // Generate Embed Configuration.
            var embedConfig = new EmbedConfig()
            {
                EmbedToken = tokenResponse,
                EmbedUrl = report.EmbedUrl,
                Id = report.Id
            };

            return View(embedConfig);
```

JAVA Script in the Web Page

In the EmbedReport.Chtml page, which is a view web page, you need a JavaScript section to embed the content into the page. Here is the JavaScript code:

```
    // Read embed application token from Model
    var accessToken = "@Model.EmbedToken.Token";

    // Read embed URL from Model
    var embedUrl = "@Html.Raw(Model.EmbedUrl)";
```

```
// Read report Id from Model
var embedReportId = "@Model.Id";

// Get models. models contains enums that can be used.
var models = window['powerbi-client'].models;

// Embed configuration used to describe the what and how to embed.
// This object is used when calling powerbi.embed.
// This also includes settings and options such as filters.
// You can find more information at https://github.com/Microsoft/
    PowerBI-JavaScript/wiki/Embed-Configuration-Details.
var config = {
    type: 'report',
    tokenType: models.TokenType.Embed,
    accessToken: accessToken,
    embedUrl: embedUrl,
    id: embedReportId,
    permissions: models.Permissions.All,
    settings: {
        filterPaneEnabled: true,
        navContentPaneEnabled: true
    }
};

// Get a reference to the embedded report HTML element
var reportContainer = $('#reportContainer')[0];

// Embed the report and display it within the div container.
var report = powerbi.embed(reportContainer, config);
```

As you can see, Embed Token is required for the embedding part. In addition, the embed content comes from the controller.

Testing Application

If you run the sample application, you can check and see how the embedding Report in application works. It should work perfectly, as shown in Figure 14-16.

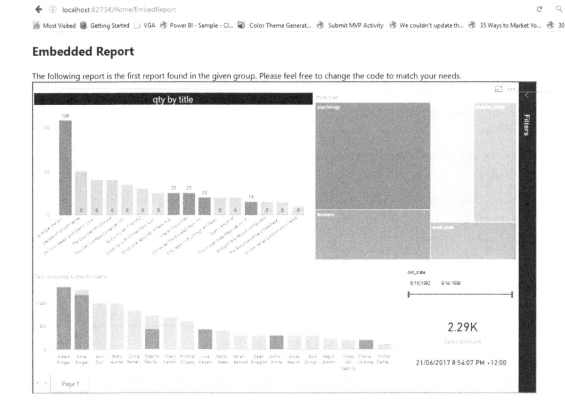

Figure 14-16. *Report Embedded into the application*

As you can see, the report is integrated into my application, which is running on my localhost. This method of embedding works with any report, sourced from any data source with any connection type.

Getting a List of Dashboards

There is a function that returns a list of dashboards for you, and you can easily select dashboards you want. The functions GetDashboardsInGroupAsync or GetDashboardAsync, along with others highlighted in Figure 14-17, provide you information about dashboards.

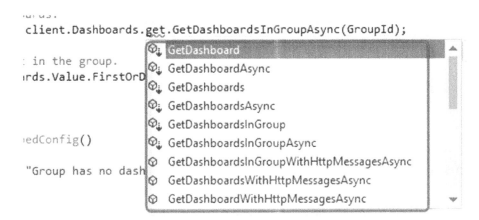

```
client.Dashboards.get.GetDashboardsInGroupAsync(GroupId);
```

Figure 14-17. *Dashboard functions for Power BI REST API*

After fetching a list of dashboards, that list can then be presented for a user to view through the following script:

```
// Get a list of dashboards.
var dashboards = await client.Dashboards.get.GetDashboards
InGroupAsync(GroupId);

// Get the first report in the group.
var dashboard = dashboards.Value.FirstOrDefault();

if (dashboard == null)
{
    return View(new EmbedConfig()
    {
        ErrorMessage = "Group has no dashboards."
    });
}

// Generate Embed Token.
var generateTokenRequestParameters = new GenerateToken
Request(accessLevel: "view");
var tokenResponse = await client.Dashboards.Ge
nerateTokenInGroupAsync(GroupId, dashboard.Id,
generateTokenRequestParameters);
```

```
            if (tokenResponse == null)
            {
                return View(new EmbedConfig()
                {
                    ErrorMessage = "Failed to generate embed token."
                });
            }

            // Generate Embed Configuration.
            var embedConfig = new EmbedConfig()
            {
                EmbedToken = tokenResponse,
                EmbedUrl = dashboard.EmbedUrl,
                Id = dashboard.Id
            };

            return View(embedConfig);
```

Embed Dashboard

Finally embedding a dashboard is similar to embedding a report. Here is the code to embed a dashboard:

```
// Read embed application token from Model
var accessToken = "@Model.EmbedToken.Token";

// Read embed URL from Model
var embedUrl = "@Html.Raw(Model.EmbedUrl)";

// Read dashboard Id from Model
var embedDashboardId = "@Model.Id";

// Get models. models contains enums that can be used.
var models = window['powerbi-client'].models;

// Embed configuration used to describe the what and how to embed.
// This object is used when calling powerbi.embed.
// This also includes settings and options such as filters.
// You can find more information at https://github.com/Microsoft/
    PowerBI-JavaScript/wiki/Embed-Configuration-Details.
```

```
var config = {
    type: 'dashboard',
    tokenType: models.TokenType.Embed,
    accessToken: accessToken,
    embedUrl: embedUrl,
    id: embedDashboardId
};

// Get a reference to the embedded dashboard HTML element
var dashboardContainer = $('#dashboardContainer')[0];

// Embed the dashboard and display it within the div container.
var dashboard = powerbi.embed(dashboardContainer, config);
```

Figure 14-18 shows a dashboard that's been embedded into an application.

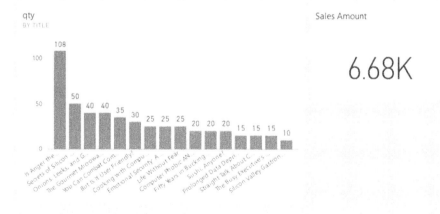

Figure 14-18. *Dashboard embedded into an application*

Getting Tiles

You first need to have the dashboard object to get tiles under it. Figure 14-19 highlights some of the functions relating to tiles.

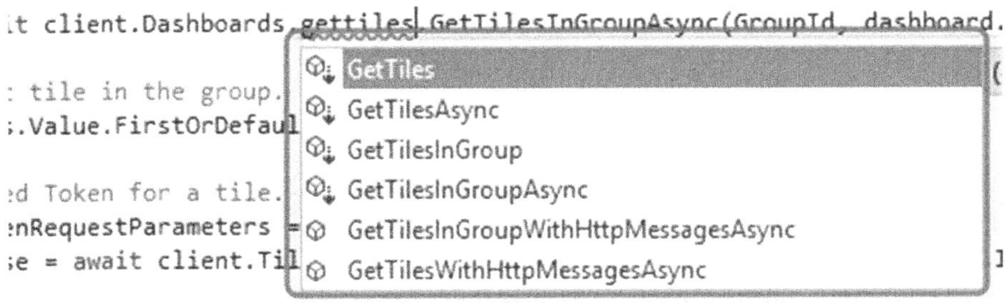

Figure 14-19. *Tile functions of the Power BI REST API*

As you can see, some functions fetch Tiles from the Dashboard and group. The following code will fetch the first tile in a dashboard and pass it to the view page:

```
var tiles = await client.Dashboards.
GetTilesInGroupAsync(GroupId, dashboard.Id);

// Get the first tile in the group.
var tile = tiles.Value.FirstOrDefault();

// Generate Embed Token for a tile.
var generateTokenRequestParameters = new GenerateToken
Request(accessLevel: "view");
var tokenResponse = await client.Tiles.Generate
TokenInGroupAsync(GroupId, dashboard.Id, tile.Id,
generateTokenRequestParameters);

if (tokenResponse == null)
{
    return View(new TileEmbedConfig()
    {
        ErrorMessage = "Failed to generate embed token."
    });
}
```

```
// Generate Embed Configuration.
var embedConfig = new TileEmbedConfig()
{
    EmbedToken = tokenResponse,
    EmbedUrl = tile.EmbedUrl,
    Id = tile.Id,
    dashboardId = dashboard.Id
};

return View(embedConfig);
```

Summary

Power BI Embedded brings Power BI into your application. Imagine the analytical power of Power BI combined with your custom application. The result would be revolutionary. You can leverage your users, interact with the embedded object of Power BI from your web application, and implement many scenarios such as customized refresh and many other features. This method, however, works on a different licensing plan, and you would need a web developer for it.

CHAPTER 15

Power BI Sharing Methods

You have published your Power BI report and want to share it with others. Now you see that you can share it through basic sharing, workspaces, Apps, Publish to Web, Power BI embedded, and SharePoint online. The wide range of this variety of methods for sharing makes it confusing to choose the right method. I have done some conference sessions explaining the difference between methods in details, and I feel this is important to know before sharing content with users. In this chapter, you will learn about all the different methods of sharing, pros and cons of each, and scenarios that you can use with each method. At the end of this chapter, you will be able to choose the best sharing mechanism for sharing your Power BI reports.

What Sharing Methods Will Be Covered in This Chapter

In this chapter, you will only hear about sharing methods that are interactive and cloud based. We won't talk about sharing the *.pbix file with others; that is a method of sharing obviously, but it is not what we consider a proper sharing method. We won't talk about exporting a Power BI report into a PowerPoint slide and sharing with others because it is not interactive. We won't talk about taking a screenshot of Power BI report and sharing with others. Also, we won't talk about sharing through on-premises solutions with the Power BI report server. That is a separate topic. In this chapter, we just focus on cloud-based, interactive methods of sharing Power BI reports. This chapter only covers methods of sharing:

- Basic Sharing
- Workspace
- Power BI App

© Reza Rad 2018
R. Rad, *Pro Power BI Architecture*, https://doi.org/10.1007/978-1-4842-4015-1_15

- Publish to Web

- Embed in SharePoint online

- Power BI Embedded

Basic Sharing of Dashboards and Reports

Basic sharing is the most common way of sharing the Power BI content. However, it is not always the best way of sharing. Basic Sharing is very simple and easy to use. You can simply click on the Share button – shown in Figure 15-1 – in the dashboard or report, and then share it with other users. This method of Sharing gives users two levels of access: Read-only, or Read-only and re-share.

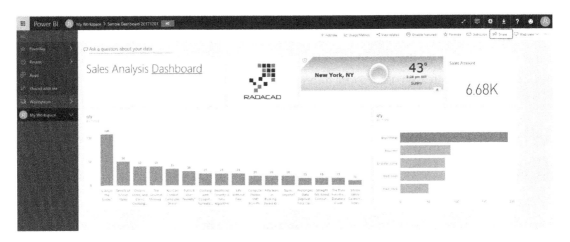

Figure 15-1. *Basic Sharing*

By default, when you share a Power BI dashboard with this method, then the report and the dataset will be shared as well. However, you can go to Manage Permissions and set up permissions specifically for every item if you want, as shown in Figure 15-2.

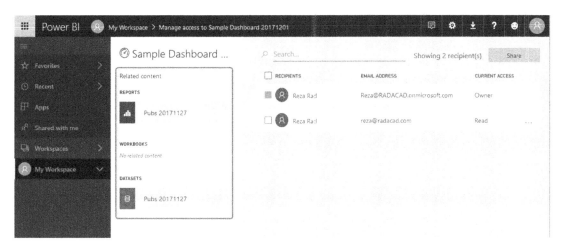

Figure 15-2. *Manage Permissions*

Users can easily click on the "Shared with me" section of their profile. By doing so, they will see all reports and dashboards shared with them. Figure 15-3 illustrates.

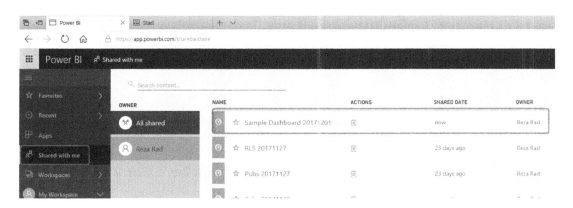

Figure 15-3. *Shared with Me*

Advantages of Dashboard Sharing

Dashboard sharing is the most basic way of sharing content in Power BI. This method is quick and easy to set up. You don't need a lot of steps to set up sharing of the dashboard. The ability to share it very quickly makes this method the most common method of sharing for testing.

If you have created a Power BI content and want to share it with others easily just for Testing, one of your first options is Dashboard sharing.

Disadvantages of Dashboard Sharing

Dashboard sharing is simple; however, it has many drawbacks, which makes it hard to be used in production. I do not recommend using this method to share Power BI content with users in a production environment because of the following:

- **No Edit Access**: With Dashboard sharing, you cannot specify edit access. For end users, you never want to give edit access; however, if you are working with a team of developers, and you want to provide them with access to edit the content, you cannot do that with dashboard sharing. You have to use other methods of sharing.

- **Share Objects one at a time**: You can only share one dashboard at a time. What if you wanted to share hundreds of dashboards? You must go to each dashboard and share items individually. Sharing every single dashboard would add a lot of maintenance overhead to your work. The best would be having all contents under a group and sharing it with all others at once.

Chapter 9, earlier in the book, talks about dashboard sharing in more detail.

Workspaces

Workspaces are created to cover the main two limitations of the basic sharing, allowing you to edit access and the sharing of multiple objects. With a workspace, you can share as many like items you have in that workspace at once. You can also decide the access level of the workspace to be either Edit or Read-Only. Workspaces because of these two features are heavily used as collaborative development environments.

You can have two levels of access for a workspace: Edit and Read-Only. Figure 15-4 shows a workspace being configured for edit access.

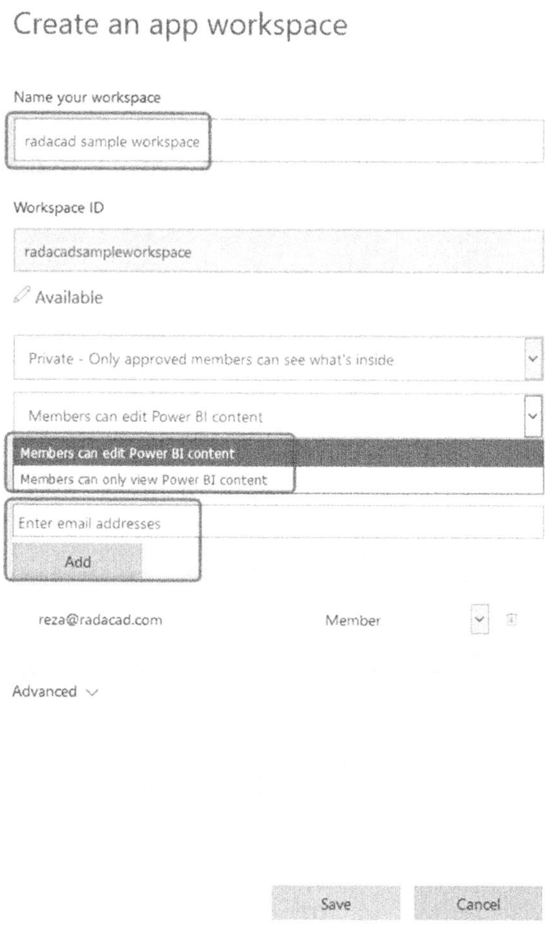

Create an app workspace

Name your workspace

radacad sample workspace

Workspace ID

radacadsampleworkspace

✎ Available

Private - Only approved members can see what's inside   ⌄

Members can edit Power BI content   ⌄

Members can edit Power BI content
Members can only view Power BI content

Enter email addresses

Add

reza@radacad.com   Member   ⌄   ⊞

Advanced ⌄

Save   Cancel

Figure 15-4. *Creating Workspace*

Workspaces also have advantages and disadvantages; let's check these out.

Advantages of Workspaces

The use of workspaces has a number of advantages. These include:

- Sharing multiple Contents with Team: You may have shared a dashboard with a couple of your colleagues in your organization, and after few weeks a need for a new dashboard comes up, and you share that dashboard with them. A couple of months later, another member of your team asks for access to a dataset in Power BI to be able to create a report and share with some others. Power BI workspaces enable you to share content (dashboard, report, and dataset) with all members of a group. You don't need to share each dashboard with each user; groups make it easy for you.

- Multiple Workspaces: It is s hectic environment when you are part of multiple teams, and each team has their own set of dashboards, reports, and datasets. Your "shared with me" section in Power BI will be hundreds of items and finding something there would be a problem. Power BI workspaces create a separate environment for all members of the group. You can easily switch between workspaces in Power BI.

- Isolated User/Group Administration: When you share content with an individual in the organization, if that person leaves the company, or is replaced by someone else from another team, then you have to remove sharing from a previous user account and assign it to the new user account. The best practice is to share content with groups. And members of groups then easily can be managed by an administrator. Power BI workspaces are fully synchronized with Office 365 groups. Once you used a group in Power BI, then it is only an admin's task to add/remove members from it.

- Best Developer Environment: For a team of developers, you need an environment to share multiple Power BI content. Everyone needs to have edit access to the content provided by the team. A Power BI workspace is the perfect solution for the development environment. You can create a workspace as a development environment and then share it with other members of the developer team with Edit access. Then you all have access to the same content in your development workspace.

Power BI workspaces are the perfect solution for the development environment.

Disadvantages of Workspaces

However, there are some drawbacks to workspaces to be aware of. These drawbacks include:

- Not good for End Users: Workspaces are not good for sharing content with end users. You may wonder why is that? You can give users of the workspace read-only access to the content. However, this is half of the requirement. In an end-user sharing environment, one of the primary requirements is to have the development and user environments separated from each other. Assume that you have created a workspace and shared it with end users. If you suddenly make changes in the workspace while they are using it, then their view of the world breaks and changes. With one workspace, your development and user environment are the same. You cannot use one workspace to be shared between developers and users. Creating multiple workspaces also brings another challenge.

- Overhead of Multiple workspaces: If you have multiple workspaces, then moving or copying content between workspaces is not possible (at the time of writing this book it is not possible, but very soon it will be available). The limitation above means you must re-create your dashboards in every workspace. The overhead maintenance costs of such scenario are high.

To learn more about Workspaces, read Chapter 10.

Power BI Apps

Workspaces are a great way of sharing content with users, but when it comes to having a development and user environment, then managing workspaces are not easy. Power BI App is the solution for multiple environment approaches. With Power BI App, your development environment (workspace), and user environment (App) are isolated from each other.

Publishing an App for a workspace is very simple. Figure 15-5 shows the Publish app button that begins the process.

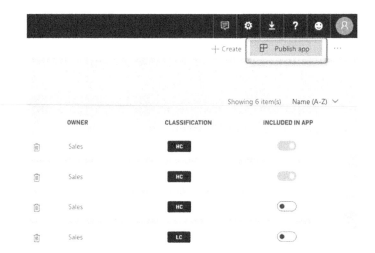

Figure 15-5. *Publishing a Power BI App*

Once an app is published, users can easily access it through the Apps section of their Power BI account. Figure 15-6 shows a sample app as users would see it.

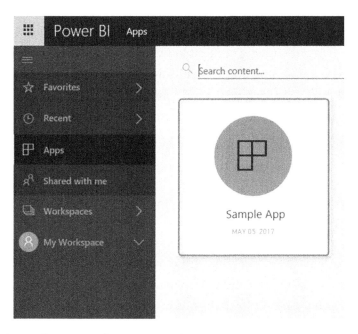

Figure 15-6. *Accessing Apps from users view*

Apps are a great sharing method for multiple environments and the best way of sharing for users in a production environment. However, Apps also have pros and cons as below.

Advantages of Power BI Apps

The use of Apps brings a number of advantages. These include:

Separate Environments for Developer and End user: The greatest benefit of this method is to have two separate environments: an environment for developers to edit the Power BI content in a collaborative workspace, and another environment for end users to consume the report. End users will be able only to view the reports, and developers will be able to make changes.

Power BI App is the best solution to have an Isolated developer and end user environment.

Controlling multiple Power BI content: Similar to the workspace, with the Power BI app, you can share multiple dashboards, reports, and datasets at the same time. Controlling multiple contents means less maintenance overhead compared to dashboard sharing, which is one dashboard at a time.

External Sharing: Another great benefit of Power BI app is the ability to integrate with Azure B2B services and provide external sharing. If you want to share Power BI content with people outside of your company, you can do that with a combination of Azure B2B and Power BI app.

Cons of Power BI Apps

Power BI Apps are one of the newest ways of sharing in Power BI, and because of that, the use of Apps comes with some limitations. The use of Apps is a replacement for Power BI Content Packs. However, the use of Apps still has some flaws:

- **Power BI Apps are not a full replacement of Content Pack**: Users cannot Make a Copy as they could in the content pack. You might say: What is the benefit of copying? The answer is this: Power BI is all about self-service. There are always some users who want to be able to create their version of the report. With Content Pack that was simply possible. They could make a copy, and change their copy without touching the original report. (read this blog post to learn how). With the new app, they cannot change anything. They cannot make a copy. Or if they are part of the group with edit access to the workspace, then they CAN CHANGE the original! It is either too much power for them or nothing.

269

- **Immediate need for the app workspace administrator**: Users who are not the admin of the group, but only have Edit access, can publish an app! Updating or publishing an app is too much access. Consider a situation that users are using a published app, and suddenly someone by mistake updates the app! It is critical that the admin of app workspace be the only person who can publish the app or at least can give this permission to a specific group of people.

- **Changes in the Dataset Applies immediately**: Power BI app is separating developer and end-user environments, and the changes in a report in a workspace don't affect the end user until you update the app. However, this functionality doesn't work with the dataset in that way. Power BI app and the workspace are sharing the same datasets, so any changes on the schedule refresh or structural changes will apply on both.

Publish to Web

Sometimes, you don't need a secure way of sharing, so you may search for an easy and free way of sharing, and your content is not confidential or sensitive. Publish to the Web is your friend in such a situation. Publish to Web is the only free way of sharing in Power BI, but be aware that this method is not secure.

The Publish to Web method gives you an embed code, which you can use in any web pages to embed the Power BI report into the page. Figure 15-7 shows how the embed code is presented to you when you decide to share a report in this manner.

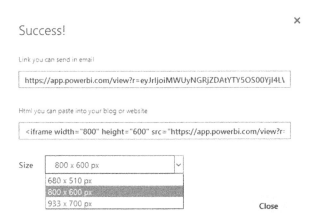

Figure 15-7. *Generating the embed code for Publish to Web*

The embedded content in this way would be available for anyone who has access to that page. Figure 15-8 shows how a user can share such a report.

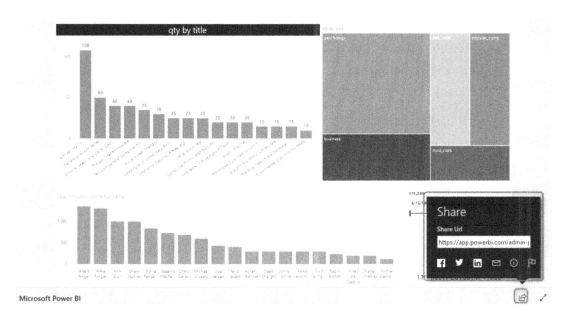

Figure 15-8.   *Publish to Web; how to access*

Security Thoughts of Publish to Web?

Publish to Web is a free method of sharing. However, it's not a secure method. Following are some things to think about when using this method.

- What You Share is for Everyone: The first thing you might think of is usually security. How can you manage security on this? The short answer is there is no security here. The report is shared through the Web, or email, with EVERYONE. So, everyone who has the link or embeds code can access the report. They cannot edit it. But they can view it with no restriction.

- All Report Pages Are Visible: If you have a report with 10+ pages, all of them would be visible to browsers. You cannot limit which pages you want to show and which you don't. As an example, the report you see above has more than one page, and you can view all of them. I recommend creating different reports if you want to restrict some pages and share them separately.

- Users can share it with others: A report that is published to the Web has a share section at the right bottom-hand side. Everyone can share this report with anyone else through all social media channels; Facebook, Twitter, LinkedIn, sharing the link directly! This method of sharing is not secure. I do only recommend using this method of sharing if the data that you want to publish is a public report on your company's or organization's website.

Chapter 12, earlier in the book, covers Publish to Web in greater detail.

Embed in SharePoint Online

If you are using SharePoint online as a portal for document management and some other reasons already, then consider the using Embed in SharePoint Online feature of Power BI reports. This method is secure, and you can share the report only with the Power BI users you want.

Power BI content can be easily embedded into a SharePoint online page. Do so by selecting Power BI as the source, as shown in Figure 15-9.

Figure 15-9. *Embedding a Power BI content into SharePoint online*

Managing security and sharing of this content needs to be done in two different places: SharePoint Site and Power BI. Figure 15-10 shows Power BI content as it appears in SharePoint.

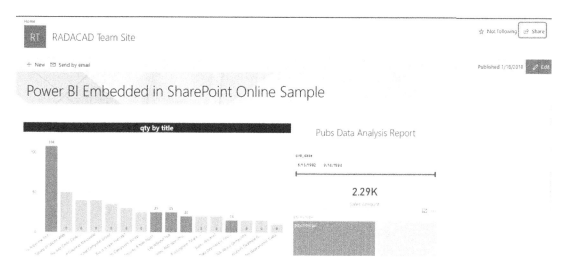

Figure 15-10. Sharing from SharePoint

Advantages of Embed in SharePoint Online

Advantages of sharing via Embed in SharePoint Online include:

- **One portal for all content**: With SharePoint online, you can share other documents as well. Why not use it for all other documents and also the Power BI report? You can have one portal that is the central sharing portal for your Office 265 tenant. Users usually love the integrity.

- **Embedding is simple**: Unlike Power BI Embedded, embedding in SharePoint online is easy. You just get the URL and embed it into a Power BI object in the SharePoint online. You don't need to write a single line of code for that purpose, but with Power BI Embedded you do need a developer.

Disadvantages of Embed in SharePoint Online

There are some disadvantages to using Embed in SharePoint Online. These include:

- **Power BI Service Golden Plate is missed**: One of the great aspects of Power BI components is the service. If you use embedding in the SharePoint, then users will use that as the portal for reports. Power BI Service has many exciting features, which may not be well used in this scenario, such as Alerts, feature dashboards, the dashboard itself, Q&A, and many other items. Users can still log in to Power BI service and see the report, but the experience that you create for them with SharePoint online would not be there.

- **Two places for managing permissions**: At the time of writing this book, you need to manage permission in Power BI Service, and also in SharePoint online. Controlling security in two different places would take some time for maintenance and also some reconciliation to check to see if those people who have access to the page are always permitted to read the report or not. Hopefully, this issue resolves quickly in the next few version upgrades of Power BI Service.

Chapter 13 earlier in the book discusses Embed in SharePoint Online in detail.

Power BI Embedded

Sometimes you want to embed the Power BI content into your custom application, and you want the content to be secured. In most of the cases, you want to leverage the custom user management of your current application rather than Power BI accounts. Power BI embedded gives you all of these features. The only side effect of that is the need for a web developer.

Power BI Embedded uses an API that we call Power BI REST API, and it has many great features for interacting with a Power BI content. Figure 15-11 shows some of the REST API objects.

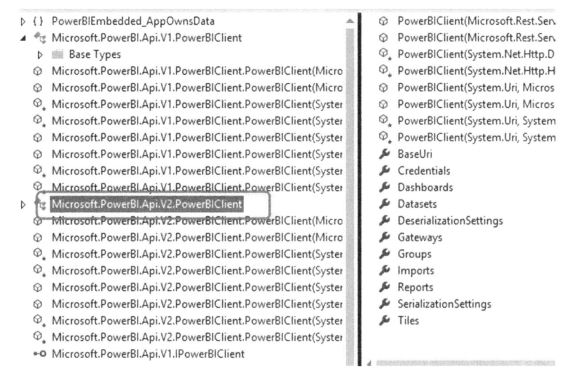

Figure 15-11. *Power BI REST API objects*

Users can easily access reports just through your application, as shown in
Figure 15-12.

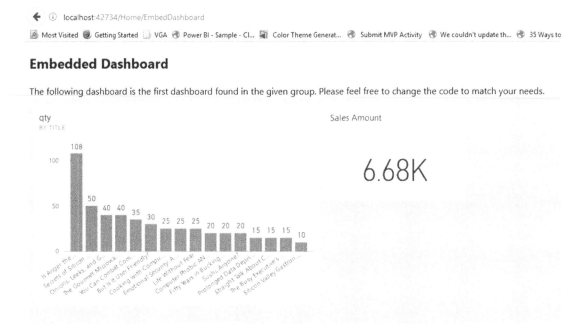

Figure 15-12. *Embedding dashboard with Power BI Embedded*

With Power BI Embedded, you get a fully customizable solution. You can do whatever you want inside your application with Power BI content. You can embed reports, dashboard, tiles, and even Q&A. You can interact with those elements from the web page.

Power BI Embedded can work without the need for Power BI accounts. If you have a set of users without accounts or your users are not part of a single company, then Embedded can be a really big advantage.

Power BI Embedded implementation needs a web developer. It is not just about one-off embedding your first content, every change after that, or every new functionality you add to your application, needs a web developer's touch.

To learn more about Power BI Embedded, read Chapter 14.

Comparing All Methods of Sharing

So far, you've learned in summary what every method does; now let's see their differences all in one place. Table 15-1 presents an at-a-glance view of what each method provides.

Table 15-1. *Comparing All Methods of Sharing*

	Basic Sharing	Workspace	Power BI App	Publish to the Web	SharePoint Online	Power BI Embedded
FREE				Yes		
No Power BI account needed				Yes		Yes
Access Levels	Read	Read/Edit	Read	Read	Read	Read/Edit
Can share with others	Yes (if allowed)	Yes (if edit access)	No (for end users)	Yes	Yes (if has access to do so)	No
Secure	Yes	Yes	Yes		Yes	Yes
Dev/User Environment		Yes, but maintenance cost is high	Yes			
Sharing Multiple Items		Yes	Yes			
Extras						The need for a Web Developer

Which Method to Choose?

With so many pros and cons, you might despair of having to wade through so much detail in order to make the right choice about how to share content. Fear not! Choosing ends up being simpler than it appears. Table 15-2 presents a cheat sheet of heuristics that I recommend using to quickly hone in on the correct choice for any given scenario.

Table 15-2. *Cheat Sheet of Power BI Sharing Methods*

Basic Sharing	Fast and quick method of sharing for testing reports and dashboards.
Workspace	Great option for collaborative development environments between Power BI Developer teams.
Power BI App	Best option to share reports with end users in a user environment that is isolated from developer environment.
Publish to Web	Free way of sharing; best for public datasets where the nature of data is not confidential.
SharePoint Online	Good choice when SharePoint online is the current portal for users in the organization.
Power BI Embedded	An option to bring Power BI content into your application, when the user management can be done in the application specifically.

Summary

This chapter was a wrap of all chapters from 9 to 14. In this chapter, you learned about pros and cons of each method of sharing Power BI content. You've learned differences between Basic sharing, Workspaces, Power BI Apps, Publish to Web, Embed in SharePoint online, and Power BI Embedded. At the end, you've learned what are the main differences, and how to choose the right sharing method for your Power BI solution. The next chapter starts the security section with an example of Row-Level Security.

PART IV

Security

CHAPTER 16

Row-Level Security

Another aspect of sharing is the security of the dataset. Enabling different roles and giving users access to different levels of data is called Row-Level Security. This chapter explains the details of this security method and how to configure it in Power BI Desktop. You then learn how to continue configuring this security in Power BI service. You will learn about the row-level security through a sample report.

Row-Level Security enables you to apply security to roles and adds users to each role. An example is helpful when you want people from one branch, city, department, or store to be able to only see their part of the data and not the whole dataset. Power BI applies that through a row-level security configuration on the Power BI model itself. So regardless of what source you are importing your data from, you can apply row-level security on it.

What's Good About It?

Row-Level Security is about applying security on a data row level. For example, the sales manager of the United States should only see data for the United States and not for Europe. The sales manager of Europe won't be able to see sales of Australia or the United States. And someone from the board of directors can see everything. The reason was that Row-Level Security wasn't part of the Power BI model. Now in the new version of Power BI Desktop, the security configuration is part of the model and will be deployed with the model.

Create Sample Report

For this chapter's example, we will use the Excel AdventureWorks sample database. Let's start with creating a sample report in Power BI Desktop from the AdventureWorks Excel file. I select only the DimSalesTerritory and FactResellerSales columns for this example, and you can see that I've checked only those two items in Figure 16-1.

© Reza Rad 2018
R. Rad, *Pro Power BI Architecture*, https://doi.org/10.1007/978-1-4842-4015-1_16

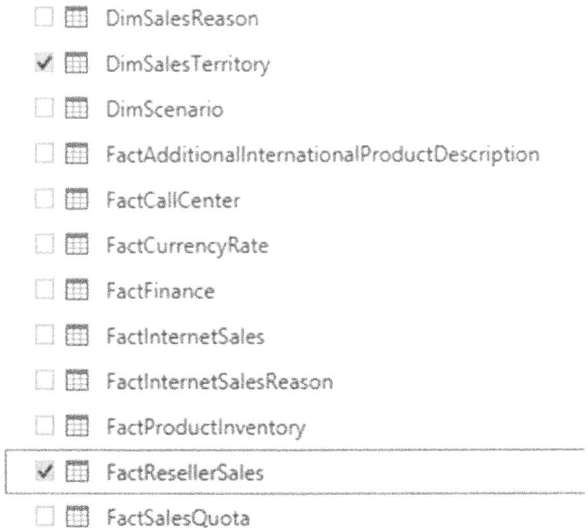

☐ ▦ DimSalesReason

✔ ▦ DimSalesTerritory

☐ ▦ DimScenario

☐ ▦ FactAdditionalInternationalProductDescription

☐ ▦ FactCallCenter

☐ ▦ FactCurrencyRate

☐ ▦ FactFinance

☐ ▦ FactInternetSales

☐ ▦ FactInternetSalesReason

☐ ▦ FactProductInventory

✔ ▦ FactResellerSales

☐ ▦ FactSalesQuota

Figure 16-1. *Select Tables from the data source*

Without any changes in the Power Query editor, let's load it in the report. Then we'll build a simple column chart with Sales Amount (from FactResellerSales), and Country (from DimSalesTerritory). That column chart will appear as in Figure 16-2.

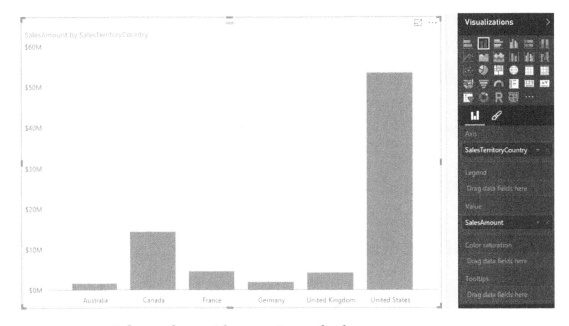

Figure 16-2. *Column chart with countries and sales*

The chart shows sales amount by countries, which can be used for creating row-level security on Geolocation information easily. Now let's add one card visualization for the total Sales Amount. We'll also add two slicers: one for Sales Territory Group and the other one for Sales Territory Region. Figure 16-3 shows the layout now of our example.

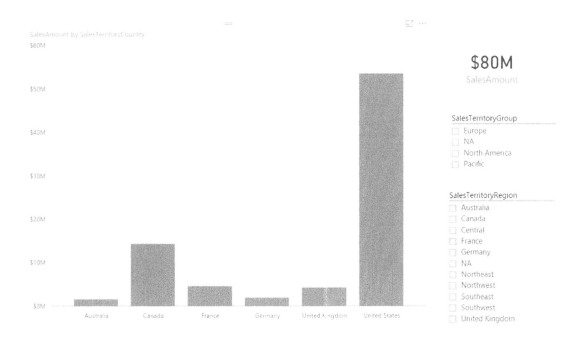

Figure 16-3. *Sample report layout*

Our total Reseller sales amount in this view is $80M. We have sales values for Australia, Canada, France, Germany, the United Kingdom, and the United States. Now let's create roles.

Creating Roles

Our goal is to build roles for sales managers in the USA and Europe. They should each only see their group or country in the dataset. Go to the Modeling tab in the Power BI Desktop. You will see a section named Security there, which is highlighted toward the right in Figure 16-4.

Figure 16-4. *Security section in Modeling tab*

Click on Manage Roles to create a new role. You will see the Manage Roles window, which has three panes as shown in Figure 16-5.

Figure 16-5. *Manage Roles*

You can create or delete roles in the first pane, and you can see tables in your model in the second pane (for this example, you will see two tables only after creating the first role). Then you can write your DAX filtering expression in the third pane. Yes, you have to write DAX code to filter data for each role, but that code can be composed of very simple DAX expressions.

Now Create a Role, and name it as "USA Sales Manager." You will see two tables in the Tables section: FactResellerSales, and DimSalesTerritory. Click on the ellipses button on each table to create DAX filters for each column. From DimSalesTerritory, create a filter for Country as shown in Figure 16-6.

Figure 16-6. *Add a USA Sales Manager Role*

Now in the DAX Filter expression, you will see an expression created automatically as [SalesTerritoryCountry] = "Value." Change the value to be "United States." Then apply the change, as shown in Figure 16-7.

Figure 16-7. *Filter expression for the USA Sales Manager*

Now create another role, and name it Europe Sales Manager. Put a filter on SalesTerritoryGroup this time, and change Value to "Europe" as shown in Figure 16-8.

Figure 16-8. Filter expression for the Europe Sales Manager role

Testing Roles in Desktop

Great; we have created our two sample roles. Now let's test them in Power BI Desktop via the View as Roles menu option shown in Figure 16-9. This option allows us to view the report exactly as the user with this role will see. We can even combine multiple roles to see a consolidated view of a person who has multiple roles. Go to Modeling tab, and choose View as Role option.

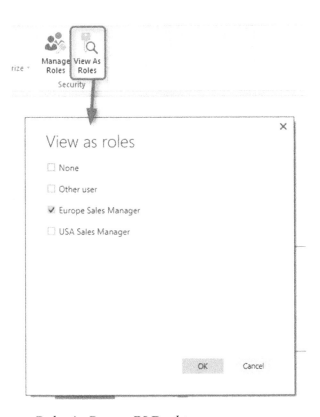

Figure 16-9. View as Roles in Power BI Desktop

Choose Europe Sales Manager, and click on OK. You will see sales for Europe, as illustrated in Figure 16-10. Those sales will total $11M, and it will include only the countries of Germany, the United Kingdom, and France.

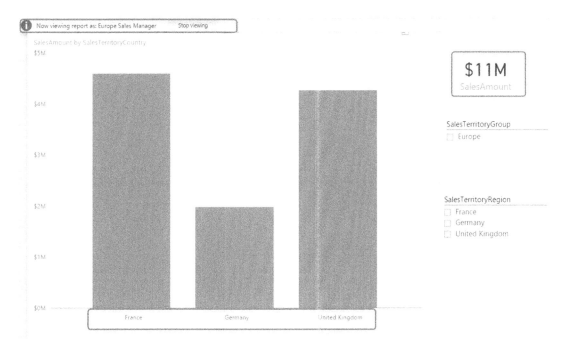

Figure 16-10. *View as Role mode for testing*

You can also see in the top of the report, there is an information line highlighted showing that the view is Europe Sales Manager. If you click stop viewing, you will see the report as normal view (total view).

Power BI Service Configuration

Roles should be assigned to Power BI users (or accounts in other words), and this part should be done in Power BI Service. Save and publish the report into Power BI. I named this report as RLS PBI Desktop. You can name it whatever you want. After publishing the report, click on Security for the dataset, as indicated in Figure 16-11.

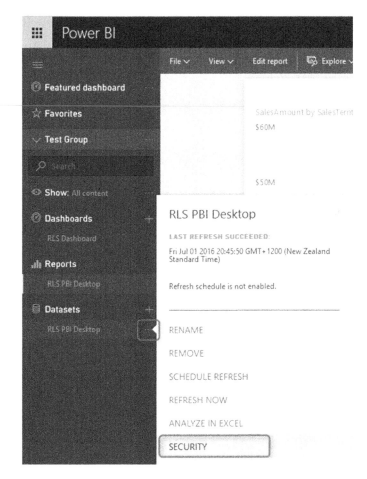

Figure 16-11. *Security tab for the data set in Power BI service*

Here you can see roles and assign them to Power BI accounts in your organization.
Figure 16-12 shows the interface for making those assignments.

Figure 16-12. *Assigning users to roles*

You can set each user to more than one role, and the user then will have a consolidated view of both roles. For example, a user with both roles for the USA and Europe sales manager will see data from all Europe and the USA.

Test Roles in Power BI Service

You can also test each role. Just click the ellipses button beside each role. Then click on Test as Role, as shown in Figure 16-13.

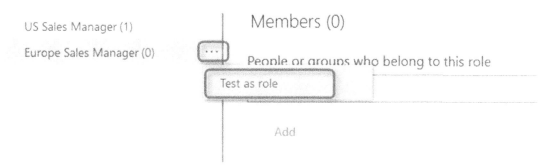

Figure 16-13. *Test as role in Power BI service*

Test as Role will show you the report in view mode for that role. The blue bar at the top of Figure 16-14 shows the "Now viewing as" role name. You can use the drop-down menu to select any of the role names to see what users in those roles will see when viewing the report.

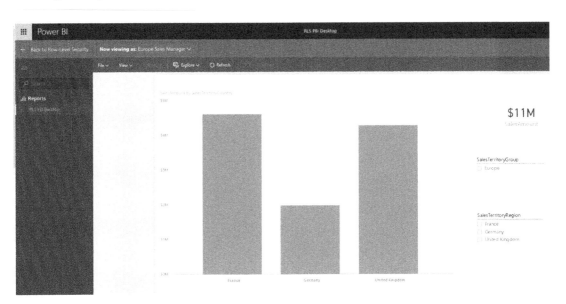

Figure 16-14. *Testing roles in Power BI website*

With setting users for each role, your role-level security is ready to work. If a user logs in with their account, they will only see data for their roles.

Republishing Won't Hurt

As I mentioned in the very first paragraph of this chapter, the great thing about row-level security is that it is part of the Power BI model. And if you publish your Power BI model again and again with changes, you won't lose configuration on the Web. You also won't lose users assigned to each role, as long as you keep role names unchanged.

Summary

Row-Level Security is giving users different views of the data from the same Power BI content. As you have learned in this chapter, implementing row-level security is simple. The reason this method is called ROW-level security is because of the DAX filter applied on the data row level.

In this chapter you've also learned about a specific type of row-level security called Static row-level security. It is called static, because the filter values are statically determined in DAX expressions. If you want to apply such a filter for thousands of roles, then maintenance costs are very high. In an ideal world, you want to be able to apply security based on the login of users automatically. In the next chapter, you will learn about Dynamic Row-Level Security, which is the next step of applying security in more complex scenarios.

CHAPTER 17

Dynamic Row-Level Security

There are different methods to use row-level security in Power BI. You can set up Row-Level Security in Power BI itself, or through a live connection from a data source such as SSAS Tabular. However, row-level security defined in the way mentioned in the previous chapter above isn't dynamic. By dynamic row-level security, I mean the definition of security is beside the user account information in the data source. For example, when John logs in to the system, based on data tables that show John is the sales manager for specific branch, he should be able to see only those branches' data. This method is possible in Power BI using the DAX UserName() or UserPrincipalName() function. In this chapter, I'll show you an example of dynamic row-level security with DAX USERNAME() function in Power BI.

Why Dynamic Row-Level Security?

The most important question is why dynamic row-level security? To answer this question, you need to think about the limitation of static row-level security. Static row-level security is simple to implement; however, if you have thousands of roles, then it would be a nightmare to maintain. For example, if you want to create a payroll Power BI report, in a company with 10 thousand users, you want every user to have his/her role. Dynamic row-level security is the answer for such scenarios.

For this chapter's example, I will use data entered in Power BI itself. There won't be any external data sources. This doesn't mean that dynamic security has an issue with external data sources. Dynamic security works with any data sources as long as we have related data rows in the tables. However, if I use on-premises data sources, then half of this example should be explaining installation and configuration gateways, or if I use

© Reza Rad 2018
R. Rad, *Pro Power BI Architecture*, https://doi.org/10.1007/978-1-4842-4015-1_17

Azure data sources, then again. I have to explain how to set up that example. So just for simplicity of this example, I'll be using data source inside Power BI.

Let's create two simple tables: Sales Rep and Transactions. Sales Rep has information about sales representatives, and transaction data are sales transactions. Obviously, each sales transaction is handled by a sales rep. So, let's create sample tables in Power BI. Open Power BI Desktop and from the External Data section, choose Enter Data as shown in Figure 17-1.

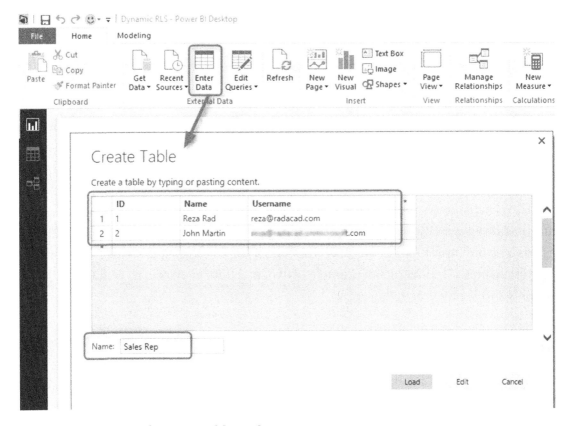

Figure 17-1. *Sample Data Table: Sales Rep*

Create a table as above with three columns and data in them. You have to use usernames similar to Power BI accounts that you want to set up security for. Name this table as Sales Rep.

Create another table for Transactions with the structure in Figure 17-2. Name the table as Transactions:

Figure 17-2. *Sample Data: Transactions*

As you can see in Figure 17-2, each sales transaction is handled by a sales rep. Again, I mention that these tables are added inside Power BI just for simplicity of this example. Tables can come from everywhere.

Load both tables into Power BI. (We don't need to do anything with Power Query at this stage.).Then go to the Relationship tab and verify the relationship between Sales Rep (ID) and Transactions (Sales Rep). Make sure the relationship that you see matches that in Figure 17-3.

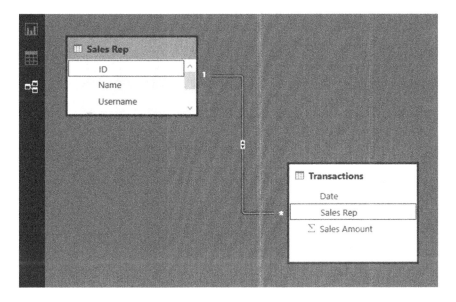

Figure 17-3. *Relationship Diagram*

Sample Report

Next, I will be using basic table visualization. The table visualization will show Date, Sales Amount (from Transactions), and Name (from Sales Rep). I also added another table visualization under that to show username and Name (both from Sales Rep). Figure 17-4 shows both visualizations.

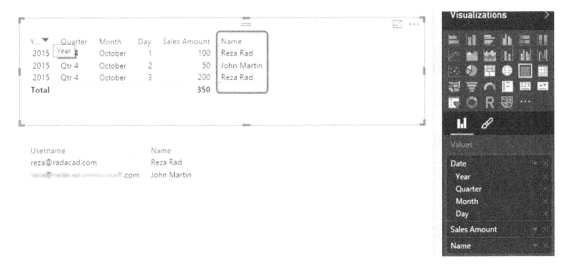

Figure 17-4. *Sample Report layout*

The main reason for these visualizations is to simply show that each user will see only their data rows from all tables. I also will add a measure for USERNAME() in DAX to see the user logged in from my report. So in Data Tab, create a new measure, and name it User, with a value of USERNAME(), all as shown in Figure 17-5.

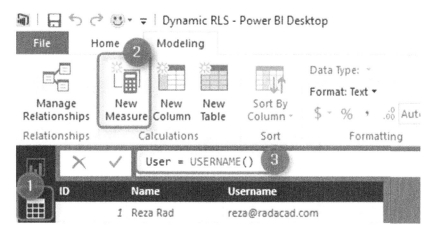

Figure 17-5. UserName() function

I also like to add the date/time of refreshing the report by invoking the DAX NOW() function. Do be aware that NOW() function will return the server's current time, not the local time on your local PC. So, let's create s new measure and name it Now, as shown in Figure 17-6.

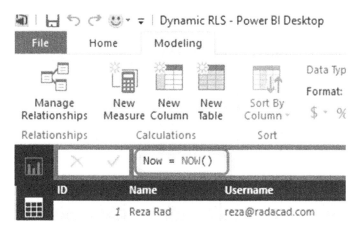

Figure 17-6. Now() function

Now let's add two other table visualizations to the report: one for User, and another for Now. Figure 17-7 shows the report's final view.

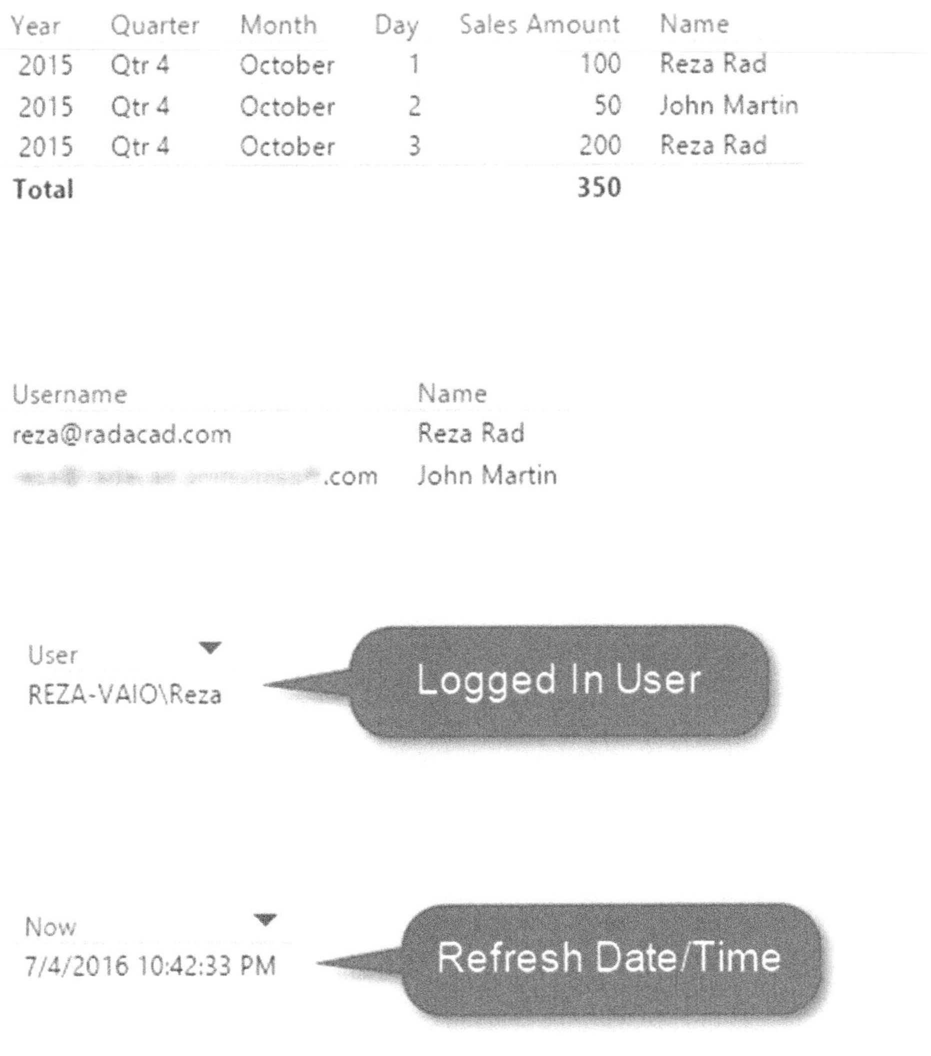

Year	Quarter	Month	Day	Sales Amount	Name
2015	Qtr 4	October	1	100	Reza Rad
2015	Qtr 4	October	2	50	John Martin
2015	Qtr 4	October	3	200	Reza Rad
Total				**350**	

Username	Name
reza@radacad.com	Reza Rad
...............com	John Martin

User ▼
REZA-VAIO\Reza   Logged In User

Now ▼
7/4/2016 10:42:33 PM   Refresh Date/Time

Figure 17-7. *Sample report execution with function results*

UserName() and UserPrincipalName()

USERNAME() function in DAX returns the username of logged-in user. However, there is a small trick for invoking it. If we don't set up row-level security for our report, USERNAME() function will return a user id, which would be a unique identifier such as in Figure 17-8. To see what I mean, publish your report to Power BI and browse the report. Without a security configuration on your report, you will see a unique identifier for the username that isn't useful.

Figure 17-8. *Username() function may return unique identifier sometimes*

UserPrincipalName() function in DAX works exactly like UserName() function with the difference that it will always return the username (not the unique identifier). So basically UserPrincipalName() is a better function for testing, but they both work the same in a production environment. Now let's set up row-level security and assign users to it to see how it works.

Row-Level Security

Chapter 16 explained how row-level security in Power BI Desktop works. Here I will use that technique to filter each role based on their username, which I determine by invoking the DAX username() function. To create security, go to the Modeling tab (you need Power BI at least June 2016 update for this example), and choose Manage Roles. Create a role and name it Sales Rep, as shown in Figure 17-9. Then define a filter on Sales Rep table, also as shown in the figure.

```
[Username] = USERNAME()
```

Figure 17-9. *One role with the usage of Username() function*

This filter simply means that logged-in user will only see his/her records in the whole dataset. As you remember, the username field in Sales Rep table defined as usernames of Power BI accounts. And the transactions table is also related to this table based on Sales Rep ID. So filtering one table will affect others. As a result, this single line filter will enable dynamic row-level security in the whole Power BI solution here.

Sharing the Dataset

Now Save and publish your solution to Power BI. In the Power BI service, go to the security setting of the dataset you just published (I named this as Dynamic RLS.) You should see results similar to those in Figure 17-10.

Figure 17-10. Security configuration of the dataset

And in Security tab, add all users to the Sales Rep role. Figure 17-11 shows one user, myself, added to the role.

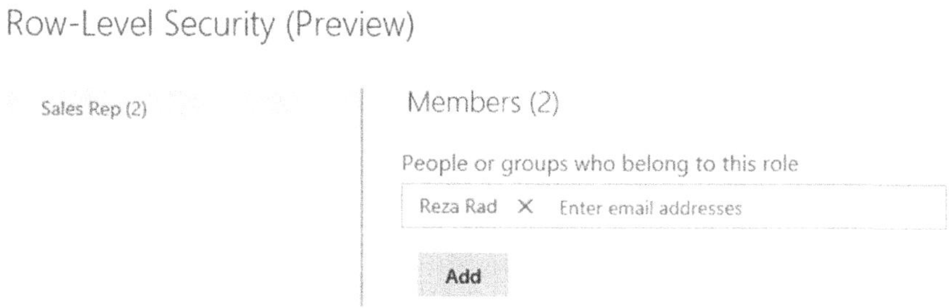

Row-Level Security (Preview)

Sales Rep (2)

Members (2)

People or groups who belong to this role

Reza Rad   X   Enter email addresses

Add

Figure 17-11. Adding users to roles

Adding a user here doesn't mean that they will see data in the report. Remember that this security is dynamic, meaning that they will see their data rows ONLY if the underlying dataset has a record for their username, and they will only see data rows related to their username, not others.

Now if you refresh the report in Power BI, you will see actual usernames. Because we already set up security for it, it doesn't show unique identifiers anymore. See Figure 7-12.

Figure 17-12. *Username() function shows the logged-in username*

Share the Dashboard

Other users should have access to the dashboard and report first to see it. Create a dashboard from the main table in the report, name the dashboard as RLS (or whatever you would like to call it), as shown in Figure 17-13.

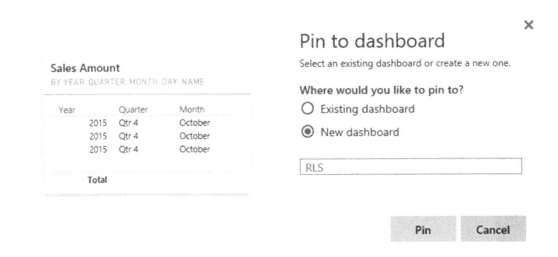

Figure 17-13. *Creating Dashboard*

Now share the dashboard with other users, as shown in Figure 17-14.

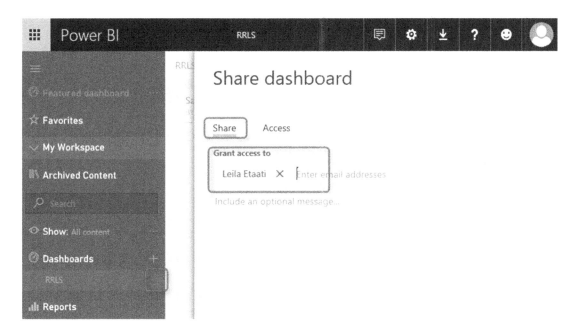

Figure 17-14. *Sharing the dashboard*

Test the Security

Now if other users open the report, and if their usernames match one of the entries in Sales Rep table, they would see their names and data rows related to that in the report. Figure 17-15 shows a user's limited view of the report.

Figure 17-15. *User's limited view of the report*

As you can see, John Martin only sees the transaction that he handled and his record in Sales Rep table. The screenshot shown above is John's view of the Power BI report. While my view of this report would be different, I will see my two transactions and my name under Sales Rep.

Summary

You have seen how easy is to use Dynamic Row-Level security in Power BI using the DAX USERNAME() or UserPrincipalName() function. With this method, users will see their view of the world. However, you need to make sure that your Power BI model has a relationship set up properly. Otherwise, people might see other table's data when there is no relationship between their profile table to those tables. Dynamic row-level security is highly dependent on your data model, so keep your data model right.

CHAPTER 18

Patterns for Dynamic Row-Level Security

This chapter is an addition to the previous chapter. We will talk about some of the patterns of Dynamic row-level security, such as Dynamic row-level security with Manager-Level Access, Users and Profiles with Dynamic row-level security, and Organizational Hierarchy access in the Dynamic row-level security.

Manager-Level Access

"What If I want users to see their data, and the Manager to see everything?," or "How do I add Manager- or Director-Level access to the dynamic row-level security?" This section will answer this question. In this chapter, you will learn a scenario in which you can implement a dynamic row-level security. In this scenario, everyone will see their own data, but the manager will see everything.

Create a Sample Dataset

To create a scenario with manager-level access and employee-level access, I created two tables. First is the Sales Rep table shown in Figure 18-1. This table has a field that is "Is Manager," and values are zero or one. If the value is one, then the sales rep is a manager and can see everything; if the value is zero, then the sales rep should be able to see his/her data rows only.

© Reza Rad 2018
R. Rad, *Pro Power BI Architecture*, https://doi.org/10.1007/978-1-4842-4015-1_18

ID	Name	Email	Is Manager
1	Reza Rad	reza@radacad.com	0
2	Leila Etaati	leila@radacad.com	0
3	David	student1@radacad.com	0
4	Mark	student2@radacad.com	1

Figure 18-1. *Sales Rep Table*

We also have a sales transactions table, which includes all transactions. Figure 18-2 shows this table, and it includes a field that is a link to Sales Rep.

Date	Sales Rep	Sales Amount
1/01/2017	1	100
1/02/2017	2	300
1/03/2017	1	50

Figure 18-2. *Transactions Table*

The relationship of these two tables is based on Sales Rep and ID field and is shown in Figure 18-3. Each sales transaction has a Sales Rep value that indicates the Sales Rep who is responsible for the transaction. Those Sales Rep values point to individual reps in the Sales Rep table.

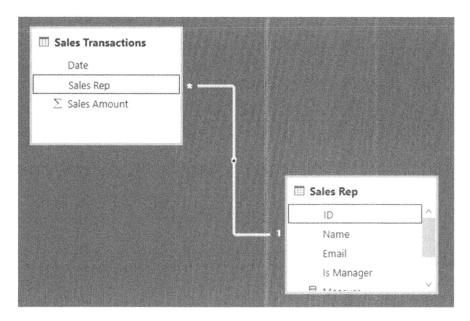

Figure 18-3. *Relationship Diagram*

Create a Role

As you can see in the Sales Transactions table, we can easily identify which sales transactions belong to which sales rep. Because of that, the logic to get only rows for every sales rep can be easily implemented with a DAX filter like this:

```
'Sales Rep'[Email]=Username()
```

The very first step is always identifying who is the person logged into the report in Power BI Service. This can be done with *Username()* or *UserPrincipalName()* functions in DAX.

We can also use a DAX expression to identify if the person logged in is a manager. The identification can be done with a simple MAXX expression as follows:

```
MaxX(
Filter(
'Sales Rep',
'Sales Rep'[Email]=Username()
)
,'Sales Rep'[Is Manager]
)
```

We are using *FILTER()* to identify all rows from the Sales Rep table, where the email address matches the logged-in user. Then we get the maximum [Is Manager] value from that using the *MAXX()* function. If the result of the expression is 1, then the person is a manager; otherwise the person is not a manager.

If the user is not a manager, then we just show the data related to him/her. This can be done through an expression like the following:

```
'Sales Rep'[Email]=Username()
```

If the user is a manager, then we show everything. An easy way of showing everything is writing a DAX expression that always returns true as a result. That expression can be as simple as the following:

```
1=1
```

Now if we combine all the foregoing code, we end up with an expression as follows:

```
If(
MaxX(
Filter(
'Sales Rep',
'Sales Rep'[Email]=Username())
,'Sales Rep'[Is Manager])=0,
'Sales Rep'[Email]=Username(),
1=1
)
```

The expression above will show everything to a manager, and it will show only limited data to non-manager users. Implement the logic by creating a role in Power BI under the Sales Rep table and using the expression just given. Figure 18-4 shows that being done, and you can see the code in the right-hand pane in the figure.

Figure 18-4. *Role expression for Manager-level access*

Test the Result

After creating the role, publish the report into Power BI. Then go to the Security configuration of the dataset as shown in Figure 18-5.

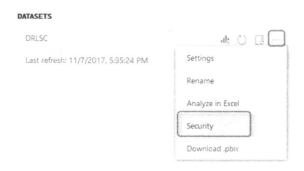

Figure 18-5. *Security configuration for the dataset*

Add all users to the role using the interface in Figure 18-6. There will be no harm in doing so. If a user is not in your Sales Rep list, they will not see anything. If they are in the Sales Rep List, they will have restricted access.

Figure 18-6. *Assigning users to roles*

Then share the dashboard also to all users. Figure 18-7 shows what Reza (the Restricted user who is not manager) will see.

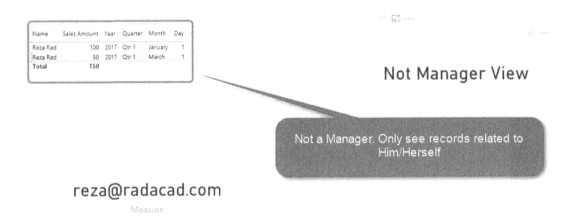

Figure 18-7. *Not Manager View or the report*

And Figure 18-8 shows what Mark (a manager user) will see.

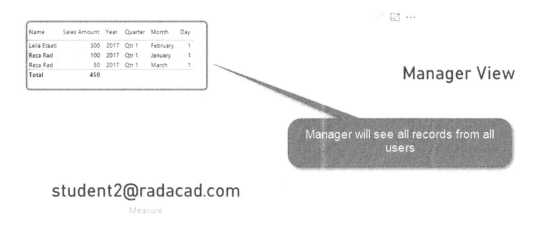

Figure 18-8. *Manager view of the report*

You've now learned how you can implement a dynamic row-level security with manager-level access. In the next two sections, you'll read about other scenarios of RLS with multiple user profiles as well as organizational hierarchies.

Multiple User Profiles

In this section, we are going to look at another type of security that deals with users and their profiles. Sometimes you have a user part of a multiple group (or profile), and also a profile contains multiple users. This Many-to-Many relationship needs to be incorporated in the way that security works in Power BI. You want all users to see data related to their profiles. Because this model includes a Many-to-Many relationship, the implementation of that is a bit different from the more hierarchical, manager-to-employee relationship.

Scenario

Imagine Mark is working in a company. Mark is part of the Sales Group in Seattle. He should see all sales transactions related to Seattle. Also, he is part of the sales group in Portland, and he should see the transactions details of Portland too. On the other side, there are other people for whom access is different. David is part of sales group of Chicago and also Seattle. This situation creates a Many-to-Many relationship between the user table and profile table such as it is illustrated in Figure 18-9.

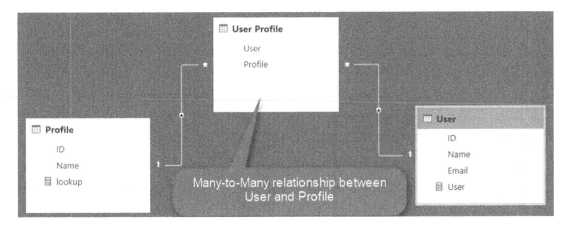

Figure 18-9. *Many-to-many relationships between users and profiles*

Figure 18-10 shows what the User table will look like and contain in this section's example.

ID	Name	Email
1	Reza Rad	reza@radacad.com
2	Leila Etaati	leila@radacad.com
3	David	student1@radacad.com
4	Mark	student2@radacad.com

Figure 18-10. *User Table*

It is important that the user table includes a column for corresponding Power BI accounts. In this example, those accounts are identified by using email addresses.

Figure 18-11 shows the Profile table. This is the table in which we record the different branches that are each managed by a sales manager.

ID	Name
1	Seattle Sales Manager
2	Chicago Sales Manager
3	Portland Sales Manager

Figure 18-11. *Profile Table*

Figure 18-12 shows the User Profile table. This table associates each user with a branch that is mentioned in Figure 18-11. The users listed in Figure 18-12 are, of course, managers. The table essentially indicates who the managers are for the different branch offices.

User	Profile
1	1
4	1
2	2
3	2
1	3

Figure 18-12. *User Profile Table*

Finally, Figure 18-13 shows the Transactions table. This is the detail table that drives our reporting.

Date	Profile	Sales Amount
1/01/2017	1	100
1/02/2017	2	300
1/03/2017	1	50
1/04/2017	3	150

Figure 18-13. *Transactions Table*

Figure 18-14 presents a visual of how all four tables relate. Every transaction is related to a profile. All users under that profile should have access to the transactions that are marked for that profile.

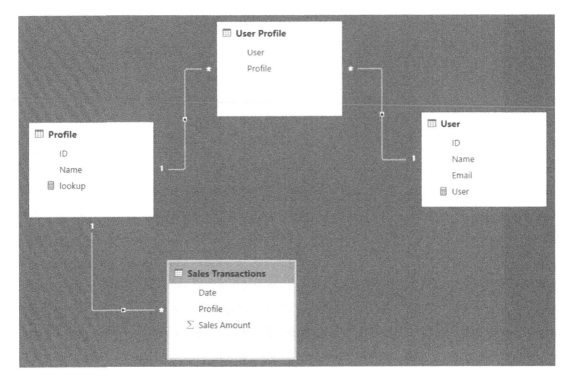

Figure 18-14. *Relationship Diagram*

The difference between this model in Figure 18-14 and a simple, dynamic row-level security model is that in Figure 18-14 we have a Many-to-Many relationship, and filter propagation is not easy as in the simple model.

Filtering Users Doesn't Work

Filtering users itself won't be a solution in this case. For example, here is a DAX invocation to filter by user:

```
[email]=UserPrincipalName()
```

And Figure 18-15 shows a role defined in the user table to filter using the above DAX invocation.

Figure 18-15. Simple dynamic row-level security

This DAX filter on the User table will filter the User Profile, but it won't filter the Profile table. As a result, the rule won't filter the transaction table at all, and Figure 18-16 illustrates this state of affairs.

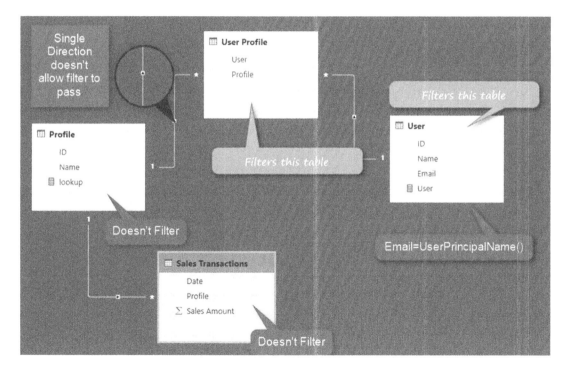

Figure 18-16. Filter propagation based on the relationship diagram

The direction of the relationship between Profile table and User Profile table doesn't allow the filter to propagate from User Profile to the Profile table. As a result, the Sales transactions table's data won't be filtered with the DAX filter defined in the user table. There are many methods so that you can get this solution working. In this chapter, I'll explain two methods.

315

The Cross-Filter Method

The so-called Cross-Filter method is not recommended because of performance issues. However, I like to explain it as the first method because it helps one to understand how relationships work in DAX. To use this method, you need to change the direction of the relationship between Profile table and User Profile table to both directional. Then you need to check the option for "apply security filter in both directions" that is shown in Figure 18-17.

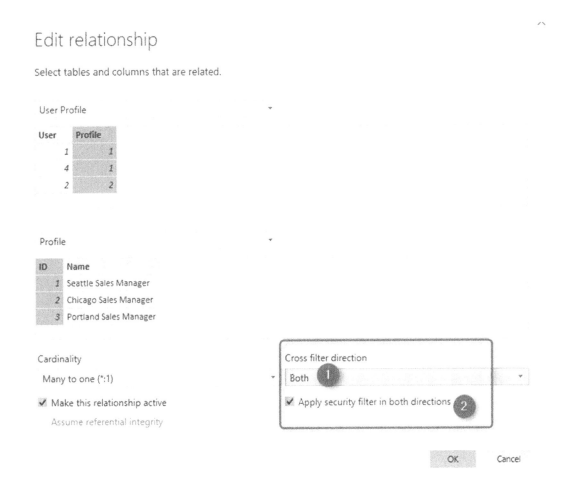

Figure 18-17. *Both directional relationship*

Now, change your row-level security configuration. It will work perfectly fine as shown in Figure 18-18.

Figure 18-18. *Effect of both directional relationship*

The diagram of the model is now passing the filter all the way to the sales transactions table. See Figure 18-19.

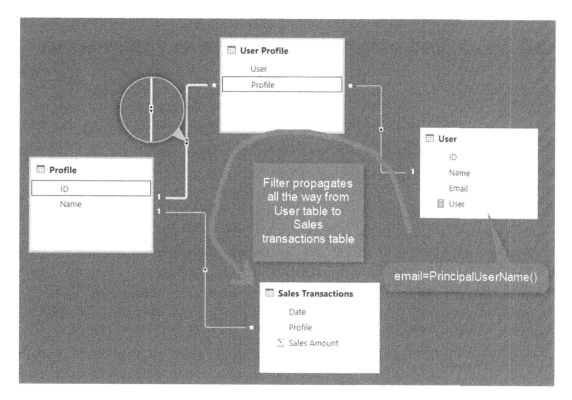

Figure 18-19. *Both directional relationships pass the filter criteria through*

This method is easy to implement. However, is not recommended. Applying both direction relationship and the security filter will slow down the performance of your Power BI solution significantly.

Filtering Data Through DAX

Filtering data through DAX is the method I recommend. There are many methods of implementing this logic with DAX. You can write a LookupValue function, a Filter function, or employ one of many other approaches. I'll explain it with a Filter function.

In this method; you don't need to change the direction of relationship to be both directions. In this method, you need to find a way to filter data in the Profile table. If you filter the data in Profile table, then the data in the Sales Transactions table will be filtered automatically. One way of filtering is to find out first all the profile IDs from the User, Profile which is related to the logged in user;

Step 1: Find All Rows in the User Profile for the Logged-In User

You can use a simple *FILTER()* function to get all rows from the User Profile for the logged-in user. Here's the code for such a function:

```
FILTER(
'User Profile',
RELATED(User[Email])=USERPRINCIPALNAME()
)
```

This code will return a subtable from the User Profile table, which are only rows that are related to the logged-in user. From this list, let's get only their Profile ID in the next step.

Step 2: Get Profile IDs from the List

Invoke the *SelectColumns()* DAX function to select the Profile column (which is the ID of the profile):

```
SELECTCOLUMNS(
FILTER(
'User Profile',
```

```
RELATED(User[Email])=USERPRINCIPALNAME()
),
"Profile"
,[Profile]
)
```

This DAX code will return a table with a single column that is the ID of the profiles.

Step 3: Filter the Profile Table on ID Matches

Now you can use the *IN* keyword to filter data from the Profile table just for the logged-in user. Here is the code to use:

```
[ID] IN SELECTCOLUMNS(
FILTER(
'User Profile',
RELATED(User[Email])=USERPRINCIPALNAME()
),
"Profile"
,[Profile]
)
```

This filter should be written into the **Profile** table as shown in Figure 18-20.

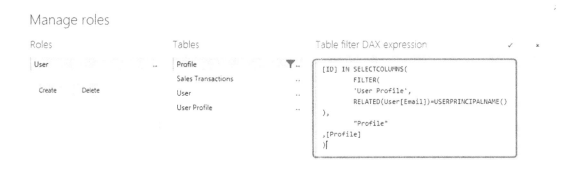

Figure 18-20. *Using IN for the DAX expression for the role*

Now see Figure 18-21. As you can see in the figure, this method works perfectly as expected.

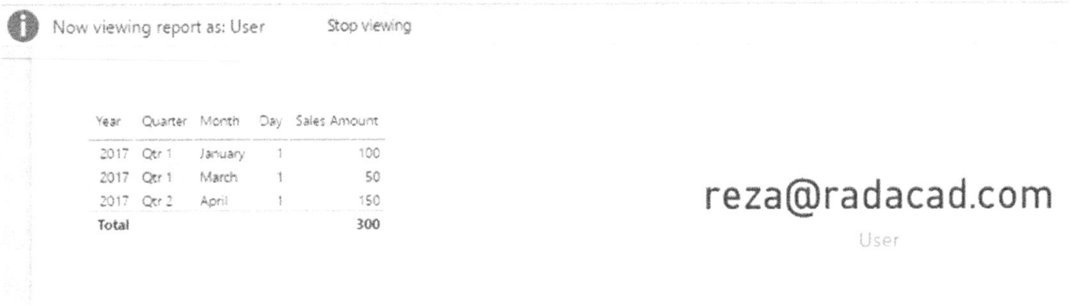

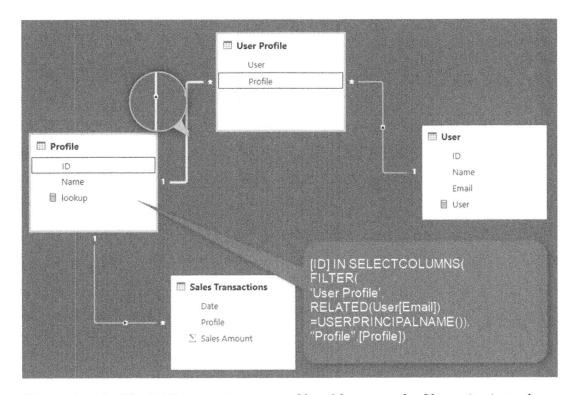

Figure 18-21. *The result of row-level security applied*

Figure 18-22 shows a diagram of this method, and you see what is a single directional relationship. However, the DAX Filter propagates all the way with the logic we've written into the role.

Figure 18-22. *The DAX expression on profile table passes the filter criteria to the transactions table*

Applying row-level security has many variations. In this section, you've learned about how to use the Users and Groups (or Profiles) concept and overcome the Many-to-Many challenge for the row-level security. You've learned about two methods and which one of them was the recommended approach. There are other ways to implement this scenario as well (with LookupValue and many other functions).

Organizational Hierarchy

In this section, I'm going to cover another common scenarios for row-level security: Organizational hierarchy for security. Through organizational hierarchy the approach is that each employee should have access to his/her data, and the manager should have access to an employee's data; there might be another higher-level manager as well. Every person should have access to all employees under him or her. In this chapter, we are going to cover this method of security in detail with Power BI.

Scenario

Every company has an organizational hierarchy, in many scenarios, employees need to be authorized to their data records only, and to the data of people whom they are managing. Figure 18-23 is an example of a typical organization chart that we'll build an example around.

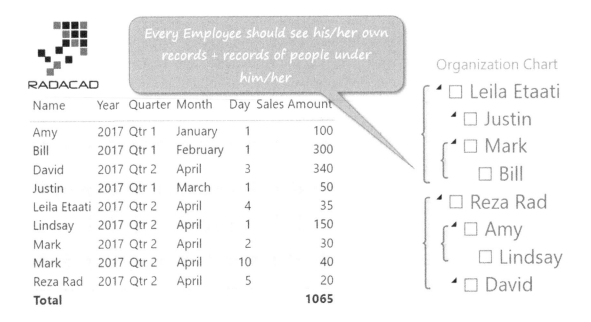

Figure 18-23. Organizational Chart example

Bill should see only one record of data. Mark should see three records: two records for himself and one record from Bill (because Bill is reporting directly to Mark). Leila should see four records: one record for herself, two records for Mark, and one record for Bill. This is how the hierarchical organizational row-level security id required to work.

Figure 18-24 shows the user table for this scenario's example. There are two main columns: the ID of the employee and the Manager ID, which points to the record that is the manager's record.

ID	Name	Email	Manager ID
1	Reza Rad	reza@radacad.com	null
2	Leila Etaati	leila@radacad.com	null
3	David	student1@radacad.com	1
4	Mark	student2@radacad.com	2
5	Amy	student3@radacad.com	1
6	Bill	student4@radacad.com	4
7	Justin	student5@radacad.com	2
8	Lindsay	student6@radacad.com	5

Figure 18-24. User table for organization hierarchy

Figure 18-25 shows the Sales Transaction table. For every employee, there might be one or more sales transactions in the transactions table.

Date	User	Sales Amount
1/01/2017	5	100
1/02/2017	6	300
1/03/2017	7	50
1/04/2017	8	150
2/04/2017	4	30
3/04/2017	3	340
4/04/2017	2	35
5/04/2017	1	20
10/04/2017	4	40

Figure 18-25. *Transactions Table*

Figure 18-26 presents a diagram of the model, which is a fairly simple model composed of just the two tables.

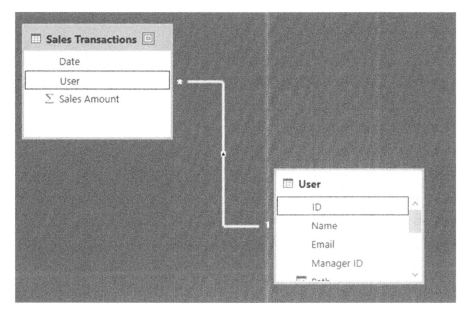

Figure 18-26. *Relationship Diagram*

Sample Report

Figure 18-27 shows a glance at a sample report. The report shows all records from all employees, as well as the full organizational hierarchy.

Figure 18-27. *Sample report layout*

Path Functions in DAX

One of the most common ways of implementing row-level security in this scenario is by using Path functions in DAX. Path functions are powerful functions that can navigate through an unknown level of hierarchy based on an ID and Parent ID structure. The structure of your data table usually is constructed based on two columns: ID and Manager ID, as in Figure 18-28.

ID	Name	Email	Manager ID
1	Reza Rad	reza@radacad.com	null
2	Leila Etaati	leila@radacad.com	null
3	David	student1@radacad.com	1
4	Mark	student2@radacad.com	2
5	Amy	student3@radacad.com	1
6	Bill	student4@radacad.com	4
7	Justin	student5@radacad.com	2
8	Lindsay	student6@radacad.com	5

Figure 18-28. *Manager ID is pointing to the same table*

To learn how path functions work, let's explore a couple of these functions.

Path()

The Path() function will go through an ID and parent ID structure, and it will reveal the whole hierarchical path into a delimited string. To use this function, you can simply create a calculated column in the user table with an expression like the following:

```
Path = PATH(User[ID],User[Manager ID])
```

Figure 18-29 shows then, what the function's output looks like.

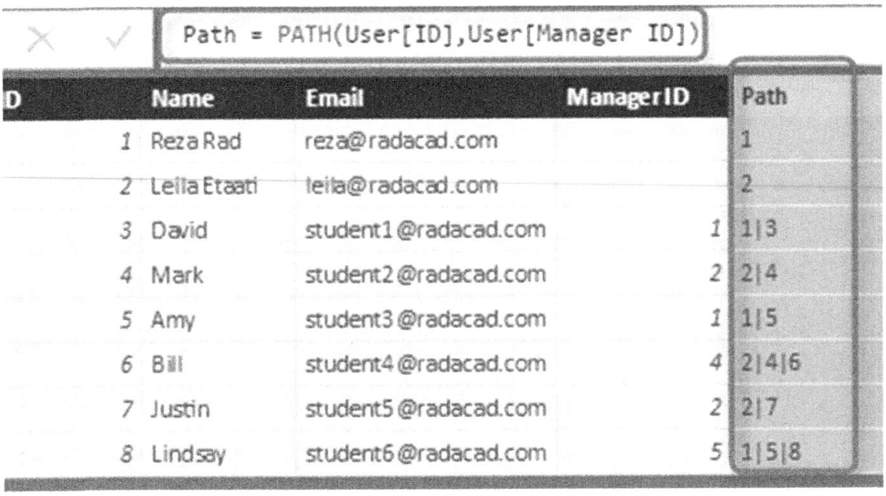

D	Name	Email	ManagerID	Path
1	Reza Rad	reza@radacad.com		1
2	Leila Etaati	leila@radacad.com		2
3	David	student1@radacad.com	1	1|3
4	Mark	student2@radacad.com	2	2|4
5	Amy	student3@radacad.com	1	1|5
6	Bill	student4@radacad.com	4	2|4|6
7	Justin	student5@radacad.com	2	2|7
8	Lindsay	student6@radacad.com	5	1|5|8

Figure 18-29. *Path function output*

This function will give you the whole path for the hierarchy with a delimited text value. The id of every employee in the path is separated in this text by a vertical line (|).

PathItem()

The *PathItem()* function will give you a specific item in a path. Here is an example showing how to fetch the second-level manager for a given user:

```
PATHITEM(User[Path],2,1)
```

You can then combine this method with a LookupValue function to find out the name of the person at that level:

```
LOOKUPVALUE(
User[Name],
User[ID],
PATHITEM(User[Path],2,1)
)
```

You can then create calculated columns such as in Figure 18-30 for every level of organization hierarchy. Figure 18-30 shows calculated columns for all three manager levels.

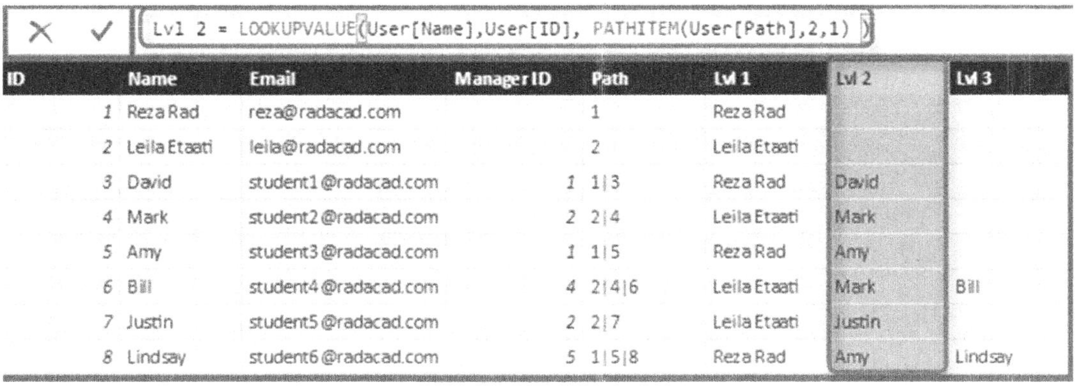

ID	Name	Email	Manager ID	Path	Lvl 1	Lvl 2	Lvl 3
1	Reza Rad	reza@radacad.com		1	Reza Rad		
2	Leila Etaati	leila@radacad.com		2	Leila Etaati		
3	David	student1@radacad.com	1	1|3	Reza Rad	David	
4	Mark	student2@radacad.com	2	2|4	Leila Etaati	Mark	
5	Amy	student3@radacad.com	1	1|5	Reza Rad	Amy	
6	Bill	student4@radacad.com	4	2|4|6	Leila Etaati	Mark	Bill
7	Justin	student5@radacad.com	2	2|7	Leila Etaati	Justin	
8	Lindsay	student6@radacad.com	5	1|5|8	Reza Rad	Amy	Lindsay

The formula bar shows: `Lvl 2 = LOOKUPVALUE(User[Name],User[ID], PATHITEM(User[Path],2,1) )`

Figure 18-30. PathItem and LookupValue together can fetch the manager's name

PathContains()

Now the important function of this post is PathContains. *PathContains* will check if an ID exists in the path or not. PathContains is the function that you need to implement row-level security. All you need to find out is the ID of the person who is logged in. We already know how to get the email address of the person who is logged in: we use the *UserName()* or *UserPrincipalName()* function for it.

Find Out the ID of Person Logged In

You can use a *Filter* function and Iterator function in DAX to find out who logged in to the system. Here is how the Filter Function can be used to fetch the logged-in user's record:

```
Filter(
User,
[Email]=USERPRINCIPALNAME()
)
```

After finding the record for the current user, you can use MaxX or MinX to find out the ID of that user:

```
MaxX(
Filter(
User,
```

```
[Email]=USERPRINCIPALNAME()
)
,User[ID]
)
```

Finally, you can now use this ID in a PathContains function to check if the user's ID exists in a path or not:

```
PATHCONTAINS(User[Path],
MaxX(
Filter(
User,
[Email]=USERPRINCIPALNAME()
)
,User[ID]
)
)
```

Figure 18-31 shows how to add this logic to a role in the User table. The DAX expression in the figure will check the full path of organization hierarchy to see whether there are any records in the user table that have a given user ID in their Path column.

Figure 18-31. *Row-level security expression for organizational hierarchy*

Testing Result

As a result, if you switch to that user, you will see only the logged-in user with records related to him/her. See Figure 18-32.

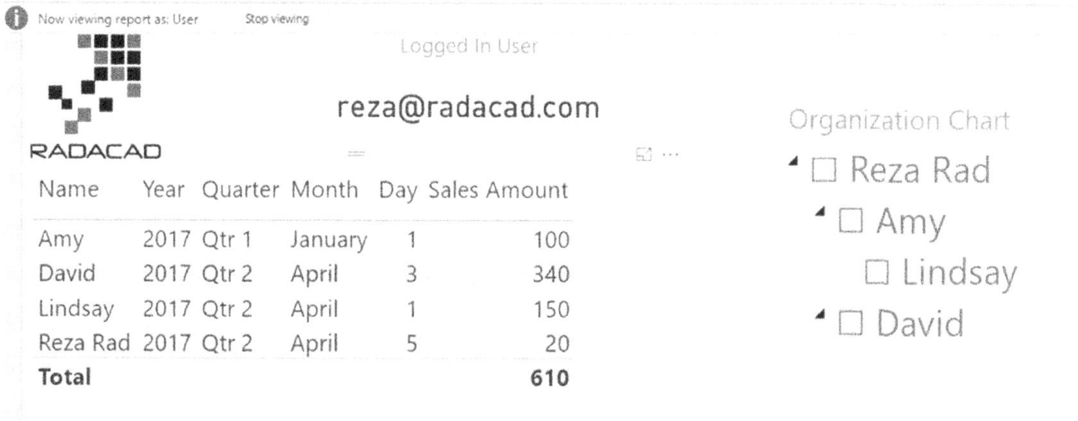

Figure 18-32. *The result of organization hierarchy row-level security*

There are other methods of implementing such logic; you can use other functions and expressions to find the current records ID. This post explained one way of doing this. As you can see in the above screenshot, Reza only has access to see records for himself, Amy, and David (his direct reports), and Lindsay (who reports directly to Amy).

Applying row-level security has many variations. In this chapter, you've learned about how to use organization hierarchy and Path functions in DAX to implement row-level security based on a hierarchy.

Summary

In this chapter you've learned three of the most common scenarios and patterns for dynamically applying row-level security: with manager-level access, users and profiles, and organizational hierarchies. The main important factor in all of these dynamic row-level security patterns is to be professional in DAX and be able to write the DAX code and filter required for that scenario. The next chapter is about row-level security in SSAS Tabular Live Connection.

CHAPTER 19

Row-Level Security with Analysis Services Live Connection

You can define Row-Level Security in Power BI itself (Chapter 16), However, sometimes you do use SQL Server Analysis Services Tabular as the source for Power BI through the Live connection. SSAS Tabular allows you to create the same type of Row-Level Security. In situations that SSAS Live connection is used, it would be much better to use Row-Level Security defined in Tabular from Power BI, rather than duplicating that in Power BI. In this chapter you'll learn an end-to-end solution.

Note that this method is different from defining Row-Level Security in Power BI Desktop. In fact, we won't use that method. To learn more about basic row-level security, read Chapter 16.

For this chapter's demo, I will be using my demo machine, which has SSAS Tabular and Enterprise Gateway installed. I will also use the SSAS Tabular's example database: the AW Internet Sales Tabular Model 2014.

Create the Data Source Under the Gateway

We want to create a Data Source in the gateway. You might think that one gateway is enough for connecting to all data sources in a domain. That is right. However, you still need to add a data source to that gateway per each source. Each source can be an SQL Server database, Analysis Services database, etc. For this example, we are building a data source for SQL Server Analysis Tabular on premises. Before going through this step, I have installed AW Internet Sales Tabular Model 2014 on my SSAS Tabular and want to connect to it. If you don't have this database, follow the instruction in the prerequisite section.

© Reza Rad 2018
R. Rad, *Pro Power BI Architecture*, https://doi.org/10.1007/978-1-4842-4015-1_19

For creating a data source, first select the gateway that you wish to use. Then click on Add Data Source in the manage gateways window, as shown in Figure 19-1.

Figure 19-1. *Add a data source to the gateway*

Then enter details for the data source as I have done in Figure 19-2. I named this data source as AW Internet Sales Tabular Model 2014, and I enter my server name and database name. Then I use Windows authentication with my domain user <domain> \username and the password. You should see a successful message after clicking on Apply. The domain name that I use is BIRADACAD (my SSAS Tabular domain), and the user is PBIgateway, which is a user of BIRADACAD domain (username: BIRADACAD\ PBIgateway) and is an administrator for SSAS Tabular (explained in the next few paragraphs).

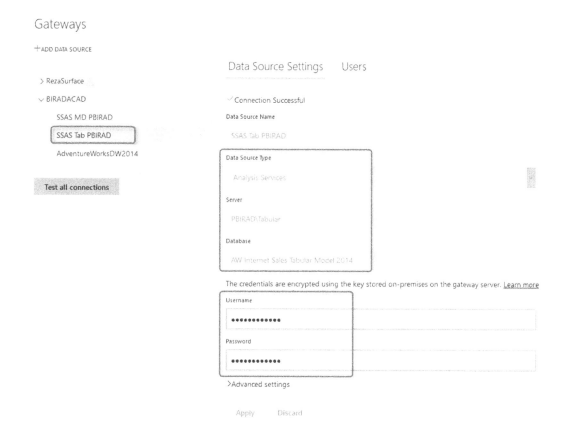

Figure 19-2. *SSAS Tabular connection settings in the gateway*

Note that the user account that you are using here should meet these conditions:

- It should be a Domain User.

- The domain user should be an administrator in SSAS Tabular.

You can set administrator for SSAS Tabular by right-clicking on SSAS Tabular instance in SSMS and goinh to the Properties window that is shown in Figure 19-3.

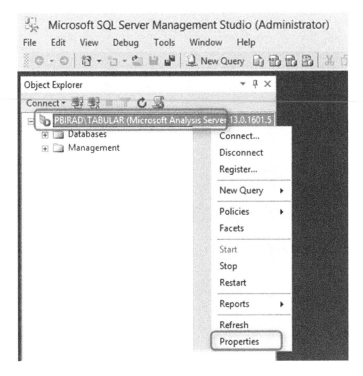

Figure 19-3. *Setting the Properties of the Analysis Services Tabular*

Then go under settings and select the Security tab as shown in Figure 19-4. Add the user to administrators list. In Figure 19-4, I've added BIRADACAD\PBIgateway to the list.

Figure 19-4. *Security configuration of the SSAS Tabular*

Effective User Name

A gateway account is used for accessing Power BI cloud service to on-premises SSAS Tabular. However, this account by itself isn't enough for the data retrieval. The gateway then passes the EffectiveUserName from Power BI to on-premises SSAS Tabular, and the result of the query will be returned based on the access of EffectiveUserName account to SSAS Tabular database and model.

By default, EffectiveUserName is the username of the logged-in user to Power BI, or, in other words, EffectiveUserName is the Power BI account. This means your Power BI account should have enough access to SSAS Tabular database to fetch required data. If Power BI account is the account from the same domain as SSAS Tabular, as shown in Figure 19-5, then there is no problem, and the security configuration can be set in SSAS Tabular (explained later in this chapter). However, if domains are different, then you have to do UPN mapping.

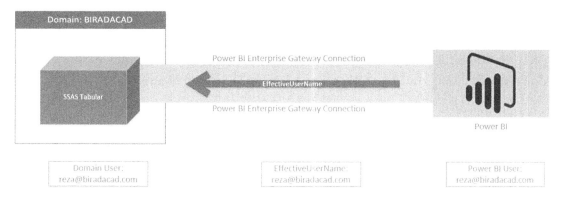

Figure 19-5. *EffectiveUserName when domain user and Power BI user are the same*

UPN Mapping

Your SSAS Tabular is part of a domain (it should be, because that's how Live connection works), and that domain might be the domain that your Power BI user account is. If you are using the same domain user for Power BI account, then you can skip this step. If you have a separate Power BI user account than the domain account for SSAS Tabular, then you have to set the UPN Mapping as illustrated conceptually in Figure 19-6.

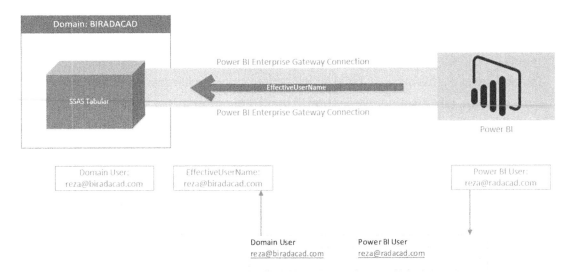

Figure 19-6. *UPN Mapping table is needed if domain user and Power BI users are different*

UPN Mapping in simple definition will map Power BI accounts to your local on-premises SSAS Tabular domain accounts. Because in my example I don't use the same domain account for my Power BI account, I set up UPN as in Figure 19-7.

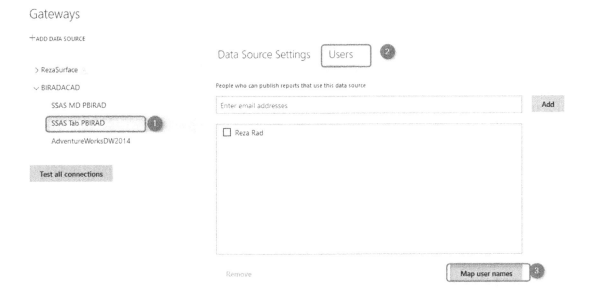

Figure 19-7. *Map User Names under the data source in the gateway settings*

Then in Mapping pane, I create a new mapping that maps my Power BI user account to reza@biradacad.com, which is my local domain for SSAS Tabular server. You can see this mapping in Figure 19-8.

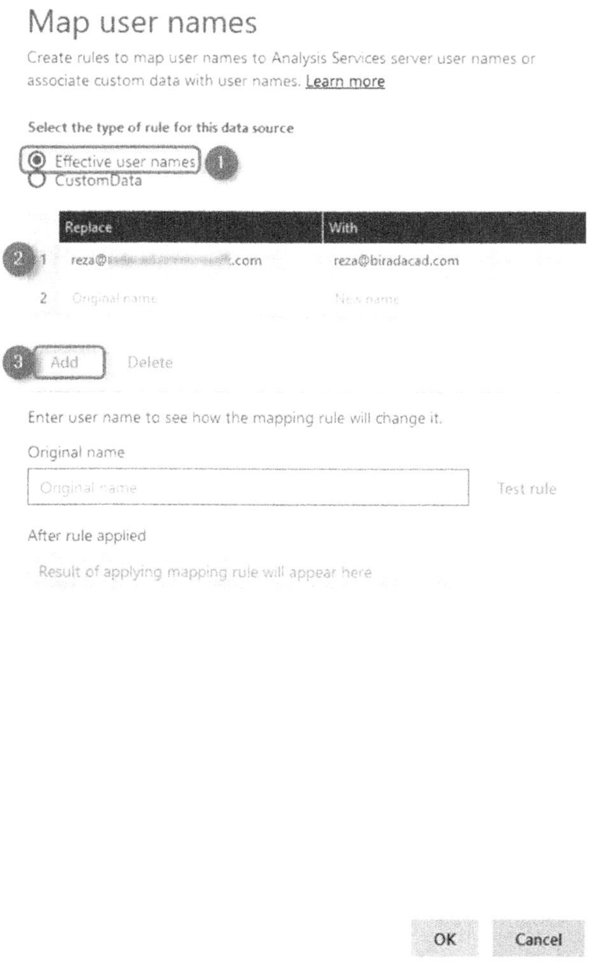

Map user names

Create rules to map user names to Analysis Services server user names or associate custom data with user names. Learn more

Select the type of rule for this data source

- ⦿ Effective user names **①**
- ◯ CustomData

Replace	With
② 1 reza@∎∎∎∎∎∎∎∎.com	reza@biradacad.com
2 Original name	New name

③ [Add]   Delete

Enter user name to see how the mapping rule will change it.

Original name

Original name	Test rule

After rule applied

Result of applying mapping rule will appear here

[OK]   [Cancel]

Figure 19-8. *UPN mapping configuration*

Now with this username mapping, reza@biradacad.com will be passed as EffectiveUserName to the SSAS Tabular.

Configure Row-Level Security in SSAS Tabular

Open SSAS Tabular in SSMS. Then expand the AW Internet Sales Tabular Model 2014, and create a New Role as shown in Figure 19-9.

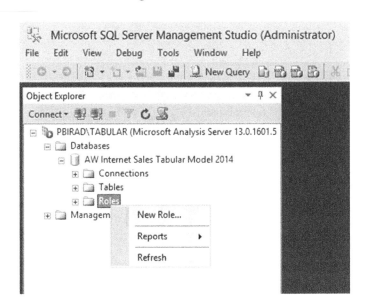

Figure 19-9. *Adding Role in SSAS Tabular*

We want to create a role for users who don't have access to Bike sales across the database. So let's name the role as No Bike Sales Manager; this role has Read access to the database. You can see the role definition in Figure 19-10.

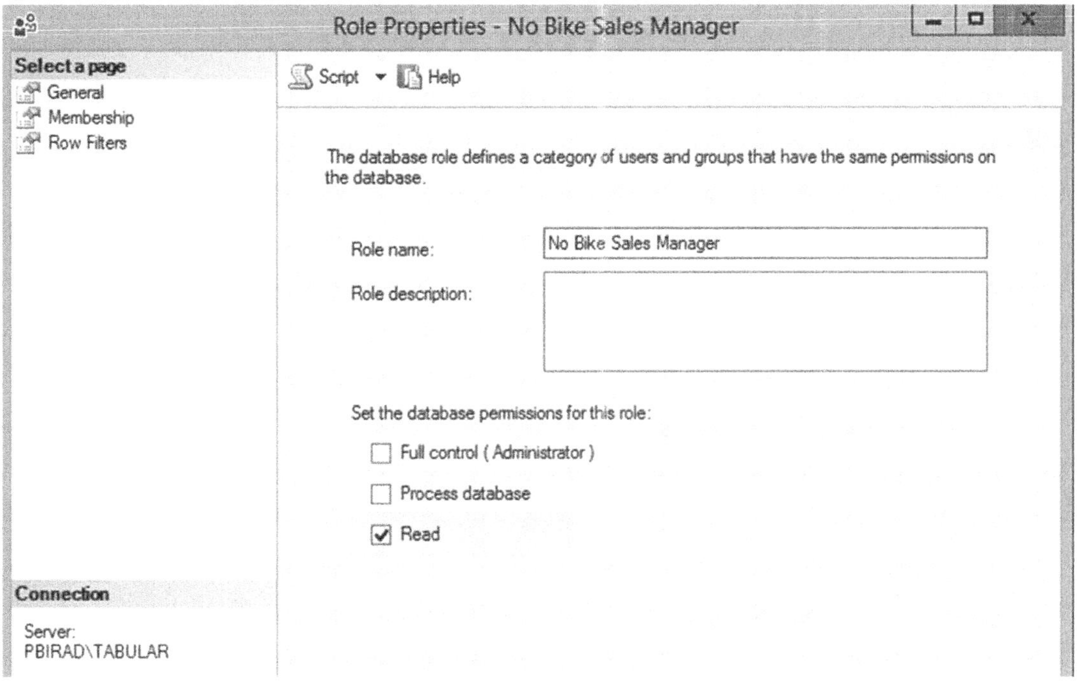

Figure 19-10. *Assigning Read access level to the role*

In the membership section, you can add users to this role as in Figure 19-11. Users should be domain users that you get through EffectiveUserName from Power BI (if Power BI accounts aren't domain users, then create a UPN mapping for them as explained above in the UPN mapping section). I add user BIRADACAD\Reza here. (Note that I've created a UPN mapping for this user, so each time the Power BI user associated with this mapping logs in, this domain account will be passed through EffectiveUserName to SSAS Tabular.)

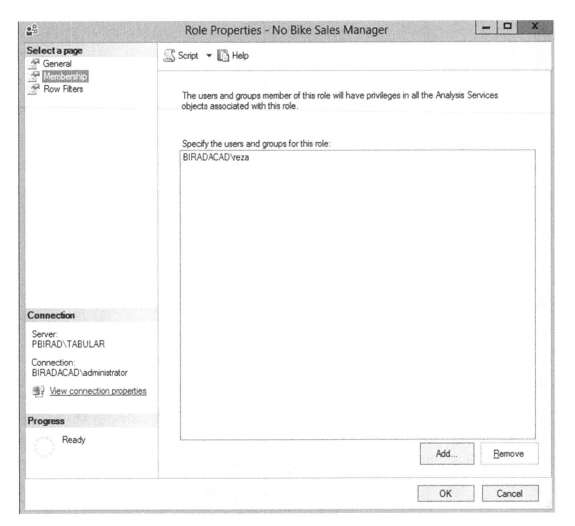

Figure 19-11. *Adding local user as a member of SSAS role*

Now let's define Row Filters with a basic filter on Product Category. Here's the filter to use:

```
='Product Category'[Product Category Name]<>'Bikes'
```

Figure 19-12 shows the filter in the Row Properties dialog.

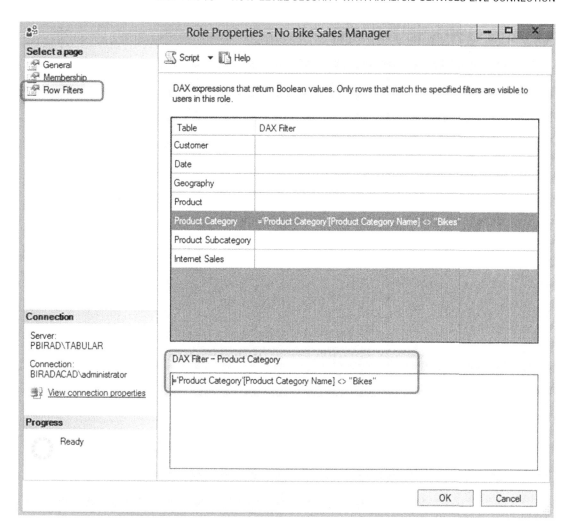

Figure 19-12. *Setting the DAX expression for the filter of role*

Now that we defined row-level security in SSAS Tabular, let's build a sample report to test it.

Create Sample Report

Our sample report here will show a Pie chart of Product Categories Sales. Create a Live connection to SSAS Tabular from Power BI Desktop as shown in Figure 19-13.

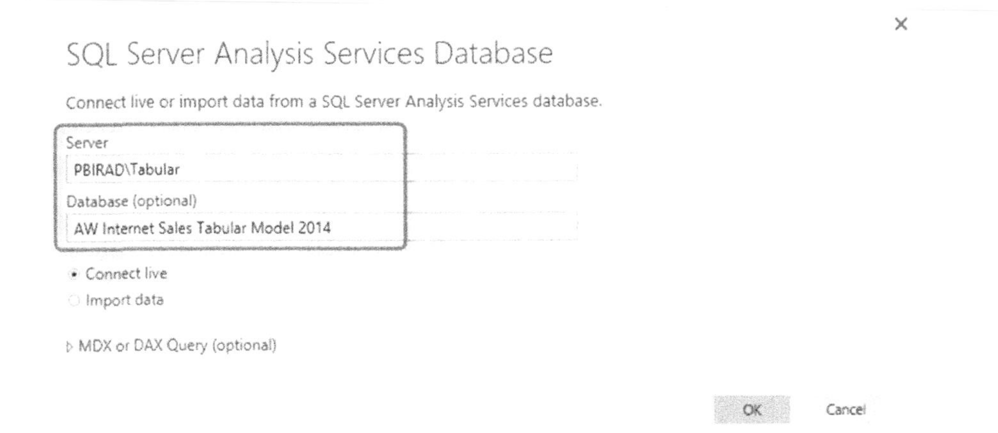

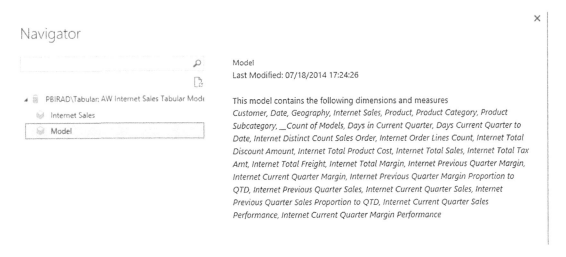

Figure 19-13. *Live Connection from Power BI Desktop*

Then choose the model, which in this case is named Model. You can see that I have the model highlighted in Figure 19-14.

Figure 19-14. *Selecting the model from SSAS Tabular*

After creating the connection, you should see the Live Connection: Connected status in Power BI Desktop down the right-hand side corner. Now create a simple Pie chart such as in Figure 19-15. Include the Product Category Name (from Product Category table) as Legend and Sales Amount (from Internet Sales table) as Values.

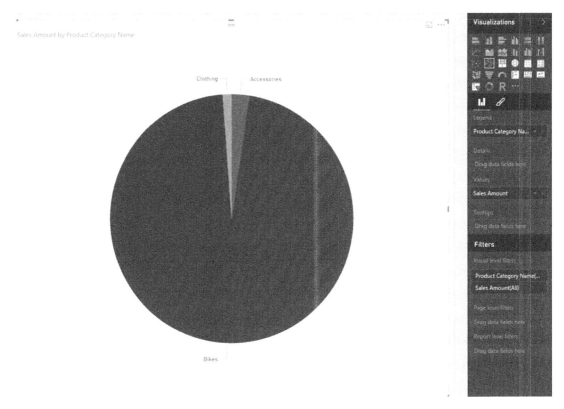

Figure 19-15.   *The sample report in Power BI Desktop*

Save the Power BI file, for example, as SSAS Tab Live Ent DB.pbix, and publish it.
Remember that you shouldn't set up Row-Level Security in Power BI itself. RLS
configuration in this scenario fetched from the Live Tabular connection.

Test the Result

In Power BI website or service, when you log in and refresh the SSAS Tab Live Ent DB
report, yuou won't see any sales from Bikes. You will only see sales of Clothing and
Accessories, as in Figure 19-16.

Figure 19-16. *The result of report with row-level security effective in the Power BI service*

How Does It Work?

What happened here is that my Power BI account mapped to reza@biradacad. com domain user, and this domain user passed through enterprise gateway as the EffectiveUserName to the SSAS Tabular on-premises. SSAS Tabular identified that this user has only one role, which is No Bike Sales Manager, and this role has a restricted view of sales for everything but Bike. So, the data returned from SSAS Tabular to Power BI report doesn't contain Bike's sales.

Summary

SSAS Tabular as a Live connection source for Power BI is used in many enterprise solutions for Power BI. There are different reasons for that, for example:

- Some organizations already have SSAS Tabular models ready, and they are using that for their on-premises reporting and data analysis. So, they want to use the same source of truth.

- The scale of data is larger than it fits into Power BI model. (Read step beyond 10GB limitation for Power BI as an example).

- And many other reasons.

In this chapter you've learned how Row-Level Security defined in SSAS Tabular will be passed through EffectiveUserName to Power BI accounts. This method will authorize users to only view part of the data that they are authorized to see.

PART V

Administration and Licensing

CHAPTER 20

Power BI Administrator Configuration

In the world of Power BI, there are many configurations in the Desktop tool and some on the website. None of these configurations are as critical as the Tenant Settings of the Power BI administrator panel. Tenant settings have a list of highly important configurations across your Power BI tenant. If you miss configuring the settings properly, it may result in leaking the data, authorizing people who should not be authorized to see reports and many other catastrophic scenarios. In this chapter, you will learn the configurations available in Tenant settings and the recommendation options for each.

Power BI Administrator

By default, the Office 365 administrator is the Power BI administrator. however, this can be changed by selecting the Power BI administrator role in Office 365 Portal. Here are the details of assigning the Power BI administrator role to a user.

Log in to `http://portal.office.com` with an Office 365 administrator account. Then find the user in the list of active users, and select that user from the list. You should now see a view similar to that in Figure 20-1.

© Reza Rad 2018
R. Rad, *Pro Power BI Architecture*, https://doi.org/10.1007/978-1-4842-4015-1_20

Figure 20-1. *Office Portal*

Then click on Edit in the Roles section. Select Customized administrator, and then from the options, select Power BI service administrator, as shown in Figure 20-2.

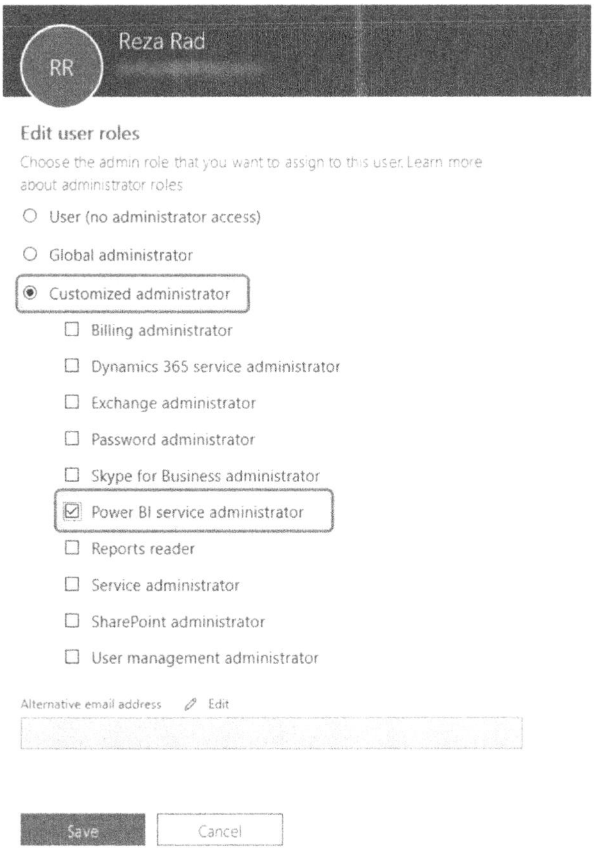

Figure 20-2. *Adding Power BI service administrator role to the user*

Tenant Settings

The Power BI Administrator can access tenant settings from the Power BI Service. Click on the setting icon and select Admin Portal as shown in Figure 20-3.

Figure 20-3. *Admin Portal*

From Admin Portal, you will be able to click on Tenant Settings as shown in
Figure 20-4. (Note that you can access this page only if you are a Power BI Administrator.
To learn how to be a Power BI administrator, read the earlier section of this chapter.)

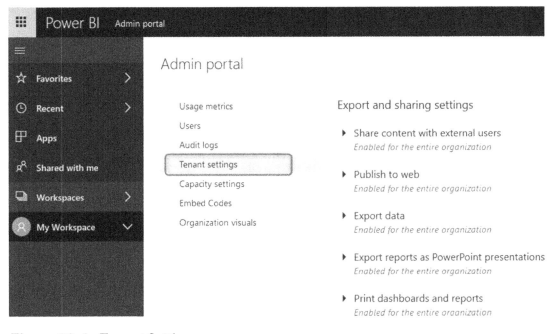

Figure 20-4. *Tenant Settings*

Configurations of Tenant Settings are categorized into groups as described in the sections to follow.

Export and Sharing Settings

In this section you can access any configuration setting relating to sharing across your tenant. The exceptions are settings for content packs and apps, which are found in another section.

Share the Content with External Users

This option by default is ON. It means that users of your organization can share Power BI content with external users. If you don't want this to happen, make sure to restrict it for everyone or for a group of people.

Publish to Web

The Publish to Web configuration by itself can be enough reason for you to access the tenant setting page. By default, everyone in your organization can publish their reports to web! If you don't know about Publish to Web, read Chapter 12. Publish to Web will make the Power BI content publicly available. This is a very dangerous option to be ON always. You have to make sure that you either disable this option or allow a restricted group of people to use this option. Figure 20-5 shows the option being set to allow a restricted group of people.

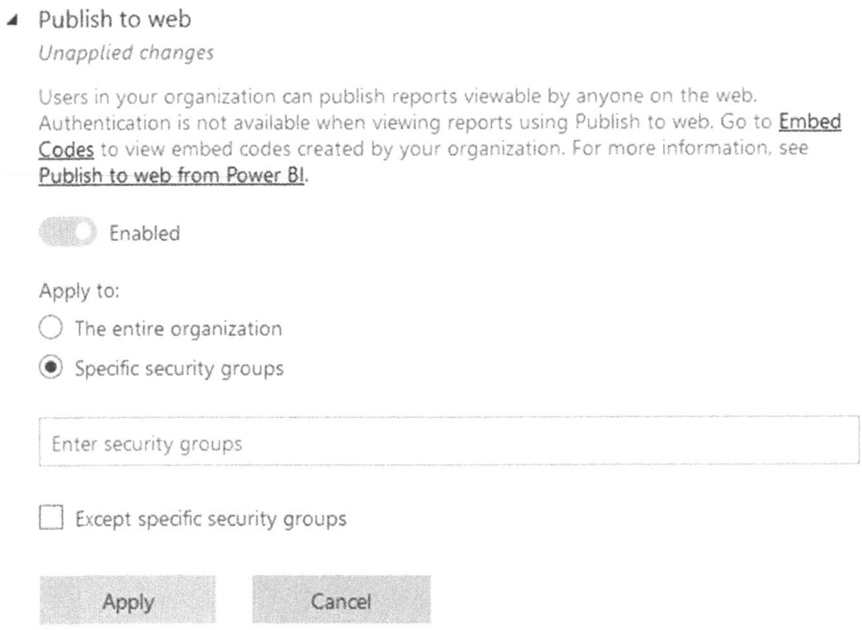

▲ Publish to web
Unapplied changes

Users in your organization can publish reports viewable by anyone on the web.
Authentication is not available when viewing reports using Publish to web. Go to **Embed**
Codes to view embed codes created by your organization. For more information, see
Publish to web from Power BI.

(•) Enabled

Apply to:
◯ The entire organization
◉ Specific security groups

Enter security groups

☐ Except specific security groups

Apply   Cancel

Figure 20-5. *Publish to Web Setting*

Export Data

Exporting data from charts or visuals, which export the data from the data set behind the scene, is by default ON. You can change the option here.

Export Reports as PowerPoint Presentation

Power BI reports can be exported to a PowerPoint slide deck file. The PPTX file won't be an interactive report like a Power BI report. If you want to change that option, here is the configuration to set.

Print Dashboards and Reports

Printing dashboards are not usually a harmful option to be turned on. However, in case you want to change it, you can modify the option.

Content Pack and App Settings

Content Pack and Power BI Apps are ways of sharing Power BI reports. The Content Pack method is almost obsolete, but Power BI App method is a very common way of sharing these days. In this section, you have options to configure for these two methods of sharing.

Publish Content Packs and Apps to the Entire Organization

By default, a content owner can publish an app to the entire organization. If you want to change this behavior and limit this ability to a specific group of people, then add their group information to the list of specific security groups as shown in Figure 20-6.

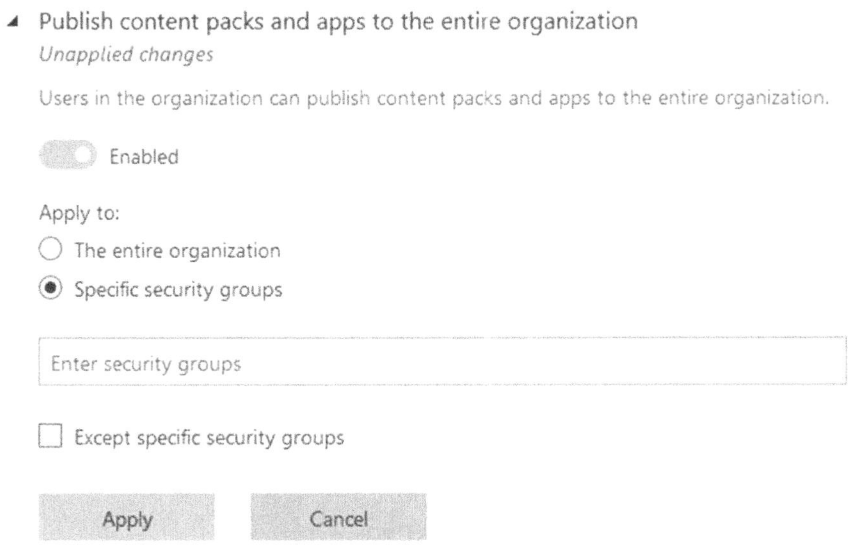

Figure 20-6. *Publish App Settings*

Create Template Organizational Content Pack and Apps

For changing the ability to create a template for content packs and apps, you need to change the setting in this section.

Push Apps to End Users

The Push apps to end users option in Figure 20-7 is one of the very new options added to the tenant settings. Without this option selected, Power BI apps won't automatically be pushed to the end user's apps section. By turning this option ON, any apps created will be automatically pushed to users. You won't need to go and GET the app from each user's profile individually. This is a very good option to be turned ON.

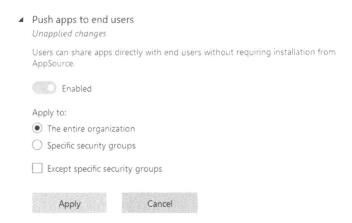

Figure 20-7. *Publish App for the entire organization*

Integration Settings

Configurations in the Integration settings are related to integrating Power BI with other technologies, such as Cortana, ArcGIS, Excel, etc.

Ask Questions About Data Using Cortana

If you don't want your users to interact with the Q&A feature of Power BI with Cortana, then disable this option. However, this is a good option to be kept on.

Use Analyze in Excel with On-Premises Datasets

Analyze in Excel gives the users ability to explore the dataset through a self-service PivotTable and PivotChart view of the Excel. This is a favorite feature of Power BI for Excel users. This option provides the access of Analyze in Excel for even data sources that are connected live to an on-premises data source. It is a very good option to be ON.

Use ArcGIS Maps for Power BI

If you intend to use ArcGIS maps in Power BI, then you need to select this option. This basically is an acknowledgment that ArcGIS servers might be processing your data in another country. ArcGIS map is one of the most powerful map visuals in Power BI. I highly recommend using ArcGIS map if you have a lot of geolocation analysis requirements.

Use Global Search for Power BI

This option integrates Azure Search with Power BI.

Custom Visual Settings

Custom visuals are one of the great add-ins for Power BI visualization. Custom visuals are built by third parties. Not all of the custom visuals are supported continuously in a satisfactory status. Also, some of the custom visuals are paid visuals. As a Power BI administrator, you may want to restrict the usage of custom visuals in your tenant by changing this option. Figure 20-8 shows the option as enabled.

Figure 20-8.   *Custom Visual Setting*

R Visuals Settings

R Visuals became the necessary part of Power BI report development. You can gain machine learning insight and enhanced visuals with leveraging R visuals in Power BI. There are many existing visuals for R, and Leila Etaati also has written a book about R and Power BI together. This option is a recommended option to be ON.

Audit and Usage Settings

You may have seen the usage metrics report of a Power BI dashboard or report. The usage metrics work with audit logs and gives you a detailed analysis of usage consumption of your Power BI content. Options in this section are related to the audit log and usage metrics.

Create Audit Logs for Internal Activity Auditing and Compliance

The audit logs will be created by this option, and users of organization can use it for monitoring and data analysis

Usage Metrics for Content Creators

Content creators are people who create Power BI reports, dashboards, and datasets. By default, content creators have access to the usage metrics report monitoring the usage of their content. If you want to turn off this feature, you can change the option here.

Per-User Data in Usage Metrics for Content Creators

Usage metrics data can also include the per-user individual metrics. Per-user data is useful especially if you want to monitor usage by user to see are they using the content shared with them or not. Figure 20-9 is an example of a usage metrics report with per-user data.

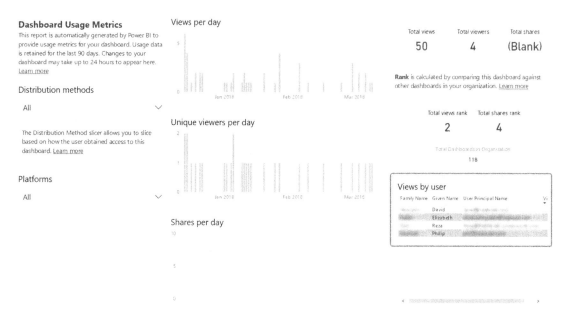

Figure 20-9. *Per-user usage metrics*

Dashboard Settings

Data Classification, shown in Figure 20-10, is a method for labeling dashboards for users. You can add labels such as Highly Classified or Normal and make it visible beside the name of a dashboard. Data classification is not security, it is just a method of labeling for users, so they know how to treat that dashboard. In this section you can create classifications such as the ones below.

Dashboard settings

◢ Data classification for dashboards
Unapplied changes

Users in the organization can tag dashboards with classifications indicating dashboard security levels.

Enabled

DEFAULT	CLASSIFICATION	SHORTHAND	SHOW TAG	URL	
◉	Highly Classified	HC	✓		🗑
○	Unclassified	LC	✓		🗑
	+ Add classification				

Apply   Cancel

ⓘ This setting applies to the entire organization

Figure 20-10. *Data Classification*

Then the classification created can be assigned to every dashboard, as shown in Figure 20-11.

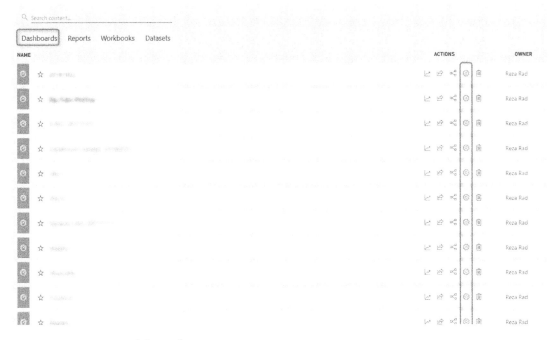

Figure 20-11. *Dashboard Settings*

360

In the settings page of the dashboard, you can choose the classification. Figure 20-12 shows a section of Low Classified, which means the data is not particularly sensitive.

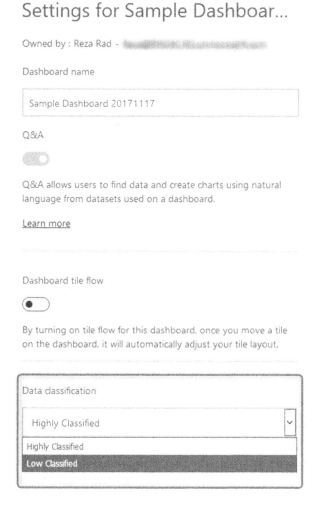

Figure 20-12. *Assign the data classification to a dashboard*

Making the setting in Figure 20-12 will create a corresponding label beside the dashboard as shown in Figure 20-13.

Figure 20-13. *Data classification labels of each dashboard*

Data Classification is not Security, it is just a method of labeling to make users aware about the type of content in the dashboard.

Developer Settings

There is only a single developer setting, and that setting relates to embedded content in apps. As a Developer, you can leverage Power BI Embedded API and embed reports or dashboards into an application. This is a powerful feature, which can be turned on or off from the developer settings.

Usage Metrics

The Admin portal has also some other sections, which are useful for a Power BI administrator. One monitoring part of the Admin portal is the usage metrics for all Power BI content across the tenant. These are shown in Figure 20-14 and can be accessed by going to the Admin Portal, and then choosing Usage Metrics.

Figure 20-14. *Usage Metrics*

The usage metrics here are different from the usage metrics for each dashboard and report. The usage metrics for Power BI administrator gives an overall monitoring view of which users view most of the content and which dashboards or reports have been used most. How many dashboards, reports, or datasets exist in the tenant, and it will reveal some information about workspaces and a lot of other information.

Embed Codes

If you enabled the Publish to Web feature of Power BI in the tenant settings, then you need to monitor what are the content users published with this option. The Embed Codes section of Admin portal is shown in Figure 20-15 and will tell you which report is published to web by which user. You have the option to see the report or delete the embed code. (Deleting the embed code will not delete the report, it will only un-publish it from the web link.)

Admin portal

	Embed Codes				
Usage metrics					
Users	View embed codes that have been created by your organization. To change users ability to use publish to web, see Tenant settings.				
Audit logs					
Tenant settings	Report name	Workspace name	Published by	Status	Actions
Capacity settings					
Embed Codes		Reza Rad	Reza Rad	Active	↗ 🗑
Organization visuals		Reza Rad	Reza Rad	Active	↗ 🗑
		Reza Rad	Reza Rad	Active	↗ 🗑
		Reza Rad	Reza Rad	Active	↗ 🗑
		Reza Rad	Reza Rad	Active	↗ 🗑
		My Test Group	Reza Rad	Active	↗ 🗑
		Leila Etaati	Leila Etaati	Active	↗ 🗑
		Leila Etaati	Leila Etaati	Active	↗ 🗑
		Leila Etaati	Leila Etaati	Active	↗ 🗑
		Leila Etaati	Leila Etaati	Active	↗ 🗑

Figure 20-15. *Manage all Embed Codes*

Organization Visuals

You can add a Power BI visual that is designed by your organization in the Admin portal section on Organization visuals that is shown in Figure 20-16. You will need a *.pbiviz file to upload from this section, describing the visual that you wish to make available.

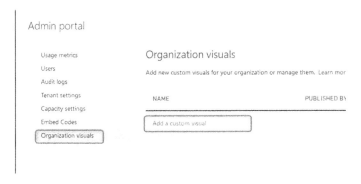

Figure 20-16. *Organization Visuals*

Then you can enter the details of the visual into the Edit custom visual dialog as shown in Figure 20-17.

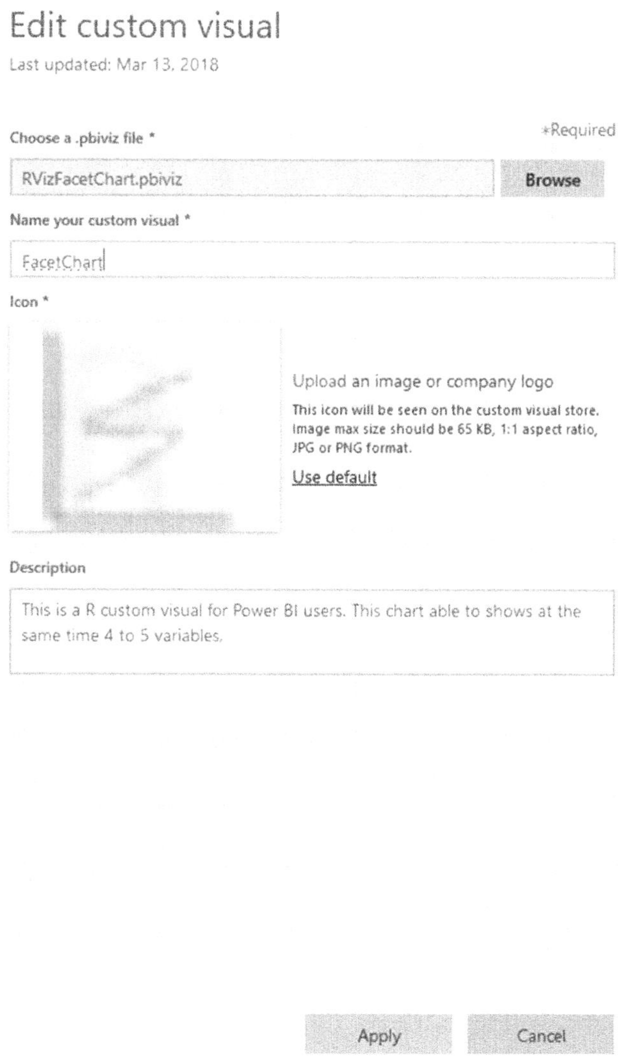

Edit custom visual

Last updated: Mar 13, 2018

Choose a .pbiviz file *   *Required

| RVizFacetChart.pbiviz | Browse |

Name your custom visual *

| FacetChart |

Icon *

Upload an image or company logo

This icon will be seen on the custom visual store.
Image max size should be 65 KB, 1:1 aspect ratio,
JPG or PNG format.

Use default

Description

This is a R custom visual for Power BI users. This chart able to shows at the
same time 4 to 5 variables.

Apply   Cancel

Figure 20-17. *Adding an organizational visual*

These visuals then will be available in Power BI Desktop. Figure 20-18 shows a
FacetChart visual that is available from the My Organization tab.

Figure 20-18. *Using My organization's visuals from Power BI Desktop*

Summary

The Power BI administrator has access to specific parts of the Admin portal such as Tenant Settings, Manage Embed Codes, Organization Visuals, and Usage Metrics. Tenant Settings has many configurations, so you need to be careful of those options. For example; Publish to Web or Integration Settings are important options to consider. Admin portal and tenant settings are getting updated in each version of Power BI service. Hopefully we will have some new features in this list soon.

CHAPTER 21

Usage Metrics

One of the features of Power BI Service is a usage metrics report on a dashboard or report. The usage metrics report will give you an analysis of how many times the content is viewed or share, through which platforms, and by which users. You can also create your monitoring report based on the model of usage metrics. In this chapter, you'll learn how easy it is to use the usage metrics or even create your report from it.

Usage Metrics

The usage metrics report in the Power BI service will give you some analysis on the views and shares of the Power BI content. (You can see an example in Figure 21-1.) This report can be turned off or on in the Power BI Administrator tenant setting configuration. You can also choose if you want the individual per-user data analysis for that to be visible or not; this configuration can also be determined in the tenant settings. To learn more about tenant settings, read Chapter 20.

The report has some sections that mainly explain to you how users consumed this report; you can slice and dice by Distribution methods (sharing, workspace) or by Platform (Mobile, Web). The report gives you an overall analysis as well as a per-day analysis. Here is a look and feel of a usage metrics report.

© Reza Rad 2018
R. Rad, *Pro Power BI Architecture*, https://doi.org/10.1007/978-1-4842-4015-1_21

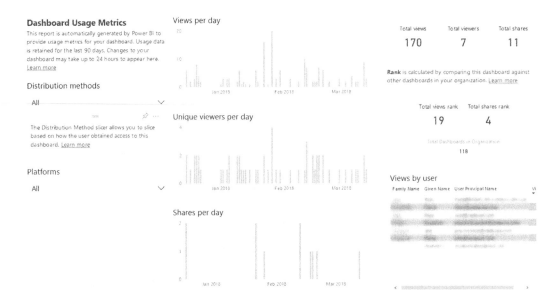

Figure 21-1. *Usage Metrics*

You can access the usage metrics report by clicking on the Usage Metrics icon as shown in Figure 21-2.

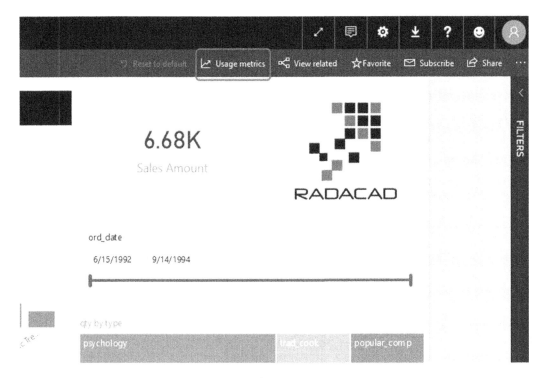

Figure 21-2. *How to Open Usage Metrics report*

Do It Yourself!

You can create your own version of a usage metrics report if you want. You just need to use the existing model and build visualization on top of it. To start, you need to create a copy of the usage metrics report. For doing this, open the usage metrics report, and then click on File, and Save As. See Figure 21-3 for an example.

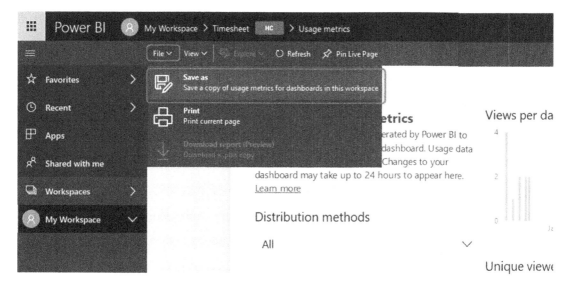

Figure 21-3. *Save a copy of usage metrics report*

Save the new report with a different name, and then open it. You can now see and click on the Edit option on the top of the report, as shown in Figure 21-4.

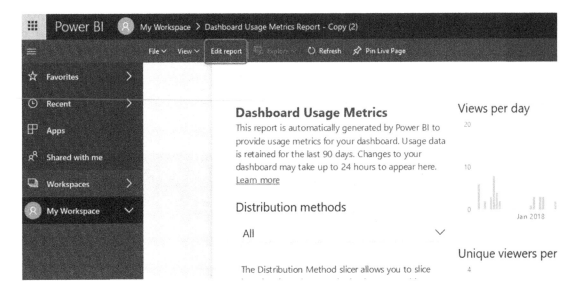

Figure 21-4. *Edit the copied report*

Going to Edit mode, and you then see the tables and fields in the dataset that has the monitoring information. Figure 21-5 shows an example of what you will see at this point.

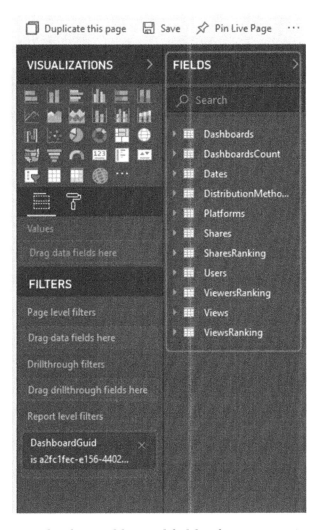

Figure 21-5. *Access to the data tables and fields of usage metrics model*

Unfortunately, you cannot download this report in Power BI Desktop at the moment to develop your report there, but you can develop the report in the website of Power BI. You can even remove the existing Report level filter as in Figure 21-6 to bring in monitoring data for all reports and dashboards.

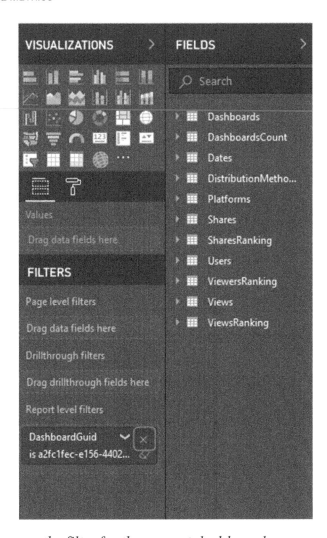

Figure 21-6. *Remove the filter for the current dashboard*

Everything after this step depends on your creativity to create your report with whatever visuals you want. Figure 21-7 shows an example of a usage metrics report version that I created in a few minutes.

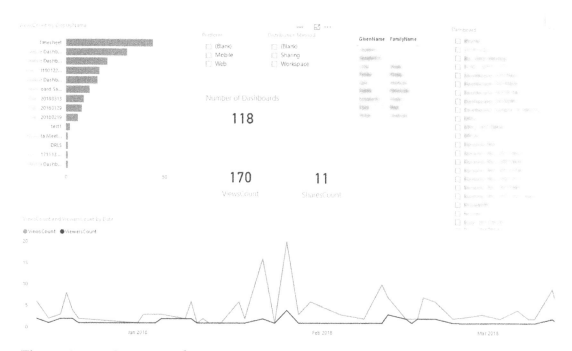

Figure 21-7. *Customized usage metrics report*

As you can see in Figure 21-7, the report includes all dashboards. I can click on a dashboard in the slicer and see the detailed monitoring analysis of that content.

Summary

Usage metrics is a report of monitoring usage data of Power BI content. You can use the existing report or create your report. In the next chapter, you will learn about licensing of Power BI.

CHAPTER 22

Power BI Licensing Guide

Licensing in Power BI is not a complicated one; however, understanding which features are included in which licensing plan is always a question from users. In this chapter, you will learn about all different licensing plans in Power BI, the scenarios to use the licensing for, and scenarios for which you may need to change your licensing. This chapter is intended to help you decide the most cost-effective licensing plan for your requirements. In this chapter, you will learn about Power BI per-user licensing such as free and Pro. You will also learn about capacity-based licensing such as embedded and premium.

Power BI Free

If you are new to Power BI, and you've heard that Power BI is free, then probably one of your first questions is this: "What features do I get with the free Power BI account?" Let's start with answering that question. With Power BI free, you get features such as the ones below.

Power BI Desktop

Power BI Desktop (Figure 22-1) is the developer tool for creating and authoring reports. This tool is free to use, and no licensing is needed for that. You can build Power BI solutions with Power BI Desktop as much as you want with any size of data you want as long as it is on the Desktop. Licensing charges usually start when you start sharing from the service.

375

© Reza Rad 2018
R. Rad, *Pro Power BI Architecture*, https://doi.org/10.1007/978-1-4842-4015-1_22

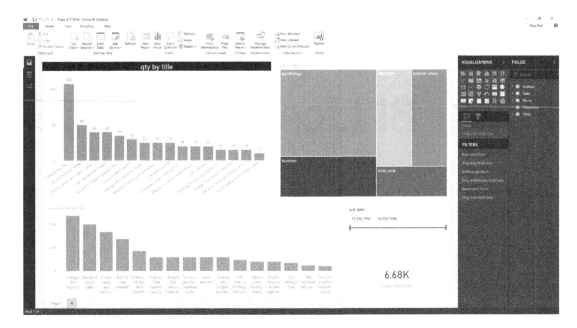

Figure 22-1. *Power BI Desktop is available for Free*

Publishing to Power BI

You can use the same Free license of Power BI to publish your reports into Power BI. If you want to create a Power BI report yourself, publish it in the Power BI service, and view it from a web browser, then doing so doesn't cost you anything. Figure 22-2 shows a Workspace about to be published to Power BI online.

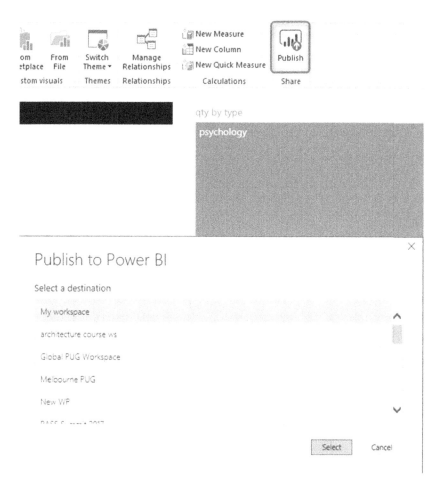

Figure 22-2. *Power BI reports can be published to service for Free*

Publish to Web

Sharing a Power BI content in a secure way is not a free feature. The only free way of Sharing is using Publish to Web as shown in Figure 22-3, which is free but not secure. Publish to Web is sharing your content publicly. All other methods of sharing need a paid subscription.

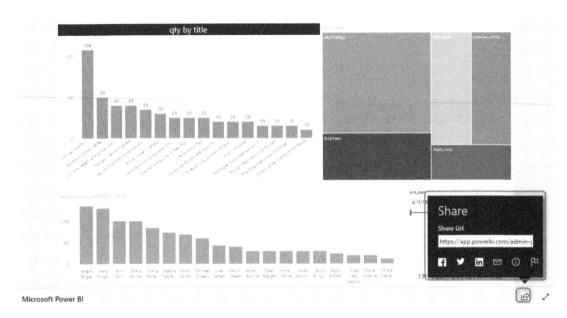

Figure 22-3. *Publish to Web is available for Free*

Power BI Free is for authoring reports with Power BI Desktop, testing it, publishing it into the service, but not sharing it securely.

Power BI Pro

Power BI Pro is the per-user subscription for Power BI. At the time of writing this book, it costs USD 9.99 per user per month. With Power BI Pro you can get everything that free account has, plus many other Power BI service features as well as other methods of sharing.

Sharing

With Power BI Pro you can use all other methods of sharing except Power BI Embedded (which comes through different licensing options). You can use Simple Sharing, Workspaces, Power BI Apps, and Embed in SharePoint Online and Teams. The important thing to know is that even for consuming a Power BI content shared with you, you need to be part of a paid subscription (the only exception is if you have access to a Published to Web Power BI content, which is free). Figure 22-4 shows a Power BI App as it is seen by a user with whom the app has been shared.

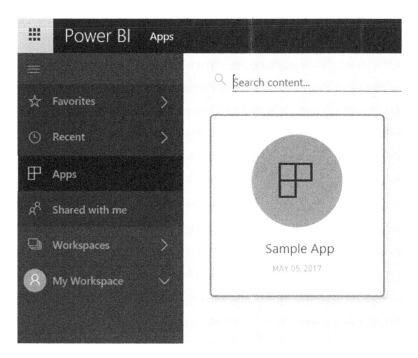

Figure 22-4. *All organizational sharing methods such as Power BI apps are accessible with Pro*

Integration

With Power BI Pro you can get some integration features of Power BI as well. An example is the Analyze in Excel feature that is shown in Figure 22-5.

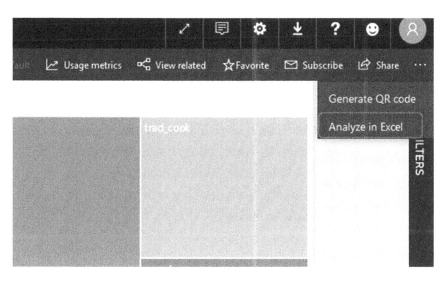

Figure 22-5. *Analyze in Excel is available in Pro version*

379

Power BI Embedded

If you ever want to embed Power BI content in a custom application and use a custom application's user management, then Power BI Embedded is the licensing plan for you. This licensing plan is not per user because there is no Power BI user requirement for embedding with a token. This licensing plan is based on page renders. Figure 22-6 shows an embedded dashboard.

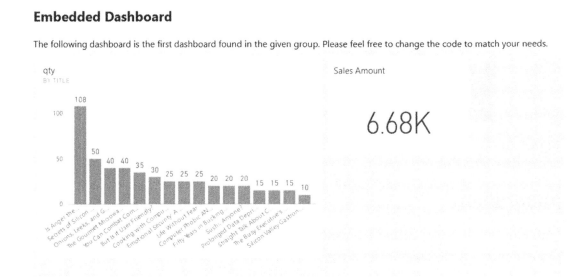

Figure 22-6. *Power BI Embedded has a different licensing plan*

Every refresh on a page that has Power BI content in it is a page render. Other events trigger page renders, too, such as when you select a slicer, or when you click on a column chart that interacts with other charts.

With Power BI Embedded you can reserve buckets of page renders per peak hour. An important aspect to consider when you think about Power BI Embedded is the hidden cost of a web developer. Power BI Embedded is bringing Power BI content embedded into your custom applications, and the web developers needed to do the work, representing a cost that you should consider.

Power BI Premium

Power BI Pro will be expensive for a large user base, and Power BI Embedded needs constant maintenance by a web developer. If you have a large user base (let's say 10,000 users), then Power BI Premium is the best licensing option for you. Power BI Premium is designed for a large user base scenario where the size of data is huge.

Calculating the Cost

Power BI Premium is not per user; it is per node. In Power BI premium you pay for nodes that have dedicated capacity and resources. Figure 22-7 shows existing node options at the time of writing this chapter. Pricing starts with P1 nodes costing USD 5K per month, and it goes up from there.

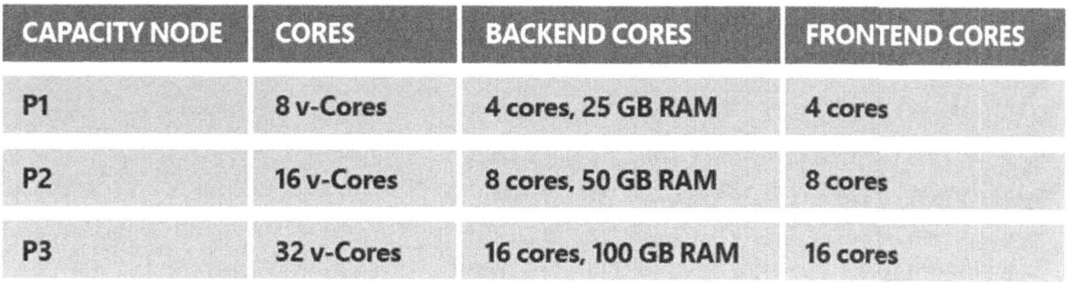

CAPACITY NODE	CORES	BACKEND CORES	FRONTEND CORES
P1	8 v-Cores	4 cores, 25 GB RAM	4 cores
P2	16 v-Cores	8 cores, 50 GB RAM	8 cores
P3	32 v-Cores	16 cores, 100 GB RAM	16 cores

Figure 22-7. *Dedicated Power BI Premium Nodes*

It is a bit hard to understand how many nodes you may need for your Power BI solution, or how large those needs must be. Fortunately, there is a Power BI Premium calculator that can help. Find that calculator at the following URL:

```
https://powerbi.microsoft.com/en-us/calculator/
```

Figure 22-8 shows an example calculation for 10,000 users.

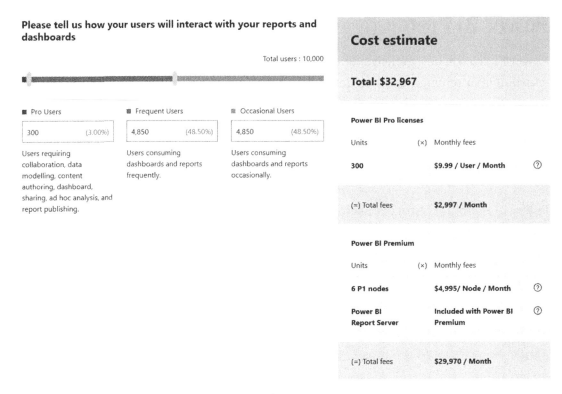

Figure 22-8. *Power BI Premium Calculator*

If you compare the total costs of $33K per month with $100K per month ($100K per month if all 10,000 users purchase Power BI pro), then you can understand how Power BI premium can be more cost-effective in a larger user-base scenario. The whole idea behind creating the Power BI premium licensing is that users who are only reading a report should not pay Pro pricing.

Extra Features of Premium

Power BI Premium will give you some extra features. Some of these features are available now, and some are still a work in progress or are simply on the road map for the future. Following are some of these extra features that are either available now or are planned for the future:

- Dedicated Power BI Resources

- Huge dataset storage and no user quotas: 100TB storage rather than 10GB per user

- More frequent dataset refresh: 48 times a day, rather than 8 times a day

- Power BI report server: Power BI on-premises

- Larger Datasets supported (not available at the time of writing this book)

- Incremental Refresh (not available at the time of writing this book)

- Pin Dataset to memory (not available at the time of writing this book)

- Dedicated data refresh Nodes (not available at the time of writing this book)

- Geo-replica and read-only replicas (not available at the time of writing this book)

- Geographic distribution (not available at the time of writing this book)

Power BI Premium licensing is designed for large user-base scenarios. This licensing will give you many extra features as well as incremental load.

SQL Server Enterprise Edition + Software Assurance

The combination of SQL Server Enterprise Edition and software assurance of that will give you Power BI Report Server, shown in Figure 22-9. You still need to have a Power BI pro account for content creators, but for on-premises sharing of Power BI content, then you can easily user the Power BI report server. I will explain more about the Power BI Report Server in another chapter. For the costing of software assurance plus SQL Server Enterprise Edition, you can contact your Microsoft contact for these products.

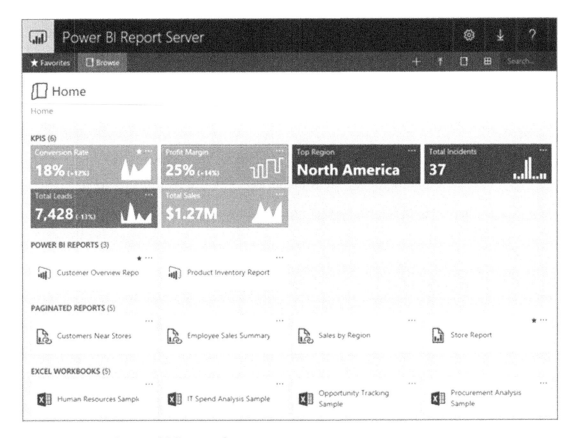

Figure 22-9. *Power BI Report Server*

If you already have SQL Server Enterprise Edition licensing in your organization, and you intend to use Power BI only through sharing on-premises with Power BI Report Server, then buying Software Assurance is a more cost-effective option.

Summary

In this chapter, you learned about five different licensing plans for Power BI. You learned what features included in each plan are, and in which situations they are cost-effective options. Table 22-1 presents a summary of features in each licensing plan.

Table 22-1. *Power BI Licensing Comparison Table*

Feature	Free	Pro	Embedded	Premium	SQL Server Enterprise Edition + Software Assurance
Developing reports with Power BI Desktop	Yes	Yes			
Publish report to Power BI service	Yes	Yes			
Publish to Web	Yes	Yes			
Export to PowerPoint or CSV	Yes	Yes			
Basic Sharing		Yes			
Workspaces		Yes			
Power BI Apps		Yes			
Embed into SharePoint Online		Yes			
Analyze in Excel		Yes			
Embed into the custom application (Power BI embedded)			Yes	Yes	
Refresh Frequency		8 times a day		48 times a day	
Power BI Report Server				Yes	Yes
Dedicated Capacity			Yes	Yes	Yes
Space allocation	10GB	10GB		100TB	
Extra Premium Features (mentioned earlier in this chapter)				Yes	

CHAPTER 23

Power BI Premium

In the last chapter, you learned about different licensing plans for Power BI. Power BI Premium is a licensing plan that has many features and needs to be explained in more detail. This chapter is about Power BI Premium. You will learn: How does it work? Is this a licensing plan that works for you or not? What is the break-even point with this plan? In this chapter, I'll answer all of these questions with a detailed explanation about Power BI Premium.

Power BI Licensing Before Premium

To look at the new licensing plan, it is best first to understand how the previous licensing worked. Before this change, the licensing plan for Microsoft was simple; it had only two plans: Free and Power BI Pro. Free was free of charge obviously. All you needed was your company's email address to get Power BI account. Pro, however, provided some additional features with a cost of about $9.99 per user per month.

The difference between these two plans was not about development work. You can do almost anything you want with Power BI free for doing the development work. But, when it comes to contribution, sharing, security, and using Power BI in a production environment, most of the features needed Pro account. Table 23-1 shows some of the current licensing details.

© Reza Rad 2018
R. Rad, *Pro Power BI Architecture*, https://doi.org/10.1007/978-1-4842-4015-1_23

Table 23-1. *Power BI Licensing Before May 2017*

Feature	Power BI Free	Power BI Pro
Space allocation	1GB	10GB *
Power BI Desktop	Yes	Yes
Development features	Yes	Yes
DirectQuery or Live Connection	No	Yes
Data Set Refresh Frequency	Up to once a day	Up to 8 times a day
Gateways - On-premises data source	No	Yes
Row-Level Security	No	Yes
Content Pack	No	Yes
Workspaces	No	Yes
Data Streaming	Up to 10K rows per hours	Unlimited

As you can see, anything regarding Developing a Power BI solution is available for free. However, to use Power BI in a production environment, most of the time you need a Pro account. Here are more details:

- If you want to use a proper mechanism to share Power BI content with others, in most of the cases, you need to use either Power BI workspaces or Content Packs, which both are Pro features.

- If you want to use Row-Level Security, which is giving access to users based on their part of the dataset, not the whole, then you need a Pro account.

- If you are using Gateways (doesn't matter if it's Personal or On-Premises) to connect to the on-premises data source, then you need a Pro account.

- For Live Connection or DirectQuery connection to data sources, you will need a Pro account. Live Connection or DirectQuery option happens a lot in an enterprise environment when the size of data and scale are so high that a Power BI 1GB model cannot host it.

- And many more as you see in the table above.

As you can see, in the production environment of using Power BI, you will hit one of the limitations above for the Free account, and then you have to use a Pro Account. It is very important to understand the statement below.

Pro account is not only for the developer but also for the consumer! If Power BI Content is Pro, then whoever uses and consumes that content should have a Pro account.

Yes, you've read it correctly. Any content that has one of the features below is considered as Pro content. And everyone who uses or consumes that content should have a Power BI pro account:

- Data from a DirectQuery dataset, such as SQL Server Analysis Services tabular data, Azure SQL Database, Azure SQL Data Warehouse, or Apache Spark for HDInsight.

- Data from a dataset that refreshes more frequently than daily.

- Data from a dataset that connects to on-premises data using the Power BI Gateway - Personal or the On-premises Data Gateway, and for which a scheduled refresh is set.

- Data from a live connection to Azure Analysis Services.

- Data (including reports, dashboards, or tiles) from a dataset that uses Row-Level Security (RLS).

- A dashboard or report that's installed from an app or an organizational content pack.

- A dashboard, report, or dataset that's contained in an app workspace.

- A dashboard that contains data streamed at a rate above 10k rows/ hour.

Source from: `https://powerbi.microsoft.com/en-us/documentation/powerbi-power-bi-pro-content-what-is-it/`

Why Premium?

With a list of limitations for Power BI free and also the pro account, it is almost obvious why we need another licensing plan (Premium). I point a few of the reasons here for more elaboration.

Large User Base

Limitations in Pro Content as above means that if you are working in a large organization with 10,000 users, you have to pay 10,000 * $10 per month, which would be $100K per month! Or $1.2 million per year! The licensing costs as above sound scary!

Power BI Model Size Limitation

Also, as you might already know, with a Pro account, you get 10GB space in your Power BI account. However, each Power BI Model (or let's say a file) cannot be more than 1GB! The limitation mentioned means that you have to combine Power BI with other technologies such as SQL Server Analysis Services for Live Connection, or a premier database provider such as SQL Server, Oracle, Teradata… for DirectQuery Connection. And that means paying for licenses for those products, too, because in an enterprise environment, it is very likely that the size of a Power BI model rises to more than 1GB.

Readers or Consumers

In most of the implementations of Power BI, the majority of users are just readers or consumers of the report. Readers or consumers CAN interact with the report, they can use charts and visuals interactively and analyze the data, but they won't create or update reports. There is always a small number of developers who do the development work. In this licensing plan, every user who is using Pro content, regardless of the role (developer or consumer), should be a pro account.

What Is Power BI Premium?

Now that you know about the previous licensing plan of Power BI, I can start talking about Premium. What is the premium? Power BI Premium is simply a licensing plan that covers limitations of a Power BI pro account. It is a licensing plan that helps overcome what you couldn't easily achieve with a Power BI pro account. The license starts at higher ground, and at the time of writing this chapter it is $5K, but don't be scared of this high cost; we will get into details of that shortly.

Are Power BI Pro and Free Gone Now?

No! Power BI Free and Pro are still there. However, there will be some changes in features supported by each type of account. I assure you here that all you can do with Power BI pro, you can still do it with Pro, so you don't need to upgrade to Premium if you don't want to.

Features that might be taken away from the free account are more about collaboration, such as sharing. So, in the feature for sharing Power BI content, you might need at least a Pro account.

Is Premium the Only Option Now?

Are you using Power BI Pro and worried that Power BI Premium is going to be your only option? Do not worry. You can continue using Power BI Pro. Pro gives you all you have already; you won't lose anything. And you don't have to upgrade to Premium. However, using Premium gives you some more options and features, so let's look at them below.

Benefits of Power BI Premium

Power BI Premium is an additional licensing plan. Additional means that you can use it or not; but if you use this plan, then you would get some benefits that help you to sometimes reduce the costs of your BI solution. But, first, you need to know what these features are. These features might be superb features for some companies but not essential for others.

Dedicated Power BI Resources

First, and one of the most important features of Premium, is that you get dedicated resources, such as capacity, cores, and processing units. Normal Power BI Free or Pro accounts are publishing content into SHARED Power BI servers. These servers are high-performing servers with great cores and capacity. However, it is not dedicated.

With Power BI Premium, you can choose the type of node that you want, and you can configure your own Power BI node. Figure 23-1 shows the current node configurations that are available.

CAPACITY NODE	CORES	BACKEND CORES	FRONTEND CORES
P1	8 v-Cores	4 cores, 25 GB RAM	4 cores
P2	16 v-Cores	8 cores, 50 GB RAM	8 cores
P3	32 v-Cores	16 cores, 100 GB RAM	16 cores

Figure 23-1. *Power BI Premium Dedicated Nodes*

Larger Datasets Supported

As you already know from Pro limitation, even with a Pro account you cannot have a model with more than 1GB of size, and your total space is about 10GB. With Power BI Premium, you can have up to 100TB space to fill in! Your model can simply be sized 50GB or add more shortly. The statement above means that you might not need to be paying for an additional SQL Server or another database technology for developing a large-scale BI solution.

More Frequent Dataset Refresh Rate

With Free, you can refresh up to once a day. With Pro, you can refresh up to 8 times a day. With Premium, you can refresh your data set up to 48 times a day. The minimum frequency for refreshing data was 30 minutes, which is lifted in Premium. You can schedule on a minute level now with this new plan.

Readers or Consumers Plan

Power BI Premium is a licensing plan for readers and consumers. Readers can enjoy consuming content that is still Pro content but with a licensing that costs less than Power BI Pro per user. So, if your company has 10K users, you don't need to pay $100K per month, you would pay far less than that. I will get into the details of costs shortly.

Power BI Report Server

Power BI Report Server (discussed in Chapter 26) is without a doubt one of the best offerings of Power BI Premium. Previously I have written about Power BI reports On-Premises with Reporting Services. This functionality will be available as a new feature called Power BI Report Server. Power BI Report Server will be part of Premium licensing, enabling you to host your reports on-premises. More details about costs will come. But the good news is that you will have Power BI on-premises. Figure 23-2 shows a report running in Report Server.

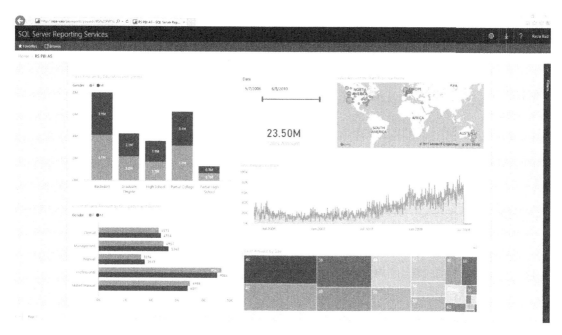

Figure 23-2. *Power BI Report Server*

Upcoming Features for Premium

Power BI Premium would be the best offering of Power BI, and there are lots of awesome features coming in for it shortly, such as the ones we talk about below. Note that at the time of writing this chapter, features below are not available yet. But these are on the road map.

Incremental Refresh

When we are talking about a dataset more than 1GB of size, then incremental refresh matters. You don't want to populate that amount of data in every refresh. With Premium, you will have this option shortly to use incremental load and update only the changed set.

Pin Dataset to Memory

Power BI, by default, allocates memory to models based on their usage. This automatic allocation sometimes might cause users to wait for their old report to load. In this feature, you will have the option to pin those datasets that you think are important and critical for a business to memory and configure performance of Power BI based on your requirements.

Dedicated Data Refresh Node

You would be able to dedicate specific nodes for data refresh, while other nodes are providing a response to report. The option mentioned above will help the performance of report loading to be high while the dataset is refreshing.

Geo-Replica and Read-Only Replicas

You will be able to distribute replicas of the Power BI model geographically, and in other ways, so your users get the best performance.

The Most Important Topic! Costs of Premium

Cost of Power BI Premium is the most important topic to discuss. When Premium announced it the first time, I saw lots of people scared from the $5K entry point of it. Let's get into details of costing and see how it is working.

There is a calculator (shown in Figure 23-3) that helps you understand the costing based on your requirement. The costing is based on how many developers (Pro) accounts you have, how frequent its users, and how many readers. The reason to separate frequent users and readers is mainly to understand how many cores you will need for Power BI Premium.

Let's go through an example. Consider an organization with 10K users. Out of these 10K uses, only 300 of them are developers (they will create or update reports), and the rest are just consuming reports (let's say 4.8K frequent consumers and 4.8K occasional). Based on the calculator for such a requirement, you will need to have 300 Pro users (this is obvious) and 6 P1 nodes to cover readers. Each P1 Node costs $5K per month.

So, as a result, it would cost about $32K.

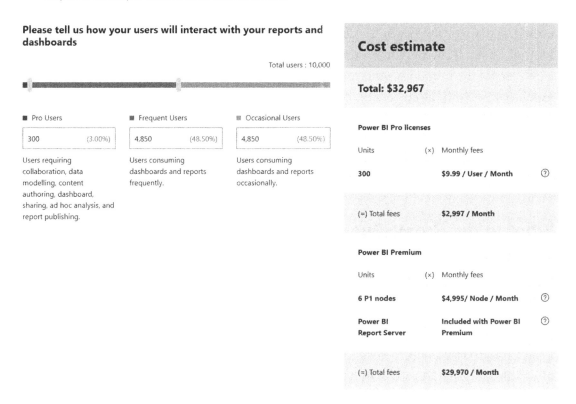

Please tell us how your users will interact with your reports and dashboards

Total users : 10,000

Pro Users	Frequent Users	Occasional Users
300 (3.00%)	4,850 (48.50%)	4,850 (48.50%)
Users requiring collaboration, data modelling, content authoring, dashboard, sharing, ad hoc analysis, and report publishing.	Users consuming dashboards and reports frequently.	Users consuming dashboards and reports occasionally.

Cost estimate

Total: $32,967

Power BI Pro licenses

Units	(×)	Monthly fees
300		$9.99 / User / Month ⑦
(=) Total fees		$2,997 / Month

Power BI Premium

Units	(×)	Monthly fees
6 P1 nodes		$4,995/ Node / Month ⑦
Power BI Report Server		Included with Power BI ⑦ Premium
(=) Total fees		$29,970 / Month

Figure 23-3. *Power BI Premium Calculator*

The costs are high, of course, but if you compare it with purchasing 10K Power BI Pro plans ($100K), it is almost one-third of that cost! As I mentioned before, you don't need to pay a price of Pro for readers, so that makes your costs lower.Also, you will notice in the calculator that this costing is including Power BI Report Server. So with this cost, you are also able to host reports on-premises.

Is Power BI Premium Always Better?

Is it always better to pay for Power BI Premium? The answer, like with many questions, depends upon the details. If you are working for a large enterprise with thousands of users, and most of the users are consumers, then it will be much more cost effective to purchase Power BI Premium licensing.

However, if you are a medium-size or small business with few hundreds of users or even less, then maybe Power BI Pro is a better option for you. If you have 50 users for Power BI, even if you purchase Pro account for them all, you have to pay $500 per month. However, for the premium, you would need to pay at least $5K, which is 10 times more expensive. So, with the current entry point of nodes (which is $5K), it is not cost effective to pay for Premium if you have such a small user base. Simply continue using Power BI Pro.

If you need to host Power BI on-premises, you might still need to consider Premium even with the small user base, because Power BI Report Server is available within Premium or with SQL Server licensing (more details to come in the future).

What Is the Break-Even Point?

One of the most common questions in this area is about when I need to use Premium and when to use Pro. What is the break-even point?

The answer to this question can be calculated easily. I cannot give you a precise number because there are many different situations to consider in terms of details. Example: Two companies have 5K users, and one of them might have 2K developers, the other one 200 only. One of them might have all users as frequent users, the other one 80% occasional users. Depending on your requirements, the number of nodes for Power BI Premium is different. And some nodes have a direct effect on the costs.

I advise you to use the calculator and enter your total number of users, frequent users and occasional users, then check if the total price with that requirement is lower than purchasing Pro account for all users; if so, then your break-even point is passed. If not, then you can simply use Power BI Pro.

I've had two examples in this chapter already. Here is a summary of those again:

- A large enterprise with 10K users, which only 300 of these users are developers, and the rest are half frequent and half occasional users. Six p1 nodes of Power BI would cover this user base, and so the cost would be: 300*$10 (per user Pro account) + 6*$4,995 (per node Premium) = $32,967. This cost is far less than 10K*$10 (per user Pro account) = $100,000. So, this organization should use Premium obviously.

- A small-/medium-size business with 50 users, even if it pays $10 for a pro account for everyone, it is paying $500 per month. However, if this company purchases premium, the minimum entry point (at the time of writing this book) is $4,995, which is 10 times more expensive. So, this company can simply continue using Power BI Pro.

Summary

In Summary Power, BI Premium is a great offering. It comes with lower pricing for enterprise-scale customers, and with many features such as dedicated server, higher dataset size, higher frequency of data refresh, Power BI on-premises, and many other options. However, not all companies need these features, and they have don't have a large user base. They can simply use the Power BI Pro license as they are using already and enjoy the current offering. If you would like to read more about details of Power BI Premium, I recommend reading the Power BI Premium Whitepaper written by Microsoft.

PART VI

Integration

CHAPTER 24

PowerPoint Integration with Power BI

Exporting a Power BI report to PowerPoint is a good way of integrating these two tools together. The analytical power of Power BI combined with the commentary and presentation features of PowerPoint enables you to present your reports differently. You can export almost any Power BI report (limitations mentioned in this chapter) to PowerPoint, and then enhance the presentation of that from there. Exporting to PowerPoint, however, has some limitations that you need to be aware of before working with it. In this chapter, you will learn everything about the export to PowerPoint feature.

How Export to PowerPoint Works

Exporting to PowerPoint only works for reports at the moment. On top of a report, you can simply click on File option and select Export to PowerPoint. (Figure 24-1 illustrates). Note that this feature is still in preview mode at the time of writing this book, and it may be subject to change.

© Reza Rad 2018
R. Rad, *Pro Power BI Architecture*, https://doi.org/10.1007/978-1-4842-4015-1_24

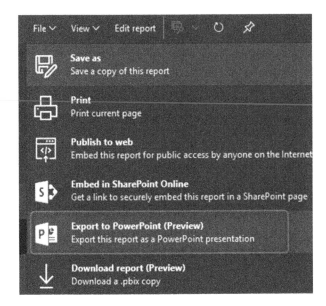

Figure 24-1. *Export to PowerPoint option in the Power BI report in the service*

Export to PowerPoint works very simply and downloads a PPTX file for you. The file will include all pages of the report, plus a summary page. The summary page will include the name of the report, a link to the report, the time of refresh for the dataset, and the download time of the report. The summary page becomes the first slide in the report and will resemble that in Figure 24-2. The "downloaded at" time will be the time on the computer that it initiated the export.

Figure 24-2. *The first slide from a report exported to PowerPoint*

Visualizations on a page will all be exported as a big screenshot of each page. That result will resemble what you see in Figure 24-3.

Figure 24-3. *Every report page will be a screenshot; it will not be interactive*

Each report page will be a slide in Export to PowerPoint: not interactive, however, just screenshots. That means you cannot click on a visual or slicer and interact with it like a normal Power BI report. Figure 24-4 shows a series of slides that once was a Power BI report.

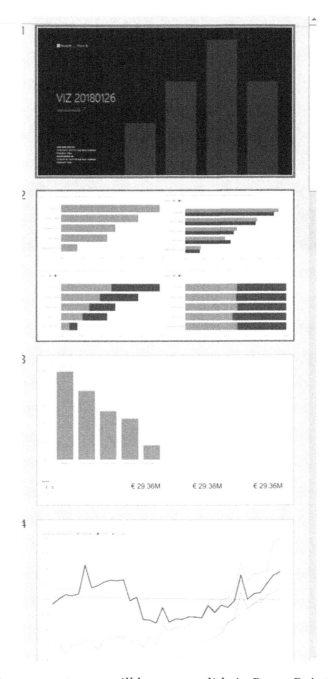

Figure 24-4. *Every report page will become a slide in PowerPoint*

What Is the Main Advantage of Export to PowerPoint?

The main benefit of export to PowerPoint is getting the great features from both products: the commentary and presentation features from PowerPoint combined with the analytical and reporting features of Power BI. After exporting to PowerPoint, you can make changes in the presentation of slides as you want. Figure 24-5 shows a slide that has been exported for use in a PowerPoint presentation.

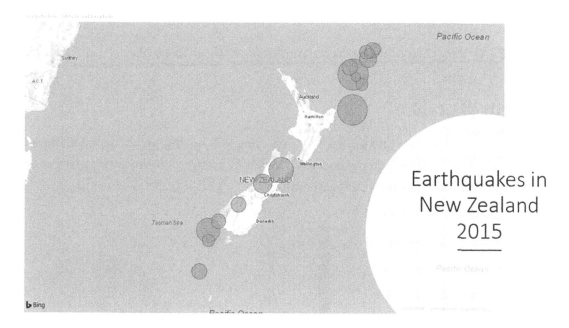

Figure 24-5. *Presentation features of PowerPoint will be combined with analytical features of Power BI*

Limitations and Important Things to Know

Export to PowerPoint is a new feature, and it has some limitations. The following sections are a list of limitations at the time of writing this book.

Number of Pages

You cannot export to PowerPoint if you have more than 15 report pages. You will get an error such as in Figure 24-6.

Figure 24-6. *You cannot export reports with more than 15 pages*

Custom Visuals

Some custom visuals won't be shown after exporting to PowerPoint, and some of them will have unusual behavior after export to PowerPoint. Figure 24-7 shows a visual that is properly supported for export to PowerPoint.

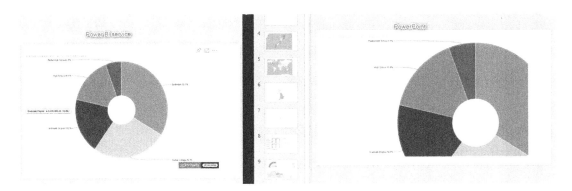

Figure 24-7. *Only certified custom visuals are supported for export to PowerPoint*

Certified custom visuals are supported fully. Infographic Designer visuals, for example, are fully supported. Figure 24-8 shows an example.

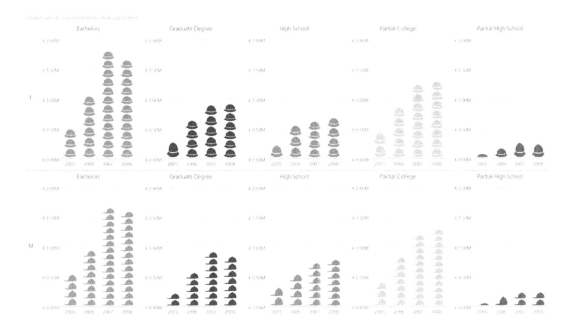

Figure 24-8. *Infographic Designer is an example of certified custom visuals*

A list of all certified custom visuals can be found online at `https://docs.microsoft.com/en-us/power-bi/power-bi-custom-visuals-certified`.

ArcGIS Is Not supported

ArcGIS custom visuals are not supported at the time of writing this book. Figure 24-9 shows one such video, along with the blank image that you'll get after exporting to PowerPoint.

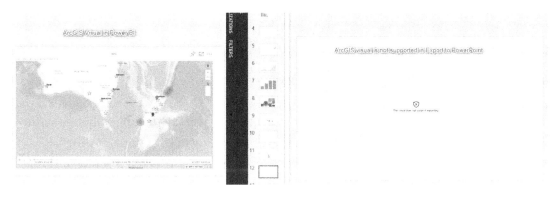

Figure 24-9. *ArcGIS map doesn't work in PowerPoint*

Export to PowerPoint Can Be Disabled or Limited

In Tenant Settings, the ability to Export to PowerPoint can be disabled or limited to a group of people. Figure 24-10 shows the settings area under Tenant settings where you would go to exert this type of control.

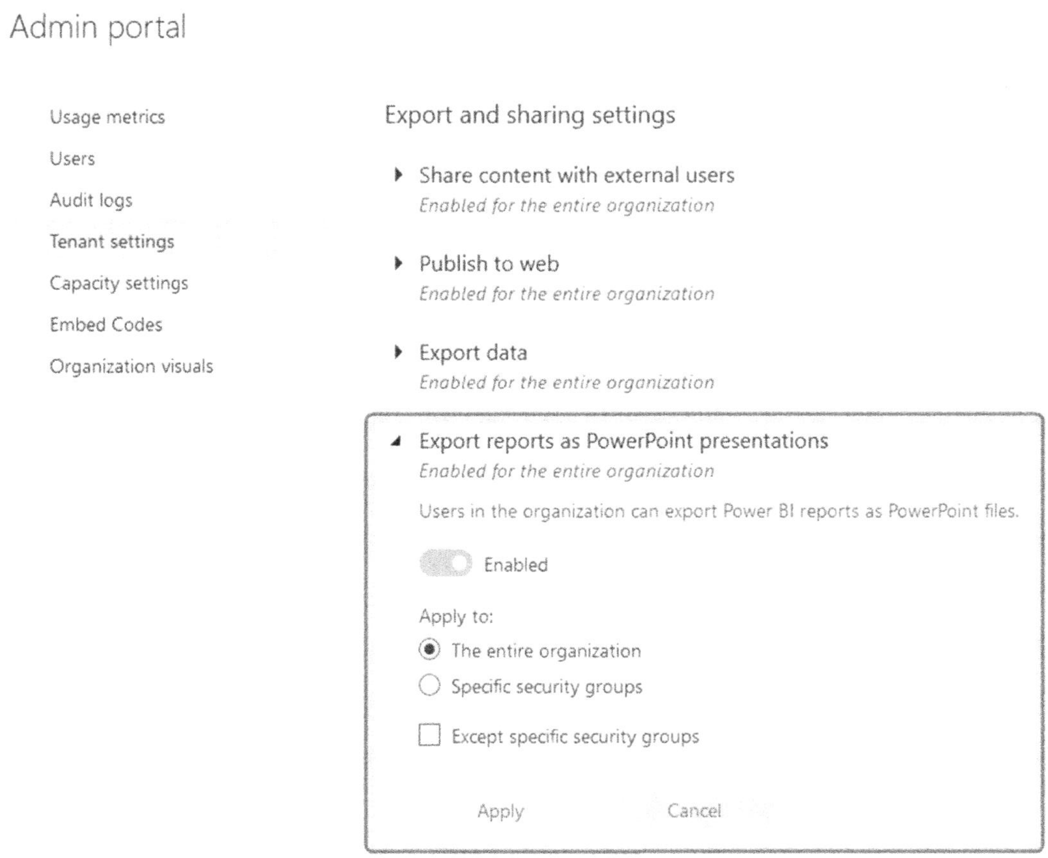

Figure 24-10. Controlling Export to PowerPoint from Admin Portal

Language Setting in Power BI

When you export to PowerPoint, the export process will use the default language settings in Power BI. If you want to change those settings, go to Power BI service, Settings, and again Settings, then Language configuration, and apply the change you want. See Figure 24-11 for an example.

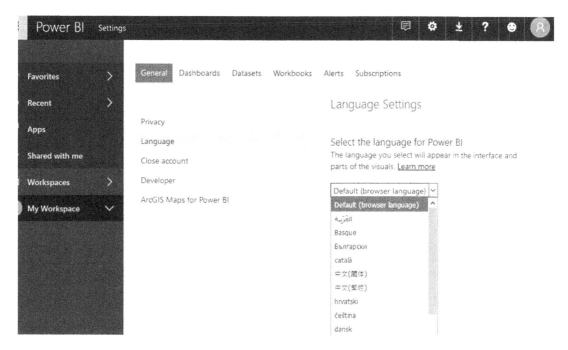

Figure 24-11. *Setting the Language for Export to PowerPoint*

Your Organization Only

If you share a report/dashboard with someone outside of your organization, they cannot use the export to PowerPoint feature. The ability to export to PowerPoint is for members of your organization only.

Still in PREVIEW Mode

The export to PowerPoint feature is still in preview mode and subject to change. The details of how the feature works may change between the time this book is published and the time the feature moves out of preview mode.

Summary

This was a very quick chapter about the export to PowerPoint feature of Power BI. The export to PowerPoint brings two products together: Power BI and PowerPoint. The result of the combination of the two products is the analytical power of Power BI combined with presentation features of PowerPoint. However, the export to PowerPoint is still in preview mode and has some limitations.

CHAPTER 25

Power BI and Excel

Power BI and Excel are longtime friends of each other, not only because Power BI components are coming from add-ins that were introduced in Excel, but also because of the way that these two tools interact with each other from the Power BI Service. This chapter is not about using Power Query or Power Pivot components in Excel. This chapter is about the interaction between Excel and Power BI through the service.

On one hand, Power BI and Excel integration through the service gives the user the ability to use Excel as their slicing and dicing tool while connected to a live Power BI dataset. On the other hand, you can pin a range of cells from an Excel document into a Power BI dashboard. Excel files also can be uploaded to the Workbook tab of the Power BI service. In this chapter, you will learn the ways explained below that Excel and Power BI interact with each other through Power BI Service: Analyze in Excel, Power BI Publisher for Excel, Upload an Excel Workbook into Power BI Service, and Import Excel into Power BI Desktop.

Analyze in Excel

In every company, you will find some users with very good experience and skillsets of Excel. Excel users can still use Excel to connect to the Power BI dataset and use Excel features such as PivotTable and PivotChart to slice and dice the data. The connection to the Power BI dataset would be a live connection, and it means that whenever users refresh the Excel file, they will get the most up-to-date data from the Power BI service.

You can start looking at Analyze in Excel from a Power BI Service report. Log in to Power BI service, and open one of the Power BI reports. In the top right-hand side, after clicking on more options, you will find Analyze in Excel as shown in Figure 25-1.

© Reza Rad 2018
R. Rad, *Pro Power BI Architecture*, https://doi.org/10.1007/978-1-4842-4015-1_25

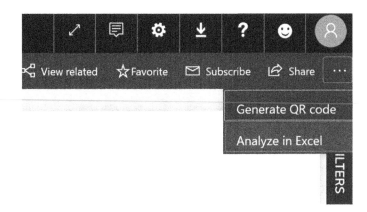

Figure 25-1. *Analyze in Excel*

You can also open Analyze in Excel from the workspace directly without opening the report. Simply click on the Excel icon beside the report's name. Figure 25-2 shows the Excel icons highlighted by a rectangle. They are under the Actions column toward the right side of the figure.

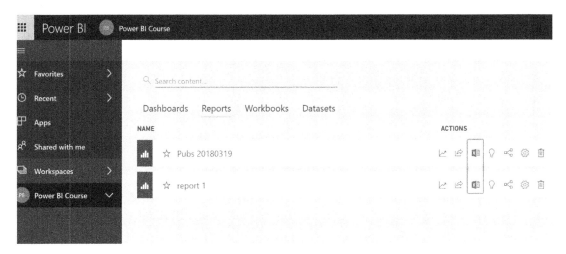

Figure 25-2. *Analyze in Excel Icon*

If this is the first time that you are using this feature on your machine, you may be asked to install a plug-in for an Office connection add-in. Figure 25-3 shows the dialog that will prompt you to install this plug-in.

I've already installed these updates

Figure 25-3. *Download OLE DB Provider for Excel*

After downloading it (which shouldn't take long), you can install the add-in. The installation is for Microsoft Analysis Services OLE DB Provider for Excel. Figure 25-4 shows the installer.

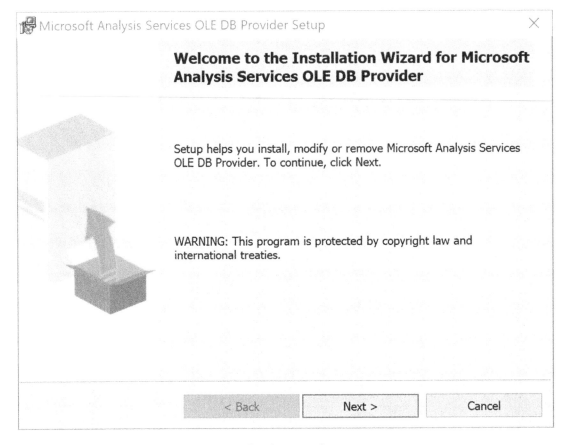

Figure 25-4. *Install OLE DB Provider for Excel*

Follow the instructions for setup. The reason that the Analysis Services OLE DB provider is required for Analyze in Excel to work is that Power BI datasets are hosted in an Azure Analysis Services instance.

After successful setup, try Analyze in Excel again, and this time you can choose the "I've already installed these updates" option as shown in Figure 25-5.

First, you need some Excel updates

To use analyze in Excel, you need to do a one-time
download and installation of the latest version of
Excel libraries. Learn more about this update

Download   Cancel

I've already installed these updates

Figure 25-5. *Downloading ODC file*

The Analyze in Excel option in Power BI service will download an Office Data
Connection (ODC) file. ODC files can be opened with Excel. Save the file as shown in
Figure 25-6. Then you can right-click on the file and choose to open it in Excel.

Figure 25-6. *Downloading ODC file*

When you open the file in Excel, you will be asked to enable the connection. The reason for the question is that you are connecting to a data source in the cloud. Figure 25-7 shows the dialog, and you can respond by clicking the Enable button.

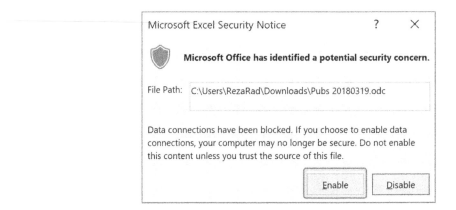

Figure 25-7. *Security Notice for connecting to online data sources*

If this is the first time you are opening the file, you may be asked to log in. Log in using the same Power BI account username and password that you used to initially create the report. After successful sign-in, you should see a PivotTable with data tables and fields fetched from Power BI model. What you see will be similar to Figure 25-8.

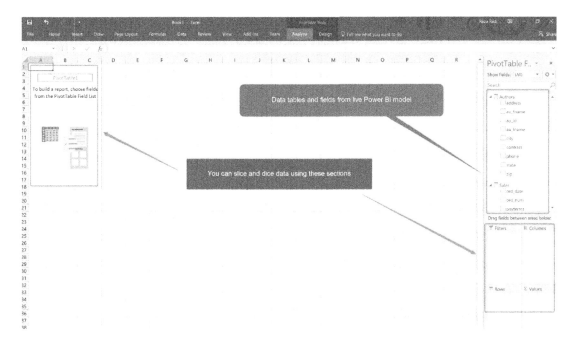

Figure 25-8. *PivotTable to explore the data from live Power BI Model*

Drag data fields into the slicing and dicing area (right under the fields pane), and you will see a result coming up in PivotTable as shown in Figure 25-9. This result is fetched live from Power BI model in the Power BI service.

Figure 25-9. *Exploring data with dragging fields into rows and columns and values*

Implicit Measures Won't Work in Excel

Implicit measures are measures that Power BI creates automatically. Power BI automatically applies auto summarization on numeric fields (that haven't been part of a relationship). Power BI behind the scenes is creating a measure for those fields; these measures are called Implicit measures. These are a measure displayed with a small Sum or Sigma icon beside their names, as seen in Figure 25-10.

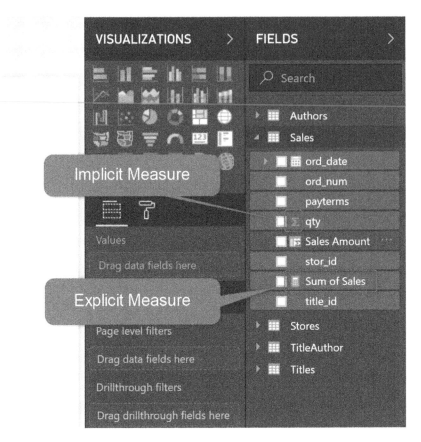

Figure 25-10. *Implicit vs. Explicit Measures*

Implicit measures cannot be used in the Analyze in Excel feature; if you try to drag them in the PivotTable, instead of seeing the aggregation or measure result, you will see individual values as shown in Figure 25-11.

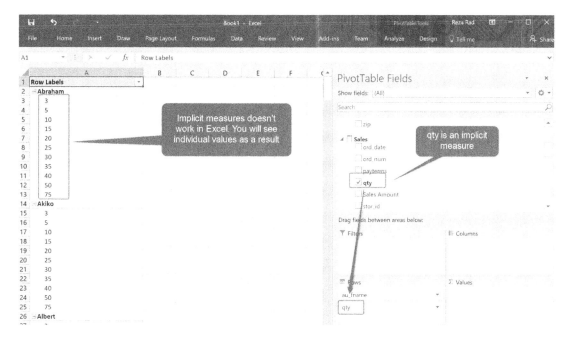

Figure 25-11. *Implicit Measures won't work in Analyze in Excel*

However, you can create explicit measures and use those from Analyze in Excel. Explicit measures are DAX measures created by you, similar to the one that is shown in Figure 25-12.

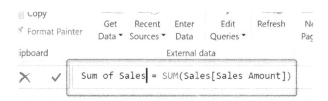

Figure 25-12. *Creating a measure explicitly*

You can use explicit measures in PivotTable in the same manner as a normal measure, and you see the correct and expected results in Excel. Compare Figure 25-13 with Figure 25-11. You can see in Figure 25-13 that the sales totals are displayed as expected, and that comes from using an explicit measure.

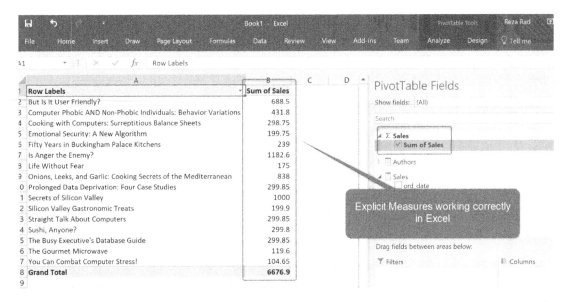

Figure 25-13. *Explicit measures work correctly in Excel*

If you want users to use Excel as their front-end tool to connect to Power BI Models, then you have to consider creating explicit measures.

Excel Is Connected Live to the Power BI Model in the Service

The wonderful thing about the Excel connection to the Power BI Service is that the connection is live. Live connection means that Excel fetches the data directly from the dataset in the Power BI service. Anytime you refresh the Excel file, you get the most up-to-date data from the service. This feature is completely different from Export to Excel. The Export to Excel option that you see on visuals in the Power BI service is only downloading data offline; however, Analyze in Excel is an online and live connection to the dataset.

You can check the connection properties in the Data tab, under Connections, in the Properties section. Figure 25-14 shows this section.

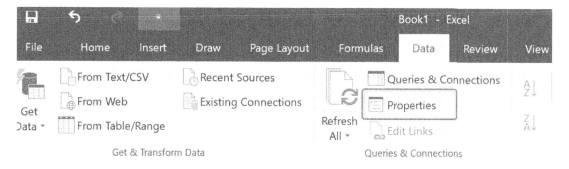

Figure 25-14. *Connection Properties in Excel*

The Connection properties will have an Azure address along with the ID of the dataset in the Power BI service. Look at Figure 25-15 for an example. You can use the connection in any other Excel file to connect to the same dataset.

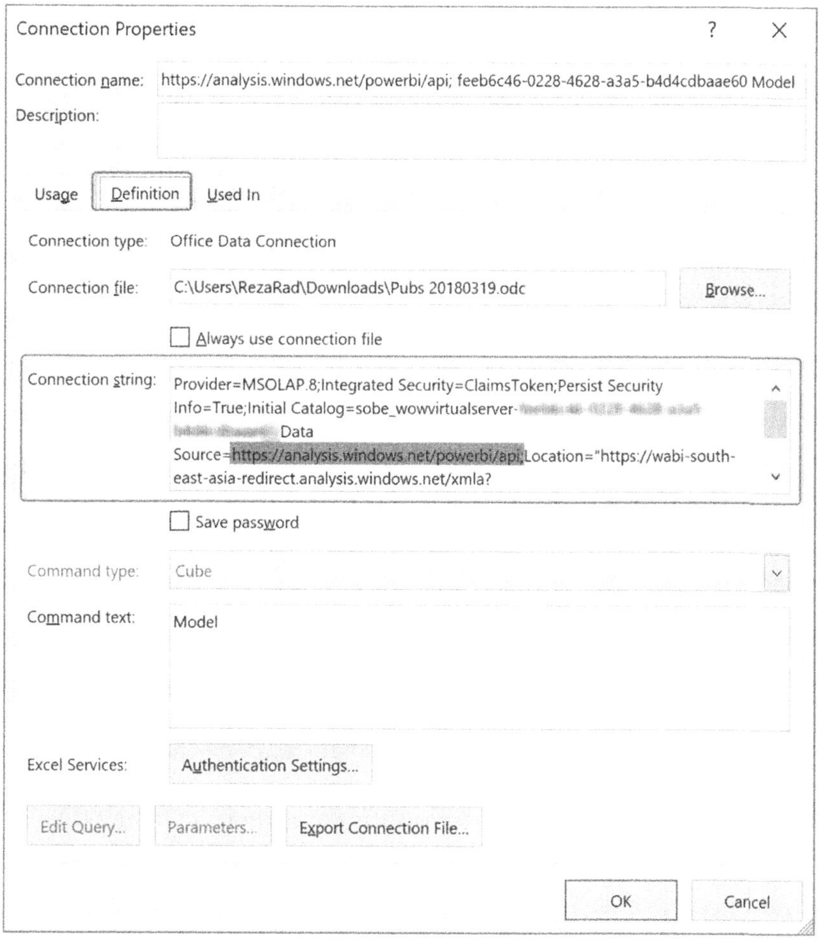

Figure 25-15. *Connection String points to the Power BI Model in the service*

Power BI Publisher for Excel

There is an add-in for Power BI integration with Excel, named Power BI Publisher for Excel. Power BI Publisher for Excel is a free add-in, which enables the two-way integration of Excel and Power BI. With Power BI Publisher for Excel, you can pin a range of cells into a Power BI dashboard, and this range of cells will be updated on a scheduled basis. You can also use the ability to connect to a data model in Power BI and start slicing and dicing it (same as Analyze in Excel). The steps below show how Power BI Publisher for Excel works.

To use the Power BI Publisher for Excel, download the add-in for free from here:

`https://powerbi.microsoft.com/en-us/excel-dashboard-publisher`

Figure 25-16 shows the download page as it exists at the time that I'm writing this chapter.

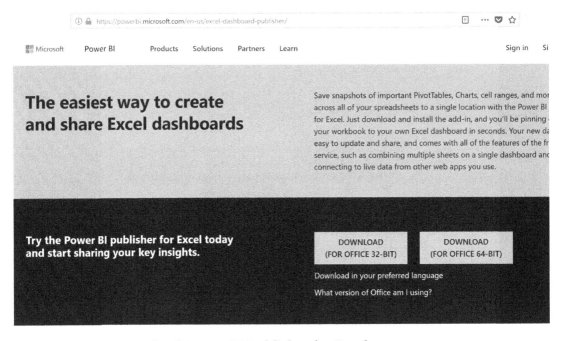

Figure 25-16. *Download Power BI Publisher for Excel*

Download the installer, run it, and follow the setup steps to install the Power BI Publisher for Excel. Figure 25-17 shows the beginning of the install process.

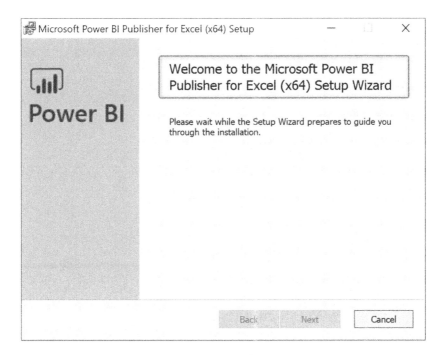

Figure 25-17. *Installing Power BI Publisher for Excel*

After installation, you can open a blank Excel document, and you will see a Power BI tab there. Figure 25-18 shows what that looks like.

Figure 25-18. *Menu options of Power BI Publisher for Excel*

The Power BI tab has two main action items: to connect to a model in Power BI or to pin an item into Power BI service.

Connect to Data

Connecting to a model in Power BI service is very similar to Analyze in Excel. When you click on Connect to Data, you will be asked to log in to your Power BI account information. Figure 25-19 shows the login prompt.

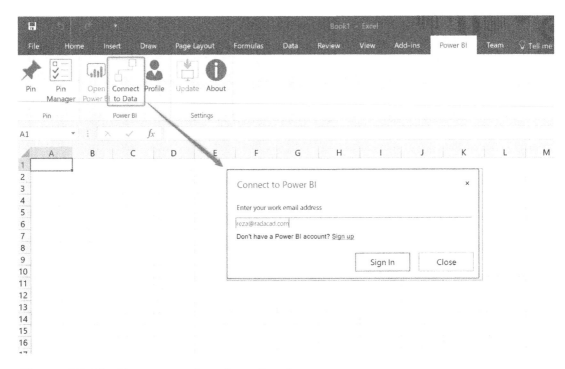

Figure 25-19. *Connect to data from Excel*

You then will be asked to choose a workspace, and then a dataset or report to connect to connect to that workspace. Figure 25-20 shows me connecting to a workspace named Power BI Course.

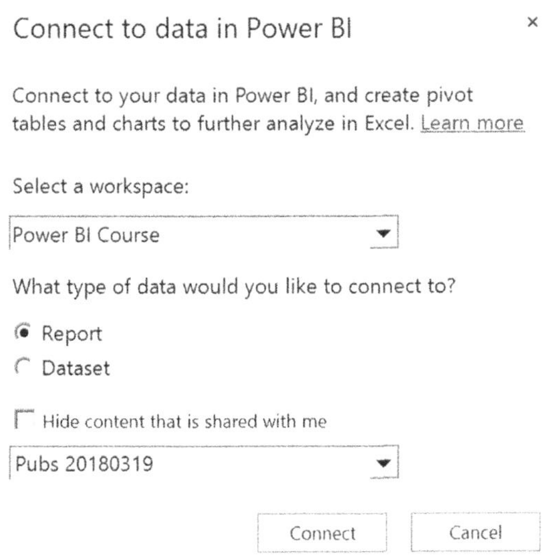

Figure 25-20. *Connecting to a report or dataset in the Power BI service*

Then the dataset will be accessible through a PivotChart, similar to the way in which Analyze in Excel works. In fact, there is no difference between Analyze in Excel and the Connect to Data in Power BI Publisher for Excel. Figure 25-21 shows an example, including the pivot table fields.

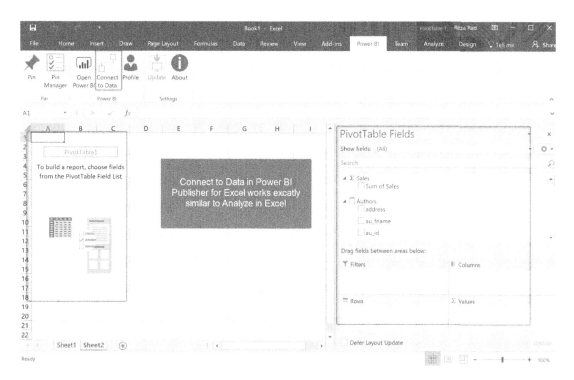

Figure 25-21. *Connect to Data works similar to Analyze in Excel*

Pin to a Power BI Dashboard

Another feature in Power BI Publisher for Excel (which is not available in Analyze in Excel), is that you can select a range of cells in Excel and Pin them to a Power BI Dashboard. Figure 25-22 shows a range of cells that are selected, and you can see the Pin option in the toolbar toward the upper left of the figure.

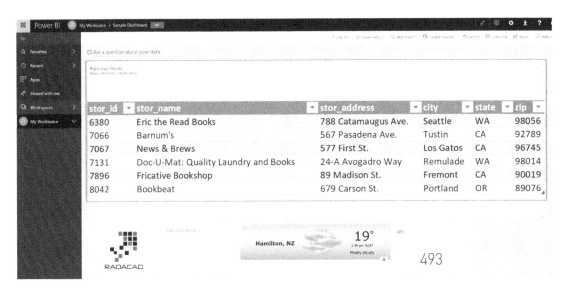

Figure 25-22. *Pin a range of cells to the dashboard*

You can either create a new dashboard or pin it to an existing dashboard. The range of cells then will be part of your dashboard, as shown in Figure 25-23. However, the range will not be interactive or editable. It will be more like a screenshot than editable values.

Figure 25-23. *Excel range of cells pinned to a Power BI dashboard*

The Excel range, however, will be updated in Excel. You can see the configuration in the Pin Manager menu option of the Power BI Publisher for Excel. Figure 25-24 shows this option.

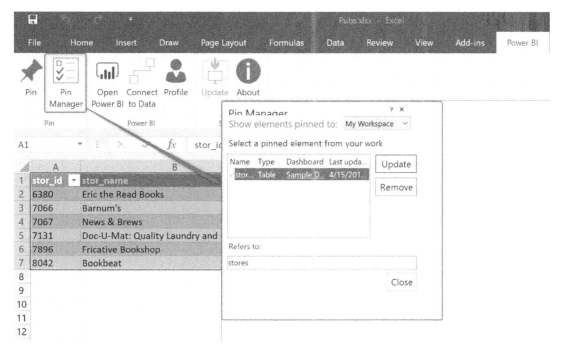

***Figure 25-24.** Pin Manager to check updates*

To get the pinned range of cells up to date, you need to save the Excel file. Figure 25-25 provides an example.

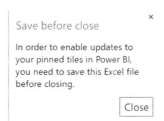

***Figure 25-25.** Saving Excel file to get the pinned items updated*

Power BI Publisher for Excel enables two-way integration between Power BI and Excel. You can connect to a Power BI model from Excel and slice and dice data with it, or you can pin part of an Excel spreadsheet into a Power BI dashboard.

Upload an Excel Workbook into Power BI Service

It is not that common to upload an Excel workbook into a service. However, if you want to have a single portal to share Excel workbooks, as well as the Power BI reports, this option would be a useful option to leverage. An Excel workbook uploaded into the service can be opened and edited with Excel Online or a local version of Excel. Here is an example of uploading an Excel workbook into the service.

In Power BI Service, click on Get Data, as shown in Figure 25-26.

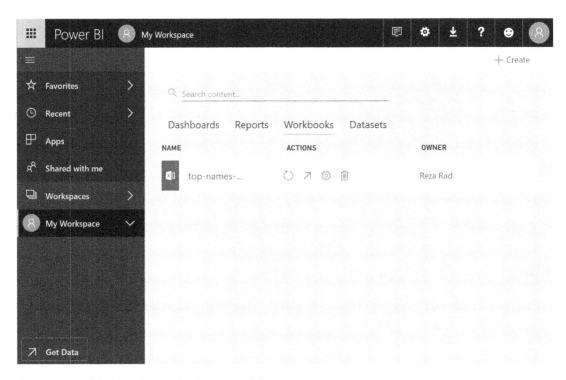

Figure 25-26. *Get Data in Power BI Service*

Select Files as a Data Source and then choose an Excel file. Figure 25-27 shows that Files has been selected as the data source.

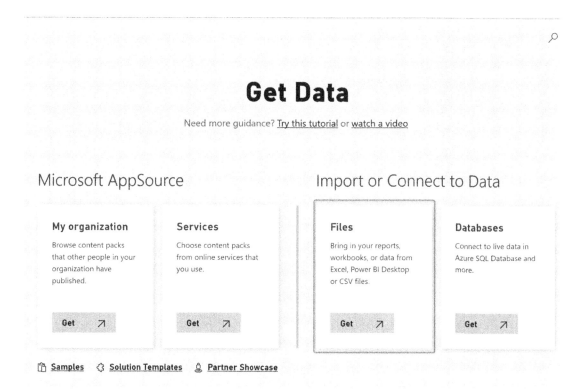

Figure 25-27. *Get Data from Files*

After selecting a specific file, then choose to Upload your Excel file into Power BI. Figure 25-28 shows this option.

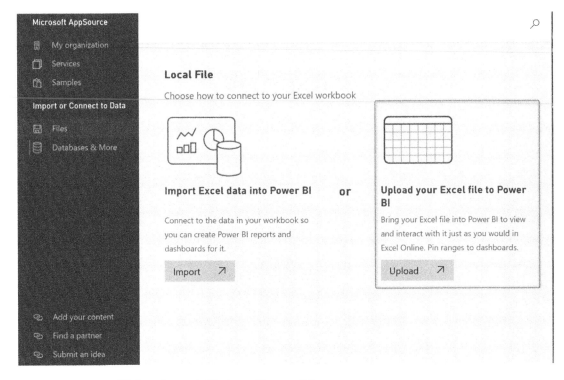

Figure 25-28. *Upload excel file into Power BI*

The Excel file will be then visible in the Workbooks tab of Power BI service. Figure 25-29 shows two such files, named Pubs and top-names-by-year.

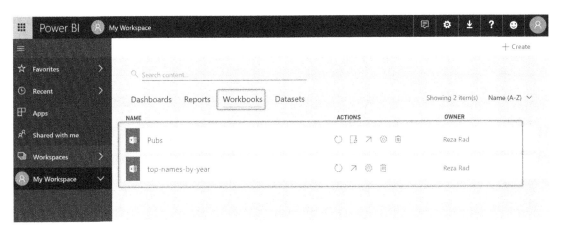

Figure 25-29. *Uploaded excel files are listed under Workbooks*

You can now click on the Excel file and edit it with Excel Online. Figure 25-30 shows the editing interface.

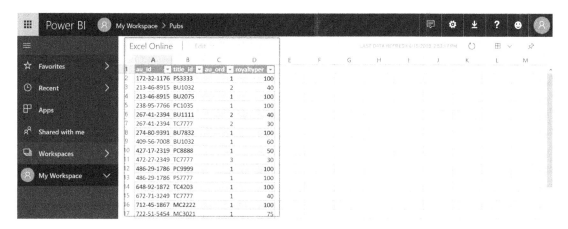

Figure 25-30. *Editing workbooks with Excel Online*

Having the Excel workbook uploaded into the Power BI service gives you the ability to interact with it using Excel Online, edit it, and change it while it is hosted in the same portal that Power BI reports are hosted there (Power BI service).

Import Excel into Power BI Desktop

We cannot talk about all integration options between Excel and Power BI without mentioning the most important developer option. You can import an Excel model that includes a Power Pivot model into Power BI. The Import into Power BI doesn't mean Get Data from Excel, it means the entire model including all the tables, relationships, and calculations will be imported into a Power BI report. Figure 25-31 shows how you navigate to the option of importing an Excel workbook's contents.

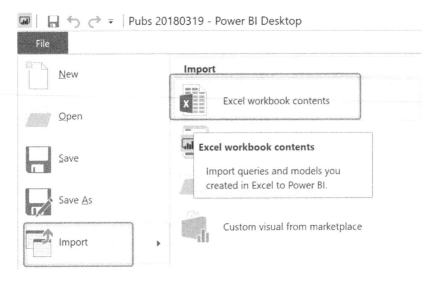

Figure 25-31. *Import Excel workbook content into Power BI Desktop model*

Importing an Excel workbook is a very easy and straightforward process. The only important note in this process is that your Excel file should not be password protected.

Summary

In this chapter, you've learned four methods that allow Excel and Power BI to work together. Each of the modes of integration will give you some features. Analyze in Excel will give you the ability to slice and dice the data model of Power BI service easily from Excel through PivotTable and PivotChart. Power BI Publisher for Excel has one step, also, to Analyze in Excel, which is pinning part of Excel content into a Power BI dashboard and updating it. Both these features mentioned will be highly well received by your business users who are good with Excel as a front-end tool.

You can upload your Excel file into the workbooks section of Power BI service; this feature will give users the ability to access the Excel content from the same portal that Power BI reports are hosted and edit the content with Excel Online. Last, but not least, you can import an entire Excel Power Pivot model with all its tables, relationships, and calculations into a Power BI report instead of re-creating it.

CHAPTER 26

Power BI Report Server

Power BI is not only a cloud-based reporting technology. Due to demand for some business for having their data and also reporting solutions on-premises, Power BI also has an option to be deployed fully on-premises. Power BI on-premises is called Power BI Report Server. This chapter is about using Power BI in a fully on-premises solution with Power BI Report Server.

In this chapter, you will learn everything you need to know about the on-premises world of Power BI. You will learn how to install Power BI Report Server, you will learn all requirements and configurations for Power BI Report Server to work correctly, and you will see all pros and cons of this solution. At the end of this chapter, you will be able to decide if Power BI on-premises is the right choice for your or not, and if it is, then you will be able to set a Power BI on-premises solution up and running easily.

What Is Power BI Report Server?

Power BI Report Server is a specific edition of SQL Server Reporting Services that can host Power BI reports. For running Power BI Report Server, you don't need to have SQL Server installation disk; the Report Server comes with its setup files. You can download setup files (explained in the very next section). Power BI Report Server can host Power BI reports as well as Reporting Services (SSRS) Reports.

With Power BI Report Server, there will be an instance of Power BI Desktop installation. The Power BI Desktop edition that comes with the report server should be used to create Power BI reports. Otherwise, reports cannot be hosted on the report server. The good news is that Power BI Desktop Report Server edition is regularly updated, and its experience will be very similar to the Power BI Desktop.

© Reza Rad 2018
R. Rad, *Pro Power BI Architecture*, https://doi.org/10.1007/978-1-4842-4015-1_26

Requirements for Setup

You need to download the latest edition of Power BI Report Server from this link:

`https://powerbi.microsoft.com/en-us/report-server/`

You will have two installation items: Power BI Report Server and Power BI Desktop Report Server edition (which comes in 32- and 64-bit versions).

Installing Power BI Report Server

Installation of Power BI Report Server is simple; just run the setup file, and continue the instructions. Figure 26-1 shows the beginning of the install process.

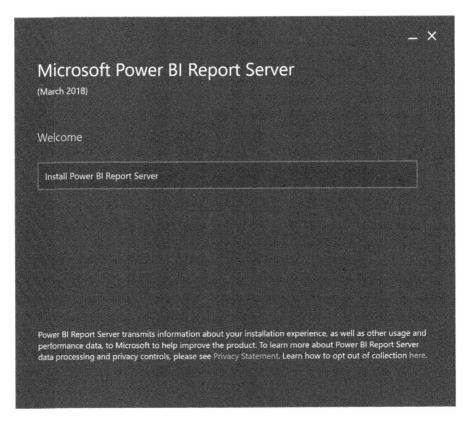

Figure 26-1. *Installing Power BI Report Server*

You can choose to have the evaluation edition (valid for six months) or to install the licensed version (licensing of Power BI Report Server comes later in this chapter). Figure 26-2 shows that I've chosen the evaluation edition.

Figure 26-2. *Choose the Edition*

Earlier in this chapter, I mentioned that you don't need to have SQL Server installed to get the Power BI Report Server. However, The SQL Server database engine is needed for the report server to run. If you don't have SQL Server installed, then don't worry; the Report Server setup process will install the database engine for you, as shown in Figure 26-3.

Figure 26-3. An instance of SQL Server database engine is required for the report server to work

The remaining steps of installation will be easy to go through to get the setup completed. Figure 26-4 shows the various packages being unpacked and installed.

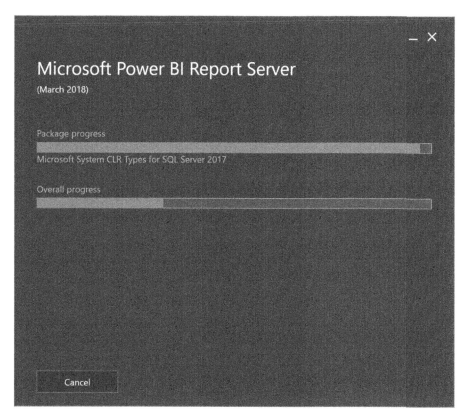

Figure 26-4. *Installation in progress*

After completing the setup, you can then open the configuration section by clicking on "Configure Report Server" as shown in Figure 26-5. The instructions, however, ask you to restart and then go to the report server. Both options are fine. If you decided to restart your server, then after restart, go to Start ➤ Programs ➤ Report Server Configuration Manager.

Figure 26-5. Configure report server

Configuring Power BI Report Server

To Configure the Report Server, you need to connect to the server that you've just installed. Usually, the instance name of this server is PBIRS. Figure 26-6 shows a connection being made.

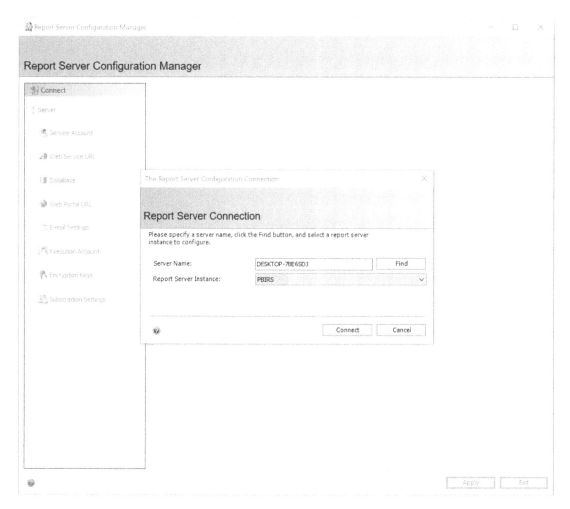

Figure 26-6. *Connect to the Report Server Configuration Manager*

After connecting, it is time to configure the server. The very first step is to configure a database. To configure a database, Click on Database in the left side tabs, and then click on Change Database as shown in Figure 26-7.

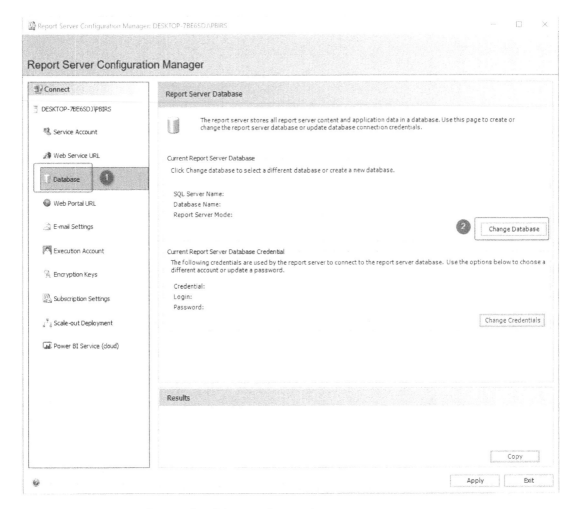

Figure 26-7. *Database tab of the configuration manager*

Database Setup

In the Change Database wizard, you can create databases for the report server. Select the option to "Create a new report server database" as in Figure 26-8. Then click on Next.

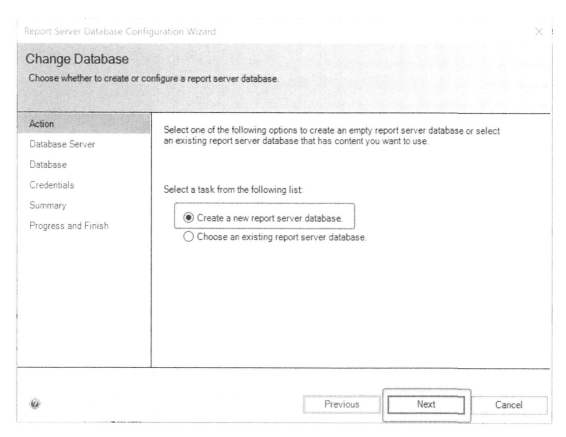

Figure 26-8. *Creating report server databases*

In the next step, shown in Figure 26-9, you need to connect to the SQL Server database instance that report server databases will be created there. If you have only one local instance of SQL Server database, then you can connect to it with a single dot (single dot means the local database server). If not, then you should enter the database server and username and password required for that. You can also test the connection afterward to make sure everything is correct.

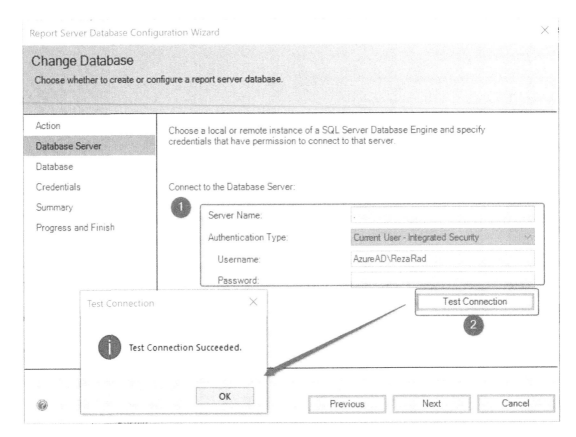

Figure 26-9. *Connecting the database engine*

Then, as illustrated in Figure 26-10, specify the database name and continue.
Figure 26-10 shows the default database name of ReportServer.

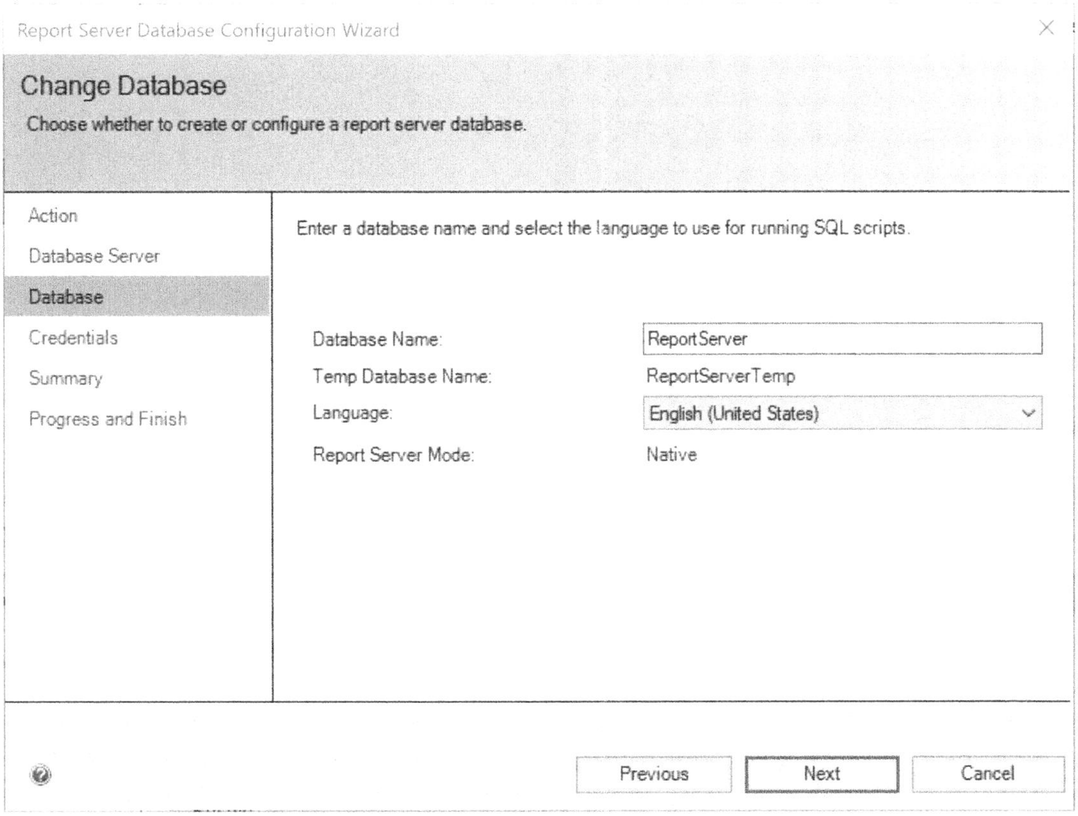

Report Server Database Configuration Wizard   × :

Change Database

Choose whether to create or configure a report server database.

Action	Enter a database name and select the language to use for running SQL scripts.
Database Server	
Database	
Credentials	Database Name: ReportServer
Summary	Temp Database Name: ReportServerTemp
Progress and Finish	Language: English (United States) ⌄
	Report Server Mode: Native

[Previous]   [Next]   [Cancel]

Figure 26-10. *The default name for the database is Report Server, but you can change it if you wish*

There will always be a second database called Temp database; you don't need to configure anything about it. Continue the wizard. In the next step, just set your credentials and continue. You can specify a username and password as shown in Figure 26-11.

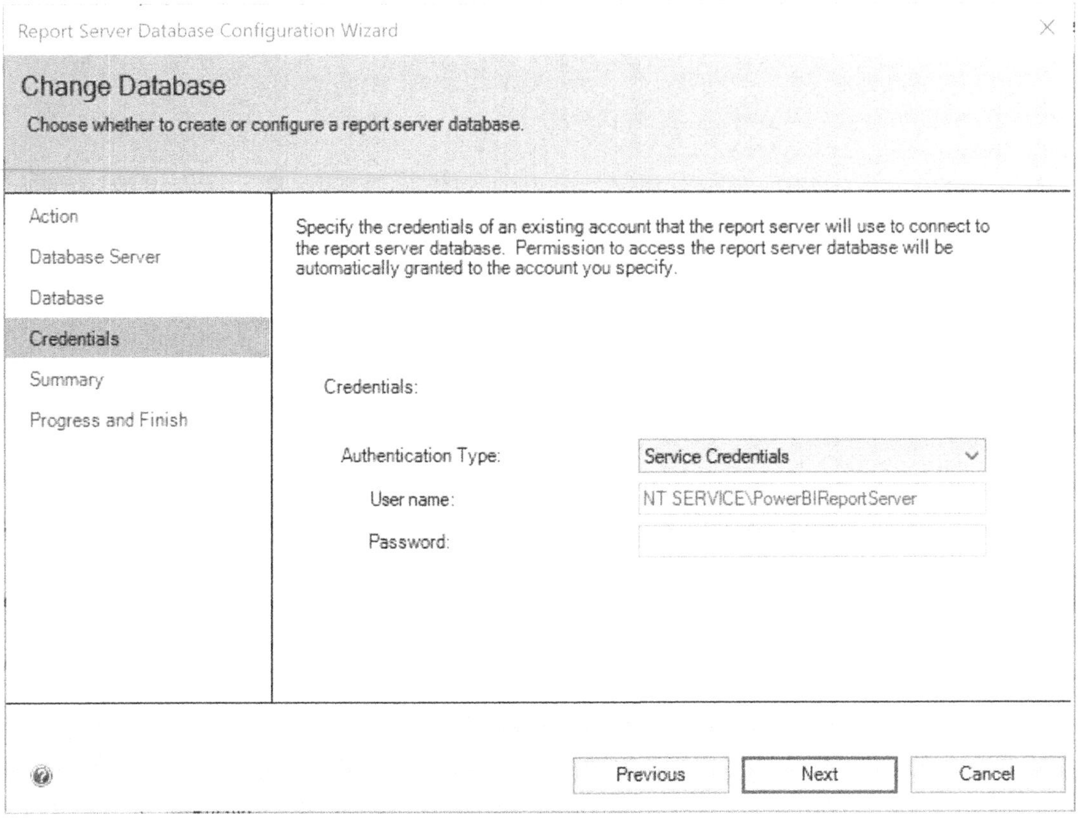

Figure 26-11. *Credential configuration for the database server*

After confirming things in the Summary step, the setup will continue and finishes soon after. The window in Figure 26-12 shows a successfully setup of database creation.

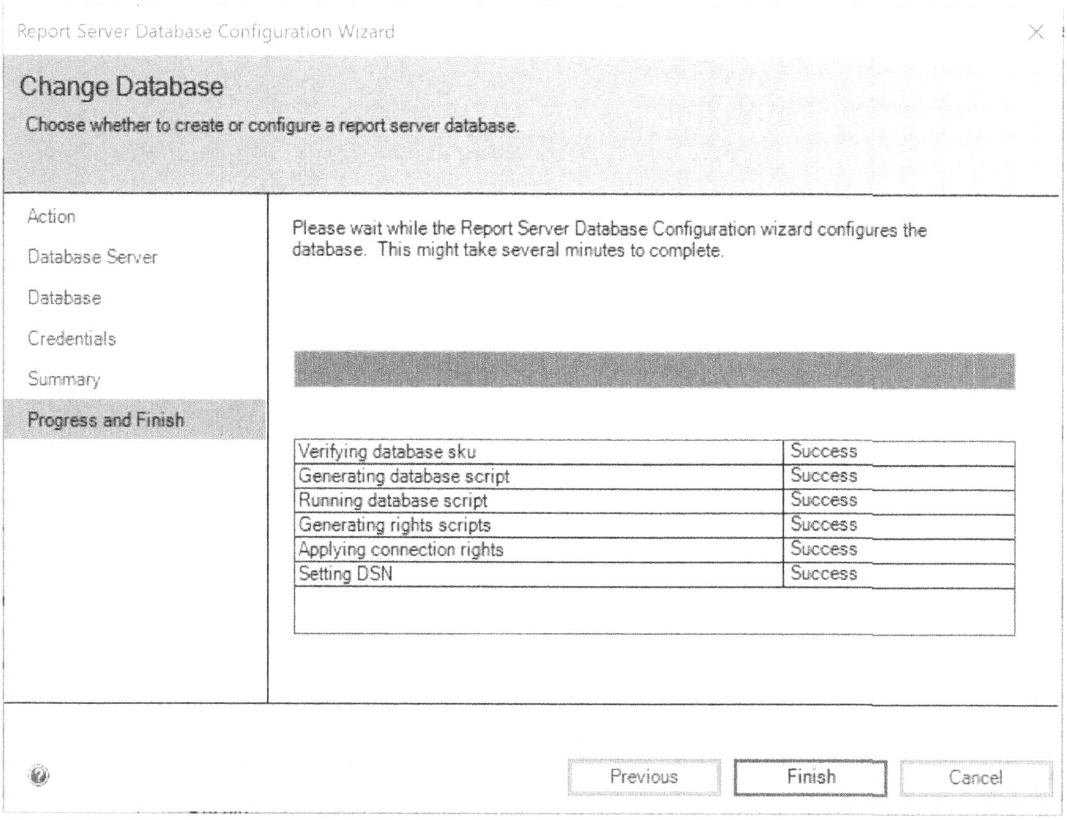

Figure 26-12. *Databases for report server set up correctly*

Click on Finish. Create database setup is done now. Your next step is to set up URLs.

Web URL Setup

Report Server needs to get the web URLs to work. There are two URLs that you must configure. The first is for the web service. The next is for the web portal.

Web Service Setup

To create the web service, click on the Web Service URL in the left side tab. Figure 26-13 shows the Web Service URL configuration page.

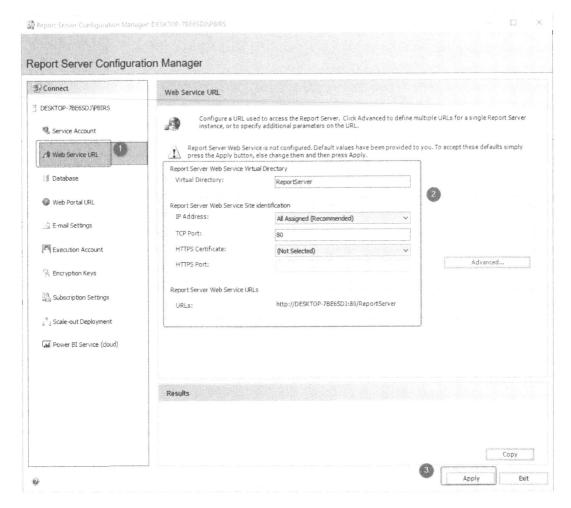

Figure 26-13. *Web Service URL configuration*

You can set up configurations such as the address of the server, the port that this web service will be running, and any other configurations. If you go ahead with a basic setup, you don't need to change anything here; just click on Apply.

Changing the configuration in the above screenshot is only required when you want to set it up on a different port, or different server, with a specific configuration. If you want to do that, it is best to consult with a web admin in your organization.

After a successful setup for this step, you should see messages and a URL that you can click on to open the report server's web service. Notice, for example, the highlighted URL in Figure 26-14.

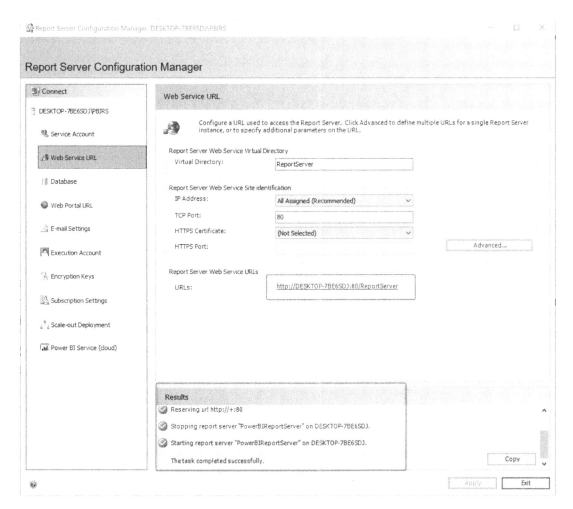

Figure 26-14. *Creating the Web Service URL*

If you click on the URL, you should see the web service's page open and run without any issues or errors. Figure 26-15 shows an example of what that service page will look like.

Figure 26-15. *Web Service URL browsed in a web browser*

In the report server's page, you won't see anything except the version of the Report server and the name of it. Later when you upload Power BI files, you'll be able to see the content there.

Web Portal Setup

To set up the web portal, click on Web Portal URL in the left-hand side tabs. You can then configure the service as needed using the interface in Figure 26-16. When you're done, click on Apply.

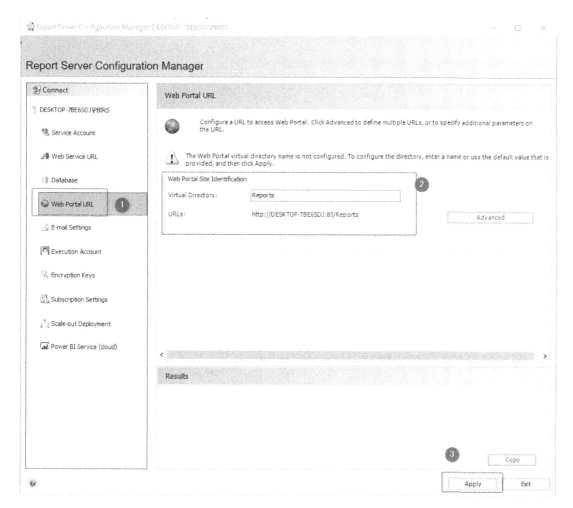

Figure 26-16. *Web Portal URL configuration*

If the configuration process finishes successfully, you will see a success message such as is shown at the bottom of Figure 26-17. Then you can click on the Web Portal URL to open it in a browser window, as in Figure 26-18.

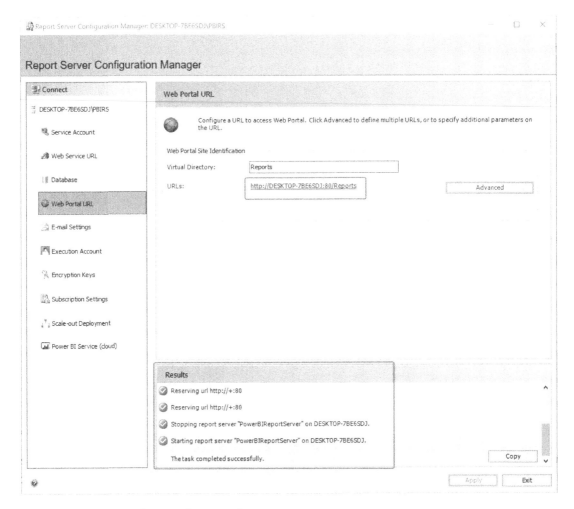

Figure 26-17. *Web portal created*

The web portal should show you the environment of Power BI Report Server's admin view. There is no content in the server yet. Later on in this chapter, we'll be adding content to this server.

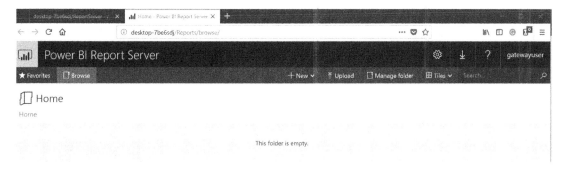

Figure 26-18. *Power BI Report Server Web Portal*

Installation and configuration of the Power BI Report Server are now finished. You can close the Report Server Configuration Manager.

Installing Power BI Desktop Report Server

Power BI reports that you can host in the report server need to be developed with a specific edition of Power BI Desktop called Power BI Desktop Report Server. You get this edition of Power BI Desktop from the same link that you download the report server from. Figure 26-19 shows the installer.

Figure 26-19. *Installing Power BI Desktop for the Report Server*

451

After a successful installation, you can open the Power BI Desktop Report Server. The Power BI Desktop Report Server appears as in Figure 26-20. The interface is similar to the normal Power BI Desktop interface.

Figure 26-20.   *Power BI Desktop Report Server looks very similar to normal Power BI Desktop*

Developing Reports with Power BI Report Server

You can start creating a report in the Power BI Desktop Report Server similar to the way that you do it in a normal Power BI Desktop. The report development experience in these two editions is very similar. You can even open a report developed with normal Power BI Desktop in the Power BI Desktop Report Server. Figure 26-21 shows an open report.

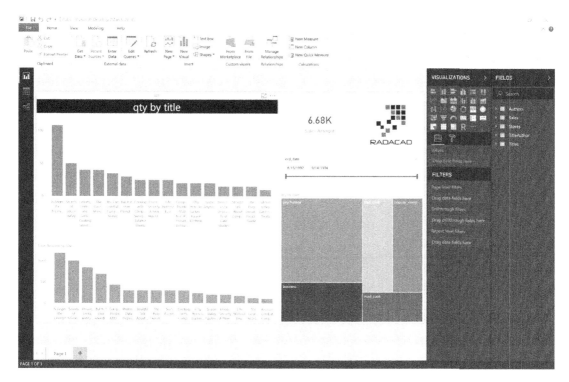

Figure 26-21. *A report from Power BI Desktop opened in Power BI Desktop Report Server*

You can run normal Power BI Desktop and the Power BI Desktop Report Server at the same time on your system. Power BI Desktop Report Server is slightly behind the Power BI Desktop. It often takes a few weeks for features added in Power BI Desktop to be implemented in Power BI Desktop Report Server. Figure 26-22 shows some of the differences that you will see in the available Options for the two products.

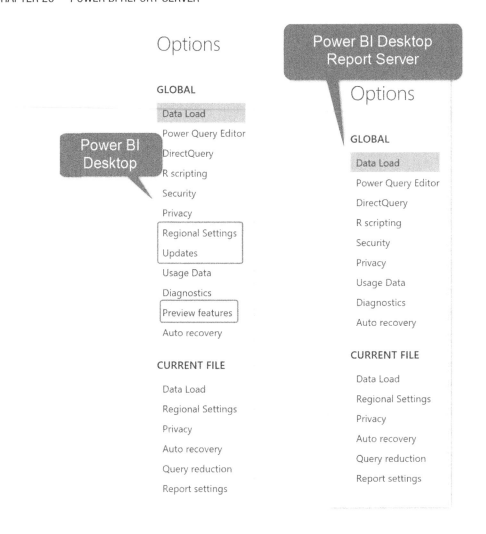

Figure 26-22. *Differences between Power BI Desktop and Power BI Desktop Report Server*

Publish Report to the Report Server

There are two ways to publish the Power BI report to the report server. One way is from the Power BI Desktop Report Server edition. First, you need to set up the URL to your report server. Go to File menu, and from Open, select Power BI Report Server as shown in Figure 26-23.

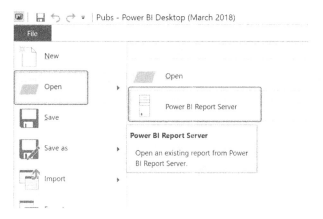

Figure 26-23. *Connecting to Power BI Report Server from Power BI Desktop*

In this window, you can connect to a report server. Enter the Web Portal URL from the step of configuring the report server. Figure 26-24 shows such an address at the bottom of the page.

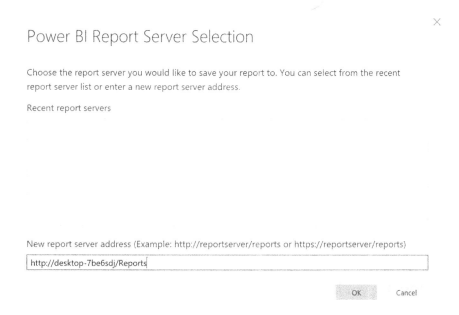

Figure 26-24. *Report Server URL is needed to connect to the Power BI Report Server*

After successful deployment, you will see a message with a link to the report. Figure 26-25 shows an example.

Figure 26-25. *Publishing to the Power BI Report Server*

Figure 26-26 shows an example of a report hosted on Power BI Report Server. The report will be a fully interactive report like a Power BI report hosted in the service.

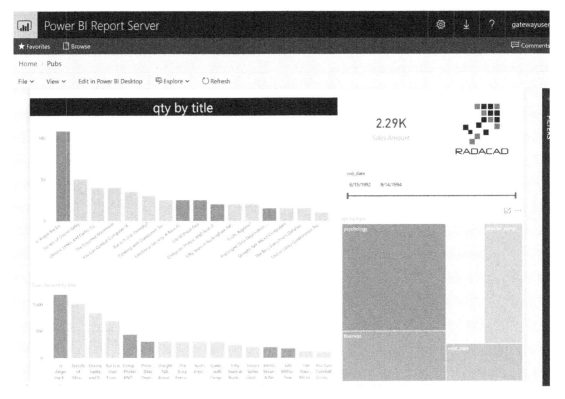

Figure 26-26. *Reports are fully interactive in the Power BI Report Server*

Figure 26-27 shows another way to publish a Power BI report to the report server. You can do so by choosing the Upload option from the web portal's toolbar.

Figure 26-27. *Uploading Power BI reports to the Report Server*

Managing Datasets on the Report Server

A Power BI report published to the report server can be configured to refresh. To do this configuration, open the report server web portal, and click on the more options of the Power BI report. See Figure 26-28 for an example.

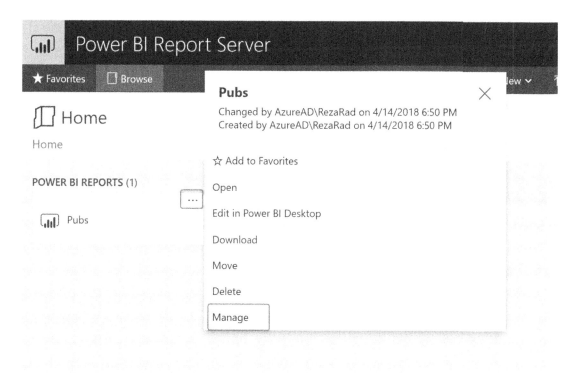

Figure 26-28. *Manage the dataset of the report on the Report Server*

In the Manage tab of a report, you can configure things such as data source configuration, connection to the data source, and schedule refresh if required. Figure 26-29 shows the Manage tab for a report named Pubs.

457

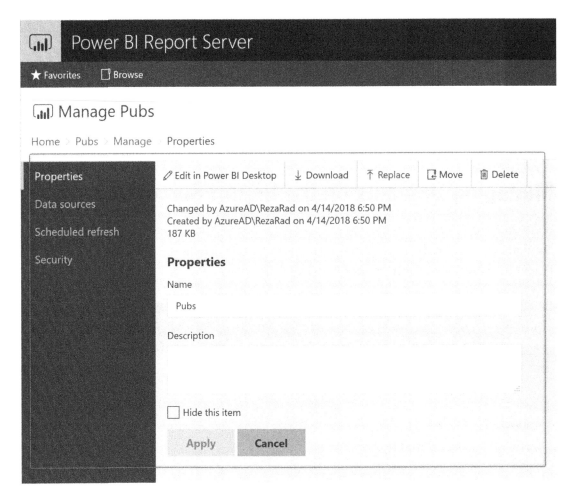

Figure 26-29. Dataset properties configuration in Power BI Report Server

Schedule Refresh Requirement

If your report is sourced from a file, then you may have some requirements to schedule the report for a refresh. You first need to source the file from a network path, as shown in Figure 26-30.

Figure 26-30. *Scheduled data refresh is only available for files with a shared network drive path*

If you use a network shared path to access to the source file, then you can set up the connection to the file as shown in Figure 26-31.

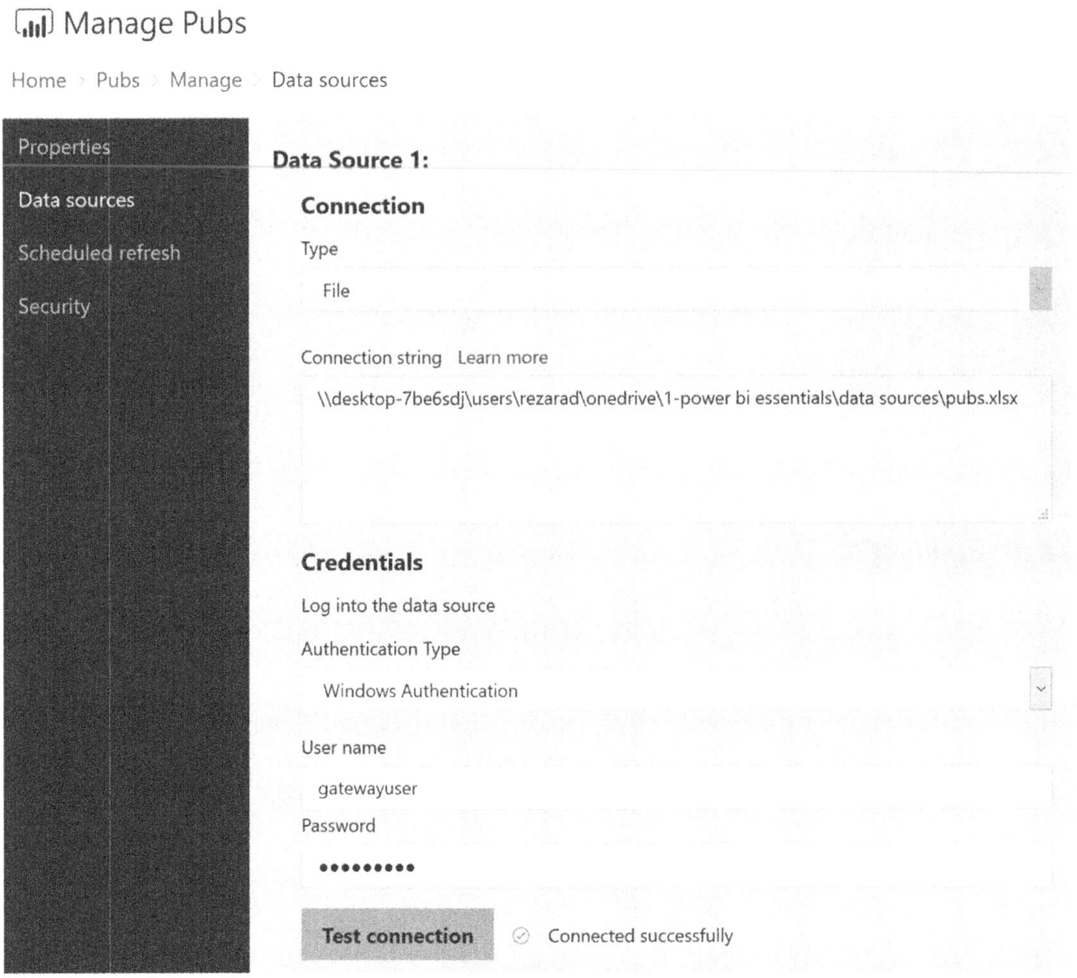

Figure 26-31. *Setting up credentials for the data source connection and testing the connection*

Make sure to click on Save after this step. Otherwise, you won't be able to schedule the refresh process.

Then click on the Scheduled refresh option in the left sidebar, as shown in Figure 26-32. From there, you can create a scheduled refresh plan.

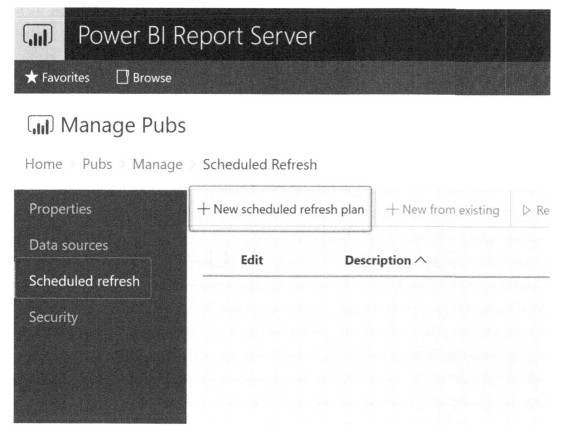

Figure 26-32. *Creating scheduled refresh plan for the dataset*

The scheduled refresh configuration of the report server has many more options compared to the Power BI Service; you can choose to schedule hourly, daily, weekly, monthly, or any custom period. You can choose the start and end dates and many other configurations. Figure 26-33 shows some of the scheduling options that are available to you.

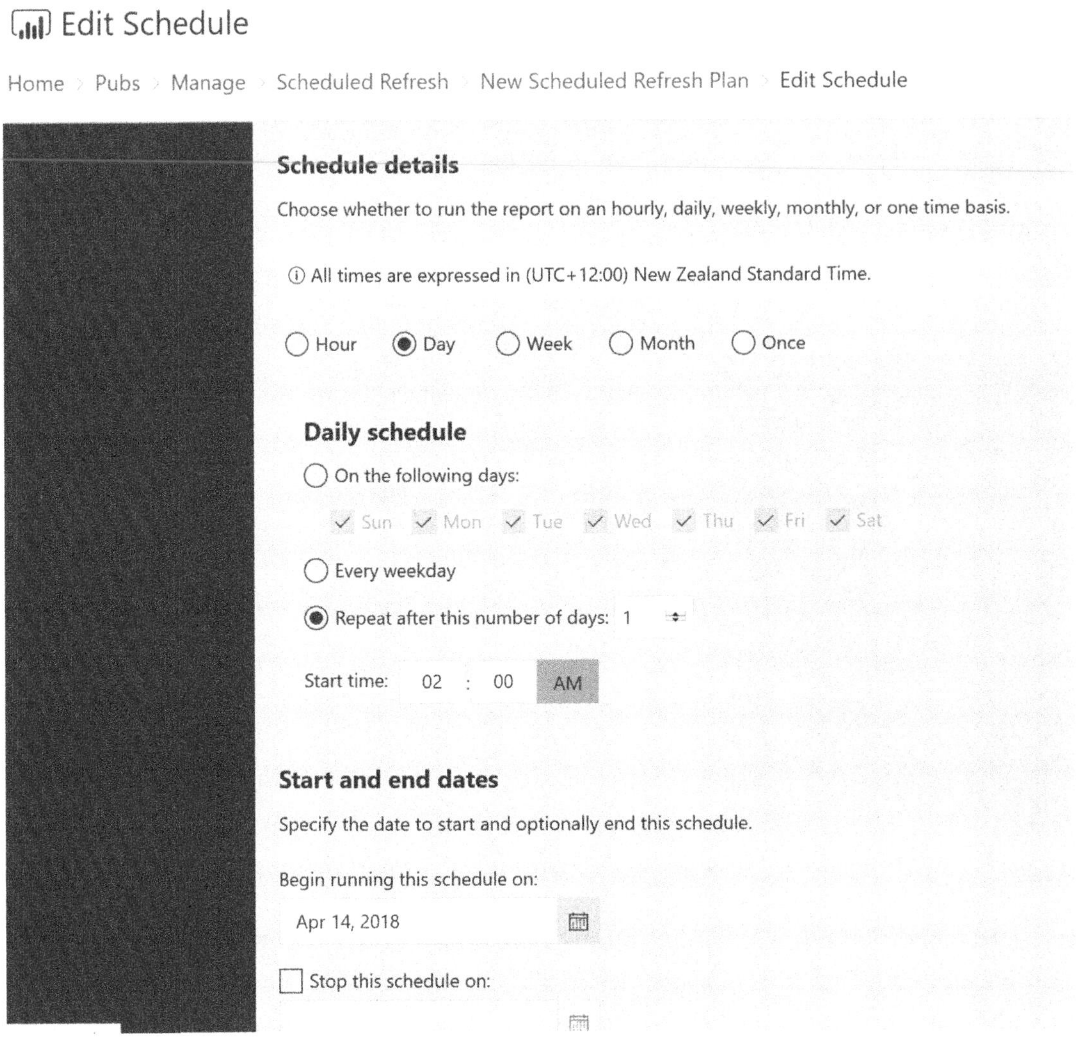

⌊ⅆⅉ Edit Schedule

Home > Pubs > Manage > Scheduled Refresh > New Scheduled Refresh Plan > Edit Schedule

Schedule details

Choose whether to run the report on an hourly, daily, weekly, monthly, or one time basis.

ⓘ All times are expressed in (UTC+12:00) New Zealand Standard Time.

○ Hour   ⦿ Day   ○ Week   ○ Month   ○ Once

Daily schedule

○ On the following days:

☑ Sun ☑ Mon ☑ Tue ☑ Wed ☑ Thu ☑ Fri ☑ Sat

○ Every weekday

⦿ Repeat after this number of days: 1

Start time: 02 : 00   AM

Start and end dates

Specify the date to start and optionally end this schedule.

Begin running this schedule on:

Apr 14, 2018   🗓

☐ Stop this schedule on:

🗓

Figure 26-33. *More detailed scheduling options are available with Power BI Report Server*

The important point for the scheduled refresh plan to be successful is that the SQL Server Agent service should be up and running.

In the Scheduled Refresh section, you will also be able to see a list of configurations and their status. Figure 26-34 shows such a list, with just one entry named Daily Refresh.

Figure 26-34. *Monitoring scheduled refresh plans*

Pros and Cons of Report Server

Power BI Report Server comes with advantages and disadvantages. These are each briefly described in the following sections.

No Gateway Needed

Yes, you read it right; with Power BI Report Server, you do not need a gateway. A gateway is only for all connections from Power BI Service. A gateway is responsible for connecting the dataset from Power BI Service to the data source on-premises. With the Power BI Report Server, everything is hosted on-premises. You do not need to install or configure the gateway.

All Types of Connections Are Supported

At the very early releases of Power BI Report Server, you could have only created a live connection to SQL Server Analysis Services from Power BI reports. Nowadays, you can use any types of connections. The example you have seen earlier in this chapter used Import Data and then scheduled the report to refresh. You can also use the DirectQuery connection or the Live Connection to Power BI Report Server.

The screenshot in Figure 26-35 is an example of data source management for a Live Connection Power BI report.

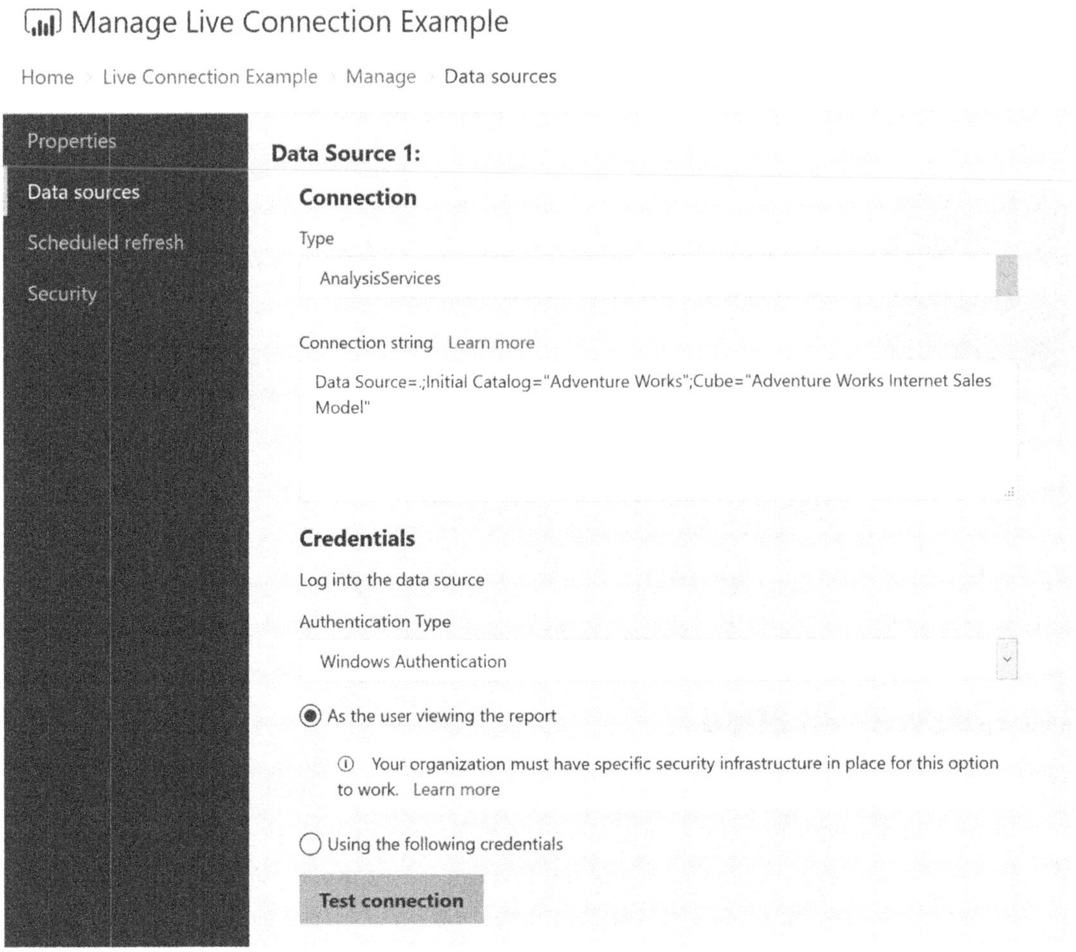

Figure 26-35. Connecting to Analysis Services with Power BI Report Server

Power BI Report Server Is a Fully On-Premises Solution

I am writing this chapter while I am flying on a 17-hour flight: my first leg from New Zealand to the United Kingdom with no Internet connection. All of the examples, and screenshots you have seen running are without any Internet connection. Power BI Report Server is a fully on-premises solution. You will not publish your reports to Power BI website, and you will not need any cloud-based technology for that to work.

Power BI Report Server is an on-premises technology choice for companies who are not yet ready to move to cloud-based technologies.

Power BI Service Features Are Not Available

Power BI Report Server has many great features. However, it also has some drawbacks. One of the main drawbacks of the Power BI Report Server is isolation from the Power BI Service. You won't get great features of the Power BI website on the report server. In the website, we have features such as usage metrics of the report, Power BI apps, Q&A and quick insights, and many other features, which are not available at the moment in the report server.

The Report Server team, however, is working hard to make these features available in the on-premises version sometime in the future.

Licensing of the Report Server

Power BI Report Server comes in only two types of licensing: Power BI Premium or SQL Server Enterprise License with Software Assurance. I have explained about the licensing requirements in the licensing chapter.

Summary

The Power BI Report Server is an on-premises reporting technology. With the Power BI Report Server, you bring interactive Power BI reports into on-premises servers. This type of technology is based on SQL Server Reporting Services technology. You will need to set up Power BI Report Server alongside with a specific edition of Power BI Desktop.

There are some pros and cons for the Report server. With Power BI Report Server, you can host reports fully on-premises with no need for a Power BI website. You will not need a gateway, and all types of connections (Scheduled Refresh, DirectQuery, and Live Connection) are supported. The Power BI Report Server, however, doesn't have all the features and functionalities available in the Power BI Service.

The Power BI Report Server needs a specific licensing, which comes either from Power BI Premium or SQL Server Enterprise License with Software Assurance.

CHAPTER 27

SQL Server Reporting Services

Power BI Report Server can host Power BI reports on-premises, and you've learned about it in the previous chapter. There is another integration between SQL Server Reporting Services and Power BI service; this integration brings tiles from SSRS reports pinned to a Power BI dashboard with scheduled updates from SQL Server agent. The integration of SSRS reports into Power BI service will create a link from the Power BI dashboard to SSRS detailed reports.

In this chapter, you will learn what the requirements are to get the SSRS report's elements pinned to a Power BI dashboard, and you will learn about the process in detail. Integrating SSRS reports into Power BI dashboards will create one single portal to access a reporting solution. Users will be able to open the Power BI dashboard and navigate from there to the detailed paginated SSRS report.

Setup Requirements

For SSRS Integration to work with Power BI, you will need:

- SQL Server 2016 or higher

- SQL Server Reporting Services 2016 or higher

- SQL Server Agent should be up and running

- Only charts, gauges, and maps can be pinned to Power BI Reports

- Power BI Integration should be enabled

- Stored Credentials should be used for the data sources of SSRS reports

Let's look at these requirements through an example.

467

© Reza Rad 2018
R. Rad, *Pro Power BI Architecture*, https://doi.org/10.1007/978-1-4842-4015-1_27

Prerequisites for the Example

To run this chapter's example, you will need to have SQL Server Reporting Services installed and available. You will also need an instance of SQL Server running the Adventure Works example database.

Enable Power BI Integration

The first action for the integration is to enable Power BI Integration in the Reporting Services Configuration Manager. Open Reporting Service Configuration Manager, and then go to the Power BI Service tab at the left-hand side as shown in Figure 27-1.

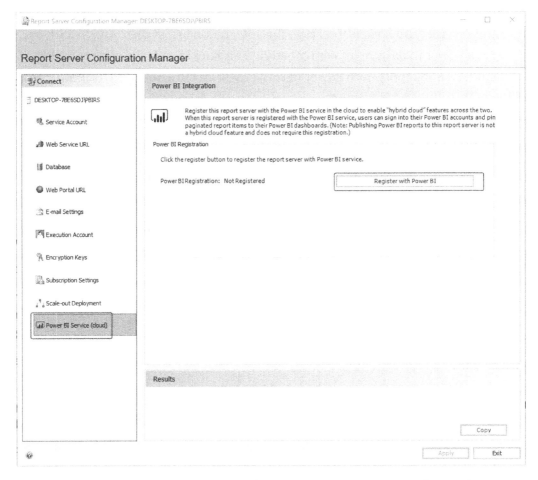

Figure 27-1. *Power BI Integration in the Reporting Services Configuration Manager*

Click on Register with Power BI and log in to your Power BI account. After registering with your account, you will see a screen such as in Figure 27-2.

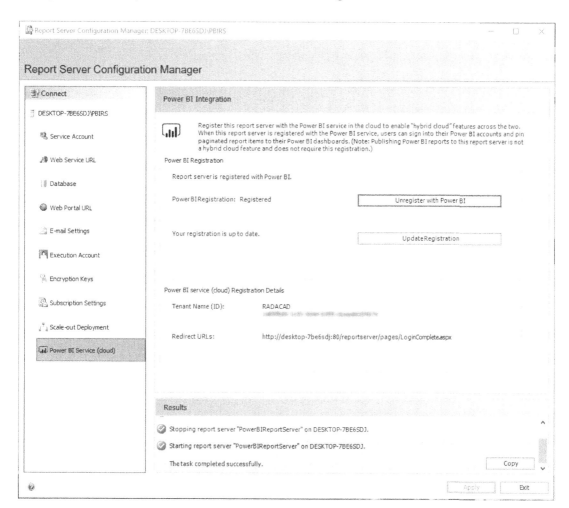

Figure 27-2. *Power BI Integration is enabled*

Pin Report Elements into Power BI Dashboard

If you open an SSRS report, you will see the Power BI pin option at the top of the report in the reporting services portal. Figure 27-3 shows the pin icon, which is highlighted by a square, red box.

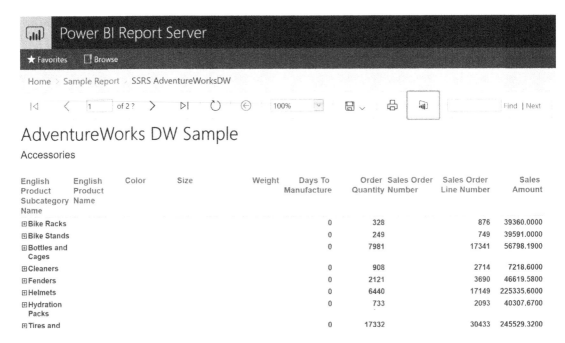

Figure 27-3. *Power BI pin icon in the Reporting Services*

You can click on the Power BI icon to start pinning elements into the Power BI service. If you don't have any charts in your report, you cannot pin any item on the dashboard. Only charts can be pinned. If you have no charts available to be pinned, you'll receive a message like that in Figure 27-4.

Figure 27-4. *Only Charts, gauges, and maps can be pinned*

When you pin an item for the first time, you will be asked to log in with your Power BI username and password. Figure 27-5 shows the login prompt.

Figure 27-5. *Sign in to Power BI*

After signing in, you will be asked to authorize SSRS to access Power BI account information, as shown in Figure 27-6.

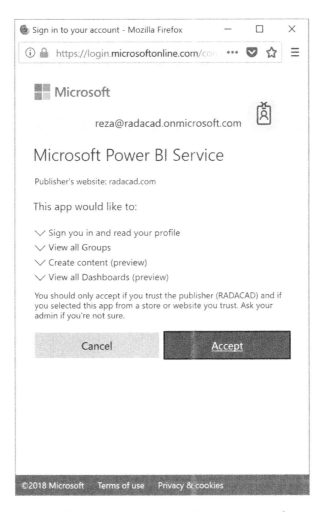

Figure 27-6. *Authorize SSRS to access Power BI account information*

After going through the login process, you will see all items that you can pin to the dashboard. Figure 27-7 shows such a list, and you can click on items to pin them.

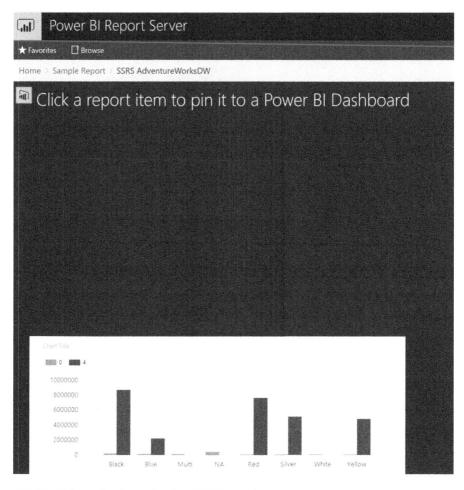

Figure 27-7. *Select the item in the SSRS to pin*

When you click on an element to be pinned, you will be asked which workspace and dashboard you want the element to be pinned to. You'll also be asked to specify the refresh frequency. Figure 27-8 shows a report item being pinned to a dashboard named Big Data Meetup in the workspace named My Workspace. A refresh interval of Daily has been specified, so the pinned item will refresh each new day.

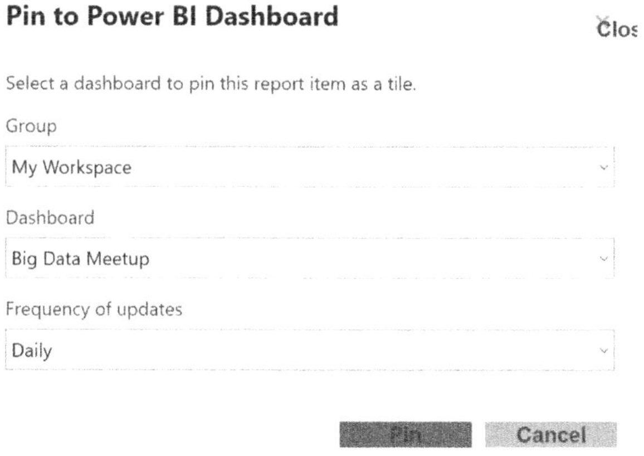

Pin to Power BI Dashboard

Select a dashboard to pin this report item as a tile.

Group

My Workspace

Dashboard

Big Data Meetup

Frequency of updates

Daily

Pin   Cancel

Figure 27-8. *Select dashboard to pin the SSRS element*

An important part of pinning items to Power BI from SSRS is that your SQL Server Agent Service should be up and running. The agent service is responsible for updating the tile in the Power BI dashboard.

After successfully pinning the item, you will see a message such as in Figure 27-9, explaining the process was successful.

Pin Successful

The visual has been successfully pinned to "Big Data Meetup".

See it in Power BI here.

Close

Figure 27-9. *Pin successful*

You can then open the dashboard in Power BI, and you will see the chart element from SSRS pinned there. Figure 27-10 shows an example of a pinned element as it appears in a dashboard.

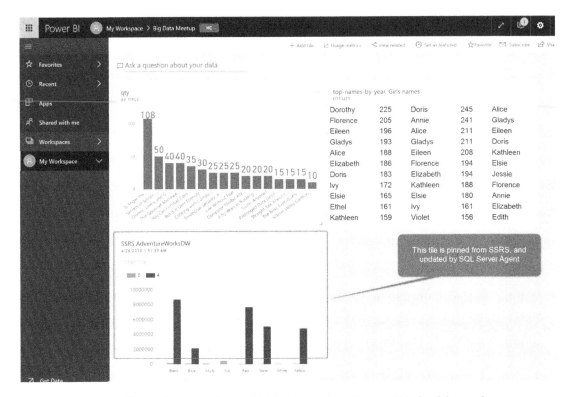

Figure 27-10. *Chart element from SSRS pinned to Power BI dashboard*

The tile will be updated from SQL Server agent. Every time you click on the chart, you will be redirected to the SSRS report. If you click to edit details of the tile, you can see the link to the SSRS report as shown toward the right in Figure 27-11.

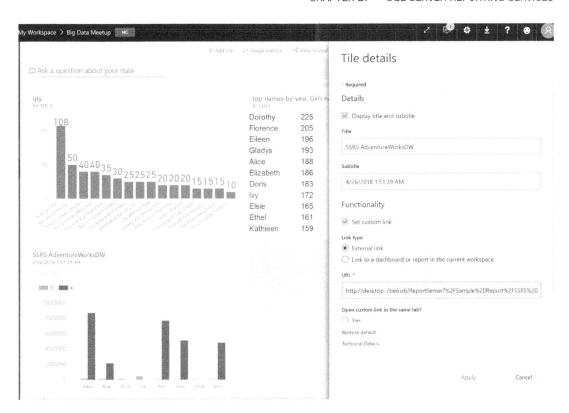

Figure 27-11. *Tile in Power BI redirects users to SSRS report*

SQL Server Agent

As you learned earlier in this chapter, the SQL Server agent is responsible for keeping that tile up to date in the Power BI Dashboard. After pinning the SSRS report element into Power BI, you can check SQL Server Agent and see that there is an agent job created for this process. Figure 27-12 shows such an agent job that has been created for a pinned item.

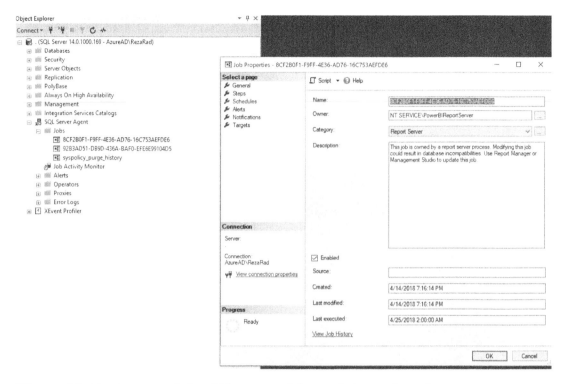

Figure 27-12. *An agent job will be created for each item pinned*

The SQL Server agent also has a schedule as shown in Figure 27-13. You can change the schedule to match your needs.

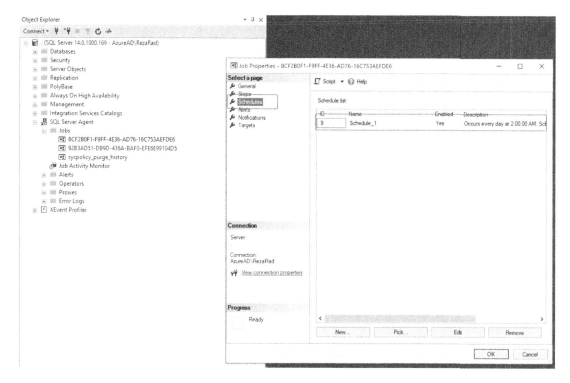

Figure 27-13. *Changing schedule of the update*

Summary

This chapter was a quick chapter about how charts from SSRS reports can be pinned into a Power BI Dashboard. For using this functionality, some requirements need to be met. You have to use SQL Server 2016 or a higher version. Your dataset of the report should be using saved credentials. SSRS reports should have charts, gauges, or maps, because only charts, gauges, and maps can be pinned to the dashboard. Power BI Integration in the reporting services configuration manager should be enabled. And finally; SQL Server agent should be up and running because Agent is responsible for keeping that tile up to date.

Using the integration of SSRS and Power BI, you can have tiles in the Power BI dashboard that point to SSRS reports for the detailed paginated report. Power BI users will use normal tiles for interactive reports, and they can use SSRS tiles when they want to see the more detailed paginated report in SSRS. The integration of SSRS and Power BI creates a single portal to access all reporting items, which would be from the Power BI dashboard.

CHAPTER 28

Real-Time Streaming with Power BI

One of the methods for creating a real-time dashboard is using Azure Stream Analytics. The Azure Stream Analytics can be combined with Azure IOT and Event Hub to get data from IoT (Internet of Things) devices. In this chapter, I'll explain to you all steps necessary to push output from a .NET application through Azure Event Hub, and Azure Stream Analytics to Power BI. You will see how to create a real-time dashboard with this method.

There is a prerequisite. You need an Azure account for running a sample of this chapter. The Azure account can be created with a free trial of one month. To create an Azure account, go to Portal.Azure.com.

You also need Visual Studio 2015 Professional or Community. This is because a .NET application will be used as the source of the data.

Architecture

The diagram in Figure 28-1 shows the architecture of this chapter's example.

Figure 28-1. *Architecture for the solution*

© Reza Rad 2018
R. Rad, *Pro Power BI Architecture*, https://doi.org/10.1007/978-1-4842-4015-1_28

IoT Devices or Applications can pass their data to Azure Event Hub, and the Azure Event Hub can be used as an input to Azure Stream Analytics (which is a data streaming Azure service). Then Azure Stream Analytics can pass the data from input based on queries to outputs. If Power BI is used as an output, then a dataset in Power BI will be generated that can be used for the real-time dashboard.

As a result, anytime a new data point from application or IoT device comes through Event Hubs, and then Stream Analytics, the Power BI dashboard will automatically update with new information.

Azure Event Hub

Azure Event Hub is the entry point of the data from applications. Start by creating an Event Hub. First go to Portal.Azure.com. Then in the Azure portal, select New, then Data + Analytics, and click on Event Hubs as shown in Figure 28-2.

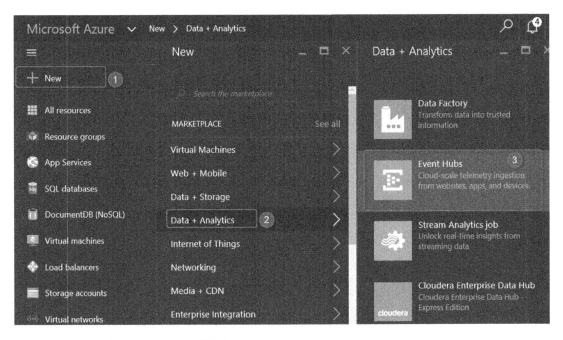

Figure 28-2.   Creating Event Hub

An Event Hub needs a Service Bus, and this first step creates the namespace for that service bus. Set a namespace in the new blade. For example, set the name PBIRadacad in Figure 28-3.

Now choose a pricing tier. For this example, you can choose Basic. Select a resource group (or create if you don't have one), and set a location. Again, see Figure 28-3.

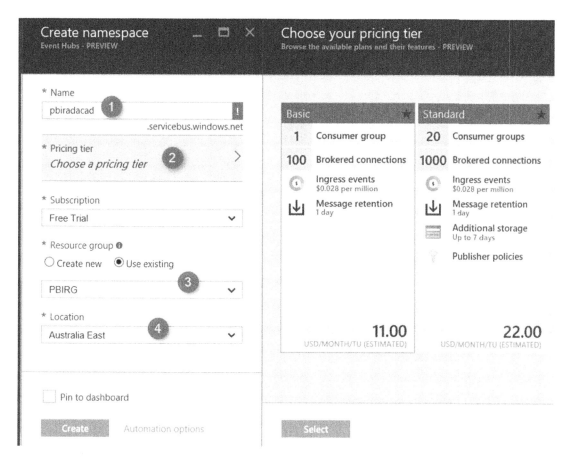

Figure 28-3. *Event Hub Configuration*

Your Event Hubs namespace can include multiple Event Hubs. Create your first Event Hub here, by Adding an Event Hub as shown in Figure 28-4.

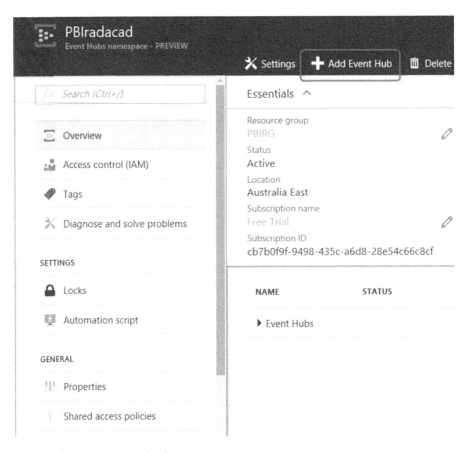

Figure 28-4. *Adding event hub*

For the new Event Hub, just set a name. Figure 28-5 uses the name pbi, for example. And leave other settings as is. You can change these settings if you want to change partitions and the number of days to retention.

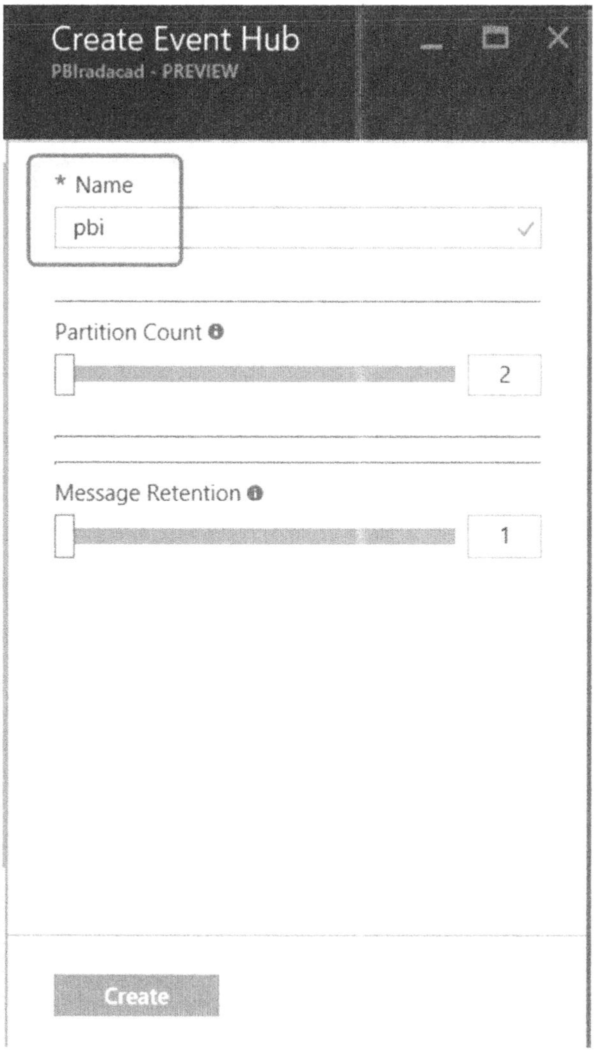

Figure 28-5. *Name for the event hub*

After creation, the Event Hub should be listed under whatever name you set for the namespace. Figure 28-6 shows an event hub in the namespace PBIradacad. (The namespace is given in the very upper left of the image.)

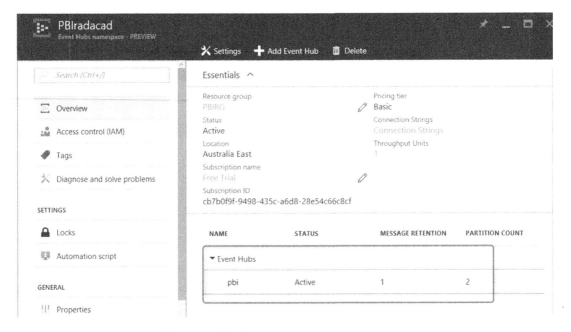

Figure 28-6. *Viewing the event hub status*

For simplicity, we keep all configuration and settings as is. So far, you have created the Event Hub, which can be used as the data entry input point. Now let's create an Azure Stream Analytics Job.

Azure Stream Analytics

Stream Analytics is a data streaming technology under the Azure list of services. With this technology, you can pass data from an input (such as Event Hub) to one or more outputs. Note that Stream Analytics is not data storage. If you want the data to be stored, you have to pass that to a storage output, such as Azure Blob Storage or Azure SQL Database or Azure SQL Data Warehouse.

Create an Azure Stream Analytics Job from the Azure portal under New, and Data + Analytics, as shown in Figure 28-7.

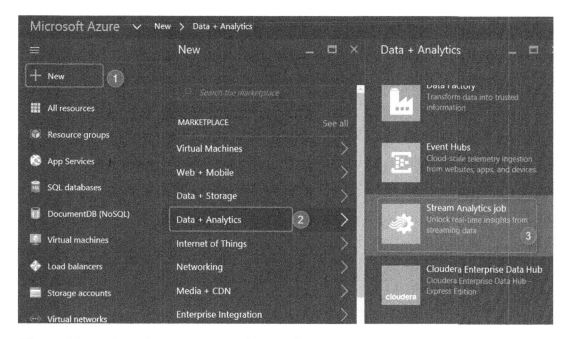

Figure 28-7. *Creating Stream Analytics job*

Set a Name, Resource Group, and Location for the Stream Analytics Job.
See Figure 28-8 for an example.

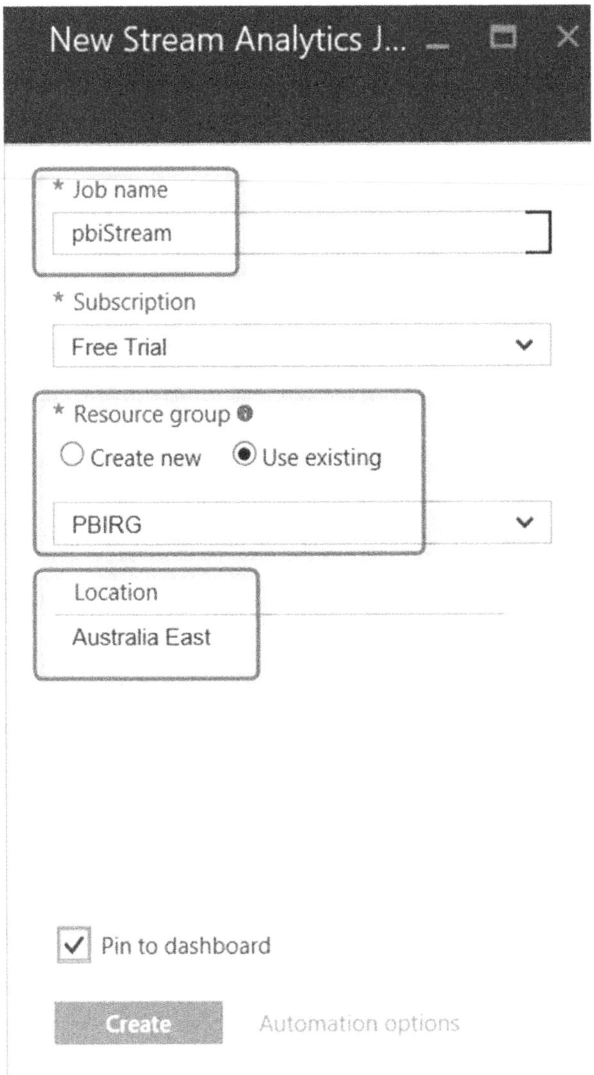

Figure 28-8. *The configuration of the Stream Analytics job*

After creating the job, you will be redirected to the job's blade as shown in Figure 28-9. The job in Figure 28-9 is named DeviceTemperatures, but you can, of course, name your jobs as you like.

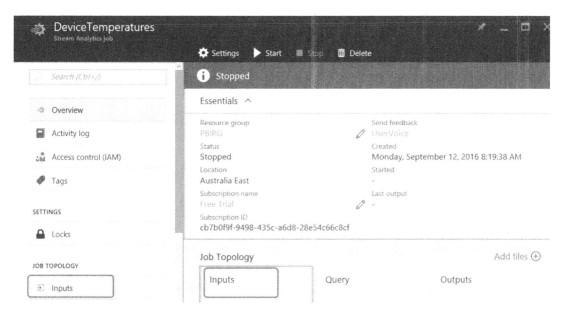

Figure 28-9. *Setting inputs for the stream analytics job*

Input from Event Hub

From Job, Topology clicks on Inputs and then Add an Input to the new blade. In the New Input blade, set a name. Set Source to Event Hub, and choose the service bus namespace as the namespace you entered earlier in this chapter (PBIRadacad). Then select the event hub as pbi. Figure 28-10 shows these settings.

Figure 28-10. *Setting up input for the streaming analytics*

Leave the event serialization format as JSON and encoding as UTF-8. With the settings in Figure 28-10, Stream Analytics reads input from the Event Hub.

Output to Power BI

Go to the Stream Analytics main blade and create an Output this time. Set a name such as PBIOutput, and set Sink to Power BI, as shown in Figure 28-11. Now Stream Analytics will output to Power BI as a dataset.

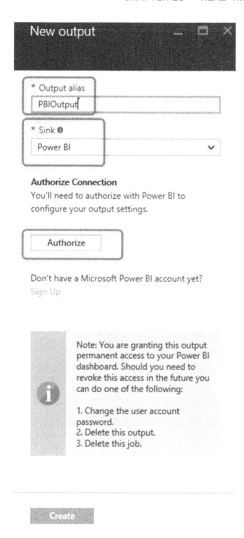

Figure 28-11. *Output to Power BI from stream analytics*

Click on Authorize to map the Power BI account that you want to use here. You will be prompted to log in with your Power BI username and password. The account you log in with can be different from your Azure account.

After authorization, you will see a list of all groups in the Power BI account, and you can choose where the dataset will be published to. By default, the dataset goes to My Workspace, but you can specify a different target group or workspace.

Set a name for dataset, for example, StreamAnalyticsDS. See Figure 28-12 for an example. Notice that if a dataset with the same name exists, that dataset will be overwritten. Next, set a name for a table. Figure 28-12, for example, specifies the name MyTable. Finally, create the output.

Figure 28-12. *Choosing the workspace, dataset, and table from Power BI service*

After creating output and input, you will see both under the Stream Analytics blade, as shown in Figure 28-13. But you can't start the job yet. There is one step more.

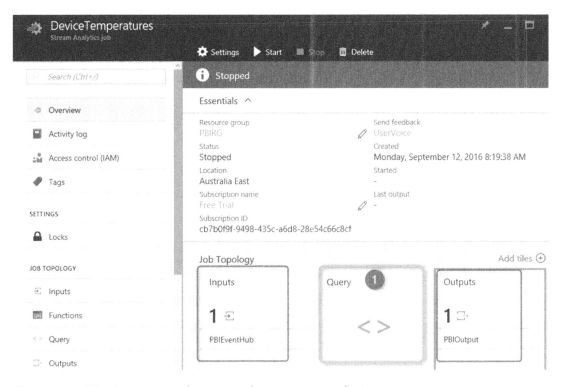

Figure 28-13. *Setting up the Query for stream analytics*

Stream Analytics Query

Stream Analytics passes data from input to output through a query. Without a query, you cannot start a Stream Analytics job. For this example, we use a very simple query that selects everything from the input and passes everything to the output.

Click on Query item in the Stream Analytics main blade. See the item tagged as #1 in Figure 28-13. That item is the Query item.

Change the default query to the following:

```
SELECT
    *
INTO
    [PBIOutput]
FROM
    [PBIEventHub]
```

You should now be seeing a configuration much like that in Figure 28-14.

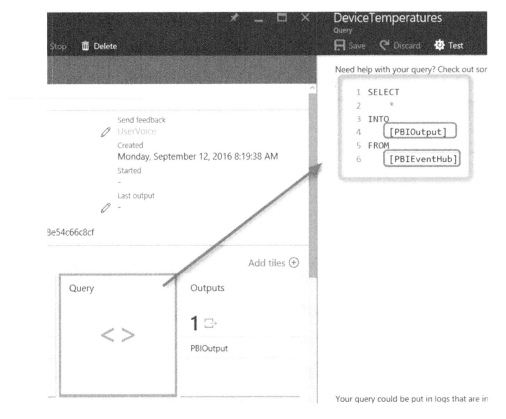

Figure 28-14. *Writing the stream analytics query*

Notice that the query selects everything from the input. You have to put your input name after the FROM clause. The query will also insert the result into the output. Thus, you need to put your output name after the INTO clause. If the input and output names aren't valid, you will get a failure error message at the time of starting the job.

Don't test the query. Save it and Start the job. It will take few minutes for a job to start. Wait and check if the job started successfully. Otherwise, failure might be related to input, output, or the query. You should, though, see a job in the RUNNING state as in Figure 28-15.

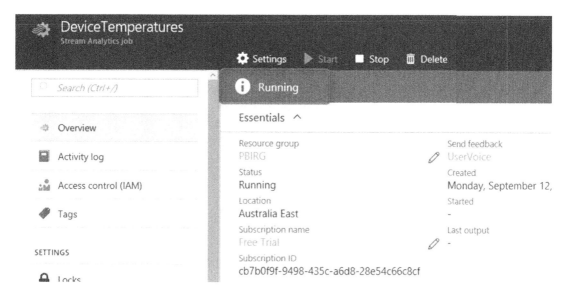

Figure 28-15. *Stream Analytics job is running*

Push Data Application

As I mentioned earlier in this chapter, I'll be using a .NET C# console application to pass the data to Event Hub. Let's create the sample application by opening Visual Studio 2015 Professional. Create a New C# Console Application as shown in Figure 28-16.

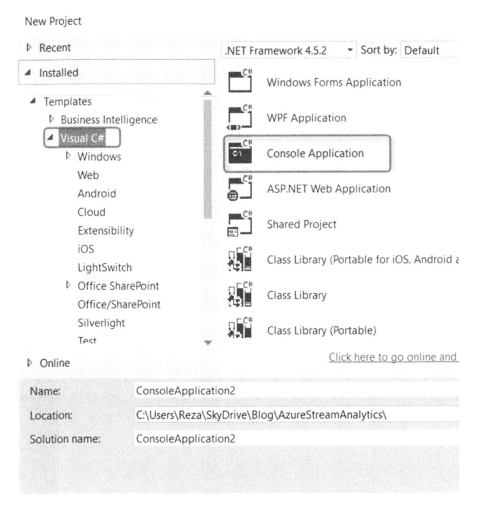

Figure 28-16. *Creating a custom console application*

Name the application something. Then when the application is opened in Solution Explorer, go to References, right-click, and select Manage NuGet Packages. Do these things as shown in Figure 28-17.

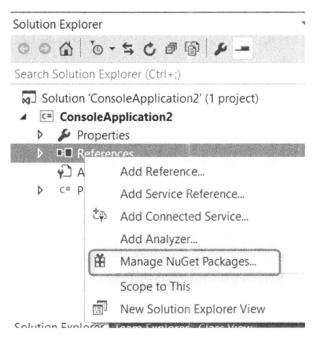

Figure 28-17. *Manage NuGet Packages*

Click on Browse, Search for Azure Service Bus, and install it. Figure 28-18 illustrates how to begin the install process.

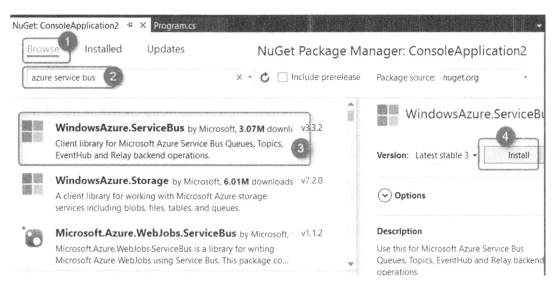

Figure 28-18. *Install Azure SDK*

After installation, open the App.Config file and search for appSettings near the end of the file. The connection string to Azure Service Bus is in the value beneath this section, and you can see that connection string highlighted in Figure 28-19.

```
App.config    ┬ X   NuGet: ConsoleApplication2        Program.cs
    1      <?xml version="1.0" encoding="utf-8"?>
    2    ⊟<configuration>
    3    ⊟    <startup>
    4            <supportedRuntime version="v4.0" sku=".NETFramework,Version=v4.5.2"/>
    5        </startup>
    6    ⊞    <system.serviceModel>...</system.serviceModel>
   47    ⊟    <appSettings>
   48            <!-- Service Bus specific app setings for messaging connections -->
   49    ⊟        <add key="Microsoft.ServiceBus.ConnectionString"
   50                value="Endpoint=sb://[your namespace].servicebus.windows.net;SharedAccessKeyⱤ
   51        </appSettings>
   52    </configuration>
```

Figure 28-19. *Setting up endpoint in the app.config*

The highlighted line should be changed to your service bus connection string. To find your service bus connection string, go to the Azure portal. Then find the service bus (we've created it in Event Hub section) under All Resources, as shown in Figure 28-20.

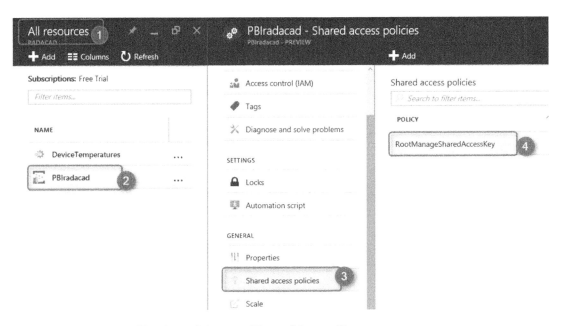

Figure 28-20. *Finding RootManageSharedAccessKey*

Under RootManageSharedAccessKey, you'll find the Primary Key, as in Figure 28-21.

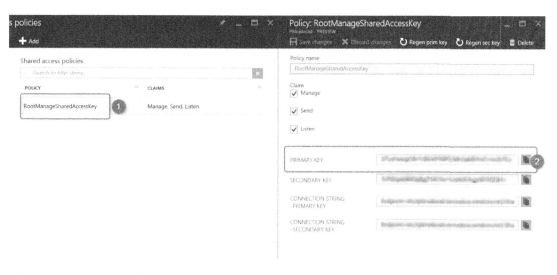

Figure 28-21. *Finding primary key*

Copy the value of the primary key here, and replace the value in the app.Config file as shown in Figure 28-22. Save the App.Config file after the change, and close it.

```
App.config  ⊉ ✕  Program.cs
    1      <?xml version="1.0" encoding="utf-8"?>
    2    ⊟<configuration>
    3    ⊟    <startup>
    4            <supportedRuntime version="v4.0" sku=".NETFramework,Version=v4.5.2"/>
    5        </startup>
    6    ⊞    <system.serviceModel>...</system.serviceModel>
   47    ⊟    <appSettings>
   48            <!-- Service Bus specific app setings for messaging connections -->
   49    ⊟        <add key="Microsoft.ServiceBus.ConnectionString"
   50                    value="Endpoint=sb://PBIradacad.servicebus.windows.net;SharedAcces
   51        </appSettings>
   52    </configuration>
```

Figure 28-22. *Adding the primary key in the app.config*

Then right-click on the references folder in the solution explorer and add a System. Configuration reference as shown in Figure 28-23.

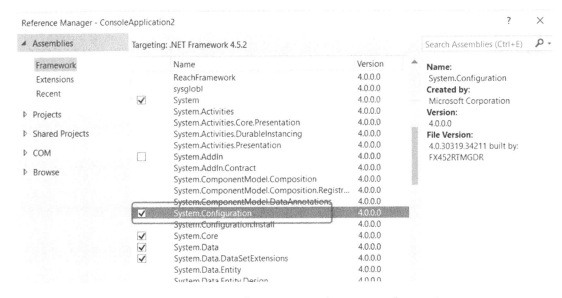

Figure 28-23. *Adding System.Configuration reference to the project*

Now open the Program.CS file and add your two namespaces as follows:

```
using System.Configuration;
using Microsoft.ServiceBus.Messaging;
```

Also add the following code under the Main method:

```
string ConnectionString = ConfigurationManager.AppSettings["Microsoft.
ServiceBus.ConnectionString"];
        EventHubClient client = EventHubClient.CreateFromConnectionStri
ng(ConnectionString, "pbi");

        // Declare values that we're about to send
        Int32 unixTimestamp = (Int32)(DateTime.UtcNow.Subtract(new
DateTime(1970, 1, 1))).TotalSeconds;
        Random r = new Random();
        int currentValue = r.Next(0, 100);

        // Generate string in JSON format
        string postData = String.Format("[{{ \"ts\": {0}, \"value\":{1}
}}]", unixTimestamp, currentValue);
```

```
// Send the Message
client.Send(new EventData(Encoding.UTF8.GetBytes(postData)));

Console.WriteLine("Message sent. Press Enter to Continue.");
Console.ReadLine();
```

The first Line in the code reads the connection string from app.config. The second line creates an instance of EventHubClient with the connection string. Note that in this line, the connection was created to Event Hub with the name "pbi."

The next three lines create a random integer value with a timestamp and then the line with the String. The format invocation will generate a JSON-formatted string. Finally, the Client.Send method sends the string in UTF-8 encoding to Service Bus (Event Hub).

Execution of this application will pass only one data point to Event Hub. To add another data point, you have to run the application again. Now the application is ready to run. Let's run it for the first time, and you should see a result similar to that in Figure 28-24.

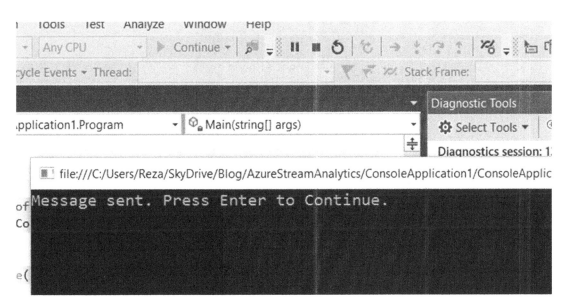

Figure 28-24. *Message sent from the application*

After the execution, we expect Power BI to show something. Let's see.

Power BI Real-Time Dashboard

Log in to Power BI service with the account you have used in the Stream Analytics Authorization section. In My Workspace (or any other group you've selected in Stream Analytics Output section), you'll find the new dataset. If you've been following along, that dataset should be named StreamAnalyticsDS, as shown in Figure 28-25.

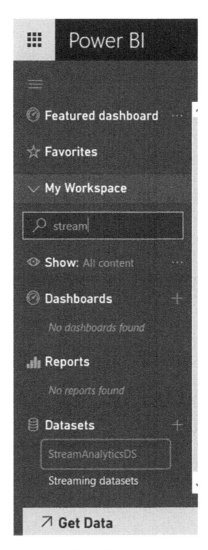

Figure 28-25. *The dataset connected to the streaming analytics*

Open the dataset, and you'll see the table under the dataset with two fields we've passed (ts and value) plus other fields from Event Hub (EventEnqueuedUtcTime, EventProcessedUtcTime, and PartitionId). See Figure 28-26 for an example.

Figure 28-26. *Table data coming from stream analytics*

As you can see, the structure can be anything sent from Event Hub and Stream Analytics. Now create two simple visualizations as shown in Figure 28-27. Create one Card Visualization with a distinct count of ts. The visual will show the number of the data point (execute the console application) from Event Hub.

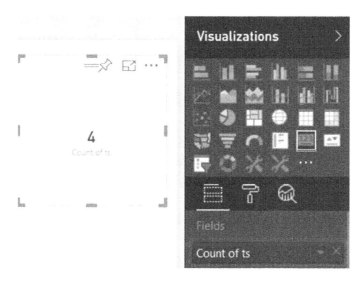

Figure 28-27. *Creating visuals*

Also, there is a Column chart with TS at the Axis and Value as the Value of chart. Figure 28-28 shows that being done.

Figure 28-28. *Creating line chart by timestamp and value from the streaming dataset*

Save this report, and Pin your two visualizations into a new dashboard as shown in Figure 28-29.

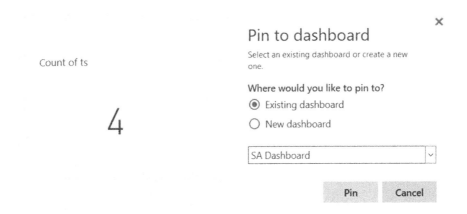

Figure 28-29. *Pinning the visual to the dashboard*

Now go to the dashboard. While the dashboard is open, execute the console application. After a few seconds of execution and sending the message, you will see how the dashboard shows the result. You should see a result similar to that in Figure 28-30, indicating that you've just built an Azure Stream Analytics and Power BI real-time dashboard.

Figure 28-30. *Dashboard shows real-time changes as messages come*

Summary

The real-time dashboard with Power BI, Azure Stream Analytics, and Event Hub opens the path to many possible solutions. You can analyze Twitter data in real time. Or you can pass data from an IoT device with an IoT Hub into a real-time dashboard. Come with ideas of what a real-time dashboard with Stream Analytics can do and start leveraging these powerful technologies to implement them.

CHAPTER 29

Power BI REST API

You have learned about some features of Power BI Rest API earlier in this book. You've learned steps that you need to implement a Power BI Embedded solution. In this chapter, we want to explore more about what the REST API has to offer. You will learn about other features of REST API such as refreshing a dataset and controlling objects in the Power BI service such as data source management and gateway management. You will also learn how the REST API can be helpful to push data into a streaming Power BI service (similar to the way that we used Power BI and Azure Analysis Services).

Refresh Dataset with REST API

Power BI REST API is not just for embedding content or getting a list of dashboards and reports. It also has many functions to work with datasets, gateways, and data sources. As one of the many exciting features of that, you can easily refresh a dataset from an application. You can refresh it as many times you want and with any frequency you want. You can refresh your dataset after ETL runs through a console application. Or you can have a service application that kicks off refresh even every single minute! There is no limitation on your data refresh anymore! Let's check it out.

Prerequisite

For running samples of this chapter, you need first to register your application and then authenticate through REST API. To learn more about the options mentioned, read Chapter 14 of this book.

The sample code for this example can be downloaded from the following URL:

```
https://github.com/Microsoft/PowerBI-Developer-Samples/tree/master/
App%20Owns%20Data
```

© Reza Rad 2018
R. Rad, *Pro Power BI Architecture*, https://doi.org/10.1007/978-1-4842-4015-1_29

Get Dataset

With Power BI REST API version 2, you can access many objects from the Power BI service. One of these object types is a dataset. You can get a list of datasets, and you can then apply some operations on it, such as refresh. After authenticating, the code below gets a list of datasets:

```
var datasets = await client.Datasets.GetDatasetsInGroupAsync(GroupId);
```

GetDatasetsInGroupAsync simply gives you a list of all datasets, and you can then iterate through them. As I've mentioned before, Group ID should be the guide of the group. You can then find the particular dataset you want. The code below just gets the very first dataset in the list:

```
var datasets = await client.Datasets.GetDatasetsInGroupAsync(GroupId);

            var dataset = datasets.Value.FirstOrDefault();

            if (dataset == null)
            {
                return View(new EmbedConfig()
                {
                    ErrorMessage = "Group has no datasets."
                });
            }
```

This dataset is already in a group in my Power BI account. Figure 29-1 shows how that dataset appears when I view it in the list.

Figure 29-1. *The dataset in the Power BI*

The dataset in Figure 29-1 is named Pubs 20170529, and it refreshed last on the 21st of June 2017. Figure 29-2 shows how you can right-click in your code and find information about the dataset from the drop-down menu.

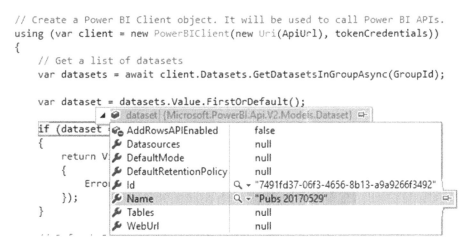

Figure 29-2. *Getting Dataset information from the REST API*

After finding the dataset, you can easily refresh it.

Refresh Dataset

You can even directly refresh a dataset; you'll just need the ID of that dataset. One way to find the dataset ID is through the application. Another way is from the URL of the Power BI service. If you go to settings for the dataset, you can find the ID of it easily, as shown in Figure 29-3.

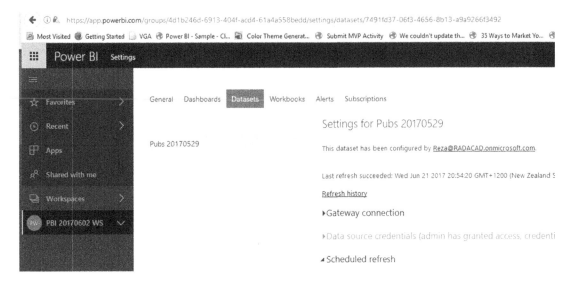

Figure 29-3. *Dataset ID on the website*

The code to refresh a dataset is very simple:

```
object result= await client.Datasets.RefreshDatasetInGroupAsync(GroupId,
dataset.Id);
```

As a result of a refresh, you can see the dataset is refreshed successfully. See that the time has been updated in Figure 29-4 as compared to that in Figure 29-1.

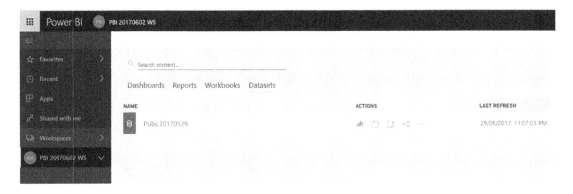

Figure 29-4. *Last refresh time of the dataset updated after execution of the code*

The last refresh time is now the 29th of June 2017, 11 p.m., which is the time of writing this chapter.

An important note to consider here is that this dataset is an IMPORT DATA dataset, and it is working through the gateway. So I need the gateway to be up and running. However, even if you are connected to a cloud data source through import data, then even without the gateway you can refresh the dataset. So, any dataset can be easily refreshed. The fascinating fact is: this: you can refresh your dataset from an application at any time you like or at any frequency you like; and it can be after the ETL run or on a scheduled basis.

Refresh History

The new REST API is an evolution in Power BI integration. You can even read the history of the refresh for a dataset. Here is the code for which to do that:

```
var history = await client.Datasets.GetRefreshHistoryInGroupAsync(GroupId,
dataset.Id)
```

Running this code will return the whole history of refresh for that dataset, as shown in Figure 29-5. You can easily see the type of refresh and time and status of each.

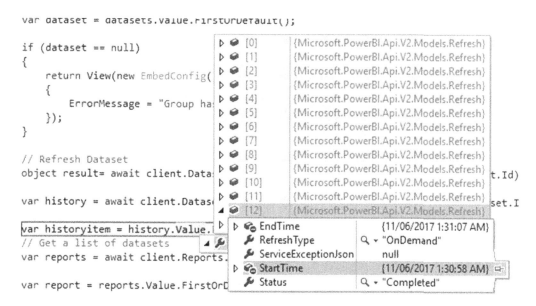

Figure 29-5. *Fetching dataset refresh history details from REST API*

The same refresh history is in the Power BI service. Figure 29-6 shows the history as viewed from the service.

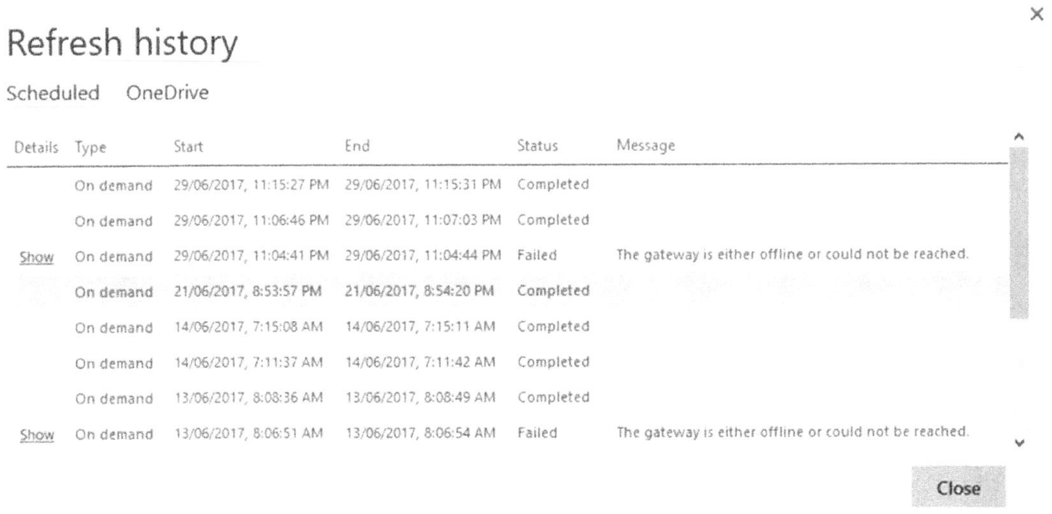

Figure 29-6. *Refresh history in the Power BI service*

Accessing refresh history from API means you can easily write an application that refreshes the dataset anytime. You can also check the refresh history for troubleshooting.

Data Source Management

The new REST API of Power BI is revolutionary. In addition to embedding content in the Power BI and the ability to refresh the dataset from API, it also gives you many functions to work with Gateways and Data Sources. With this API, you can set up new data sources, clone datasets, check the credentials of a data source, get a list of all data sources under a gateway, and do many other operations. In other words, Data Source Management can be fully automated with REST API. Continue reading this chapter if you'd like to learn more about this.

Get List of Gateways

A list of gateways is accessible through a function under Gateways, called GetGatewaysAsync. You can easily fetch a list of gateways (on-premises gateways, not personal), and then loop through them in your code.

Here is the function invocation to obtain the list of gateways:

```
var gateways = await client.Gateways.GetGatewaysAsync();
```

And Figure 29-7 shows how the results appear when you execute the function in Power BI.

Figure 29-7. *Getting the gateway information with Power BI REST API*

This function, as you can see in the above code screenshot, will give you a list of all on-premises data gateways defined under your account. Then you can loop through each gateway and get the information of that gateway: for example, the name of the gateway, ID of it, and some information such as version.

Figure 29-8 shows a list of gateways under my own Power BI account.

Figure 29-8. *Gateway name in the Power BI website*

As you can see, all of the gateways listed in Figure 29-8 can be accessed through the REST API.

Get List of Data Sources

Under a gateway, you can access all data sources with a GetDataSourcesAsync function. For example:

```
var dashboards = await client.Dashboards.GetDashboardsInGroupAsync(GroupId);
```

Figure 29-9 shows the results of executing the function.

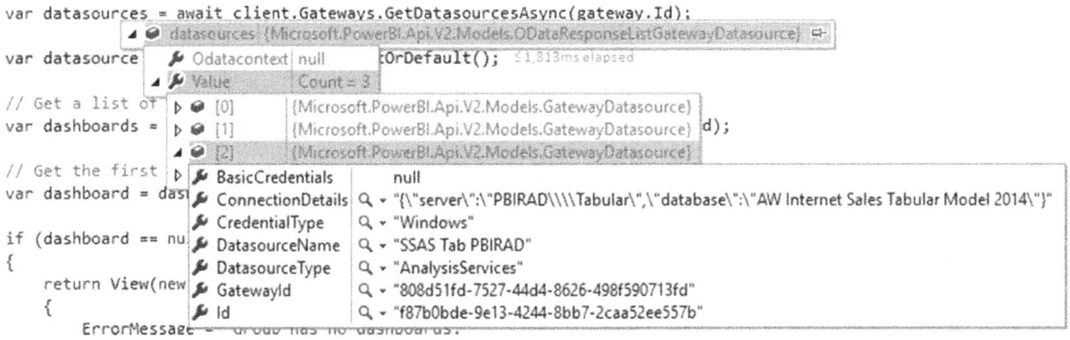

Figure 29-9. *Controlling data source information under a gateway with REST API*

The sources retrieved using the GetDataSourcesAsyn function matche exactly the configuration of that data source in the Power BI service. See Figure 29-10 for an example.

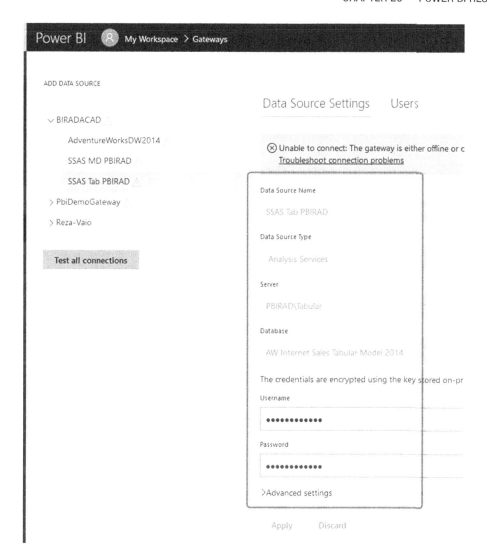

Figure 29-10. Data source information in the Power BI service

As you can see, there are also properties for accessing the credentials or even changing them.

Data Source Management

In addition to the reading list of data sources, you can do some other operations such as creating a data source, setting up credentials for it, and even binding a data source to a gateway.

Create Data Source

There is a function to create a data source, called CreateDatasourceAsync. You need to specify a data source through a new object of PublishDatasourceToGatewayRequest to create a data source. This object can contain a type of dataset and connection information about it, including credentials. Figure 29-11 shows an invocation of CreateDatasourceAsync to create a new source using the REST API.

```
var newdatasource = await client.Gateways.CreateDatasourceAsync(gateway.Id,
    new PublishDatasourceToGatewayRequest(
        "Sql",
        "{\"server\":\".\",\"database\":\"AdventureWorksDW2014\"}",
        new CredentialDetails(
            "                                                        ",
            "Basic"),
        "AdventureWorksDW2014"
    )
);
```

Figure 29-11. *Creating a new data source using REST API*

Binding Dataset to a Gateway

After creating the data source, you can then bind a dataset to that gateway. For finding the particular dataset, please read the previous section of this chapter. When you have the dataset key, then you can easily use the BindToGatewayInGroupAsync function:

```
client.Datasets.BindToGatewayInGroupAsync(GroupId, datasetKey, new
BindToGatewayRequest(gateway.Id));
```

Real-Time Streaming and Push Data

In this section, you will learn one of the functionalities of REST API, which is pushing data to the Streaming dataset. In the previous chapter you've learned how to do real-time streaming using Azure Streaming Analytics and Power BI. However, this chapter explains real-time functionality, just with the REST API. You will not need Azure services when using a REST API.

Streaming Dataset

In Power BI, you can create different types of datasets. The normal dataset that everyone knows about is a dataset that automatically generates when you create a Power BI Desktop solution and publish it on the website. However, there is another very important type of dataset called a Streaming dataset. This dataset is used for pushing data into Power BI in a real-time scenario.

How to Create a Streaming Dataset

Go to the Power BI Service (`http://powerbi.microsoft.com`) website. Log in to the website with your Power BI Account. When logged in, create a new **streaming dataset**, as shown in Figure 29-12.

Figure 29-12. *Creating a streaming dataset*

There are three ways to create a streaming dataset. In the previous chapter, you've learned about the Azure Stream Analytics method. For this example, choose API as I have done in Figure 29-13.

Figure 29-13. *choosing the type of streaming dataset as REST API*

Figure 29-14 shows the next part where you specify the name of your dataset, and add fields to it. Your fields can be of type DateTime, Text, or Number. With adding every new field, you will see a JSON format being created underneath, which is the format that the data needs to be sent through REST API.

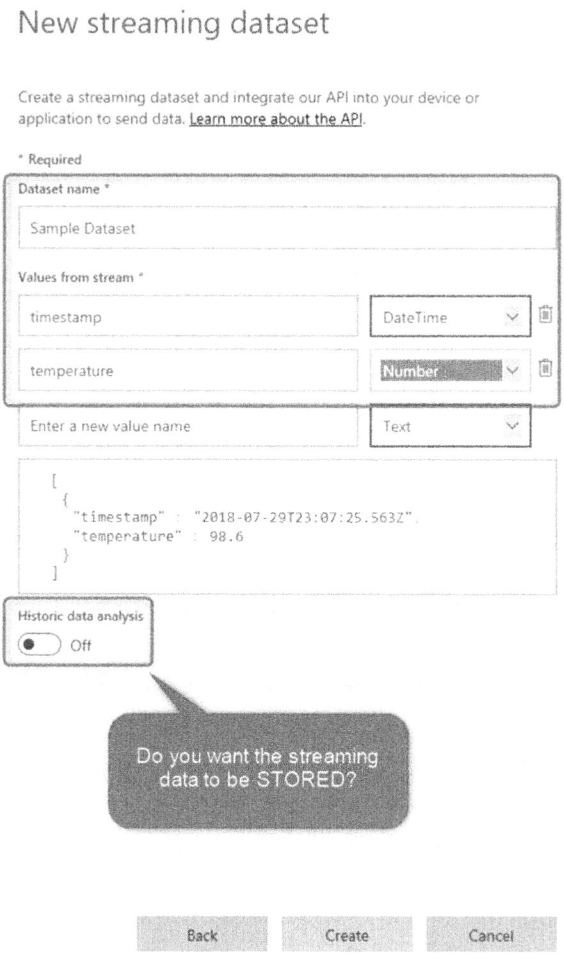

Figure 29-14. Configuring fields in the streaming dataset

Push, Hybrid, or Streaming?

One very important option to choose is the Historical Data Analysis. By default, this option is off. It means the streaming data will not be stored anywhere. Service keeps up to 200,000 rows of data. When row # 200,001 comes in, the first row will be deleted. If you want the history to be saved, you have to switch this option to On. When you turn on this option, your dataset changes from a streaming dataset into a Hybrid dataset. Figure 29-15 shows the API Access column in which the type of dataset – hybrid, streaming, or push – is indicated.

Datasets				Showing 4 item(s) Name (A-Z) ⌄
ACTIONS		LAST REFRESH	NEXT REFRESH	API ACCESS
.ılı: ⓘ ✎ 🗑		6/11/2017, 2:48:05 PM	N/A	Hybrid
.ılı: ↻ ▱ ⤳ ⋯		6/12/2017, 6:05:09 AM	N/A	Push
ⓘ ✎ 🗑		6/21/2017, 9:04:44 PM	N/A	Streaming
.ılı: ⓘ ✎ 🗑		6/14/2017, 7:23:35 AM	N/A	Hybrid

***Figure 29-15.** Different types of streaming dataset*

Streaming Dataset

A streaming dataset only streams the data rows, and it keeps up to 200,000 rows. First In, First Out. When row #200,001 comes in, row #1 will be removed. It cannot be used easily in reports because there is no historical data.

Hybrid Dataset

A Hybrid dataset streams the data and also keeps the data rows. You will have the rich experience of a Power BI Report with this option. Because data is stored, you can interact with that easier from a report.

Push Dataset

A Push dataset is created when publishing from the Power BI Desktop with data imported into it. This dataset is not a streaming dataset. It stores the data. The data should be then scheduled to refresh. We are not talking about this type of dataset in this chapter.

In this example, it doesn't matter which option you choose.

Create a Dashboard and Report

After creating the dataset, you need to create a report with a simple line chart with a value and timestamp on it, and then save it and pin it to a dashboard. The dashboard's chart at the moment will be blank because there are no data entries in it for now. In the next step, we will be adding rows into this dataset from an application.

Connecting to the Dataset from REST API

When the application is ready (after registration, and authentication), you can a add few lines of code to pass data through REST API. Here is some example code to do that:

```
// Create a Power BI Client object. It will be used to call Power BI APIs.
        using (var client = new PowerBIClient(new Uri(ApiUrl),
        tokenCredentials))
        {
            // Get a list of dashboards.
            var datasets = await client.Datasets.GetDatasetsInGroupAsyn
            c(GroupId2);

            // Get the first report in the group.
            var dataset = datasets.Value.FirstOrDefault();

            if (dataset == null)
            {
                return View(new TileEmbedConfig()
                {
                    ErrorMessage = "Group has no datasets."
                });
            }

            Random random = new Random();

            for (int i = 0; i <= 5000; i++)
            {
```

```
var requestBody = new RowsRequestBody()
{
    rows = new List<OnlineData>()
    {
        new OnlineData() { ts = DateTime.Now, value =
        random.Next(0, 100) }
    }
};

await client.Datasets.PostRowsInGroupAsync(GroupId2,
dataset.Id, "RealTimeData", requestBody);
    System.Threading.Thread.Sleep(1000);
}
```

A majority of the code here is about finding the dataset (which you learned about earlier in this chapter). After finding the dataset, I used a loop (highlighted lines,) to create a random number from 0 to 100 and passed it to the service and dataset with a function named **PostRowsInGroupAsync**. This process is in a loop and happens every second for 5 minutes. As a result, now you can see the dashboard data changes, as in Figure 29-16.

Figure 29-16. *The real-time dashboard shows the even results instantly*

Summary

In this chapter, you learned that Power BI REST API is not just for embedding reports and dashboards into a web page. Power BI REST API can connect to most of the objects in the service including dataset, data source, gateway, etc. With Power BI REST API, you can control the refresh of your dataset, and you can control the credentials of a data source under the gateway. You can also use REST API to push data into a real-time streaming Power BI dataset.

PART VII

Architecture

CHAPTER 30

Power BI Architecture Guidelines

Implementing a Power BI solution is not just about developing reports, creating a data model, or using visuals. Power BI, like any other technologies, can be used in a correct or incorrect way. Any technology can be used more effectively if it harnesses the right architecture. A right architecture can be achieved after a gathering requirements and designing aspects and components of the technology to fit the requirements. In this chapter, you will learn about some of the most common architectures to use Power BI. You will learn about using Power BI in different architecture guidelines such as Sharing architecture, Self-service architecture, and Enterprise architecture.

The architecture diagrams and blueprints in this chapter are only generic examples of recommended methods of using Power BI. For designing architecture in a real-world scenario, every single requirement should be considered specifically. Because different businesses have different requirements, you need to tweak and change the design and architecture, particularly for every business-use case scenario.

Disclaimer   The advised architecture in this chapter is a general recommendation. For every solution and implementation, it is always best to tweak the architecture based on the specific requirements. A general architecture only explains what the best overall methodology is.

Power BI Sharing Architecture

Considering all sharing methods that you already know about Power BI, it is a hard decision sometimes to choose a sharing mechanism or architecture for Power BI implementation. This chapter explains a blueprint of a recommended architecture.

© Reza Rad 2018
R. Rad, *Pro Power BI Architecture*, https://doi.org/10.1007/978-1-4842-4015-1_30

Developer Team

Sharing Power BI content with a team of developers can be effectively done with a shared workspace. Everyone in the team of developers can have edit access to this workspace. The shared workspace will be like a collaborative development environment. Developers can make changes to the Power BI content in this workspace without affecting another user's environment. Figure 30-1 shows a screenshot of a developer sharing architecture.

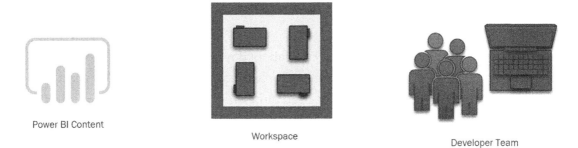

Power BI Content

Workspace

Developer Team

Figure 30-1. *Sharing architecture for a developer team*

Test User

For a test user, an easy way of sharing without too much hassle is usually the best way of sharing. Sharing of dashboards and reports as in Figure 30-2 is easy and simple to do. Test users can be notified that Power BI content is shared with them. Test users then can give feedback to the developer team, who can then iterate changes back through another cycle of development.

Power BI Content

Simple Sharing of dashboard or report

Test User

Figure 30-2. *Sharing architecture for test users: simple dashboard and report sharing*

Organizational or External Users

After going through some development/test cycles, the Power BI content becomes gold. Gold Power BI content is content that has been developed based on requirements, tested, and successfully passed all the requirements with high quality. This gold content can be shared with end users (which can be in the organization or even external) through Power BI Apps, as shown in Figure 30-3. For sharing the content with people outside of the organization, Azure B2B services should be leveraged. Power BI app users will be end users who only consume the content as read-only.

Figure 30-3. *Sharing architecture for end users (internal or external)*

Public Users

In every business, there might be a set of reports and datasets available for the public to use: for example, an overall annual report of a company without any confidential data. The public report can be shared through Publish to Web functionality of the Power BI service, as illustrated in Figure 30-4. The most important tip about this way of sharing is that the public report should use a completely isolated dataset that doesn't have any confidential data in it. Because even if the data is not exposed in the report, users can access the data rows with the export or view rows option of the Publish to Web.

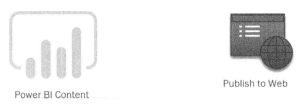

Power BI Content   Publish to Web   Public Users

Figure 30-4. *Sharing architecture for public content*

SharePoint Users

If in your company, the culture is nurtured that users use SharePoint Online as their portal of accessing content and documents, then Power BI content is best to be shared through the same portal as illustrated in Figure 30-5. The best way of sharing is the way that users can feel familiar with it. When users are used to SharePoint Online portal, then embedding the Power BI content in SharePoint Online is usually a great option.

Power BI Content   Embed in SharePoint online   SharePoint Users

Figure 30-5. *Sharing architecture for SharePoint users, Embed in SharePoint Online*

Custom Application Users

For ISVs and many other types of businesses, the portal for users is a custom application such as is in Figure 30-6. The custom application has been used for some time, and thus it is probably the best place to share the Power BI content. Embedding content into an application would also create a single sign-on sharing solution for the users. Power BI embedded into the custom application will give users a seamless experience of their web application. Users can view the Power BI content easily through the application without the need to log in to Power BI.

Power BI Content

Power BI Embedded

Custom Application Users

Figure 30-6. *Sharing architecture for custom application users*

On-Premises Organizational Users

If Power BI Report Server has been used in an organization, then content can be shared through the report server with users of the active directory. Figure 30-7 illustrates this architecture. This way of sharing doesn't need users to have Power BI accounts. However, the licensing should be either Premium or Software Assurance of the SQL Server Enterprise. This method of sharing is for companies whom are not yet ready for cloud and want to leverage the Power BI content on-premises.

Power BI Content

Power BI Report Server

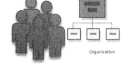

Organizational Users

Figure 30-7. *Sharing architecture for on-premises solution: Power BI Report Server*

Sharing Architecture Is Not One Method

As you have learned so far, each method of sharing gives you part of the architecture; workspace is good for the developer environment. Simple sharing is good for sharing with test users, Power BI Apps is good for end users, and other methods give you other options. When you think about the sharing architecture, don't limit yourself to only one or two methods; you can use multiple methods. You can use a different method for Dev environment and another method for Prod environment. The main objective is to ease the access for users, meet the requirements, and isolate the developer environment.

Self-Service Architecture

Power BI is a self-service tool, and you don't want to take this power of self-service from your users. In every business, some users know the business well, and they are also good at analyzing data; we call these users power users. A power user is someone who may not model the data, and may not right DAX calculations or M expressions, but can (and want to) do some visualization. Power users can leverage the self-service capabilities of Power BI and build their reports from the dataset that the developer team provided for them.

Power BI Desktop

Get Data from Power BI service is a feature that enables power users to use Power BI Desktop to connect to an existing data model live from the Power BI service. Figure 30-8 illustrates this approach, and the approach allows users to connect to a dataset without being able to modify the dataset, change the model, change the calculation, or even change relationships. Users can only build visualizations on top of the existing models.

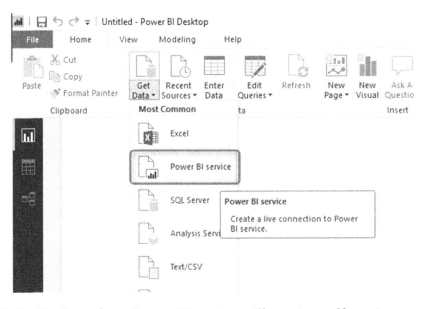

Figure 30-8. *Get Data from Power BI service will create a self-service experience from Power BI Desktop for Power Users*

Users, however, can write their measures if they want; these measures are called report-level measures. Accessing the centralized model from Power BI service is one of the ways that can build an architecture with one data modeler and multiple data visualizers in the team. Figure 30-9 shows how one dataset can feed multiple reports.

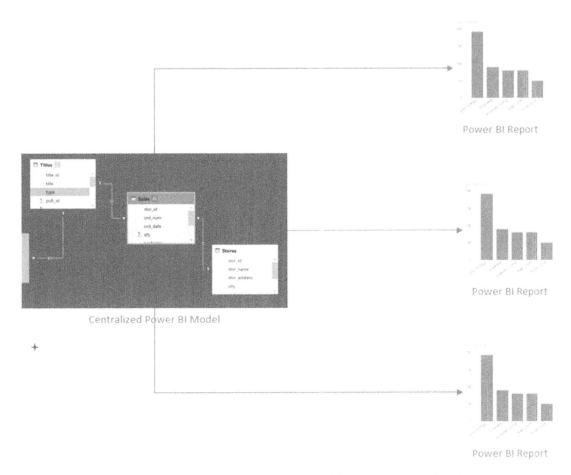

Figure 30-9. *One Power BI dataset can be used for creating multiple reports*

Excel

Some of the power users might be very familiar with Excel as a slicing and dicing tool. In another chapter, I explained how the integration between Excel and Power BI works. Excel users can connect directly to the Power BI model in the cloud using Analyze in Excel feature or use the Power BI Publisher for Excel add-in for Excel.

Excel users are able to use the PivotTable and PivotChart in Excel to slice and dice the data from Power BI service, as shown in Figure 30-10. Excel users can save their sample Excel file and reuse it later. Excel users can connect to Power BI models even if they have read-only access to the model.

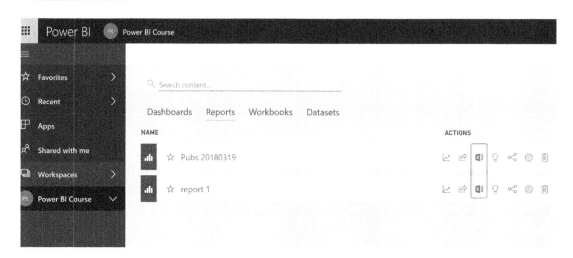

Figure 30-10. *Analyze in Excel for slicing and dicing the data from a dataset live in Power BI service*

Power BI Service

Power users also can create a report directly from the website, as shown in Figure 30-11. Creating reports directly from the service is a very good option for non-Windows power users because Power BI Desktop can be only installed on a Windows machine (at the time of writing this chapter).

Figure 30-11. *Create a report in the Power BI service*

Self-Service Architecture

Combining the three methods mentioned so far, you can give power users the ability to slice and dice the data of the Power BI model. They can build new visualizations or even sometimes new calculations using the architecture illustrated in Figure 30-12.

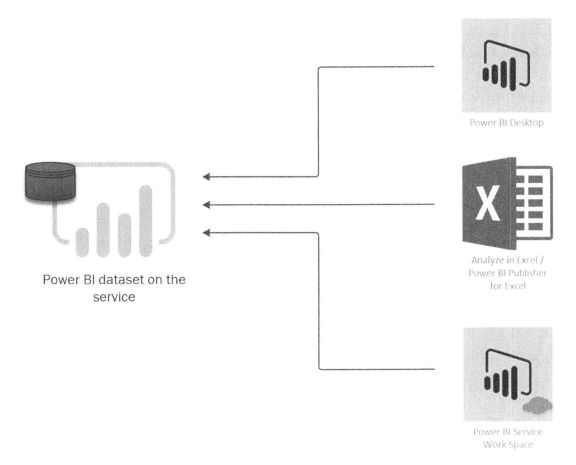

Figure 30-12. *The self-service architecture of Power BI*

Self-service users need edit access to the dataset to be able to create reports on it, except for Excel users who can access the content even with read-only permission. In all methods of self-service mentioned above, users need to have a Power BI Pro license.

Enterprise Architecture

Using Power BI in an enterprise environment usually comes with some types of requirements that may not be available in a small- or medium-scale business. In an enterprise-scale business, usually, the size of data is huge. Power BI (without premium licensing) only allows up to 1 GB for a model, which may not be enough for the enterprise clients. Also; enterprise clients most probably already have a data warehouse and data model in place. Another requirement of the enterprise clients is printing reports, which is the main functionality of SSRS reports. Combining all these requirements, usually, we have an architecture for enterprise clients with components such as those shown in Figure 30-13.

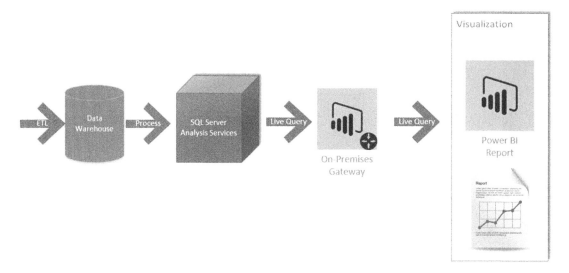

Figure 30-13. *Power BI architecture for enterprises*

As you can see from the figure, in large organizations, most business intelligence applications draw data either directly or indirectly from a data warehouse that is populated on some regular basis from operational data. The data is then passed through Analysis Services, then through on on-premise gateway, and finally the data passes into Power BI where it is presented in the form of visualizations that users can draw upon to make sound business decisions.

Index

A, B

P

Made in the USA
Coppell, TX
02 August 2021